Theory, Politics and the Arab World

Critical Responses

Edited by
Hisham Sharabi

D0829453

Routledge
New York and London

Published in cooperation with the Center for Contemporary
Arab Studies, Georgetown University

First published in 1990 by

Routledge
an imprint of
Routledge, Chapman & Hall, Inc.
29 West 35 Street
New York, NY 10001

Published in Great Britain by

Routledge
11 New Fetter Lane
London EC4P 4EE

Library of Congress Cataloguing-in-Publication Data

Theory, politics, and the Arab world : critical responses / edited by
  Hisham Sharabi.
      p. cm.
    "The papers were presented at a faculty study group held at the
  Center for Contemporary Arab Studies, Georgetown University, during
  the academic year 1987–88"—Pref.
    "Published in cooperation with the Center for Contemporary Arab
  Studies, Georgetown University"—P.
    Includes bibliographical references and index.
    ISBN 0-415-90361-0.—ISBN 0-415-90362-9
    1. Arab countries—Study and teaching—Philosophy. I. Sharabi,
  Hisham, 1927– . II. Georgetown University. Center for
  Contemporary Arab Studies.
  DS37.6.A2T48   1990
  956—dc20   90-35848

British Library Cataloguing Publication in data also available.

Contents

Editor's Preface

In the last decade or so, mainstream academic scholarship on the Arab world, the Middle East, and Islam has come under severe criticism as a new generation of scholars, raised and trained in a different political and intellectual milieu, came of age. The new criticism, largely fashioned by the concepts and vocabularies of postmodernist paradigms—continental theory, neo-Marxism, structuralism, poststructuralism, and feminist theory—has called into question some of the fundamental assumptions, methodologies, and ways of writing, teaching, and research of established scholarship.

Within closely guarded traditional disciplinary boundaries, conventional scholarship has maintained itself by preserving hierarchical structures within carefully delimited fields defined by certain kinds of expertise and sanctioned by established disciplinary authority. In the various fields and subfields, competition for power and position has been governed by implicit and explicit ideological and professional values set by the scholarly institution. In this situation, development within the various disciplines has remained limited and uneven. For example, in history the focus has been mostly on political history, the state, and high culture; in political science, on Islamic institutions and current developments; in anthropology and cultural studies, on literary history, old-style ethnography, and religion; in sociology and social psychology, on the kinship system, tribal and family structures, and modernization. In its theory and method the general field of Arab or Middle East studies has remained—despite some borrowing from Max Weber and recent social theory—anchored in the concepts and vocabulary of nineteenth-century historiography and social science.

The older generation of scholars belonged to the pre–World War II and immediate postwar periods. Some of its members had emigrated from continental Europe before the outbreak of the war to Britain and the United States; during the war, some served as specialists and advisors on Islam and the Middle East. The "Middle East" as an academic field flourished in the postwar era, which was marked by United States hegemony and the Cold War, when liberalism, anticommunism, and modernization emerged as the dominant ideological undercurrents. Not surprisingly, these historical and intellectual circumstances shaped much of the structure and orientation as well as areas and modes of research in Middle East studies.

The present cleavage within Middle East scholarship between what may be termed "traditionalists" and "innovators" became perceptible in the early 1970s. The former generally held on to old-time conventions and views—the canons of European Orientalist scholarship, Anglo-American positivist humanism, anticommunist ideology, "area studies" approaches, and so on—while the latter stressed new perspectives derived from the experience of the 1960s—Vietnam, the student movement, the Arab-Israeli war of 1967, and the accompanying intellectual upheavals.

The writers of these papers were invited to participate in a collective effort to examine from different disciplinary standpoints the implications of these upheavals for Middle East and Islamic writing and research. Along with a critique of the mainstream scholarship, these essays provide a description of some of the methodologies, theories, and changing patterns of thinking and writing in the various disciplines. Before a few notes on some of these, a word about the way the project was carried out.

The papers were presented at a faculty study group held at the Center for Contemporary Arab Studies, Georgetown University, during the academic year 1987–88. Faculty members and graduate students from neighboring universities were invited to participate in the study group. Before each session, a draft of the paper to be discussed was made available to the participants. The first part of the meeting was devoted to a presentation by the writer, followed by a vigorous and sometimes heated discussion. The papers were revised in light of the discussions prior to being submitted in their final form.

A certain rule should govern the reading of these essays. They should be read not only as an expression of a profound crisis within the field of Middle East studies, but also as a comprehensive multidisciplinary effort at reconstructing this field.

In their tone and style, all of the essays gathered here express self-conscious skepticism regarding writing, reading, and interpretation, in stark contrast to the self-assured and placid authoritarian attitude of established scholarship. The new critical approach is perhaps best expressed in Lila Abu Lughod's characterization: "a reading and writing from a particular place, from an individual who is personally, intellectually, politically, and historically situated."

Despite differences in assumptions and points of view, these papers attempt a single critical project. In most of the essays, the old tendency to totalize has been largely abandoned and closure has been displaced by self-reflexive criticism. In rejecting the Olympian all-knowing point of view of the old scholarship, the younger scholars do not intend to subvert science as such, or to undermine meaning and truth, but only to frame them differently, by underscoring the historicality of truth and knowledge and the perspectival character of science. For them, the politics of theory extend beyond considerations of explicit content and into those of form. From this standpoint the authority of mainstream scholarship and its hegemonic claims can no longer be taken seriously.

What is, from the vantage point of the different disciplines represented here, the current state of scholarly writing in the field of Arab, Middle East, and Islamic studies?

In political science most mainstream scholarship is largely descriptive, consisting mainly of diplomatic history and journalism focused on current politics and the ruling elites ("the regional counterpart," in Lisa Anderson's terms, "of contemporary Kremlinology"). Anderson attributes the poverty of American political science not so much to the difficulty of the languages of the region or the inaccessibility of certain of its parts to American writers and scholars, as to American foreign policy and its effect on political writing and research on the Middle East. Although she is not overly optimistic about fundamental changes taking place in her field—which "remains unsystematic and even unself-conscious"—she does see some significant shifts occurring in current research, redirecting focus from "the state" to "a revival of political economy in both international relations and comparative studies," from "crisis management" to structural "trends and patterns," from prediction of "what is coming and how it will get here" to analysis of political practice, "where conceptions of accountability and responsibility are defined and realized."

In a similar tone, Samih Farsoun and Lisa Hajjar decry the disarray of American sociology on the Middle East as "undeveloped" and "underdeveloped." It is a "distorted" sociology, applying concepts and modes of analysis developed not in the study of the Middle East itself but in the course of the West's own transformation—a distortion found in most Western social science disciplines. To this aberration is added the Orientalist syndrome, which has in Western sociology "earned a new lease on life." Perhaps more than any of the other writers, Farsoun and Hajjar detail the destructive consequences of Orientalism within mainstream writing in their field, but they are more optimistic than Anderson about their discipline's prospects for change. They see an emerging scholarship already successfully challenging established concepts and approaches and laying the ground for a new radical sociology of the Middle East.

This emerging scholarship is adumbrated in Halim Barakat's analysis of social-psychological writing. Taking a position close to Farsoun's and Hajjar's, he describes a "dynamic approach" which he envisions already replacing the static approach of institutional scholarship. In this approach he sees a process taking place simultaneously of "learning and unlearning," producing a radically new mode of reading and writing.

A similar division between "new style" and "old style" writing is evident in Judith Tucker's careful elaboration of the new social history perspective, where she focuses on precisely what traditional scholarship has neglected most: the history of ordinary people, of families, classes, peasants, women. In both theory and method the social history she describes, "history from below," represents perhaps the most direct challenge to the established forms of writing and research. And, reading from the left, Peter Gran presents an account of why political economy, so rich an interpretive tool in other fields, has failed to develop an autonomous approach on the Middle East. Attributing this failure to the acceptance by many Marxist-oriented scholars of some of Orientalism's basic assumptions as well as of the "liberal trade theory" or simultaneously of Anglo-American positivism, Gran gives a trenchant critique of some left writing in the field.

Lila Abu Lughod's criticism of mainstream anthropology takes a softer, non-agonistic form, addressing the limits of theory and communication rather than the specific failures of established anthropology. Her essay exemplifies the sort of self-critical consciousness to which the emerging interdisciplinary writing in the field aspires, giving the most sensitive treatment of the epistemological and linguistic problems that writing about the Other has to confront. This theme is the focus of my introductory essay, dealing with the problem of the scholarly point of view, and of the role of politics, perspective, and paradigm in shaping representation and meaning. The introduction focuses on the rising critical movement in Arab scholarship, which is largely influenced by the self-same upheavals in Western epistemology and linguistics mostly ignored by Western mainstream scholarship.

Some readers may think some of these essays have gone a little too far in their contestation of established conventions and in their criticism of prevailing academic scholarship. Such a view would only reinforce the conservative trend entrenched in the field and encourage those who still reject skepticism on principle and who dismiss "nihilistic" theories out of hand.One thing is certain: The division between the emerging scholarship and conventional scholarship is likely to grow deeper and take new oppositional forms.

But it is important to reiterate that this collective effort is not concerned with just attacking established scholarship; its aim is to arouse mainstream thinking, writing, and research to the implications of the conceptual upheaval wrought by recent theory. Its main point is that traditional rationality, with its *a priori* certainties and common sense convictions, along with the old modes of writing, teaching, and research it embodies, must be called into question and reconstructed.

Already, the language and vocabulary of conventional scholarship have to a large extent been destabilized. Between signifier and signified, sign and referent, a gap has opened up which cannot be bridged simply by a "return"—by renewed commitment to plain language and unproblematic theorization. To maintain that the present crisis is a passing phase and scholarship will revert to normal practice, is to refuse to confront postmodern reality.True, intellectual fads come and go; but some will not easily go away until they have transformed the prevailing paradigms (as classical Marxism and Freudism did earlier in the century). The poststructuralist phenomenon—in its semiological, psychoanalytical, Marxist, deconstructionist, feminist, and other forms—may be a fad, but it is not likely to disappear before it has played out its impact and has changed some of the existing modes of our representation and meaning.

1

The Scholarly Point of View: Politics, Perspective, Paradigm

Hisham Sharabi

I. Critique of Academic Scholarship

The Question of Perspective

The following critique of Western academic scholarship on the modern Arab world and Islam derives from a familiar assumption, namely, that scholarly interpretation is never neutral or objective but is always linked to certain theoretical and methodological perspectives that determine the course of understanding and interpretation. It is precisely this connection between perspective and interpretation in which I am interested here, not just in order to find whether the connection can be broken and interpretation freed from its constraints, but rather to examine the constraints themselves and to see how they actually affect understanding and interpretation. My contention is that although it might be quite legitimate to distinguish between what is explicitly or unconsciously political or ideological and what is clearly epistemological or methodological, it is frequently the case that theory and method, far from being free of politics and ideology, and thus autonomously constituted, are often grounded in convictions, preferences, and interests framed in various paradigmatic styles and forms.

Thus the point of departure of this exposition may be defined as "perspectivist," the term taken in its most comprehensive sense. Let me briefly outline the sense in which I employ this term.

Clearly, perspective shapes understanding and interpretation most decisively under the aspect of spatio-temporal determination; thus what we may see and what we may know are circumscribed by history and geography, by culture and physical conditions, i.e., by factors and forces that come together to form a determinate perspective. Above all, the fact of perspective denies transcendence, a position "outside" or "above," and affirms historicity, temporality, and the relativity of all interpretive discourse.

Thus if it is legitimate to speak of a Western perspective (in general as well as in specific terms), of a specifically Western framework and understanding of the Other, how do a non-Western culture and society get interpreted in a Western perspective? How is the relation between Self and the Other established in the interpretation from such a perspective? For example, what is the colonial mode of interpretation, and what is the post-colonial mode?

Two points we often tend to forget must be kept in mind in this context. First, the scholarly disciplines in the humanities and social sciences are all initially products of Western experience and thought. Second, the kind of knowledge that the Other, the object of Western knowledge—in this case Arab society and culture—has of itself is therefore essentially Western knowledge even when it is locally produced. Modern Third World scholarship is basically derivative scholarship, producing and re-producing a Western knowledge. This latter fact sheds strong light on one of the major impulses of fundamentalist Islam and its insistence on the need for a total break with the West and return to Islamic values and categories—that is to say, to independent interpretation and scholarship.

Against this background the current movement of secular cultural criticism in the Arab world presents itself not as a synthesis or a compromise binding Western-type modernity to Arab and Islamic modes of thought, but rather as an oppositional discourse seeking to transcend *both* Western hegemony and fundamentalist resistance through systematic critique. This new critical consciousness, still in its formative stage, seeks, on the one hand, to go beyond mainstream Western scholarship—which has dominated Arab scholarship and training in most Arab countries since the nineteenth century—and, on the other hand, to establish its own independent perspective. But before dealing with this movement— which expresses in embryo the most radical extant approach to established scholarship and which might well serve as a sounding board to the nascent critical movement in Middle Eastern studies as a whole—we must examine Western academic scholarship and characterize its implicit politics, perspective, and mode of writing.

Knowledge of Self and Other

Let us pose the question again: How can knowledge be "objective" when it is knowledge of an Other? Academic scholarship has generally approached its subject matter (here, Arab society and culture) as though from a position of timeless knowledge. A distinctive feature of the notion of perspective is the implicit assumption of *perspectiveless* knowledge, of an Archimedean point in space from which truth is grasped in its Hegelian, universal form. For a very long time we have been taught that social and historical reality can be grasped and objectively represented in the disciplines of history, sociology, anthropology, psychology, etc., if only we follow valid theory and rigorous method.

The point of radical criticism is that it is not just ideology or stereotyping or hidden interests that distort understanding and interpretation of the past and present of the Other, but also the way established academic scholarship is constituted. To begin with, Western knowledge is the product of European expansion and of world domination. Self-knowledge (the way Western scholarship understands its own Western culture and history) is achieved in terms of categories and assumptions that are centered on the Self and as such essentially different from those that constitute the knowledge of the Other. Thus the social-science disciplines developed in pursuit of knowledge of non-Western cultures and peoples are based on forms and categories of analysis designed *specifically* for grasping the Other, as in ethnology, the prototypical Western discipline invented for understanding non-Western (primitive) cultures. Once recognized, the outlook implicit in this orientation readily reveals how values cultivated within established scholarship could create the cultural contrasts and oppositions between the Self and the Other (primitive/civilized, backward/advanced, traditional/modern) that serve to justify Western practices in a non-Western world.

In its current form, radical criticism in the West aims at questioning the validity of the perspective in which this scholarship functions and thrives. Western *radical* criticism, from Marx to Derrida, is not satisfied with merely revealing the political or ideological content of bourgeois scholarship: a good deal of this criticism centers on the questions of perspective (for Nietzsche the determining condition of "truth" in all the "human" sciences), which is no longer seen as innocently determined by the way the subject matter is presented or approached; it is rather the result of certain conscious and unconscious choices made by the observer that determine both the methodological approach and the type of analysis embarked upon.

An example of the privileged self-view implicit in the European perspective is provided by Edmund Husserl in his important book *The Crisis of the European Sciences and Transcendental Phenomenology*, published just before World War II. In it, Husserl asserts that only European man enjoys the historical privilege of philosophy; he describes non-Western cultures as primitive and prescientific and in any case congenitally incapable of philosophical reflection. Husserl assumes the qualitative superiority of the European perspective as a starting point, never for a moment thinking of putting the privileged viewpoint of European consciousness into question. "This," as Paul de Man points out, "although by his own definition philosophy, as unrestricted reflection upon the self, necessarily tends toward a universality that finds its concrete, geographical correlative in the formation of supratribal, supernational communities such as, for instance, Europe. Why this geographical expansion should have chosen to stop, once and forever, at the Atlantic Ocean and the Caucasus, Husserl does not say" ("Criticism and Crisis," pp. 15–16).

A most telling element resulting from the way perspective is constituted in this sense is the determination of what is attended to and what is excluded by it—of what one wishes to see and what one turns away from. As the Marxist critic Terry Eagleton puts it: "What you choose and reject theoretically . . . depends upon what you are practically trying to do . . . In any academic study we select the objects and methods of procedure which we believe the most important, and our assessment of their importance is governed by frames of interest deeply rooted in our practical forms of social and political life" ("Political Criticism," p. 286).

Again, it is not the validity of the conventional discourse that is being questioned, but the standpoint and the unspoken assumptions that give rise to it. In whatever disciplinary form it may be expressed, the conventional scholarship I am referring to proceeds from a perspective in which two basic assumptions seem to be always implicit: that the non-Western Other is behind but will *catch up* (i.e., is always behind), and that this Other has a *separate* destiny (i.e., will always be Other). The first assumption is in its discursive construction modeled on the specifically Western experience of transformation and change understood as progress—modernization, science, technology, economic development. The second proceeds from the view that non-Western cultures somehow belong to a different order of existence and develop according to a different impulse. Both assumptions imply a qualitative difference between Self and Other, indefinitely deferring equality or identity of West and non-West.

Another Reading of Texts

In this section I shall attempt a *reading* of a few Western texts on Arab society and culture representative of mainstream academic scholarship. The disciplines these texts exemplify are history, anthropology, social psychology, sociology, and intellectual and institutional history. Taken together they fairly represent the three main tendencies of conventional academic scholarship: Orientalism, area studies, and liberal humanism. The representative samples below are by André Servier, Raphael Patai, Carlton Coon, Clifford Geertz, Daniel Lerner, Gustav von Grunebaum, H. A. R. Gibb, Albert Hourani, and Jacques Berque.

This reading consciously supersedes both the reading of the abstract general reader and that of the academic specialist. It is the reading specifically of a critical Arab reader approaching these texts from a perspective in which the premises and assumptions, attitudes and goals of the Western general reader and specialist are no longer the natural or conscious frame of reference. It is a reading, however, that is not shut in on itself but fully mindful of its own perspective and that insists on a nonconventional, nonacademic, and non-Western interpretation of scholarly texts.

In this reading my purpose is to give specific, brief examples of how the relation of Self and Other may determine the perspective and thus the orientation and language of scholarly writing on Arab culture and society. The fact that the relation itself is anchored in, to use Frederick Jameson's term, a "political unconscious" helps to elucidate how perspectives (conscious or unconscious) can influence the forms as well as content of scholarly texts. This same relationship will be later considered from the other side—the side where the Other appears as Self—by means of similar textual examples taken from recent Arab critical texts.

Let me outline very schematically what such a reading will reveal about the writing of mainstream academic scholarship.

First, that conventional scholarship is characterized by a mode of writing in which narrative description tends to be dominant and concepts and their "objective" referents are taken unproblematically: history and social reality are presumed to be transparent and fully graspable provided one applies the appropriate rules of research.

Second, that it is a scholarship grounded in the language and conceptual framework of nineteenth-century (Western) thought. Even when academic scholarship questions its categories and methods, it does so by means of concepts embedded in the traditional discourse from which it stems. Categories such as subject, object, reality, concept, cause, effect, etc. (in which recent linguistic criticism has revealed profound ambiguities and inconsistencies) are taken at face value and almost never subjected to radical criticism; when they are, they always get reinstated practically unchanged in the conventional discourse.

Third, that it is a scholarship that consciously grounds itself in authority ("scholarly" or "scientific") and expresses itself in "correct" modes of writing and exposition, remaining generally unmindful of its own ideological or political biases or of the consequences of its own rhetoric and mode of discourse.

And finally, that it is fundamentally a patriarchal scholarship, rejecting or eliding the feminist claim, viewing with sarcasm all new or different readings, and pretending to establish only one *correct* reading (there are only true or false readings).

Colonial Scholarship: Servier and Patai

The first two texts we shall deal with, André Servier's *La psychologie du musulman* (published in English translation in 1924) and Raphael Patai's *The Arab Mind* (1973), belong to the late-colonial and early–post- (or neo-) colonial periods of mainstream scholarship; one is in cultural history and the other in anthropology. Although Servier's and Patai's texts belong to the same field, the two writers use markedly different "languages" in their analysis. Servier's text illustrates the kind of mainstream scholarship that was prevalent in the final stages of imperialism and a type of writing that is anchored in the hegemonic Self, directly and frankly contemptuous of the non-Western Other. It is paternalistic in its approach, with no self-doubt about its scholarly legitimacy or the integrity of its interpretation. Thus *La psychologie du musulman* will not only contribute, as Louis Bertrand puts it in the preface, to historical knowledge as such, but will also "enlighten the natives themselves to their own past history" (p. vii). This history is constituted on the basis of two simple assumptions: the natural inferiority of the conquered Other, and the natural superiority of the conquering Self. Thus, in Servier's assertion, "the inferior Arab has borrowed everything from other nations, literature, art, science, and even his religious ideas. He has passed it all through the sieve of his own narrow mind, and being incapable of rising to high philosophic conceptions, he has distorted, mutilated and desiccated everything" (p. 73). Similarly, Islam is not "an original doctrine but a compilation of Greco-Latin traditions, biblical and Christian; but in assimilating materials so diverse, the Arab mind has stripped them of all poetical adornment, of the symbolism and philosophy he [*sic*] did not understand, and from all this he [*sic*] evolved a religious doctrine cold and rigid as a geometrical theorem: God, The Prophet, Mankind" (p. 12).

It is easy to see how this kind of writing would drive a generation of Arab intellectuals and writers to anger and frustration as well as to an enormous outlay of energy to disprove these claims and to prove their opposite: the greatness and splendor of Arab history and culture. The apologetic obsession in all contemporary Arabic writing may be traced to a reaction to this kind of late colonial scholarship, of which André Servier's text is perhaps an exaggerated but a clear example.

Raphael Patai's book *The Arab Mind*, written after the 1967 Arab-Israeli war, is more sophisticated only because expressed in social scientific language. In Patai's text, as in Servier's, Arab society, history, culture, appear thoroughly transparent and comprehensible. The similarity underlying the structure of the two texts derives from the perspective they share based on the facts of power and domination. From this perspective the Other, conquered and subdued by force, must simultaneously be conquered by knowledge. For only by grasping the history, religion, psychology, etc., of the native can the conqueror truly overcome and control. It is a perspective that calls for a special kind of knowledge, one already determined by a given conjuncture of historical forces and circumstances, a knowledge that is necessarily totalizing, essentialist, and reductive, in which the Other can appear only as essentially different, as simultaneously monolithic and mosaic, both socially and psychologically.

Patai, as a knowledgeable scholar, approaches Arab culture from *within*. Throughout the text he quotes Arabic terms and phrases to demonstrate his close familiarity with the language and the culture. From his preface we learn that he studied Arabic "twice a week for an hour" with the famous German orientalist Carl Brockelmann at the University of Breslau and again in Palestine, where he studied and "taught Arabic at a high school in Talpyot." Yet, curiously, he uses no Arabic sources in his book, and his quotations are mostly oral or secondhand, interesting not so much for their content as for the kind of messages they convey about the culture and the psychology of the people he is dealing with. One of the proverbs he quotes illustrates the point: "I and my brothers against my cousin; I and my cousins against the stranger (or 'against the world')." This is an acute comment on the Arab traits of family cohesion and hierarchical loyalties. A proverb current in Syria and Lebanon comments on Arab pride: "Even if I have to see the worm of hunger emerge from my mouth, I shall not debase myself [i.e., by asking help]" (p. 22). And he adds, "A study of these proverbs would yield a fascinating folk view of the Arab character and would set forth the Arab value system as applied to personal conduct" (*ibid.*).

Patai quotes opinions given by various individuals, in one instance those of one 'Abdul-'Aziz Zubi ("Deputy Minister of Health in the Israeli government") on Arab "emotionalism." Again, what is of interest is less Mr. Zubi's insights than the portrayal of Arab "behavior" and "psychology." Mr. Zubi declares that one of the bad characteristics of the Arabs is their tendency to exaggerate: " 'Our hearts do the job of our brains,' were his words. 'We exaggerate in both love and hate. We are emotional rather than coldly analytical. Honor is exaggerated at the expense of the real need. We would *like* to see certain things [so] we think they *are*' " (p. 52, emphasis in original).

The Arab "mind" is represented as a unified, finished, static structure, and the Arabic language as a reflection of Arab "psychology": a language of "predilections," "exaggeration," "hyperbole," and "repetition" (pp. 51–53). An Arab, according to Patai, remains captive of this state of mind and language even when he studies other cultures and succeeds in mastering a foreign tongue. Though some Arab authors may have managed to acquire a true mastery of a European language, including not only its vocabulary, grammar, and style, but also its spirit, they still have difficulty ridding themselves of the Arab linguistic tradition of exaggeration, even when writing in a European tongue (p. 55).

Patai's conclusion: "Arab thought processes are . . . more independent of reality than the thought processes typical of Western man" (p. 311).

Hegemonic Anthropology: Coon and Geertz

Carleton Coon and Clifford Geertz are two anthropologists whose texts accurately reflect the similarities and the differences within Western hegemonic anthropology of the postcolonial period.

Coon's *Caravan: The Story of the Middle East* (1952) reflects the relation between Self and Other as no longer that of European and native (colonialist and colonized), but between the developed industrialized West and the underdeveloped or developing Third World. Though not motivated by the imperialist ideology of Servier or the ambivalent anxieties of Patai, Coon is nevertheless keenly sensitive to the American structure of power on which this relationship is based in its new postcolonial form.

In Coon's perspective, Arab or Middle Eastern society appears as a static, mosaic structure. The concept *mosaic,* the opposite of united or uniform, reflects the implicit contrast between the structure of modern, industrialized societies and the premodern ethnic and religious diversity of Third World societies. Thus such categories as *sect, tribe, ethnic group, village, peasant, nomad,* and so on become central signifiers in the social and cultural analysis of those societies. On this view, these societies seem to lack an inner core or center: individuals and groups have no distinctive identity and appear only as manifestations of the religious, ethnic, and linguistic mosaic of which they are faceless products. If mosaic traditional society is defined by the lack that differentiates it from Western society, it is this lack that at the same time bestows on it a special symbolic value: "Caravan" becomes a metaphor of a society that offers "wisdom long ago forgotten," "basic truths about man's relations to man," "basic principles of human behavior" (p. 344), and so on.

As an analytical category, changelessness is central to this perspective; Coon is not interested in what might be a basic feature of Middle Eastern society—rapid social change. He wishes to approach Arab or Middle Eastern society or culture "at rest" and to turn away from problems posed by "the newly Westernized Muslim intellectuals" (p. 349). He places "Westernized intellectuals" in quotation marks because they do not represent the authentic traditional, mosaic society to which he assigns value. For him "the automobile and the movies and the parliament and the radio broadcasts" represent the real issues—and they are not the ones Westernized "intellectuals" talk about (p. 8). But even these aspects of modernization are not given systematic treatment, as they fall beyond the horizon of Coon's perspective.

Coon thus submits to the archetypical temptation of Western ethnography: to bracket history (historical social time) in order to facilitate synchronic analysis of "symbolic systems." Instead of a living society in the throes of transformation, we have a "system in equilibrium" endowed with "automatic controls" by virtue of an organization of production based on what Coon describes as a "fivefold division of labor." This is an organization that presumably affords every member of society a chance "to specialize in one way or another, and thus to channel his energy, whether he realize[s] it or not, into the most efficient utilization possible of the landscape by the greatest number of people, at a preindustrial level of technology" (p. 345).

Despite his liberal values (or maybe because of them), Coon ends by projecting a picture of the Arab or Middle Eastern Other that is so alien as to make the gap between West and non-West seem practically unbridgeable. Though he nowhere talks of Western as opposed to Arab "thought processes," he seems to find it natural that Arabs will for some time yet find it difficult to comprehend Western ways: Arabs or Middle Easterners "are amazed and shocked at our behavior. They cannot understand why we insist on driving our own jeeps and trucks, and why we go around in dirty, patched-up trousers, why we get down in the trench and do some of the excavating ourselves, and why we are always in a rush. Mad emissaries of the inscrutable West" (p. 8).

For whom does Coon write? Not just for those who are "interested" in the Middle East or who "are about to go out there," but also for those concerned with "the foreign relations of the United States in this area" (p. 342). He strives to be neutral, to be above the differences and conflicts he encounters in the field: for him "both Sunni and Shi'a dogmas are equally virtuous," and the "troubles between the Israelis and the citizens of the Arab states are none of [his] business" (*ibid.*). What *is* his business? It is to help those "who are planning to build dams or who are estimating the costs and efficiency of local labor for factories in which they are thinking of placing investments" to understand what the people "they or their clients will be dealing with, *are really like*" (*ibid.*, emphasis added).

Clifford Geertz is an innovative stylist and goes far beyond Coon in establishing a distinctive ethnographic perspective for the exploration of the Islamic Other. With the publication of *Islam Observed: Religious Development in Morocco and Indonesia* (1968), Geertz produced a new kind of ethnographic writing about Islam and Muslims: two traditional Muslim societies at the opposite ends of the Muslim world are here *observed* and "thickly" described as they search for identity and a place in the Western sun. The chief characteristic of the conflict is an "intermixture of radical fundamentalism and determined modernism," which Geertz considers "so puzzling to Western observers." The conflict itself is seen as a basically simple opposition between religion and secularism, thought and practice. In a language and a style that obscure the somewhat ordinary character of his conclusions, Geertz consciously tries to avoid "on the one hand . . . the pallid mindlessness of radical relativism and, on the other . . . the shabby tyranny of historical materialism" (p. xii), assuming a position that lies outside—and above and beyond—the object of his observation.

In substance, if not in style, Geertz's focus and approach are conventional. Typically, like Patai and other Orientalist scholars, he is not interested in "Westernized" intellectuals but in the conservative Muslim fundamentalists, the "*'alims* and *kijajis.*" The nationalist or radical revolutionaries exist only on the margin of his scholarly interest; hence his distance from the central concerns of modern Muslim society. From this distant and patronizing perspective, Muslims, compared to Westerners, appear backward, ineffective, and self-deluding. "Stepping backward in order to better leap is an established principle in cultural change; our own reformation was made that way. But in the Islamic case the stepping backward seems often to have been taken for the leap" (p. 69). He quotes a Muslim *'alim* who tells him that the Declaration of Human Rights and the secret of the atom are to be found in the Qur'an, which leads him to this essentialist conclusion: "Islam, in this way, becomes a justification for modernity, without itself actually becoming modern. It promotes what it itself, to speak metaphorically, can neither embrace nor understand" (*ibid.*).

Geertz's text is neither naive nor misinformed in the manner of Servier or Patai. Here the observed is reduced to a function of the observer's description, a description that derives its central meaning less from the phenomena observed than from the self-conscious voice giving it expression: this is truly a text about another text, a "reality" consciously fashioned by the mode of its representation.

Daniel Lerner: Modernization Theory

Daniel Lerner's *The Passing of Traditional Society* (1958) is an outstanding example of modernization theory and of the area studies approach in general. It is grounded in the same American hegemonic liberal perspective of the post–World War II period we have seen reflected in Coon's text. The Other in this perspective consists of the developing—the not-yet complete (or equal)—societies of the Third World. "What the [West] is, in this sense, the Middle East seeks to become" (p. 47).

But Lerner, unlike Coon or Geertz, is interested not in "traditional" society, society "at rest," but in its opposite, in society undergoing rapid transformation. For Lerner—as for such varied modernization theorists of the 1950s and 1960s as Martin Lipset, Lucien Pye, Karl Deutsch, Walt Rostow, and Samuel Huntington—traditional society in itself is of little interest, relevant only insofar as it provides the context in which social, economic, and political transformation occurs. In this respect Lerner's text comes closer to addressing the concerns with which the contemporary Arab critics have been mostly involved, but from a wholly different standpoint.

Lerner arrives at his idea of "traditional society" and its mode of modernization in Grunebaum's definition of the *challenge* modernization represents to Arab society: the infusion of "a rationalist and positivist spirit against which Islam is absolutely defenseless" (p. 45). This "rationalist and positivist spirit" penetrated Arab society at first only in its upper strata, "affecting mainly leisure-class fashion" (*ibid.*), but after World War II and the spread of mass media it took a global form, affecting society at large. Thus "today's Middle East 'chaos' is largely due to the shift of modernist inspiration from the discreet discourse of a few Oxford colleges and Paris salons to the broadcast exhortations among the multitudes by the mass media" (*ibid.*). Lerner eschews what he calls "the great debate over Permanence versus Change" and focuses on "the *personal* meaning of social change" (pp. 45–46, emphasis added). Though he admits that it is "large historical forces" that are responsible for the postwar social upheaval, he fails to address these forces—precisely because of his perspective, in which attitude and individual psychology, not "historical forces," form the basic categories of analysis.

Modernization for Lerner *is* in reality nothing but Westernization, "becoming what the West is." The reason he uses the term "modernization" instead of "Westernization" is, as he puts it, political and pragmatic. "[For] some [Middle Eastern] leaders, when convenient for diplomatic maneuver, to denounce the West is politically important and explains why we have chosen to speak of 'modernization' rather than 'Westernization' " (pp. 46–47). For Lerner, as for other modernization theorists, the speed at which modernization/Westernization is being carried out is too high. Why? Because "some Middle Easterners seek to accomplish in years . . . what happened in the West over centuries." But more significantly, Middle Eastern Westernizers want to modernize according to their "own way," by taking "new routes" and risky "by-passes" (the nature of which he doesn't specify) and by allowing "xenophobic nationalism," "hatred created by anti-colonialism," and rejection of "foreign tutelage" to guide their action (p. 47).

Lerner's study illustrates not only the substantive aspects of the process of modernization but also the methodological approaches whereby modernization theory has sought to validate its claims—the statistical surveys, questionnaires, and interviewing techniques as well as the theoretical frameworks and conceptual models elaborated in the various subfields, e.g., politics, social integration, economic development, and child-rearing. In the text before us, the quest was to investigate the conditions and forces for and against modernization and change in the traditional/transitional societies of the post–World War II Middle East. The study represents a major undertaking carried out under the auspices of two leading American social scientists, Paul Lazarfeld and Robert Merton. The 300 interviews conducted in Turkey, Lebanon, Jordan, Egypt, Syria, and Iran represent several months' fieldwork, during which respondents were queried in their native tongue about "their habits and preferences with regard to the mass media of communication, their attitudes toward foreigners and foreign countries, their general outlook on life, as well as certain features of their daily life" (p. vii).

Lerner admits to the limited number of the interviews and to their flawed, unrepresentative character, i.e., in terms of "men against women, town and city dwellers as against rural inhabitants, readers and radio listeners against non-readers and non-listeners" (p. 1). The study sought to answer questions such as these: "Why were some countries (e.g., Lebanon) changing so fast while others seemed to falter at rapid modernization (e.g., Iran)? . . . Why were some countries (e.g., Turkey) able to maintain stability while rapidly acquiring mobility, whereas others (e.g., Egypt) seemed to accomplish any step toward modernization only along an erratic course of violent fluctuations involving personal anguish and social dislocation?" (p. viii).

Self-imposed "value neutrality" and avoidance of "taking sides" thus establish a definite type of perspective from which it seems difficult to see alternatives to "modernization" as solutions to the existing social and political problems. If the primacy of the psychological over the social, and of the individual over the group, endows this approach with a certain concreteness, as it sometimes does, it at the same time conceals the essentially conservative ideology of the liberal modernization approach. Far from accelerating the process of social change, it often bolsters the status quo, implicitly opposing radical transformation.

Grunebaum and Lewis: The Empathy Factor

The two texts we will now examine belong to powerful representatives of European/American Orientalism, Gustav von Grunebaum and Bernard Lewis. In *Modern Islam: The Search for Cultural Identity* (1962), a collection of articles written in the 1950s, Grunebaum addresses such themes as Islam's power of expansion and adaptation, Westernization and nationalism, acculturation in Arabic literature, and so on. Lewis's book, *Semites and Anti-Semites* (1986), covers many of the same topics but in light of the changed conditions of the 1980s.

Grunebaum exhibits little interest in the underlying political issues which would later inform Lewis's main concerns; he is mostly occupied with attempts to theorize on cultural diffusion and transmission (see, e.g., pp. 13–29, 30–72) by using philological approaches and concepts taken from mainstream American social science. Like Lewis, he is eager to exhibit his familiarity with different European and Eastern languages and his erudition in a fussy, mannered style. Somewhat as Geertz does, he approaches his object of study as almost secondary to the analytical form he bestows on it in the course of his investigation, and like Geertz's, his authorial presence is primary to the text. It is difficult not to feel the chill that his indifference toward his subject matter (the Other) evokes. Both he and Lewis seem at home only with historically distant and long-dead Arabs, or with non-Arab Muslims, and comfortable only in abstract theorizing about Islamic symbolism, cultural patterns, diffusion, and so on.

Let me illustrate this effect by the following quotation, in which Grunebaum ironically describes how modern Arabs see themselves and their history:

> The creed of Pan-Arab nationalism, genetically but not inherently connected with democratic aspirations, may be sketched somewhat as follows: This community (to Arabs, that is) of the Arabic-speaking peoples, stretching from the Persian Gulf to the Atlantic, inhabits regions that possess considerable geographical similarities and great economic potentialities. The population represents a young race that has its origin in the harmonious fusion of various human strains which Islam brought together in one crucible. Within this community there is no distinction of color or race. The blood mixture has resulted in a great similarity of intellectual and moral aptitudes even though the variety of physical types has been maintained. This Arab "race" is extremely prolific, courageous, enthusiastic, enduring, patient, and guided by the spirit of fairness. The absolute superiority of Arabic over all other languages allows it a great civilizational role. The influence of Islam confers on "Arabism" a sense of spiritual values which sets it off against the materialism of the West. What internal divisions exist, such as sects or tribes, are but the result of ignorance or foreign interference. Add to this the claim, made with varying degrees of conviction, that the most outstanding features of modern civilization in the West have

their origin in the Arab-Muslim tradition and their peculiar feelings of being a chosen people derived from their central position within Islam, and you have all from which historical constructs are constantly being devised and revised, all designed to justify aspiration and hope for the future in terms of past achievement (pp. 211–12).

The message in this passage is clear: "Pan-Arab nationalism" and "democracy" are "not inherently connected"; "blood mixture" and naive racial conceptions are constitutive of Arab nationalism; the Arabs' exaggerated regard for their language, religion, and culture leads to an unrealistic assessment of themselves and of their proper place in the world; Arabs take their political fragmentation and weakness as due to mere "ignorance" or "foreign interference," rather than to their own division into "sects and tribes"; they compensate for their impotence by claiming that "modern civilization in the West has its origin in the Arab-Muslim tradition"; they have "peculiar feelings of being a chosen people"; they constantly "devise," "revise," and "design" history to fit their "aspiration and hope for the future"; and they view the future only "in terms of past achievement."

As for Lewis, after 1967 he (like other European and American scholars with a special concern for Israel) entered what might be described as a revisionist phase. Modern Arab history, after Israel's victory and its emergence as a hegemonic power in the region, undergoes some important revision. For example, Lewis now wishes to show that the modernization of the Arab countries took place not under the influence of democratic and parliamentary models derived from Britain and France (as has generally been supposed), but under the impact of totalitarian Germany (and Italy). Thus, "The situation in German lands, especially in the nineteenth century, compared much more closely to the ethnic confusion and political fragmentation of the Middle East; German-style nationalism, for the same reasons, was more intelligible and more appealing than British- or French-style patriotism" (p. 146). And by the 1930s and 1940s "political parties of the Nazi and fascist type began to appear, complete with paramilitary youth organizations, colored shirts, strict discipline, and more or less charismatic leaders" (p. 148). In Syria and Lebanon, as well as in Egypt and Iraq, Nazi ideology and organization, not liberal democracy and parliamentary government, were the forces shaping political doctrine, life, and institutions. Lewis quotes with satisfaction the Syrian politician Sami al-Jundi, who affirms: "We were racists: we admired Nazism, read the books and the sources from which its ideas derived, particularly Nietzsche" (p. 147). And in Egypt, "Not least among the borrowings of Young Egypt from Young Germany was its racism and anti-Semitism. This included support for Nazi philosophy, viciously anti-Jewish propaganda in the party press, and the organization of boy-cotts and harassment directed against the Jewish community in Egypt" (p. 149).

There inevitably followed Arab "anti-Semitism," deriving from "a wide range of anti-Semitic literature, all of it of Christian and European or American origin. It included the products of clerical and anti-clerical, right-wing and left-wing, socialist fascist anti-Semitism" (p. 199). This in turn led to indigenous anti-Semitic writing, which, "purporting to be scholarly, reveal[ed] dreadful secrets about Jews and Jewish religion . . . writers of popular fiction and drama create[d] an array of malignant Jews worthy to take their place beside the Jewish rogues' gallery of literary Europe" (p. 200). "The demonization of the Jew in modern Arabic writing goes further than it had ever done in Western literature, with the possible exception of Hitlerite Germany" (p. 201); but, paradoxi-cally, only a "few of the major figures of modern Arabic literature are among its authors . . ." (*ibid.*).

About the Arab-Israeli question, the expulsion of the Palestinians, the wars between Israel and the Arabs, the suffering and upheaval of forty years, he has only this to say: "In the summer of 1948, with the establish-ment of the state of Israel and the unsuccessful attempt by the Arab armies to destroy the new state at birth, the already bad situation of the Jews in Arab countries deteriorated rapidly" (p. 206).

More recently, Lewis, speculating about "our duty as scholars" toward our discipline, colleagues, students, and the general public, had this to say:

> What we can and should discuss [are "not the problems and conflicts which at present beset the Middle East"] but ourselves; our own role, our own duty as scholars, our duty towards our discipline, towards our colleagues, towards our students, towards the media, and beyond the media, toward the general public (*Journal of Palestine Studies* [Winter 1987], pp. 85–86).

Gibb and Hourani: Bourgeois Humanism

H. A. R. Gibb and Albert Hourani may be fairly described as the guardians of modern Middle Eastern studies, and within it, of humanistic bourgeois historiography characterized by scholarly objectivity and the canons of scientific values of research which reflect (in Gibb's terms) "the full and unprejudiced examination of *all* the relevant *facts* without attempting to place upon them any *construction* which will fit them into agreement with preconceived ideas" (*Islamic Society and the West* [1950], p. 1, emphasis added). In this perspective, the genuine scholar is one who has a firm grasp of the facts and the sources, who commands the tools of research (including the relevant languages), and who writes clearly and logically. A sense of this ideal of scholarship may be had from the introduction to the unfinished *Islamic Society and the West,* in which the essential problems of rigorous research are posed:

> A complete bibliography of this field has not yet been, and probably never will be, compiled, but the few partial bibliographies which exist demonstrate that the mass of publications dealing with these countries since 1806 is staggering. Even in the limited ground covered by René Maunier's classified *Bibliothèque Economique, Juridique et Sociale de l'Egypte Moderne (1798–1916)* the number of books and articles listed (in French, English, Italian, and German, but excluding Arabic and Greek) amounts to 6,695. When there are added to these published works relating to Turkey, Syria, and Iraq, it is evident that twenty thousand titles would be a low estimate for the period to 1919, and those written since 1919 probably amount to as many again (*ibid.,* p. 1).

In Gibb we are dealing with an ideology of scholarship as institutionalized practice. To partake of it is to become part of an esoteric profession in which master and disciple are joined by a sacred bond. In the hierarchy of authority and power, the teacher not only prescribes the correct rules of procedure and analysis, but also exemplifies the true (liberal humanistic) values whereby social and historical reality are revealed and assessed. In this perspective, antagonistic theories—especially "philosophical" and "speculative" theories, such as Marxism and the various philosophies of history—are viewed with suspicion and hostility. Here we have the pure patriarchal perspective, simultaneously totalitarian and humanistic.

Albert Hourani's *Arabic Thought in the Liberal Age, 1798–1939* (1962) provides a distinguished example of liberal scholarship. Here representation is set forth in an elegant, crystal-clear narrative that projects no ambiguity, recognizes no code, and carries no intended message. In this treatment, the course of modern Arabic thought is linear, continuous, developmental, with a clear beginning (the Napoleonic invasion of Egypt, 1798) and a definite ending (breakout of World War II)— "The West by now had carried out its *historic mission* of creating a new and unified world. The world is one" (p. 348, emphasis added). Seen in this perspective (representative of most academic, Anglo-American, liberal, humanistic scholarship), the Arab encounter with the West is a problem of secular modernization and reform, of social and political liberalization, and, in its final stages, as purely a problem of "education" and "technology": "for the first time in modern history it had become possible for eastern states, if they wished, completely to break their connections with the West."

Ironically, at the very moment that this liberal conventional mode of scholarship was celebrating the coming of age of Middle Eastern studies (see Leonard Binder [ed.], *The Study of the Middle East: Research and Scholarship in the Humanities and the Social Sciences* [1976]), the impact of the new critical and deconstructive approaches in philosophy, linguistics, and psychoanalysis was already subverting some of its central values and assumptions.

Berque: The Other as Self

Jacques Berque stands in an intermediate position between liberal conventional scholarship and the new criticism of the Arab cultural critics. Berque focused on North Africa and Islam, which his compatriot André Servier had written about in the 1920s; juxtaposing Servier's *La psychologie du Musulman* and Berque's *Les Arabes d'hier à demain* (1960) will give a clear idea of the distance separating colonial and postcolonial Western scholarship. In Berque's writing we see reflected a conceptual transformation paralleling the political one that took place in the post–World War II period. But in his more recent writings Berque goes beyond established scholarship and comes very close to the position of the Arab critical writers. Indeed, Berque saw himself, and was seen by many Arab scholars and intellectuals, as a virtual member of the Arab critical movement. As he himself wrote:

> I feel myself, in Cairo and Beirut, almost a member of that Arab intelligentsia. This undoubtedly means renouncing the classic exploits of absentee scholarship. But on the other hand it means adapting our field of study to the measure of my method. I have in fact sought to rely only on personal observation or local sources. In other words, on first-hand experience. And also on communicated experience, since the greater part of the facts I have collected or the opinions I have quoted come straight from their context of feeling, from which they must not be abstracted (*Les Arabes d'hier à demain*, p. 7 [trans., pp. 17–18]).

Berque believed that the task of scholarship is to "serve [society] by analysis and comparison" and by provoking criticism to help "those it aims at serving to make progress in self-study" (p. 10 [trans., p. 20]).

The limit reached in turn by Berque himself is the one separating internal criticism from external critique. No matter how closely Berque came to identify himself with the Arab position, he remained objectively rooted in a different cultural soil, in a foreign perspective. For, as I emphasized earlier, it is not only ideology—political, ethnocentric, or racist—but also conceptual frameworks, sensibility, and paradigm that account for the way the Western scholarly perspective and its discourse are ultimately formed and consequently differentiated from those of the observed Other.

II. Western Certainties and Non-Western Questionings

The Problem of Received Knowledge

The knowledge that Arab society has had of itself in the modern epoch, along with the scholarship on which it is based, is largely a received knowledge, a knowledge based on European "scientific," truth-seeking, post-Enlightenment social science, now under attack on its own home ground. What is being questioned in the "human and social sciences" is not just this or that aspect of epistemological or ontological theory or method, but the axiomatic certainties of Western thought itself and its central categories, with their claim to objective and universal validity.

Over the past two decades, conventional academic scholarship in its Orientalist, area-studies, and bourgeois humanistic forms has come under severe criticism from different positions. A new generation of American and European scholars, raised and trained in a different political and cultural climate and exposed to divergent values and points of view, began to put forward new questions in theory and approach and to turn to areas of research that the established scholarship had hitherto ignored or consciously deemphasized. This trend, absorbing concepts and vocabularies derived from linguistics, radical critical theory, and cultural criticism, has now developed into a more or less independent scholarly and critical perspective.

In this section I shall focus on the emergent scholarly critique as it is expressed in the avant-garde Arab writers and academics who have been influenced directly or indirectly by the radical critical debate in the West during the last two decades. My concern here will be not only to describe the content of the new critical discourse, the "meanings produced," but also—and more important—to examine the process of "production of meaning," that is, the way in which language and culture, concepts and method, have come to constitute the interpretations and meanings contained in the new critical Arab discourse.

But first I wish to establish an explicit framework in terms of which such an analysis may be undertaken. The essential element of this framework is the opposition between the Western and non-Western perspectives, between Self and Other, leading to the questions of similarity and difference in discursive practices, "logic," ways of *thinking*, and methods of *articulation* and communication. Here the issue is not only difference between a traditional, universalist, totalizing view of history and culture and a view based on difference, change, and impermanence, as in the difference between the established academic scholarship and the new radical criticism, but differences among "divergent rationalities" that are separate, independent, and nonuniversal.

Divergent Rationalities

The first question concerns the universality of concepts and experience in different cultural contexts. In his insightful study "Divergent Rationalities," the anthropologist Richard Shweder argues that certain rational processes are not universal but culture specific. These processes include the presuppositions and premises involved in reasoning, the metaphors and models used for explanation, and the models and categories for describing and classifying objects and events, so that "the version of reality we construct is a product of *both* the *universal* and the *nonuniversal* rational processes . . ." (p. 181, emphasis added). In this view, the experience of history—the historicality of all cultures—provides the horizontal dimension within which cultures develop a common experience of reality as well as individual interpretation of it.

Knowledge emerges from the sociohistorical process and serves to order this process; but central to experience and understanding, to historicality and interpretation, is the specificity of language. Language (to use Heidegger's term) "forestructures" understanding and experience and so has a determining effect on the way we see the world and make sense of it. One's observations must be recreated within the specific sense-making devices at one's disposal (Gergen [1986], p. 150). Hence the appropriateness of the notion of divergent rationalities, even though "what is rational must necessarily be universal" (Shweder [1986], pp. 163–64). The divergence of rationalities may be seen as a result of differences in tradition, cultural practices, and historical experiences, not of essential makeup or structure. Consider, for example, the profoundly consequential correlation in the Western imagination between the baby and its mother, which is not a Freudian effect but the product of the long tradition of Madonna and child rooted in the West's "social imaginary" and objectified in its art. In Islam the equivalent may be seen in the correlation of omnipotent father and obedient son originating in the Muslim "social imaginary" and articulated in Islamic myth, custom, and religious tradition. Another example: Why has there been no institution-alized witch-hunt in Islamic society when witches, jinn, and all kinds of supernatural beings proliferated in religious and popular culture, while in Europe, where the same supernatural representations were equally widespread, witch-hunting was a common institutionalized practice?

Again, how to explain the phenomenon of madness and mental derange-
ment, which in the West figures so profoundly as a disruptive social and
discursive force (as Foucault has shown), while in Islam it is practically
nonexistent in this negative or deviant form?

So the opposition in which Otherness is produced should be understood in terms other than those supplied by ideology or discursive practice; for in its active, aggressive mode, this opposition is nondiscursive:
it is experienced directly and emotionally as foreignness, strangeness,
hatred, fear. A foreign culture in this mode, when not "understood" in
its own terms, that is, *from its own perspective*, may even be seen as psychotic
(Kohut [1985], p. 251). Only when *empathic* bridges are built can the
Other society/culture be seen as no longer "psychotic" (*ibid.*). Empathy
from the point of view of academic scholarship has always been regarded
as a tendency toward subjective judgment and, as such, unscholarly.
The only form empathy might take to acquire some acceptance in the
conventional perspective is the romantic or exotic or mystical form, for
example, which juxtaposes the "spiritual" East to the "materialist" West,
and so on.

Cultural Dependency

The central thesis of the emergent Arab cultural critique is that received or derivative knowledge, imported or borrowed consciousness,
far from liberating the mind and society, serve only to reproduce and
reinforce the relations of subordination and dependency. The new critique seeks to assert its autonomy by means of a conscious selective
borrowing from the West of such concepts and approaches as would
foster independent, creative criticism. Until the mid- or late 1960s, the
values and goals of Western bourgeois humanism, as expressed principally in Anglo-American social science, were virtually unquestioned except by a muted and marginalized Marxism largely ensconced in rigid,
conventional orthodoxy. And until the end of the 1960s, Western-trained
Arab scholars and researchers chose their research areas and topics in
accordance with goals and values inspired by their conventional training
and under the influence of American funding institutions and organizations. If the term *reification* may be used in this context, it would adequately describe the kind of scholarship practiced by the post–World
War II generation of Arab researchers and writers, focused as it was on
microsocietal and largely nonpolitical areas and topics far removed from
the burning issues of the times.

The critics of the 1970s questioned not only the subordinate and
dependent character of this scholarship and its product but also the
ideological and discursive perspective which gave it form. The revolt

against Western traditional scholarship and its bourgeois positivist and humanistic values was in large part sparked by two disparate existential political events: the radical student upheaval of the 1960s in Europe and America and the crushing Arab defeat in the 1967 war. The first event revealed the bourgeois character of the Arab intellectuals' Western *learning* and exposed them to the radical and anticapitalist texts from which they had been shielded or alienated. The second event exemplified in concrete terms the consequences of subordination and underdevelopment and cleared the way for a new critical self-awareness. Then followed in a widening circle a process of *unlearning* involving the reexamination of accepted methods, premises, and tools and the search for new ones. As we shall see, the consequences for scholarly orientation of this unlearning process have been quite significant.

In the first place, there arose a tendency to abandon abstract issues and projects, that is, issues and projects that were socially or politically irrelevant. This meant a radical shift from the individual to the social: it was no longer the psychology of the individual or aspects thereof that constituted the object of concern but socially organized exploitation, repression, and domination characteristic of Arab social reality. Simultaneously, there developed not only a movement away from the contemplative, self-reflexive debate of conventional academic scholarship but also rejection of purely epistemological and literary preoccupations. The tendency now was toward commitment, toward assault on real issues encountered in the struggle to change patriarchal society.

In the realm of interpretive practice this shift expressed itself in a deliberate stepping aside in face of certain Western concepts and approaches, *both* conventional and radical. What was rejected were not the analytical categories or methods of interpretation, whether academic or radical, but those special values and insights implicit in an exclusively Western view or perspective on the (non-Western) world. Above all, this rejection involved an attempt to replace the hegemonic Western discourse regarding the Other by an independent discourse, one produced by "our" understanding, representing "our" interpretation, and grounded in "our" experiences and concerns. Though still in the process of formation, this emerging discourse has already begun to deploy its own analytical vocabulary and to fashion its own critical approaches.

Perhaps the most significant and lasting consequence of this process of unlearning and criticism since the early 1970s is the attempt to break not only from traditional Western models but also and simultaneously from Islamic fundamentalism and "modernized" Arab neopatriarchy. With regard to the latter, this has involved, on the one hand, a gradual but systematic turning away from tradition and traditional values as the grounding and legitimating referents of social practice and discourse and, on the other, an uncompromising opposition to the claims of neopatriarchal modernization and reformism.

Arab Cultural Criticism

Now we shall examine the writings of some of the leading Arab cultural critics of the contemporary period and cite a few samples of the emerging discourse which these writings represent.* The two dozen writers I have chosen discuss different themes from several different positions, all linked in some measure to one or more of the following perspectives: the Marxist, psychoanalytical, structuralist, poststructuralist, deconstructionist, or feminist. This categorization should be taken broadly, as defining general conceptual orientations rather than fixed philosophical or ideological positions. This fluidity is largely due to the difference in conceptual orientation, which in turn is frequently the result of practical conditions and the need for adaptation to repressive social and political situations in the existing Arab regimes. When these contexts change, the themes and modes of analysis also change, hence the frequent overlapping among the different positions, in which elements in one easily assimilate into the other without ideological fuss. Thus, for example, categories such as class or class struggle, though crucial within a strictly Marxist perspective, tend to give way to other analytical categories; in social macroanalysis, for example, to categories of culture and cultural determinants, and so on.

The writers dealt with here should not, then, be strictly differentiated on ideological grounds. All, however, tend to be progressive, secularist, and deeply influenced by radical theory. This is why there is little ideological hostility within the emergent critical movement, except where specific political or personal issues obtrude. Most of the writers mentioned below are alive and active (most are relatively young), and the full impact of their radical critique has only recently been felt outside intellectual and academic circles in the Arab world.

One final observation concerning the nature of the themes addressed by these writers: these are neither *political*, i.e., dealing directly with ongoing political issues, nor *Utopian*, i.e., focusing on political ideology and myth. This is in contrast with the basic preoccupation of the previous intellectual generation, which was fundamentally political (political ideology, political organization, political activism, revolution, and so on) *and* Utopian (Arab unity, socialism, Islamic unity, and so on). This is not to say that the contemporary critics are not interested in politics or in future forms of political organization; they are very much interested in these.

---

*All works cited in this section are written in Arabic, except where otherwise indicated.

Only the political circumstances under which they live, as well as their mode of approach, differ from those of the previous generation. The postcolonial conditions of independence—and national state repression—under which the new discourse is being written tend to repress its political content and force it into nonideological formulations. Thus, its approach may be oblique and often "moderate," but its underlying long-term goal is radical and revolutionary: to subvert simultaneously the existing social and political (neo)patriarchal system and the West's cultural hegemony.

Historical Rereadings: Adonis, Laroui, Arkoun, Jabiri, Djait

The Arab defeat of 1967 for the first time (and briefly) made it possible openly to challenge the political status quo, to question its ideological claims and political legitimacy. Thus the influential poet Ahmad 'Ali Sa'id (Adonis), in a three-volume work entitled *The Permanent and the Changeable* (1978), put this challenge in the form of a radical rereading of Arab and Islamic history. In a confrontational way, Adonis's critique questioned the authenticity of the dominant patriarchal discourse in these words:

> What is authenticity [*asalah*]? How can we define the authentic? How is the relation between what is past, present, and yet to come to be properly interpreted? Why has . . . Arab culture suffered such decline? Is it only due to political disintegration and foreign influence? How are we to interpret the relationship existing between language, religion, and politics? What does modernity signify . . .? (*Ibid.*, I., p. 19).

Adonis's rereading of Arab literary and cultural history constitutes a landmark in the emergent secular discourse and its development into a full-fledged cultural critique.

At about the same time but from another angle, the Maghribi historian 'Abdallah Laroui formulated a parallel critique—put forth, however, without open confrontation. His approach, grounded in a secular, Westernized perspective, maintained itself within an uncompromisingly radical framework. He articulated the basic terms of reference of the emerging debate in his book, *L'idéologie arabe contemporaine* (1967), translated into Arabic in 1970, in which he called on Arab thinkers and intellectuals to cultivate a "critical consciousness," to question "Western technology," and to recognize that "true strength resides in collective social organization and not merely in the acquisition of the instruments of war" (p. 16). Arab society "will not change until Arab thinkers themselves change, and thus choose the future rather than the past, reality rather than fantasy, and to use their writing as an instrument of criticism, not as a means of escape" (p. 14). He must also be credited with having been among the first writers systematically to address the question of meaning and the historical relativity of conceptual categories.

The Marxist tendencies in Laroui's early works, still clear and unambiguous, for example, in *La Crise des intellectueles arabes: traditionalisme ou historicisme* (1974), became less pronounced in his later writing. In a lecture delivered in 1986 on the problem of methodology, he appeared to distance himself from both Marxists and poststructuralists, accusing the latter of the same "metaphysical" and "mystical positions" they attributed to traditional Western philosophy. Indirectly he criticized his poststructuralist Moroccan colleagues for excessive preoccupation with epistemology and literature:

> If you look deeply into what is written today on epistemology in vague and complicated styles (at least in Europe, and particularly in France, the situation in America is different), you will find that it is grounded in metaphysical and mystical positions. In my own writing [when] I reach the threshold of the problems involved I stop. It is my belief that one can settle these problems; but under the conditions in which we Arabs live, it is not necessary to settle them. I receive these epistemological works as I receive literary and aesthetic works: for pleasure or intellectual exercise (Laroui *et al.*, *Methodology in Literature and the Human Sciences* [1986], p. 17).

The question of Islam and Arab history was approached from still another point of view by Muhammad Arkoun, a French-speaking Algerian historian fully at home in both traditional Islamic historiography and Western social science. Arkoun's central concern is to break the monopoly of traditional and neopatriarchal interpretation of Islamic history and the Qur'an, which he seeks to accomplish, as he puts it in *Lectures du Coran* (1982), by enacting a new reading of the relevant texts that ignores philological and Orientalist methods and relies on linguistic, semiological, anthropological, and sociological approaches (pp. 1–26). Using Heidegger's notion of "thinking," he suggests a new way of "thinking" Islam, one that does not oppose the conventional and traditional approaches so much as sidestep them altogether: "So-called modern [conventional] scholarship remains far from an epistemological project that would free Islam from the essentialist, substantialist postulates of classical metaphysics." Specifically, he wishes to go beyond the "two dogmatic attitudes—the theological claims of believers and the ideological postulates of positivist rationalists," i.e., the patriarchal as well as the neopatriarchal positions, and to treat history as "an anthropology of the past and not just as a narrative factual account" (*ibid.*).

In a lecture given at Georgetown University in 1985, entitled "Rethinking Islam," Arkoun provided a detailed analysis of what the new approach would consist of; its key concepts are derived from Lévi-Strauss, Foucault, Derrida, Lacan, Castoriades, and other recent French theorists. He structures his approach according to the following schema:

1. Tools for new thinking.
2. Modes of thinking.
3. From the unthinkable to the thinkable.
4. Societies of the Book.
5. Strategy for deconstruction.
6. Revelation and history.

Arkoun's use of the concept of *l'imaginaire sociale* opens up new vistas for social and psychological research (*ibid.*). Arkoun proposes a scholarly undertaking which he recognizes as beyond the ability of single researchers, envisaging "teams of thinkers, writers, artists, scholars, politicians, and economic producers," whose goal is to revive "a vision of Islam which could have the same impact on the [Islamic] community as the *Risalah* of Shafi'i or *Ihya 'Ulum al-Din* of Ghazzali" (*ibid.*).

Like Arkoun, the Moroccan historian Muhammad 'Abid al-Jabiri aims at transcending the discourses of both Islamic traditionalism and "modern" Arab scholarship, patriarchal and neopatriarchal alike. In traditionalist scholarship he sees "legacy repeat[ing] itself," and in "modernized" scholarship a distorted European perspective occupying a dominant position. Jabiri's own position on the traditional legacy–West opposition rests on an attempt at a radical redefinition of its terms. In a lecture on the question of methodology (*Methodology in Literature and the Human Sciences* [1986]), he argues that the revival of the legacy of Arabism and Islam is "a necessary undertaking not only because it serves to propel society toward a better future, but also because it bolster[s] the present [and] affirms [social] existence and the Self" (*ibid.*, p. 76). But legacy (*turath*) must be correctly understood to signify not only something "inherited" (in the legal sense), but also "an intellectual and spiritual *heritage* (*tarkah*)" (p. 75, emphasis added). Interestingly, he points to the same Oedipal relation Paul Nuwiya employed in his introduction to Adonis's reading of Islamic history in *The Permanent and the Changeable* (I, 16), insisting that recognition of the above distinction is important inasmuch as it "signifies the disappearance of the father and his replacement by the son," or "the presence of the father in the son, of the dead generations in the living, of the past in the present" (*Methodology*, p. 75).

Similarly, Jabiri rejects what he considers Europe's or the West's self-assigned centrality, its claim to embody "the 'general history' of human thought" (p. 78) and its marginalization of non-Western thought "which if acknowledged at all, was seen to lie outside this 'general history' . . . a stagnant 'lake' like the Dead Sea, completely separated from the 'eternal river' gushing forth from Greece" (p. 79). And he adds: "It is true that European cultural historians of the last two centuries, whether orientalists or not, did not share the same viewpoint or the same methodology. Yet despite differences in standpoint, method, and motive they all labored within the same Eurocentric framework, which they continually reinforced . . ."

Jabiri gives some space to criticizing Western scholars known for their sensitive and empathic writing on Islam and Islamic culture, such as Louis Massignon and Henry Corbin, for their failure to free themselves from the limiting horizon of the West's self-referring perspective. Significantly, he includes Marxism, which he puts alongside Orientalism, describing it as another variety of *salafi* reading of history (described by Muhammad Waqidi, [1985], p. 106). He claims that although Marxist historians may have differed from their bourgeois colleagues in frankly affirming their ideological position, they were equally unaware of their own allegiance to the same Eurocentric perspective. "Historical Materialism," according to Jabiri, is bound to the "universality of European thought, to European history in general, . . . if not in content and orientation (which, however, rather is the case), then in basic concepts and categories . . ." (*Methodology*, p. 82). Because of that bond the Marxist understanding of Arab history and culture rests on an "external" understanding, just like that of the Orientalists (*ibid.*).

Having distanced himself from Islamic traditionalism, Western conventional scholarship, and Marxist historicism, Jabiri proceeds to chart his own course in his important Arabic-language book, *The Contemporary Arab Discourse* (1982).

> [F]rom the very beginning I decided on what kind of critique I was going to apply to the contemporary Arab discourse, an epistemological, not an ideological critique . . . When I first embarked on this task, I did not have a definite "model" to go by. For me neither Kant, Freud, Blachard, Foucault, Marx nor Derrida were the proper examples to pursue, nor were other [Western] thinkers. I let the subject matter determine the choices I made. I was careful to pay due respect to my subject matter and not to allow any referential authority to exercise domination over it. On the contrary, I preferred that the subject matter should enjoy "hegemony" over all referential authorities which bind the concepts and categories I use. I did this consciously without surrendering [to these authorities] (p. 13).

In doing this Jabiri was of course greatly influenced by precisely those "authorities" he wished to set apart. But the point is that he does not willingly allow conceptual borrowing to subject or subordinate his analysis to the *external* perspective of Western scholarship, including the new critical scholarship. In the same book he writes:

> I use different concepts, derived from different, often opposed philosophies, methodologies, and "readings," from Kant, Freud, Blachard, Althusser, Foucault, in addition to a number of Marxist concepts without which modern thought cannot breathe. Readers familiar with these theories and methods will no doubt notice that in my use of these concepts I do not limit myself to the constraints present in the original frameworks, but often utilize them with considerable freedom. I am fully conscious of this and exercise my freedom responsibly. We should not consider these concepts molds cast in iron, but tools to be used in each instance in the most productive way, otherwise I would discard them, for what is the value of any concept if it is used only as an ornament? (p. 12).

The Tunisian historian, Hichem Djait, like most of his Maghribi colleagues, writes in French. His two major works, *La Personalité et le devenir arabo-islamique* (1974) and *L'Europe et l'Islam* (1978) (the first translated into Arabic in 1984 and the second into English in 1985), raise some of the major themes with which the other Maghribi historians are concerned: the place and meaning of the cultural heritage (*turath*); the relation of historicity; the questions of religion, identity, tradition, and modernity.

Djait's starting point is the contradictory expression of "openness and repression, of tradition and modernity, of oneness and fragmentation," which characterizes Maghribi intellectual experience and history. He defines the difference between the Mashriq's and the Maghrib's experience in cultural terms: Though the Arab East is politically more advanced, having achieved independence long before the Maghrib, it remains culturally less mature. This is due to two main reasons: the lack of direct, unmediated contact with the West like that experienced by the Tunisians, Algerians, and Moroccans; and the proliferation of state repression following achievement of independence in the Mashriq. This has led to "an unstable, faulty understanding of modernity [and] to a confused view of Arab history . . . making it difficult to see the self and history with any clarity" (*al-Shakhsiyyah al-'Arabiyyah* [1984], p. 7). What makes the Maghribi experience richer and intellectually more fruitful, in his view, is the direct wrenching encounter with Europe, with the resulting social and psychological uprooting of society and the individual.

"Precisely because the Maghribi self was so uprooted it gained distance from itself and was thus better able to demystify its view of itself—the precondition for establishing any kind of truth about self and history" (*ibid*).

Djait, unlike most of the other Arab cultural critics, considers himself an Islamic reformer, but not a fundamentalist, and an Arab nationalist, but not a pan-Arabist. Stressing an identity which is at once Muslim and Arab, but whose features are distinctly Maghribi, he lays claim to a specifically "Maghribi historical thought," which he grounds in three North African thinkers belonging to three transitions in North African history: St. Augustine and the fall of the Roman Empire, Ibn Khaldun and the disintegration of medieval Islam, and Khair al-Din Pasha and the end of the Muslim Ottoman empire.

Djait characterizes his own perspective as "consecutively Westernized, historicist, ideological and spiritual" (p. 9), and refuses identification with either right or left: "Arab [intellectuals] welcome their latest discoveries with emotion and enthusiasm. If they are for modernity, everyone else [who is not] becomes the object of their contempt. If they are revolutionaries, there is no place except for revolution. And if they are critics, every constructive suggestion for the future becomes meaningless . . . as though originality were impossible and what is of value could come only from the outside or from the past" (*ibid.*).

Djait appears to be a liberal as wary of Marxism as of Islamic fundamentalism: "Arab Marxism" could be used to bestow "modern legitimacy" on the "oriental despotism" of the Arab state (p. 106). His preference is for a "secularism not hostile to Islam." The choice, as he puts it, should not be "between Islam and Westernization, or between Islam and Marxism . . . but between traditionalism and modernity" (pp. 107, 111).

In *Europe and Islam* Djait fits Islam and Europe into a common genetic structure which enables him to see Europe as the "analogue" of Islam: "Europe as historical culture and a great civilization corresponds to Islam as an international community and civilization" (p. 2). Both cultures have passed through the same historical phases: a phase characterized by the political and economic power of an imperial center followed by a phase of political decline and rising cultural influence. He then speaks of two Islams, one constituting "part of an integral world history," the other consisting of a distinct, self-contained "political and cultural organism . . . focused on its own interior life" (p. 114). From this perspective, a politically weak and fragmented Arab world could still become culturally and intellectually significant by "reclaiming its Islamic heritage" and by thus becoming "the cradle of Islamic culture" in the same way that Europe became "the cradle of modernity" (p. 2). Today the Arab world plays the same role vis-à-vis the external and peripheral Islamic societies that

Europe played in regard to its colonial outposts in the age of expansion. And like Europe after its political decline in the postcolonial age, the Arab world could now "effect a kind of transferral and shrinkage of the Islamic space into the confines of Arab space, and become charged with an emotionally powerful political, ideological content" (*ibid.*). His point is that cultural regeneration can be achieved despite political fragmentation. The historical experience of Europe and Islam provide proof of this: "[I]f Europe, in its commonplace, shrunken present-day form, can find an analogue in the Arab world, Europe as a historical culture and a great civilization corresponds to Islam as an international community and civilization" (*ibid.*).

Marxist Perspectives: Tazzini, Muruwwah, and Murqus

The Arab Marxist critique is expressed in different forms and from different standpoints, of which three stand out: orthodox Marxism, "Islamic" Marxism, and "Western" Marxism. I shall briefly characterize each of these types by referring to three leading Arab Marxist writers: Tayyib Tazzini, Hussein Muruwwah, and Elias Murqus.

Tayyib Tazzini, a graduate of Karl Marx University (Leipzig, German Democratic Republic) and professor at the Syrian University, approaches the question of cultural legacy in a global, totalizing manner, devoting to it a (projected) twelve-volume study, entitled *A Project for a New Vision of Arab Thought*. This is how he formulates the central issue in the first published volume of the study (*From Legacy to Revolution* [1979]):

> In the present phase the majority of Arab writers, historians, and intellectuals—despite their different class positions, orientations, and ideological horizons—agree that the significance of the problem of posing the question of the national "legacy" stems not from its historical nature or the requirements of scientific research or scientific truth; to some degree or another, they all view this problem in terms of its relation to the existing political, social, economic, and cultural reality of the Arab world—a relation which can be defined and whose features and horizons can be clearly outlined (p. 17).

Tazzini intends this first volume of his study to be "an introduction to the basic theoretical and methodological problems of the study of human heritage and history in general and Arab heritage and history in particular" based on the "scientific tools [of] the historical-materialist dialectic" (pp. 21, 31). Although he comes up with little that is new by way of theory or method, he makes effective use of the Marxist vocabulary to enrich his new critical exposition.

If Tazzini represents the "orthodox" materialist tendency within Arab Marxism, Hussein Muruwwah is probably its best Muslim interpreter. Muruwwah's position rests on a compromise that characterizes a growing tendency among liberal and left intellectuals: the tendency to seek a "return" to the national heritage in order to draw from it the values and principles to face the "threats" and "challenges" of the modern world. For Muruwwah and other Muslim leftists who have made their peace with religion, secularism is rejected as a form of "bourgeois nihilism," a product of Western cultural imperialism. In *Studies in Islam* (1980), he writes:

> Those in our society who put forward the theory of historical "rupture" between contemporary Arab culture and its intellectual heritage . . . aim to direct the [new] Arab generation not toward the scientific technology of the West but toward Western bourgeois ideology, toward those kinds of nihilism in Western bourgeois culture . . . in order to drive this generation away from confronting the problems posed by the conditions of the liberational and progressive battle now reaching its peak in the Arab world (p. 58).

But Muruwwah's intention is not so much to adapt Marxist doctrine to Islam as it is to apply materialist theory to the understanding of Islam and Arab history, to the interpretation of the Islamic experience in such a way as to effect social and cultural resurgence. A first step in this direction is to make clear the distinction between the sense of cultural legacy as "a quantitative accumulation of forms of consciousness . . . lacking any kind of structural unity" and one based on "a historical materialist conception of the relation of social consciousness to social existence" (pp. 40–41). This would make possible the view of cultural history as "a continuous movement of becoming, of travelling from the past to the present and into the future on a course obstructed only by temporary deviations, disruptions, turns and sudden leaps"(p. 41).

Muruwwah vehemently attacks vulgar materialism (including orthodox Marxism), accusing its practitioners of "negating the relation between past consciousness and contemporary consciousness," of seeing the latter as merely " a reflection of the present, a pure mirror reflection" (pp. 41–42). "Thus," he concludes, "we can say that we have before us two kinds of meaning of cultural legacy [*turath*]: one deriving from a metaphysical, idealistic view of the problem of consciousness and being and another based on a historical materialist view of this problem" (p. 47). It is only the latter view that can reconstruct historical reality and connect it to the present: "The present then discovers that it possesses a history, that this history is based on a territory and a fatherland with real human beings rooted in this history and fatherland" (*ibid.*).

Finally, Elias Murqus, a Christian high school teacher from Latakia and a "Western" Marxist, is primarily concerned with epistemological and theoretical issues. He asks, "Is Arab thought truly *thought?*" and directs his critique against no particular body of thought or ideology, but against the mode of analysis characteristic of nationalist, traditionalist, and old leftist thought. "It is not thought at all but rather *fiqh* [legal exegesis]," which in this context may be read to mean "dogmatism" or "ideology." "I call *'fiqh'* that kind of thought based on 'principles and conventions,' 'origins and derivations . . .' for example Stalinist 'dialectical materialism . . .' " (*al-Wihdah*, October 1984, p. 28) "Arab thought must make some transitions, of which the first must be the transition from symbolism and objectivism to conceptualization [*mafhumiyyah*] and realism [*waq'iyyah*]" (*ibid.*, p. 33).

He calls for modernization, not in the form of "Westernization," but in the form of Marxist progress—which "is not bourgeois progress emulating the West's example" (*ibid.*, p. 29). In any event, there is no alternative to moving into modernity and secularism: if Arab society fails to move forward "we will return at some future date to a former state of being, fall outside world history, and become an object . . . rather than a subject of history" (*ibid.*, pp. 32–33).

Social Being: Barakat, Zayour, and Safwan

Critical work in the fields of sociology and social psychology may be represented by the writing of Halim Barakat (Syria), 'Ali Zayour (Lebanon), and Mustafa Safwan (Egypt). Barakat's pioneering work, *Contemporary Arab Society* (1984) is probably the first systematic sociopolitical analysis of the structure and dynamics of Arab society. In his approach, Barakat breaks with the conventional mode of sociological writing—natural, statistical, descriptive—and assumes an intentionally contestatory mode. By approaching Arab society not only as underdeveloped but also as *alienated*—"a society estranged from itself and seeking to transcend its estrangement" (p. 13)—Barakat adds to the concreteness and effectiveness of the emergent cultural critique.

So does the Lebanese psychologist 'Ali Zayour in his book *The Analysis of the Arab Self* (1977), which provides the kind of analysis largely lacking in the purely historical approach. Zayour, as far as I know, is the first critic to apply psychoanalytical concepts systematically to the analysis of contemporary Arab society. Like Barakat, but from the more intimate standpoint of the *analyst*, Zayour approaches society from the inside as Self or Subject, employing, as he puts it, the tools of "observation, recording, field investigation, comparative analysis" in probing its "individual and collective unconscious" (p. 6). He stresses the relation between the collective and individual selves and discusses the latter's sociohistorical development, emphasizing the need for investigating "the sexual and religious" structures of society as much as its "intellectual and ethical systems" within the structure of class and "methods of production" (*ibid.*). He maintains that only within this kind of analytical framework can we grasp the structure of the kind of personality Arab society produces, including the methods of child-rearing, ways of family organization, patterns of repression and control, and so on, which it employs for this purpose.

The third work constitutes another pioneering premier, the Arabic translation of Freud's *Interpretation of Dreams* (1981), an event of major significance whose social and political implications have not yet been fully felt in the Arab world. The translator, Mustafa Safwan, a Lacanian psychoanalyst now living in Paris, has with this one move made available in Arabic practically the entirety of the basic vocabulary and framework of psychoanalysis. Although some of Freud's writings were translated into Arabic in the 1950s, the translation of the *Interpretation of Dreams* represents a qualitative advance in the construction of a systematic and workable psychological language in Arabic, making possible both the understanding of the Freudian corpus and the handling of an intellectual dimension hitherto absent in the critical Arabic discourse.

In the introduction to his translation, Safwan characterizes Freud's influence in the West as having touched "everything from art to philosophy to the human sciences." He asks whether the Arab world will face up to the challenge of a writer "who has revealed to us the words behind the dream and the language behind the words," quoting a phrase from Freud that reflects the challenge he (Safwan) sees Arab society facing: "Who fails to choose his past will never find his present" (p. 26).

The Structuralist and Poststructuralist Approaches: Abu Dib, Kilitu, Fihri, Waqidi, Benniss, Khatibi

Structuralism and poststructuralism, like psychoanalysis, made their appearance in Arabic only in the last decade or so, with the publication of a number of important works in which the structuralist and poststructuralist approaches were fully or partially incorporated. The first work in Arabic to give a full and systematic exposition of the structuralist movement in France was published in Cairo in 1975. This was *The Problem of Structuralism* by Zakariyya Ibrahim, a French-educated Egyptian professor who taught philosophy at Muhammad V University in Rabat. The book presents a brief but accurate description of the various structuralist schools in linguistics, anthropology, epistemology, psychoanalysis, cultural history, and Marxism, and discusses de Saussure and Jacobson (linguistics), Lévi-Strauss (anthropology), Barthes and Foucault (episte-mology and cultural history), Lacan (psychoanalysis), and Althusser (Marxism). Ibrahim's great contribution is that he introduced a wholly new set of analytical terms which became basic to the language of the new critical discourse.

Structuralism and poststructuralism have had a profound impact on the development of the critical discourse in the 1980s and are still growing in influence. In the following examples I focus on the works of six major writers who have most contributed to the formation of this orientation in the critical movement.

The first is Kamal Abu Dib, an Oxford-trained literary historian until recently a professor of literature at Yarmouk University in Jordan, who in his major work on the Arab linguist al-Jurjani (in English, *Al-Jurjani's Theory of Poetic Imagery* [1979]), demonstrates how structuralist concepts may be applied not only to the analysis of Arabic linguistic theory but also to the criticism of the thought and literature of the modern *nahda* (renaissance). In the introduction he makes clear that he intends his study to be an example of how the intellectual "lostness and confusion" of the writers and intellectuals of the *nahda* might be critically analyzed and how thought might be transformed from "one-sided superficiality" and "subjectivity" into a "structuralist" mode which will not be "satisfied with grasping isolated phenomena but seeks to define the fundamental, consti-tutive elements of phenomena—in culture, society, and poetry" (p. 8).

This is how he defines the structuralist approach, both as a method of analysis and as a tool of radical critique:

> Structuralism is not a philosophy but a way of seeing and a method of dealing with reality. Structuralism does not change language or society or poetry. But in its rigor and insistence on fundamental analysis, on multidimensional understanding and the pursuit of the real determi-nants of things as well as of the relations between them, it changes thought—in the way it deals with language and society and poetry— and transforms it into a questioning, doubting, pursuing, seeking, comprehending, dialectical thought" (*ibid.*).

French structuralism (including poststructuralism) has had its greatest impact in the Maghrib, particularly in Morocco, where a veritable renais-sance in critical writing (and publishing) is in process. Among the recent publications of the newly established Tobqal publishing house in Casa-blanca is a collection of texts (some of them mentioned above) under the title *Methodology in Literature and the Human Sciences*. These are lectures given by 'Abdullah Laroui, 'Abdul-Fattah Kilitu, 'Abdul-Qadir al-Fasi al-Fihri, and Muhammad 'Abid al-Jabiri, with an introduction by al-Tahir

Waziz, together with the questions and comments of the audience and the speakers' replies. In the introduction, al-Tahir Waziz reiterates the main theme of poststructuralism, which in the context of the prevailing Arab patriarchal discourse represents a major challenging principle: "It is no longer permissible to believe in the possibility of a single methodology . . ." (p. 5). He quotes Feyerabend's *Contre la méthode* (1975): "Methodological measures are not immune to criticism; it is possible to reexamine these, to improve on them or to replace them by better ones," concluding that "a methodology, any methodology, when it loses its fruitfulness is no longer useful in revealing anything new" (pp. 5–6).

Of the four lecturers included here, we have already touched on Laroui and Jabiri; the other two are 'Abdul-Fattah Kilitu and 'Abdul-Qadir al-Fasi al-Fihri.

Kilitu, like many of his Moroccan colleagues, draws heavily on Roland Barthes, particularly on his theory of reading. Kilitu asks: "How should we *read*, and what are the conditions and measurements of good reading?" [emphasis added]. Then he asks: "Who will judge whether a reading is good or bad, who will make the final judgment?" (p. 20). In his introduction to an Arabic translation of a collection of Barthes' essays (*Leçon*, 1978), Kilitu raises questions about literature, language, and textuality never before (as far as I know) posed in the mainstream debate:

> How has the concept of literature developed across the ages in different societies? . . . What is the relation between literature and language, between language and authority? . . . What is the relation between the literary discourse and other kinds of discourse? . . . How should the question of the social character of literature be posed? . . . How are the subject, dominant opinions, the beginning and the end in a given text to be deconstructed? . . . How should reading be carried out? (*A Lesson in Semiology* [1986], pp. 5–6).

Kilitu maintains that it is not enough just to read Barthes, one should go beyond him:

> The Arab reader should read very closely, he should even learn "by heart," but at a later stage he should "no longer remember," so that he will not fall into the trap of repetition, so that he will be able to reformulate Barthes' questions and provide new answers no one has heard before (*ibid.*, p. 6).

Al-Fasi al-Fihri is a young linguist, an MIT graduate, who teaches at Muhammad V University in Rabat. On the "legacy" (*turath*) issue, his position is one of the most clear-cut: he refuses to submit to the fundamentalist position, which he sees as repressive, leading only to "retreat from history" (*Methodology*, p. 94). His approach is based on linguistic analysis and the elaboration of "theoretical frameworks" of interpretation which may be "judged by the extent to which [they] enable us to arrive at a certain conception of the phenomenon we are dealing with" (p. 36). He criticizes Laroui for failing to formulate a clear theoretical framework for his interpretive project. "[H]ow can we speak of interpretation without mentioning theory?" (*ibid.*).

Theory is the product of scientific discourse defined not by some universal or transcendental rule, but in terms of the conditions of its production, that is to say, "in terms of the addresser, the addressee, and the context of discourse" (p. 43). As "an explanatory structure" it brings together a number of concepts and assumptions by means of a "deductive apparatus" (*ibid.*). But scientific discourse is one of several possible kinds: "One discourse defines a certain reality, another discourse defines another reality" (p. 49). Discord between different interpretive discourses—historical, scientific, literary—could only be resolved, according to al-Fihri, by linguistic analysis.

For him, methodology, like theory, is a "circumstantial experience," changeable in the way experience changes. Thus for al-Fihri the search for meaning is what makes for the "complementarity" (*takamul*) between philosophical, literary, scientific, and historical discourses, a search in which various theories and methods of interpretation compete and cooperate in arriving at "meaning" (p. 62). But underlying all meaning discovered in different discourses is what is revealed by linguistic analysis.

Muhammad Waqidi complements al-Fihri's critique from a purely philosophical standpoint. In his book *A Philosophical Dialogue* (1985), he underscores the methodological aspect, observing that "contemporary Arab philosophy has failed to confront the [crisis of] epistemology and cultural values brought about by the revolution in the human sciences" (p. 10). He laments the anemic state of philosophy in the Arab world and calls for Arab involvement in the philosophical debate going on in the West in spite of the fact that "the scientific revolution was carried out within a cognitive development outside our own" (p. 173). To grasp the inner structure of this revolution, including its own problematics and those connected with its interpretations, is a basic condition for breaking out of the state of passivity and diffidence in which Arab philosophy finds itself today.

Muhammad Benniss, literary critic and poet (author of the Arabic *Finnegan's Wake*, *Mawasim al-Sharq* [1985]), is one of the most sophisticated deconstructive critics of the Maghribi movement. He dismisses the prevailing (neopatriarchal) discourse as vague, generalized, and wholly unsuited to tackle the problematics of the modern intellectual scene.

Indeed, Benniss charges, it habitually "dismisses answers as contemptuously as it does questions" (*al-Karmil* [1984], p. 222). In his criticism of the neopatriarchal discourse, particularly its absolutist and repressive tendencies, he attacks many of the nationalist and secularist positions that date back to the early years of the *nahda*—for example, the goal of Arab unity, on the ground that it suppresses ethnic differences and minority rights. Thus: "[T]here are class differences, language differences, historical differences which various forms of knowledge in the Arab world, whether they are already dominant or on their way to becoming so, seek to suppress" (Introduction, *The Wounded Arab Name* [1980], p. 7). The only way to approach the dominant discourse is by direct confrontation, a task that, under the repressive conditions prevailing in the Arab world, only deconstruction is able to undertake.

> To deconstruct the theological ground is the first condition of effective criticism; it brings us from heaven back down to earth. It is high time that this "heaven" is made to stop hiding our body, dividing it into Light and Darkness, into Left and Right, Good and Evil, Angels and Devils. It is high time that this body be allowed to celebrate its desires and its pleasures, and to create new values not prescribed beforehand or imposed by necessity (*ibid.*, p. 8).

The central figure of the deconstructive critique is 'Abdul-Kabir al-Khatibi, a French-trained sociologist who has written exclusively in French (and whose works Benniss has partly made available in lucid Arabic). Khatibi starts out from the by-now-established position of the radical critique, that transcendence is possible through neither Western nor Fundamentalist models: "There is no profit in going . . . through the various phases traversed by Western thought; and it is futile to believe in the possibility of establishing a complete connection with Arab classical knowledge" (*Double Critique* [1980], p. 164).

Although the most "Western" of the radical critics, Khatibi insists on "violent rupture with hegemonic Western culture" (*ibid.*, p. 161). Western knowledge is inescapably tainted by ethnocentrism; it is, he maintains (quoting Derrida), "the relation of ontology to the history of Western metaphysics and its inherited categories" (*ibid.*, p. 159; Derrida, *La Structure, le signe et le jeu* [1967], p. 414). Hence the need for approaching the "language of the [Western] human sciences" with caution if not suspicion. It is never enough just "to translate and acquire [Western] scientific knowledge": a truly authentic grasp must be rooted in criticism (*Double Critique*, pp. 161–62). And Khatibi introduces here the notion of "double criticism" (pp. 157–65), which he defines as criticism directed "both outward and inward." Directed to the outside, it takes a deconstructive form, aimed at dismantling "the concepts and categories produced by the sociological writing and knowledge which speaks *about* and *for* the Arab world, and which is largely Western produced and linked to an ideology rooted in Western ethnocentricism"; directed inward, it assumes the form of self-criticism, criticism of Arab sociological and historical writing. On the latter, Khatibi writes: "[W]e must rethink history and [sociological] knowledge not in relation to a center or origin (the West)," but autonomously, on independent grounds (*ibid.*, p. 158).

Khatibi goes further than most of the Maghribi critics in opposing knowledge to criticism and in advocating a position beyond the human sciences, which he defines, following Foucault, as the field of "absolute Western knowledge."

> Arab thought retreated five centuries ago; it returns today to enter a world dominated by the absolute knowledge of the West. Instead of initiating a serious dialogue with the thought of difference (Nietzsche, Heidegger) it gets lost in the various fields of the human sciences. Doubtless, this orientalism has some benefits, but it is an orientalism that cannot lead to the creation of original thought. This is why Arab thought may be best described by its historicist and cultural tendencies (*ibid.*, p. 36).

Khatibi takes an ambivalent position vis-à-vis Marxism, which he attacks in its vulgar form (the form it generally assumes in the Arab world), because the only "lead[s] us to theology" (*ibid.*, p. 31). At the same time he sees Marxism capable of transcending its present (vulgar) form if it succeeds in incorporating difference and pluralistic thought. "And as we are waiting for this to happen, we should teach Marxism, but making sure that we teach it cautiously" (*ibid.*).

He demonstrates the meaning of double criticism by outlining some of the contents of those "internal" and "external" areas (the Self and the West) to be subjected to criticism. His starting point in the "internal" area is the notion of *unity*, the cherished unity of the Arab people, of Arab history and culture. He displaces the view of Arab disunity as just an aberration produced by Ottoman domination and Western colonialism, suggesting that the present reality of fragmentation is the product of a historical process which is "in itself neither good nor bad" (*ibid.*, p. 9). The Arab world should be accepted and understood in its difference, in its multiform and pluralistic structures. The Arab world "does not form—and cannot form in itself—an interconnected totality which may be encompassed in a single system" (*ibid.*). Nor can it fall back on archaic "originary" identity rooted in "linguistic, religious, and patriarchal origins" (*ibid.*). Both Arab society and identity are the product of internal "contradictions" and "struggles" and of "the process of learning to adapt to the modern age and opening up to the world" (*ibid.*).

Khatibi was probably the first Arab critic to raise the issue of "Orientalism" and to expose it to a rigorous deconstructive analysis in an article published in *Les Temps modernes* in 1976, which focused on Jacques Berque, one of the most "empathic" of Western Arab-oriented scholars. For Khatibi, Orientalists invented the notion of Islam, defining it as "total submission to Allah's will," when in fact Islam only served as a "compromise" rubric covering a large area of "heathendom" (*ibid.*, p. 29). "Nowadays the orientalist has become a humanist in reverse. I mean he is oriented toward 'man' as conceived by the human sciences, that conception so sharply criticized by Foucault" (*ibid.*).

In an interview published in *Le Monde* (February 14–15, 1978), Khatibi was asked whether he agreed with the statement that Arab society is not really underdeveloped but only falsely described as such. He responded that Arab society is indeed woefully underdeveloped, and that to attribute underdevelopment to the analysis of underdevelopment is mere "sophistry, or better still, demagogy." Both the traditionalist claim and the nationalist apologetic, he said, conceal through "radical negation" problems they simply cannot face (*ibid.*, p. 27).

It is worth noting that Khatibi criticized Heidegger as well, for not acknowledging his indebtedness to Arab philosophy, particularly to Avicenna's concept of Being, which profoundly influenced Duns Scotus, who in turn intimately influenced Heidegger. Khatibi attributed the latter's "forgetfulness" to the European's inbuilt ethnocentric attitude.

The Feminist Perspective: Sa'dawi, Mernissi, Sa'id

Feminism in the Arab world is still a predominantly female concern; even among radical (male) intellectuals the women's question remains a peripheral issue, one still framed in conventional political terms. In fact, the new cultural critics have very little to say that is new about the women's problem and have shown only perfunctory support for the nascent Arab women's movement. Fundamentalists, on the other hand, have exhibited keen interest in the women's issue and have argued that Islam assures women a large measure of freedom and legal protection. Fundamentalist writers seek above all to subvert the secular claims of the women's liberation movement by opposing their "Muslim concept" to the "Western secular concept" and defining the latter as idolatrous (al-Qadi [1983], p. 21). The sheer size of fundamentalist literature on the subject reveals the extent to which the problem of women constitutes a source of concern and anxiety in patriarchal consciousness.

The threat of social and ideological subversion is exemplified by three feminist writers discussed in this section, the Egyptian psychiatrist Nawal

Sa'dawi, the Moroccan sociologist Fatima Mernissi, and the Syrian literary critic Khalida Sa'id.

In the late 1960s Nawal Sa'dawi shocked the Arab world with a book entitled *Women and Sex* in which she exposed in frank, clinical language the structure of sexual oppression in Arab society. For the next two decades Sa'dawi devoted herself to establishing feminism as a fully integrated political movement in the Arab world. She opposed the fundamentalist position headlong, maintaining that the liberation of Arab women could be achieved neither by the revival of religion nor by sexual "equality," but by political and economic emancipation:

> The question of liberation of Arab women is not an Islamic question or an issue of sexual freedom; it is not based on hostility to men, or opposition to Eastern traditions. It is in essence a political and economic problem, and as such it opposes imperialism in the Arab world and the world over and stands against all forms of enslavement and exploitation, be they economic, sexual, social, cultural, or ethical (*al-Wajh al-'Ari* [1977], p. 167).

Unmoved by the fundamentalists' claim that they are the true representatives of the Islamic heritage (*turath*) and its values, she maintained that "the cultural heritage is used by various political groups according to their views and interests." For her, the cultural tradition has no meaning if it is not the possession of the entire society. In Arab society women, half of the society, are "absent" and prevented from playing a role in "the battle between tradition and modernity" (*Tahadiyyat* [1987], p. 40).

The issue of women, while suppressed and distorted by the fundamentalists, is largely marginalized by the secularists and the progressives, whether nationalist or socialist. "For the Arab nationalist movement the important struggle is the national struggle, for the socialist movement it is the class struggle; as for the struggle between male and female, it will be prevented from appearing on the scene until it is imposed by the political power of Arab women" (*Nahwa Istratijiyyah* [1982], p. 475). Though she expresses strong leftist leanings, Sa'dawi is not sanguine about socialism's solution of the problem of woman: "Changing the law is necessary but not sufficient to bring about change," she wrote in her first book, *Women and Sex* (p. 168). But, simultaneously, she maintained that only in a socialist society can women achieve equality and justice: "Women should know that their success in achieving liberation depends on the extent to which they participate in changing society and in building a true socialist order capable of realizing equality and justice among all its members regardless of color, race, or social position" (*ibid.*, p. 187). "But to be able to engage in successful action, it is necessary to possess social consciousness, which in turn depends upon attaining self-consciousness" (*Tahadiyyat,* p. 41), i.e., feminist consciousness.

Although she often uses a psychoanalytical language and generally adheres to Freudian interpretation, Sa'dawi rejects Freud's Oedipal theory on the ground that it is socially conservative and antifeminist: "The conservative Freudians as well as those of their followers who call themselves neo-Freudians try to explain away the rebellions of students, blacks, and women by referring their cause to internal, psychological disturbances and not to dysfunction in the social order itself" (*al-Mar'a,* p. 159).

Fatima Mernissi, in her book *Le Harem politique* (1987), maintains that the discussion of basic social inequalities of patriarchal society, particularly political and sexual inequalities, is central to any debate addressing the question of democratic freedoms and human rights in Arab society. She writes: "Imagine the effect of a harmless phrase such as the one [from the first article of the Universal Declaration of Human Rights] which states that 'All human beings are born free and equal in dignity and rights' in societies where the inequality between the sexes reproduces, guarantees, and maintains the ground for political inequality and affirms this as basic to [defining] culture and identity" (p. 33).

Her point of departure is the famous *hadith* attributed to Muhammad: "Those who entrust their affairs to a woman will never succeed," which she sees as emblematic of Islam's traditional attitude toward women. All groups, including liberals and secularists, by using Islamic history and traditions to support their own claims, end by bolstering the claims of the fundamentalists.

Mernissi is opposed to the way the problem is posed. In the first place, she insists, there is no point in going back to the past; the debate concerning tradition (*turath*) is just another way men seek to safeguard their domination. Invoking the past and idealizing the cultural heritage really aim at reinforcing patriarchal authority and keeping women in their "right place" (p. 34). At an all-Arab women's conference in Cairo in 1986, Mernissi rejected the concept of *turath* altogether, insisting on the primacy of the present and its secular demands, for which the past cannot provide the adequate model. "It is impossible for the forms of the past to compete with or replace the forms of the present in a cultural time grounded in history; only a mind that maintains its distance from history can properly live the past and fruitfully interact with it . . ." (*al-Dimuqratiyyah* [1986], p. 54).

She then compared the different ways in which Western and non-Western historians approach the past, the former with cool detachment, the latter with passionate involvement: "The Western [historians] use the past as something of a hobby or pastime to relieve the stress of the present. We, on the other hand, persist in making it a passion, a vocation, a horizon. By invoking our ancestors at every turn, we live the present merely as an interlude that hardly commits us" (*Le Harem*, p. 29). Obsession with the past has made Arab writers and scholars unable adequately to "read" the past: "We are no longer able to read the past, whose charms we sing like a magical litany, because we are preoccupied with superimposing on its pages our present concerns and obsessions" (*ibid.*).

In regard to woman's liberation, Mernissi is as skeptical as Sa'dawi of the idealistic formulations of liberal male feminists. Only when society has genuinely set up woman's emancipation as a political goal and mobilized the material forces for its realization can the dream of female liberation be translated into reality. As Mernissi writes in her best-known English-language book, *Beyond the Veil* (1975), "The capacity to invest in women's liberation is not a function of society's wealth, but of its goals and objectives" (p. 99). For a radical undertaking, women's liberation involves a qualitative transformation of society: "partial demands are worse than useless because they inhibit [commitment to] real struggle" (*al-Dimuqratiyyah*, p. 57).

So what is needed is a new kind of discourse, "a discourse which redefines Arab identity in a way which will make women creative, productive and equal partners with men" (*ibid.*). Nothing short of a radical "rewriting" of the cultural heritage can bring about genuine change. In a book she published under a pseudonym (*Woman in the Muslim Unconscious* [1984]), Mernissi writes: "As a woman who belongs to Muslim society and has access to writing (a male privilege and the incarnation of power), I am indulging in the indescribable pleasure of rewriting the cultural heritage—the subversive and blasphemous act, par excellence. What I mean by 'rewriting' is an active reading—that is, a process of decoding the heritage and at the same time of coding it in a different way" (p. 6).

Thus, women writers and scholars have a clear task before them: "to restore historical consciousness" by engaging in a different kind of writing, one that seeks to uncover "the silent part of Arab history, the obedient part, the past exploited by power, that is to say, the [history of the] majority that has for centuries been excluded from power and political decision" (*ibid.*, p. 57). And Mernissi adds:

> In history books there is a great deal of information about this Umayyad prince and that Abbasid wazir; we know what they wore and what they ate and how they spent their leisure time and how many dinars they gave the poet whose poetry pleased them, or to the slave girl whose looks drew their attention. But we have no information about the social or economic condition of the slave girl or the poet, let alone the condition of the butcher, the vegetable vendor, the perfumer, the peasant, the porter during the life-time of this prince or that wazir . . ." (*ibid.*, p. 56).

In the end, women must retrieve what they have lost: "Time, and talking about time, how it develops, how it changes, how it is transformed—its dynamic and the way it is consumed, its investment in future planning; but more important how it is enjoyed in the present, as a fleeting moment, a moment which could be transformed into joy" (*ibid.*, p. 58).

Khalida Sa'id is, on the technical level, perhaps the most advanced of the Arab literary critics: her grasp of the intellectual history of the modern period is comprehensive and more solid than that of most contemporary writers, and her language and terminology are polished and crystal clear. Living in Paris in the early 1970s, a period of exceptionally rich intellectual activity, enabled her to experience firsthand the transformations wrought by structuralism, structural linguistics, and poststructuralism. Her collection of essays, *Dynamics of Creativity: Studies in Modern Arabic Literary Criticism* (1979), presaged a wholly new stage in Arabic critical writing. But the issue of women inspired her first powerful assaults.

The woman in Arab society, Sa'id writes, suffers from a dual alienation, "a class alienation and alienation . . . [within] the family, where she is enslaved" (*al-Mar'a* [1970], p. 93). "The woman has no independent being. Her identity is constituted by attribution to the male. She is so-and-so's wife, sister, or cousin. What is a woman? The female of the man, his mother, his wife . . ." (*ibid.*, p. 94).

Sa'id maintains that Arab intellectuals, including left-wing critics, are still blind to the basic problems posed by feminism. Thus a leftist intellectual "may rebel against his class and struggle alongside the proletariat, but he finds it difficult . . . to overcome the residues of the psychosexual distortions he carries within him. This is why the leftist militants' attitude on the woman question is still basically religious and conservative" (*ibid.*, p. 99).

To the question, "Why don't women rebel?" she answers: because they cannot carry out the rebellion on their own. "Rebellion is useless unless it is a collective undertaking. A proof of this is the many incidents of women committing suicide in Algeria to protest [male] oppression—which, however, led to no result" (*ibid.*, p. 95). Women acting by themselves, through women's societies, will not be taken seriously and can achieve very little. The protests of women intellectuals in newspapers and books are mere curiosities classified as "women's literature" (*ibid.*).

Like Mernissi and Sa'dawi, Khalida Sa'id maintains that women's liberation is possible only through total societal commitment: "So long as society (including both men and women) is not free from *a priori* ideas about women—ideas formed across the ages, expressed in myths and nonscientific views, based on the inferiority/superiority syndrome—and so long as social structures do not provide for the emergence and development of the woman's independent personality, for an atmosphere of freedom and respect for the human person, free from discrimination and oppression because of gender or ethnic origin, as expressed in the Declaration of Human Rights; so long as all this has not been realized, this problem will remain unresolved" (*al-Mar'a*, p. 91).

At the same time Sa'id affirms that while women's liberation is far from having been achieved anywhere, firm results have been realized in many socialist countries. "The road [to liberation] is a long one, and the [liberation of the] women of the world is still in its initial stage. Still women in the socialist countries stand closer to the threshold of liberation. For Arab women to reach this threshold they must take the 'classical' steps— and whoever raises the women's problem seriously should insist on this— even though these steps may appear purely reformist" (*ibid.*, p. 100).

In the first essay of her book *The Dynamics of Creativity* (*Harakiyyat al-Ibda*), Sa'id attempts a fresh reading of the *nahda*, depicting the "Awakening" as a fundamentally conservative movement oriented toward the past rather than toward the future, "towards a center of light in the past, engendering acceptance, adulation, imitation" (p. 36). She considers Jubran Khalil Jubran (Kahlil Gibran) a singular exception among the writers of the *nahda* who represented the true spirit of awakening: "Jubran absorbed his Eastern cultural legacy without turning in upon himself and remained open to the world of other cultures without feelings of inferiority or superiority . . . He rejected the idea of historical or cultural break and took his departure from a belief in [historical] continuity and [cultural] complementarity" (*ibid.*).

Jubran is seen as a precursor of creativity and modernity, of a new vision of the individual and society, a figure similar in some ways to that projected by poststructuralist writers, like Artaud or Roussol; for Jubran too the "madman" was the privileged visionary. Sa'id portrays Jubran as the quintessential "other," the "man of imagination," in opposition to the pedestrian (liberal or conservative) "man of memory" (p. 39). She contrasts him to the great Arab poet al-Ma 'arri, who lived in the period of Abbasid decline:

> al-Ma'arri had a premonition of approaching catastrophe and breakdown . . . he foresaw the descending darkness; in his voice all longing was dead, his poetry was the obituary of a dying culture—"every house is for destruction." In al-Ma'arri's poetry we encounter a despair that goes beyond individual hopelessness; his poetry resonates with the music of disintegration and collapse. On the other side stands Jubran, with his vision of a world propelled by desire and the thirst to discover, to create, to transcend the self . . . His music conveys good tidings (*bisharah*). Jubran's greatness lies precisely in being the conscious har-

binger of good tidings. For the [true] creator is the one who either achieves something great in itself, which becomes a source of new human value, or who produces something that brings a new rhythm to life, signs of new possibilities and new ways (p. 40).

Sa'id speaks of a "new language" in modern Arabic, one relying on fresh "modes of speech" and a new "conceptual terminology," linking this new language with the innovative style of Jubran's early works in Arabic. "The new language—by which Jubran meant the new uses to which the expressions of established language are put—echoes the distinction which Ferdinand de Saussure and other modern linguists made between 'parole' and 'langue,' [the latter] considered as a sociohistorical system made up of signifying units and rules governing the signifying relations between the different units" ("al-Lughah al-Jubraniyyah," p. 168).

In Sa'id's view Jubran's greatest contribution consists in his "secularization of the text" and the unification of its "inner" and "outer" structures: "The dual text, with its mythic, religious, and mystical usage, was secularized . . . and the static relations between inner and outer displaced by a dynamic unity" (*ibid.*, p. 169). The immediate or literal signification of the text for Jubran is related to its "deep" meaning "as the metaphor is related to the truth and the part is linked to the whole" (*ibid.*).

For Sa'id, Jubran's writing is itself a metaphor representing a revolutionary and liberating gesture that has the power to effect "a radical change in the history of Arab thought" (*ibid.*, p. 171).

III.   Feminism and the Non-Western Critique

The problem of perspective, as I have tried to define it in the first part of this essay, receives striking elucidation in the feminist critique of patriarchal culture in the West. Consider, for example, this formulation by Elizabeth Gross:

> Women [assert] themselves not as object but subjects of knowledge with particular perspectives and points of view often systematically different from men's. Such perspectives or viewpoints are not simply "subjective" in the sense of individual, personal or idiosyncratic positions—"subjectivity" being seen as an interference with the "objective" procedures of knowledge in just the same way that men's theoretical productions are a function of their lived positions in the world ("What Is Feminist Theory?" [1987], p. 194).

Feminist theory seeks to uncover the "partial," "committed," and "non-universal" character of the opposing perspective by demonstrating that "patriarchal discourses are not neutral, universal or unquestionable models, but are the effects of the specific (political) positions occupied by men" (*ibid.*, p. 198). Perhaps the feminist critique's greatest contribution to the consolidation of a viable counterparadigm derives from its ability to clarify the very nature of Western "male-stream" power-knowledge and the unity of the areas of its oppression and control: class, race, and gender, and the corresponding structures in which they are rooted— capitalism, imperialism, and patriarchy. Thus, for example, what the Arab critical intellectuals encounter in Western scholarship as Orientalism, the feminist critics experience as misogyny.

Let me briefly attempt an outline of the parallel aspects in the feminist and the non-Western critical discourses.

In the first place, both positions are "outsiders" to the dominant Western discourse: the feminist to the male and the non-Western critical to the Western hegemonic discourse. Generally, in its workings and unspoken assumptions the male-dominated, Western-centered discourse is opposed to both feminist claims and critical non-Western demands; it persistently tends to devalue or ignore both. Thus in its binary mode of categorization it opposes masculinity to femininity and Western to non-Western in a parallel and equivalent manner—and tends to assign greater value to the first term.

For example, the "historian," like "man" or the "individual," is in the dominant discourse always male and Western—that is to say, phallo-Eurocentric. The virtues of this model historian, as Judith Allen puts it, "comprise a list of Western masculine qualities . . . his justice and his instincts are posed as universal, rather than partial, and mediated by the lived experience of a male body in a [Western] patriarchal culture" ("Evidence and Silence: Feminism and the Limits of History" [1987], p. 179).

Feminists and non-Western critical intellectuals also agree on the question of the subjectivity of knowledge, where history and society, the Self and Other, are objects of knowledge. Writers of both camps join in attempting to combine theoretical analyses of class with those of gender, of capitalism with patriarchy, of imperialism with religious fundamentalism. And in mobilizing their theoretical and methodological forces, both borrow selectively from Western (masculine) theories and techniques. Both engage with more or less the same radical perspectives: Marxism, critical psychoanalysis, poststructuralism, Nietzsche, Foucault, Derrida, Lacan, Frederick Jameson, Terry Eagleton. But it is worth noting that while the feminist critics, particularly in France, have approached these writers and discourses with aggressive critical scrutiny, the Arab (and other non-Western) critics have been less assertive and less self-confident in the way they have approached their Western sources.

In this context, attention should be drawn to a matter rarely examined by non-Western criticism but central to feminism: the essential difference, from the radical feminist viewpoint, between equality and autonomy. From this perspective equality (with men) appears as a false category, implying as it does a measurement according to an established male standard involving the equivalence of two or more terms, one of which is set up as the norm or model. Autonomy, in contrast, is understood as the right to accept or reject received standards or models according to their suitability to one's self-definition. The parallel problematic for non-Western critics may be described as the distinction between (political) independence and (cultural) autonomy.

The fact remains that Arab criticism's main intellectual resources, including feminism, are all *Western* in origin. Regardless of how congenial they may be from the point of view of the non-Western critics, they are all constituted by specific conditions and interests stemming from a fundamentally different context. Until it attains full autonomy—that is, the capacity for independent theorization—Arab criticism will remain tied to the changes of Western critical approaches and to the ups and downs of Western intellectual fashion.

Criticism in the West is by definition an elitist practice, largely confined to intellectual and academic circles. It speaks an idiom hardly comprehensible to the "general public." Thus one of the distinct dangers the Arab critical movement runs is mirroring the ivory-tower manner of Western criticism and its distance from social struggle. This danger is the more real when we consider the political and ideological constraints under which critical intellectuals live in most Arab and Third World countries, so that faddishness, academicism, abstraction—the ways of withdrawal from political life—become temptations to writers and scholars who must protect themselves against state surveillance as much as against militant fundamentalism. Thus to distance themselves from the "lifeworld" of political and ideological violence becomes the contradictory choice of intellectuals engaged in cultural criticism in order to change society.

The other difficulty confronting the Arab critics is an internal one. It stems from the contradiction implicit in the attempt to formulate a critique in the very language and syntax that their criticism seeks to change or displace. This ends in the paradox postulated by Derrida: "We have no language—no syntax and no lexicon—which is foreign to this history; we can pronounce not a single destructive proposition which has not already had to slip in the form, the logic, and the implicit postulations of precisely what it seeks to contest" ("Structure, Sign and Play in the Human Sciences" [1978], pp. 280–81).

Despite the inadequacy and the shortcomings of the available language in contemporary Arab society, a counterdiscourse can perhaps still be constructed to challenge and ultimately displace the established discourse. Such a counterhegemonic project does not aim merely to contest the given language and its paradigms. Its ultimate goal is really to subvert the "mentality" in which these are rooted.

The questions raised by this undertaking provide the framework by means of which the new formulations may effect the transformation of the new critique into original, autonomous theorization. The goal of the resulting discourse would not be just another alternative hegemonic norm; on the contrary, it would be to provide the necessary condition for the rise of multiple nondogmatic and nonhegemonic discourses interacting within a framework open to difference and to the mutual recognition of alterity.

A criticism of this sort would seek first of all to transcend the traditional limits of established scholarship in terms not only of perspective but also of the areas of scholarly investigation. Indeed, it is the shift in substantive writing and research that will give the questions of theory and method their concrete shape and meaning, endowing otherwise abstract theorization with specific life and form. But to whatever orientation or topical engagement the critical perspective may lead, there will be no substitute for solid, disciplined scholarship, that is to say, for rigor in seeking evidence, precision in analysis, and coherence in the signifying narrative.

If new forms of writing and research are to bring about radical transformation in understanding and interpretation, then they must ground themselves in other than purely speculative criticism. In the field of cultural and social studies, this may be achieved as much by making the proper choice among the topics of research as by pursuing the "correct" methods of research. Criticism can become constructive practice only by engaging in concrete exploration of new fields and approaches. Specifically, what might such topics be?

First of all, the topics that have been willfully ignored or devalued by conventional scholarship. For example, reassessment of the conceptual structure of the "awakening" and simultaneous review of the processes of European expansion into the region; shift of focus from the purely political to the economic and the social, that is to say, to social and economic history, from the eighteenth century into the twentieth, in terms of the general sweep of development as well as of local structures and patterns; and reevaluation of the modes of superimposition of Western social and administrative forms in the nineteenth and twentieth centuries—municipal organization, nascent parliamentary structures, legal reforms under "protectorate," "mandate," and "special treaty" conditions, and so on. In the cultural area, the central shift should be from formal, totalizing, and causal narrative, that is to say, from emphasis on "influence," "modernization," "Westernization," "development," "history from above," to analyses of mass culture, specificities of rural and peasant life, folk religion, oral traditions, urban proletarian and subproletarian existence, and so on. Of special significance in this area is research in the Arab household system, the transformation of the kinship system, the processes of urbanization, and education and health from the late nineteenth and early twentieth centuries on. An area of study that has hardly been touched and should be at the center of historical analysis and interpretation is the rise of modern systems of social surveillance and controls, and of advanced military structures in the late twentieth century, along with the impact of these developments on political power and the consolidation of the nation-state in the second half of the twentieth century. Finally, a central theme of investigation in this new body of research will be the gender issue in Arab and Islamic society—the history of women and sexuality and of the systems of patriarchy and neopatriarchy.

Bibliography

Abu Dib, Kamal. *Al-Jurjani's Theory of Poetic Imagery*. Warminster: Aris and Phillips, 1979.

Adonis. *Al-Thabit wa al-Mutahawwil: Bahth fi al-Ittiba' wa al-Ibda' 'ind al-'Arab* (The Permanent and the Changeable: A Study of Imitation and Originality in Arab Culture). Beirut: Dar al-'Awdah, 1974.

Allen, Judith. "Evidence and Silence: Feminism and the Limits of History," in Carol Pateman and Elizabeth Gross (eds.), *Feminist Challenges: Social and Political Theory*. Boston: Northeastern University Press, 1987.

Arkoun, Muhammad. *Lectures du Coran*. Paris: G. P. Maisonneuve et Larousse, 1982.

———. *Rethinking Islam*. Washington, DC: Center for Contemporary Arab Studies, 1987.

Barakat, Halim. *Al-Mujtama' al-'Arabi al-Mu'asir: Bahth Istitla'i Ijtima'i* (Contemporary Arab Society). Beirut: Markaz Dirasat al-Wihdah al-'Arabiyyah, 1984.

Barthes, Roland. *Dars fi al-Simyulujiyyah* (A Lesson in Semiology). Translated by A. Bin 'Abdul-'Ali. Casablanca: Dar Tobqal, 1985.

Bennis, Muhammad. *Mawasim al-Sharq* (Seasons of the East). Casablanca: Dar Tobqal, 1985.

Berque, Jacques. *Les Arabes d'hier à demain*. (Paris: Editions du Seuil, 1960). Translated into English by Jean Stewart, London: Faber and Faber, 1964.

Binder, Leonard. *The Study of the Middle East: Research and Scholarship in the Humanities and the Social Sciences*. New York: John Wiley and Sons, 1976.

Caws, Mary Ann (ed.). *Textual Analysis: Some Readers Reading*. New York: Modern Language Association of America, 1986.

Coon, Carleton S. *Caravan: The Story of the Middle East.* New York: Henry Holt, 1951.

Derrida, Jacques. *La Structure de signe et le jeu.* Paris: Editions du Seuil, 1967.

———. "Structure, Sign and Play in the Human Sciences," in *Writing and Difference.* Translated by Alan Bass. Chicago: The University of Chicago Press, 1978.

Djait, Hichem. *Europe and Islam.* Translated by Peter Heinegg. Berkeley: University of California Press, 1985.

———. *Al-Shakhsiyyah al-'Arabiyyah wa al-Masir al-'Arabi* (La personnalité et le devenir arabo-islamique, 1974). Beirut: Dar al-Tali'ah, 1984.

Eagleton, Terry. "Political Criticism," in Mary Ann Caws (ed.), *Textual Analysis: Some Readers Reading.* New York: Modern Language Association of America, 1986.

Feyerabend, Paul K. *Contre la méthode.* Paris: Editions du Seuil, 1975.

Fiske, Donald W. and Richard A. Shweder (eds.). *Metatheory in Social Science: Pluralisms and Subjectivities.* Chicago: The University of Chicago Press, 1986.

Geertz, Clifford. *Islam Observed: Religious Development in Morocco and Indonesia.* New Haven: Yale University Press, 1968.

Gergen, Kenneth J. "Correspondence versus Autonomy in the Language of Understanding Human Action," in Donald W. Fiske and Richard A. Shweder, *Metatheory in Social Science.* Chicago: The University of Chicago Press, 1986.

Gibb, H. A. R. and Harold Bowen (1950). *Islamic Society and the West: A Study of the Impact of Western Civilization on Moslem Culture in the Near East.* London: Oxford University Press, 1950.

Gross, Elizabeth. "What is Feminist Theory?" in Carole Pateman and Elizabeth Gross, *Feminist Challenges: Social and Political Theory.* Boston: Northeastern University Press, 1987.

Grunebaum, G. E. von. *Modern Islam: The Search for Cultural Identity.* Berkeley and Los Angeles: University of California Press, 1962.

Hartman, Geoffrey H. "Psychoanalysis: The French Connection," in Geoffrey H. Hartman (ed.). *Psychoanalysis and the Question of the Text.* Baltimore: Johns Hopkins University Press, 1978.

Hourani, Albert. *Arabic Thought in the Liberal Age.* London and New York: Oxford University Press, 1962.

Husserl, Edmund. *The Crisis of the European Sciences and Transcendental Phenomenology.* Evanston: Northwestern University Press, 1970.

Ibrahim, Zakariya. *Mushkilat al-Bunyawiyyah* (The Problem of Structuralism). Cairo: Maktabat Misr, 1976.

Al-Jabiri, Muhammad 'Abid. *Al-Khitab al-'Arabi al-Mu'asir* (Contemporary Arab Discourse: A Critical Analytical Study). Beirut: Dar al-Tali'ah, 1982.

Al-Karmil, 11 (1984).

Al-Khatibi, 'Abdul-Kabir. "Jacques Berque ou la saveur orientale." *Les Temps Modernes* (June 1976).

———. *Al-Naqd al-Muzdawij* (Double Critique). Beirut: Dar al-'Awdah, 1980.

Kohut, Heinz. *Self-Psychology and the Humanities: Reflections on a New Psychoanalytic Approach.* Edited by Charles B. Strozier. New York: W. W. Norton, 1985.

Laroui, 'Abdallah. *Al-Idyulujiyyah al-'Arabiyyah al-Mu'asirah* (Contemporary Arab Ideology). Beirut: Dar al-Haqiqah, 1983.

————. *La Crise des intellectuels arabes: traditionalisme ou historicisme.* Paris: François Maspero, 1974. Translated by Diarmid Cammell, Berkeley: University of California Press, 1976.

Lerner, Daniel. *The Passing of Traditional Society.* Glencoe, IL: Free Press, 1958.

Lewis, Bernard. *Semites and Anti-Semites: An Inquiry into Conflict and Prejudice.* New York and London: W. W. Norton, 1986.

DeMan, Paul. "Criticism and Crisis," in *Blindness and Insight: Essays in the Rhetoric of Contemporary Criticism.* Minneapolis: University of Minnesota Press, 1983 (2nd edition).

Marcus, George and Michael M. J. Fischer (eds.). *Anthropology as Cultural Critique: An Experimental Moment in the Human Sciences.* Chicago: University of Chicago Press, 1986.

Mernissi, Fatima. "Al-Dimuqratiyyah ka-Inhilal Khuluqi" (Democracy as Moral Disintegration) in *al-Tahaddiyyat allati Tuwajih al-Mar'ah al-'Arabiyyah fi Nihayat al-Qarn al-'Ishrin* (The Challenges Facing Arab Women at the End of the Twentieth Century). Cairo: Tadamun al-Mar'ah al-'Arabiyyah, 1986.

————. *Beyond the Veil: Male-Female Dynamics in Modern Muslim Society.* New York: John Wiley and Sons, 1975.

————. *Le Harem politique: Le Prophete et les femmes.* Paris: Albin Michel, 1987.

————. [Fatma A. Sabbah]. *Woman in the Muslim Unconscious.* New York: Pergamon Press, 1984.

Murad, Hussein; Mahmoud Amin al-'Alim; Muhammad Dikramb; and Samir Sa'd. *Dirasat fi al-Islam* (Studies of Islam). Jerusalem: Salah al-Din, 1980.

Murqus, Elias. "Ishkiliyat al-Manhaj" (The Problem of Method), in *al-Wihdah* (October 1984), pp. 27–46.

Muruwwah, Hussein. *Dirasat fi al-Islam* (Studies in Islam). Jerusalem: Salah al-Din, 1980.

Patai, Raphael. *The Arab Mind.* New York: Scribners, 1973.

Al-Qadi, 'Abdul-Wahid Isma'il. *Harakat Tahrir al-Mar'ah fi Misr* (The Movement of Women's Liberation in Egypt). Cairo: Dar al-I'tisam, 1983.

Sa'dawi, Nawal. *Al-Mar'ah wa al-Jins* (Woman and Sex). Beirut: al-Mu'assasah al-'Arabiyyah lil-Dirasat wa al-Nashr, 1972.

————. "Nahwa Istratijiyyah li Idmaj al-Mar'ah al-'Arabiyyah wa Ta'biatiha fi al-Harakah al-Qawmiyyah al-'Arabiyyah" (Toward a Strategy for the Mobilization of the Arab Woman in the Arab National Movement) in *al-Mar'ah wa Dawruha fi Harakat al-Wihdah al-'Arabiyyah* (The Role of Women in the Movement of Arab Unity). Beirut: Dar al-Wihdah al-'Arabiyyah, 1982.

————. "Al-Tahdiyyat al-Siyasiyyah allati Tuwajih al-Mar'ah al-'Arabiyyah fi al-Qarn al-'Ishrin" (Political Challenges Facing the Arab Woman in the Twentieth Century) in *Al-Tahadiyyat allati Tuwajihu al-Mar'ah al-'Arabiyyah fi Nihayat al-Qarn al-'Ishrin* (The Challenges Facing the Arab Woman in the Twentieth Century). Cairo: Tadamun al-Mar'ah al-'Arabiyyah, 1987.

————. *Al-Wajh al-'Ari lil-Mar'ah al-'Arabiyyah* (The Naked Face of the Arab Woman). Beirut: al-Mu'assasah al-'Arabiyyah lil-Dirasat wa al-Nashr, 1977.

————. *Al-Mar'ah wa al-Sira' al-Nafsi* (Woman and Psychological Conflict). Beirut: al-Mu'assasah al-'Arabiyyah lil-Dirasat wa al-Nashr, 1977.

Safwan, Mustafa. *Tafsir al-Ahlam* (The Interpretation of Dreams). Cairo: Dar al-Ma'rif, 1981.

Sa'id, Khalida. *Harakiyyat al-Ibda': Dirasat fi al-Naqd al-'Arabi al-Hadith* (The Dynamics of Creativity: A Study in Modern Arab Criticism). Beirut: Dar al-'Awdah, 1979.

———. "Al-Lughah al-Jubraniyyah wa al-Nass al-Muzdawij" (Jibran's Language and the Dual Text). *Mawaqif* (Beirut), No. 47–48, 1983.

———. "Al-Mar'ah al-'Arabiyyah: Ka'in bi Ghayrihi la bi-Dhatihi" (The Arab Woman: A Being for Others, Not for Itself). *Mawaqif* (Beirut), No. 12, 1970.

Servier, André. *Islam and the Psychology of the Musulman.* Translated by A. S. Moss-Bundell. London: Chapman and Hall, 1924.

Shweder, Richard A. "Divergent Rationalities," in Donald W. Fiske and Richard A. Shweder (eds.), *Metatheory in Social Science.* Chicago: The University of Chicago Press, 1986.

Tazzini, Tayyib. *Min al-Turath ila al-Thawrah* (From Heritage to Revolution). Beirut: Dar Ibn Khaldun, 1978.

Wallace, Edwin R. *Freudian Anthropology: A History and Reappraisal.* New York: International Universities Press, 1983.

Waqidi, Muhammad. *Hiwar al-Falsafah* (A Philosophical Dialogue: A Critical Reading in Contemporary Arab Philosophy). Casablanca: Dar Tobqal, 1985.

White, Hayden V. *The Content of the Form: Narrative Discourse and Historical Representation.* Baltimore: Johns Hopkins University Press, 1987.

Al-Wihdah, No. 11 (October 1984).

Zayour, 'Ali. *Al-Tahlil al-Nafsi lil-Dhat al-'Arabiyyah: Anmat al-Sulukiyyah al-Usturiyyah* (The Analysis of the Arab Self). Beirut: Dar al-Tali'ah, 1977.

2

Policy-Making and Theory Building: American Political Science and the Islamic Middle East

Lisa Anderson

The American study of politics in the Middle East leaves a great deal to be desired.[1] Although there are notable exceptions to the general rule, much of what passes for political science in Middle Eastern studies is a theoretical description: modern diplomatic history, journalism, the regional counterpart of Kremlinology sometimes known as "mullah-watching." The fundamental questions about the exercise of power and authority which constitute the core and *raison d'être* of political science as a discipline are infrequently raised in studies of contemporary Middle Eastern politics, and Middle Eastern data rarely contribute to disciplinary theory building.[2]

Describing the weakness of political science of the Middle East is easier than identifying causes or prescribing solutions. The difficulty of the languages of the region for English-speaking students constitutes a hurdle, particularly for those whose theoretical bent outstrips their linguistic aptitude, but the similarly daunting languages of East Asia do not discourage lively debates in the political science of that region. It is also true that a strong and independent indigenous scholarly community, such as those of Europe and Latin America, provides valuable collaborators and critics and not all areas of the Middle East are endowed with or tolerant of local scholars in political science. The virtual absence of independent local counterparts with whom to share political research did not prevent the flowering of sophisticated American studies of China or the Soviet Union, however, nor has the long-standing presence of such a community guaranteed good work on Tunisia, for example, or the Palestinians. Finally, the reputed inaccessibility of parts of the Middle East to American researchers, particularly of certain religions and sexes, is also said to discourage students from entering the field in the first place or from undertaking field research when they do. While real and supposed constraints on research and researchers are obvious impediments to scholarship, they are equally obviously surmountable, as American studies of the Soviet Union and China since World War II have demonstrated.

It is difficult to escape the conclusion that the poverty of American political science on the Middle East reflects politics in the region itself and particularly the position of the United States there. To some extent, of course, this region is no different from any other: American area studies, particularly in political science, have been shaped since World War II by the policy concerns of a world power.[3] American studies of the Soviet Union have been preoccupied with debates about Soviet motives and capabilities that were born in the US-Soviet rivalry, while the academic interest in economic change and political stability in development studies grew out of the American policy concern with making the Third World impervious to revolution and socialism.

Unlike other regions, however, the American position in the Middle East is based neither on the single issue of the Cold War and its ramifications in political and economic development nor, as in the somewhat exceptional case of Europe, on long and intimate contact. For forty years, American policy objectives in the Middle East have been described as threefold: prevention of Soviet expansion, assurance of access to oil, and maintenance of the security of Israel. For forty years as well, it has been argued that these objectives may be incompatible.

The complexities, not to say contradictions, of US policy in the Middle East have left political scientists in the United States without the consistent policy preoccupations which have guided the formulation of research agendas, both enthusiastic and critical, in other regional studies. In principle this should liberate the study of politics from its customary close links with policy and permit independent investigation of the exercise of political authority in the region. In practice, however, it seems to have rendered the field intellectually aimless and politically malleable: more susceptible than usual to confusion of description with analysis and conviction with rigor.

This, in turn, has opened the field to the battles of the region, which are, as is well known, many and bitter. Kenneth Stein expressed a very common view in a recent survey of Middle Eastern studies in the United States:

> Already the academic profession in various social science disciplines is torn by schools of interpretation, but doubts exist whether the venom expressed between Marxists and non-Marxists, or the level of antagonism directed at liberals by neo-conservatives and vice versa, can equate with the personal attacks that have dominated the study of the Middle East.[4]

The widespread, if undocumentable, impression that an individual's ethnic background or political persuasion may influence hiring and tenure decisions has a chilling effect on the debate and controversy that are necessary to academic political science. The perception of censorship and, perhaps more damaging, of self-censorship in the study of Middle East politics discourages students from pursuing it as a professional commitment and influences the research agendas of those who do, encouraging what Stein calls "crisis-driven" scholarship. Perhaps most importantly, it stifles the academic freedom in which intellectual creativity thrives, and contributes to work which is either too polemical or too "safe" to be anything but mediocre scholarship.

As a consequence, much of the best political science on the Middle East grows out of self-conscious efforts to link regional studies not with American policy concerns as such, or even with the regional controversies of the day, but with theoretical and intellectual agendas originating in other regions. This may account for the curious divorce of popular political commentary on the Middle East from the academic political science of the region. Unlike Latin American or even Soviet studies, where the theory building and policy-making sides of political science are closely intertwined, scholarly "responsibility" in Middle East political science is usually interpreted as demanding not political engagement but a studied distance from the fray. Conversely, the few analytical concepts that have developed in studies of the Middle East, such as the notion of the rentier state, have found a more receptive audience among academics outside Middle Eastern studies than among policy-makers concerned with the region.

This essay is principally concerned with attempts to integrate the Middle East into the broader concerns of contemporary political science and political theory rather than with policy-relevant commentary as such. This distinction is not an absolute one, of course, since in the last analysis, all American political science reflects the policy dilemmas and opportunities of a superpower in the late twentieth century, and current events are rarely far from the attention of scholars of modern politics in any event. Nonetheless the focus here is on works that aspire to contribute to theory building rather than policy-making. The development of the field—its fashions, if not its progress—is best illustrated in a chronological survey, beginning at the beginning of modern American studies of the rest of the world shortly after World War II.

The 1950s and 1960s—Political Culture and Modernization: The Early Years of Political Science and Area Studies

From the close of World War II until the early 1970s, American political science was almost exclusively concerned with examining influences on politics. This "society-centered" approach[5] relegated politics and government, which older institutional approaches had defined as the central concern of the discipline, to the status of a virtually unknowable black box and concentrated instead on examining factors that shaped the political process. The abandonment of institutional approaches in favor of the empiricism and behavioralism associated with structural-functionalism not only contributed to a dramatic shift in the way American politics was studied with its new emphases on statistical analysis and survey data, but also provided much of the intellectual infrastructure for the study of the newly independent countries of the "Third World" in what became known as modernization or development theory.

Modernization theory has been severely criticized from a variety of quarters, and the critiques need not be reiterated here.[6] Suffice it to say that in most of its numerous versions, it was a self-conscious effort to provide a liberal pluralist alternative to Marxist theories of social and political change. The theorists drew on interpretations of the modern world associated particularly with Weber, Durkheim, and Freud (though not exclusively so, since much of the discussion of class development suggests the power of Marxist analysis even among those most insistent on its rejection); on a hasty and schematic reading of Western, especially American, history and politics; and on an optimism about the future so astonishingly cheerful that it could have appeared only in a country newly anointed a world power. Modernization theory portrayed change as a linear rather than a dialectical process, emphasized shifts in social organization and psychological orientation rather than economic forces and relations of production as the instigators of political change, and predicted an essentially nonviolent trajectory culminating in—not surprisingly—liberal, pluralist democracy.

Problems in this theoretical construct quickly became apparent. Much of the more interesting work of the era was reminiscent of pre-Copernican astronomy and its myriad "epicycles," designed to "account for appearances" while remaining faithful to the earth's central place in the sky. Although the theoretical framework of development studies grew more elaborate, it was always hobbled by disabling assumptions, particularly in its contempt for history and inability to integrate the realms of "domestic" and "international" politics. If the theory was not all that enlightening, however, data collection proceeded apace and the data were often revealing.

Perhaps the most important work of this period was that on political attitudes: what were they? where did they come from? how could they be changed? This was known in the discipline's somewhat misleading jargon as "political culture" (what was meant was not really culture so much as social psychology) and the study of political culture was, and remains, particularly popular in the political science of the Middle East. The inclination toward quasi-cultural explanations probably grows at least in part out of the Orientalist tradition in Western studies of the Middle East, in which unfamiliar or unexpected political institutions or inclinations are attributed to the influence of Islamic tradition. Thus, the importance of political leadership is said to have been prefigured by the political role of the Prophet Muhammad himself, for example, while passivity among ordinary people in the face of authoritarian government is credited to Islamic precepts enjoining submission (in the Sunni case) or withdrawal (if the people in question are Shi'a).[7]

Interestingly, however, because they were not really interested in the "traditional" attitudes and beliefs, believing them little more than obstacles to modern democratic politics, political scientists during the early heyday of modernization theory neglected the scholarly tradition of European Islamic and Oriental Studies. It was not until the growth of what became known as Islamic fundamentalism in the 1970s that real debates about the nature of Middle Eastern political culture and political traditions were joined. For the modernization theorists, the specific content of traditional beliefs merited no real attention since they would become mere historical relics as secularization and rationalization proceeded. As Daniel Lerner put it in his very influential *The Passing of Traditional Society: Modernizing the Middle East,* published in 1958:

> Whether from East or West, modernization poses the same basic challenge—the infusion of "a rationalist and positivist spirit" against which, scholars seem agreed, "Islam is absolutely defenseless."

Moreover, as he continued:

> This observational standpoint implies no ethnocentrism. As we will show, the Western model of modernization exhibits certain components and sequences whose relevance is global. Everywhere, for example, increasing urbanization has tended to raise literacy; rising literacy has tended to increase media exposure; increasing media exposure has "gone with" wider economic participation (per capita income) and political participation (voting). The model evolved in the West is an historical fact . . . [t]he same basic model reappears in virtually all modernizing societies on all continents of the world, regardless of variations in race, color, creed . . .[8]

For Lerner, and for many of his contemporaries, the essense of modernity was a personality type—what Lerner called "mobile" or "empathetic"—and the more such personalities there were in a given population, the more modern was the society, since mobile personalities were literate, activist, participatory—in a (circular) word, modern.

Thirty years later, the problems with this perspective are painfully apparent. As it turned out, the model was not only far from a historically factual description of Western development (European or American). It also constituted a serious misreading of the Middle East. The equation of literacy and modernity missed the role of literacy in the premodern Islamic world; the equation of political participation, particularly voting, with modernity presumed an institutional context of very limited historical relevance even in the West. Indeed, both the historical and the structural context of political behavior are striking by their absence in early modernization theory.

Political scientists working on the Middle East who did turn their attention to institutions of any kind during this period exhibited great hopes for the "mobilizational" regimes which succeeded colonial rule. Single-party governments and "Arab socialisms" of various kinds—Ba'thist, Nasserist, even Bourguibist—caught the imagination of American scholars. Despite the assumption that democracy was the ultimate goal of political development, the absence of democratic institutions in most of the Middle East was a minor worry. Not only did the behavioral revolution in American political science give short shrift to institutions in general, many theorists believed that new organizations—mass political parties principally, but also "enlightened" military regimes—were required to break the fetters of tradition and to inculcate attitudes that would sustain democracy over the long run.[9]

The military intervention in Turkey in 1960 and the now-pale 1958 civil war in Lebanon reinforced the conviction that institutions were less important than behavioral and attitudinal variables in supporting democracy. It was the mobilizational regimes that were creating new participatory attitudes among the masses. Clement Henry Moore, for example, introduced his discussion of Tunisia's single party with the observation that "Tunisia's ruling Neo-Destour Party has achieved possibly the most effective regime in the Afro-Asian world for leading its people toward a modern society."[10] Analyses of the increasingly frequent military interventions—and here Turkey and Lebanon proved to be among the exceptions since their military rulers retired in favor of civilian governments—also contributed to the literature on military regimes that flourished during the 1960s; in contrast to the civilian bureaucracy, the military in the Middle East received a great deal of attention.

On this issue, among others, one of the most influential books of the early 1960s, Manfred Halpern's *The Politics of Social Change in the Middle East and North Africa*, illustrated the capacity of development theorists to make theoretical virtues out of empirical necessities. Although it seemed to be apparent, said Halpern, that "the traditional Middle Eastern elite of kings, landowners, and bourgeoisie is declining in power or has already yielded its place," it was not (and, to be frank, still is not) nearly so clear "who shapes politics and makes the fundamental decisions in the Middle East and North Africa." Who were the military rulers and the heads of the ruling single parties? The answer turned out to be—representatives of a "new middle class."

> Leadership in all areas of Middle Eastern life is increasingly being seized by a class of men inspired by non-traditional knowledge, and it is being clustered around a core of salaried civilian and military politicians, organizers, administrators, and experts.[11]

These were people defined not by their economic position, social status, or even particular political program (they ranged from Gamal Abdul-Nasser to Habib Bourguiba), but by their attitudes. This was a "revolutionary" class, in Halpern's words, because of its "freedom from traditional bonds and preconceptions" and because "once it controls the machinery of a modernizing state, it possesses a power base superior to that which any other class in the Middle East can muster."

As it turned out, the "modern" outlook of the military was not its only politically salient attitude. To the disappointment of the modernization theorists (and, I suspect, the secret delight of those of a more Orientalist inclination, who had been less confident of the irrelevance of "traditional" loyalties), it soon became apparent that recruitment in a number of the Middle Eastern armies had been discriminatory, favoring certain sects, regions, ethnic groups, or tribes. Far from the instrument of a class— new or old—these armies were tools of distinctly "traditional" cliques and communities.[12]

Moreover, because what constituted "the machinery of a modernizing state" was never spelled out, the policies thought to be designed for state consolidation, social reform, or economic redistribution were sometimes indistinguishable from unvarnished and self-serving coercion. The point of all the upheaval was not quite as clear as the teleology of development suggested, and the problem was exacerbated by the neglect of institution building, public administration, and bureaucracy on the part of both the political elites of the Middle East and the political scientists of the United States.

The sense of the fragility of institutions and of the contrasting power of mass sentiment that was implicit in the "society-centered" approach of development theory was reinforced in the Middle East by the importance of nonstate nationalisms. Thus were the varieties, components, and half-lives of the region's nationalisms dissected and compared with their counterparts in Asia and Africa; generational change was widely observed, for example, as interwar liberals gave way to postwar radicals.[13] Ironically, efforts systematically to identify and measure components of the popular attitudes and beliefs that impinge on politics were rare after Lerner's effort in *The Passing of Traditional Society*, and despite the relative novelty of the states themselves—only a generation had passed since the demise of the Ottoman Empire, and "French North Africa" and the United Arab Republic were still on the scene—much of the work on international relations in the Middle East was (as it still is) description of the foreign policies and policy-making processes of individual regimes.[14]

By and large, in the rare examinations of foreign policy and regional interstate relations, the same questions arose as in domestic development studies. Culture and attitudes remained important, though most work remained unsystematic and even unself-conscious in assuming that there is something in the concepts of the "Islamic world" or "Arab politics" that is more relevant to international relations than, say, the "English-speaking world" or "modern Christendom." Even today, the fact that the Middle East is the only region in American area studies whose designation reflects historical politics rather than geography—"East Asia" having long since superseded "the Far East"—reflects the continuing intellectual uncertainty about the cultural component of the area study. Geographical designations such as "Southwest Asia" cannot easily replace "the Middle East" because they do not include that important center of Islamic culture and Arab civilization, Egypt, to say nothing of the rest of Arabic-speaking northern Africa. Yet whether there is actually such a thing as "Arab" foreign policy based on cultural affinities or even on common interests in conflicts with Israel or Iran, or whether Islam provides a common focus or perspective in foreign policy-making, remain open questions.[15]

Nonetheless, during the 1950s and 1960s the notion that regional politics was an appropriate focus of analysis was buttressed by the intensity and frequency of regional calls for Arab unity. Thus could scholars like Leonard Binder discuss "The Middle East as a Subordinate International System" and Malcolm Kerr examine *The Arab Cold War* in terms of mutual influence (or interference) among the states of the region.[16] That their works were primarily descriptive did not detract from their importance in suggesting the reality of an Arab or perhaps regional system. Partly because of the decline of Arab nationalist rhetoric, however, the 1970s brought a parallel decline in political studies that took the region, or even the relations of three or four actors, as the unit and focus of analysis.

The cavalier regard for the consequences of social change implicit in much of the modernization theorists' enthusiasm for social mobilization eventually met serious criticism. As Leonard Binder, whose voice was one of the most important "Middle Eastern influences" among the development theorists in the United States in the 1960s, has recently observed,

> the liberal development theory is a radical call for virtually unlimited expansion of political participation in developing countries, and it is a radical assault on all established institutions, traditional elite and religious structures, corporate arrangements, distributive coalitions and the like. As such it was a gross distortion of what the United States was like and it was viewed increasingly as an irresponsible academic construction . . . It is easy to see why it aroused considerable opposition among conservative scholars long before the Marxist opposition got its act together.[17]

Among the first and most telling critiques of this perspective was, as Binder suggests, conservative: the emphasis on political stability and institution building in Samuel Huntington's *Political Order in Changing Societies* was an explicit effort to provide a corrective to the radical call for mass participation and destruction of tradition.[18] In part because it was published in 1968, when most campus sentiment in the United States accorded much better with liberal development theory, Huntington's remained something of a voice in the wilderness and, somewhat ironically, it was later assimilated to modernization theory by the critics of the left.

In the political science on the Middle East, the principal early challenge to modernization theory was also conservative rather than Marxist. It came not from Huntingtonian circles, however, but from those who felt a need to explain what was to most of these theorists—and not a few of the political elites of the region—the surprising, indeed, dismaying, resiliency of tradition.

The 1970s—Tradition and Dependence:
The Divergence of Political Science and Middle East Studies

For political science as a whole, the 1970s witnessed the end of the intellectual hegemony of modernization theory. The weight of both logical argument and empirical evidence suggested that modernization theory was at best too optimistic and at worst simply wrong. The results were a period of eclecticism and drift and a growing gulf between political science and Middle Eastern studies. Although it was widely agreed that the developing countries were not following the path predicted for them, scholars were divided on how to understand the problem. The discipline's theorists inclined to the position that development theory itself was inconsistent, ahistorical—in a word, wrong; for them, modernization was a scientific paradigm that had been exhausted and merely awaited a successor.

By contrast, particularly in the Middle East but to a lesser extent in the other regions of great "non-Western civilizations" as well, area specialists were less willing to condemn the theory outright and more inclined to look for obstacles to the fulfillment of its predictions in their region. From this perspective, the major problem with the theory lay not in its logical premises but in its failure to account for the unique variations of each culture. Thus, as political scientists in general turned to what would become known as political-economy approaches to politics, particularly those associated with the theories of dependency and bureaucratic authoritarianism that originated in Latin America, political scientists working on the Middle East took up the study of "tradition." From this point on, students of the region were to sense a palpable tension between their disciplinary and their regional training.

This is not to say that the critiques that influenced the rest of the discipline were entirely absent from Middle Eastern political science. By the beginning of the 1970s, it had become apparent that at least in the short run few of the once-promising mobilizational regimes of the Middle East were giving birth to democracy. Most, in fact, appeared to be moving toward conventional authoritarianism, as the single-party vehicles for popular participation withered into unresponsive mechanisms for enforcing government policy. Simultaneously, a number of the military regimes began to develop alliances with civilian technocrats. These developments prompted American political scientists of the Middle East to abandon their focus on political parties and the military as such and to look instead to the work being done on the causes and character of authoritarian regimes elsewhere, particularly Latin America.

The notion that the historical experience of imperialism was profoundly different for the colonized and the colonizer was not foreign to the Middle East, and that provided a perspective from which to examine the Marxist-inspired dependency theory which was coming out of Latin America. Having been reshaped by European imperialism in the interests rather than the image of Europe, so the argument ran, the countries of the Third World start at very different beginnings in development and enjoy much less autonomy as it proceeds than did their European predecessors. Indeed, at its most extreme, the dependency that is a legacy of imperialism may be perpetuated by a combination of local and international elites so as to prevent any genuine development at all.

In the initial formulations, the criteria for development in this approach were largely economic—self-sustaining economic growth, industrialization, higher standards of living—and the political ramifications were usually portrayed as inconsequential or self-evident: dependency supports authoritarian regimes that act in the interests of international capital; rectification of the injustice of the international economy would ensure political improvement. Eventually, particularly in work on Brazil, theorists began to develop more specific hypotheses about the relationship between economic dependency, development and crises, and various types of political regime, particularly what became known as bureaucratic authoritarianism. Unlike older autocratic or oligarchic authoritarianisms, this was a developmental regime that appeared in response to certain kinds of bottlenecks or breakdowns in economic development. By early in the 1980s, Sadat's era in Egypt had been usefully examined in light of the bureaucratic-authoritarian model by John Waterbury in *The Egypt of Nasser and Sadat.*[19]

Yet, in what promised to be very fruitful lines of inquiry in political economy, Middle East political scientists were surprisingly modest in their ambitions: theory was used to explain data rather than data to develop theory. Leonard Binder prefaced his 1978 study of Egypt, *In a Moment of Enthusiasm,* by saying that the book was a product of his resolve "to break the epistemological barrier between area studies and behavioral science," but he acknowledged that the work "never strays very far from an Egyptian immediacy" because "the purpose of theory is to elucidate the particular." In his work on Egypt, Waterbury was even less concerned with theory building: "My aim is not to generate new theories or paradigms but rather to test the utility of a few of the plethora that now exist with respect to a concrete case."

The outcome of this attention to the concrete and particular was a further refinement of the perennial debate on the class interests of the Egyptian government: Binder argued that it was not a "new" but a "rural" middle class that was served by the Nasser revolution, and Waterbury concluded with the somewhat anticlimactic observation that "class origins do not necessarily explain the bottom-line interests of any set of individuals." Much as this discussion may have revealed about the contours of Egyptian politics and society, it did not promote the development of political science theory and it probably further contributed to the isolation of Middle Eastern studies in political science.[20]

In international relations theory, the Middle East fared little better. The growing academic concern with trade and debt in the Third World in general contributed to regionally specific attention to issues as various as the impact of foreign aid in Egypt; the role of lending agencies like the International Monetary Fund in policy and politics in borrower states such as Morocco, Tunisia, and Egypt; and the consequences of the great swings in revenue earnings in oil-producing countries since the early 1970s. Labor exports to oil-producing countries also drew some attention, on both the sending and receiving side, although little comparative work was undertaken.[21] In general and with one very important exception, however, the international political economy of the Middle East was descriptive and derivative.

The exception was the impact of oil revenues. Although the transformation of the regional economy with the oil price rises of the 1970s did not receive the sustained and sober attention it merited—much of the contemporary literature reflected the crisis atmosphere of the day—it did contribute what may have been the most important addition by Middle Eastern studies to the literature on economic influences in politics: the notion of the rentier state—a state reliant not on extraction of the domestic population's surplus production but on externally generated revenues, or rents, such as those derived from oil. This concept proved quite influential and illuminated examinations of political systems as disparate as Libya, pre- and post-revolutionary Iran, Saudi Arabia, Venezuela, and Nigeria.[22]

Apart from this unusual attention to the impact of oil, however, critical studies of economics and politics were noticeably absent from Middle East political science at just the time that they were reentering mainstream American political science. Presumably, this reflected a number of causes, including the continuing empirical importance of nonclass ethnic, sectarian, and kin-based social solidarity and the difficulty of encompassing the oil-producing countries in conventional analyses of dependency or of defining monarchies as ordinary authoritarian regimes.[23] Still, the paucity of studies emphasizing the structural, particularly economic, constraints on politics is striking. For all intents and purposes, the group of scholars associated with *MERIP Reports* were the principal proponent of this sort of critical analysis and theory in the United States during the 1970s.[24]

This gap is all the more striking in light of the enormous attention devoted to understanding the culture and attitudes associated with the region's "traditions." The widely accepted proposition that the impact of imperialism was different for colonizer and colonized turned out to be understood less in economic than in psychological and cultural terms: the failure of development to proceed as predicted was thought to be explainable by the pull of traditional ties of family and religion. This perspective did not originate in American policy but it was certainly encouraged thereby. During the 1970s the U.S. commitment in the region grew dramatically, as U.S. policymakers felt compelled to fill the "vacuum" left by the British withdrawal from the Gulf in the early 1970s; to reward Sadat's turn away from the Soviets; to ensure Israel's economy after the oil-price rises of 1973–1974. That this rush into the area may have been ill-considered would suggest itself in the painfully awkward

American positions in the Iranian revolution, the assassination of Sadat, and the Israeli invasion of Lebanon. In the meantime, however, local criticism of U.S. policy was easier to dismiss than address, and this was efficiently accomplished by portraying its adherents as irrational. That, in turn, encouraged explanation based on culture, particularly religion.

The Islamic component of the Iranian revolution and the existence of Islamic protest movements elsewhere in the region, for example, permitted some observers to equate Islam with unquestioning opposition to U.S. policy or to the status quo, whatever it was. That the grievances of the protest movements might have been comprehensible as rational choices rarely figured in the literature, with the partial exception of work on Lebanon and the Palestinians. The unexpected collapse of Lebanese democracy, the eclipse of Arab nationalism, and the rise of what became known in the West as Islamic fundamentalism had been completely at odds with modernization theory's confident prediction of increasing democratization and secularization, of course, and occasioned a flood of efforts to describe and explain them. The Lebanese civil war actually received some good and thoughtful analysis, particularly from international-relations specialists whose global perspective had trained them to study political systems on the verge of anarchy and who recognized regional influences more adeptly than the comparativists, who had been taught to hold constant such "environmental factors." Thus, for example, was Michael Hudson able to draw on his early work on *The Precarious Republic* in an important article on the impact of the Palestinians, and several analysts would examine the Syrian role in Lebanon.[25]

For the rise of Islamic politics, almost every possible causal factor was invoked. Islam was said to have provided solace in the shock and disappointment of the 1967 war, to have reflected the shift in power toward conservative Gulf (or radical Libyan and, soon, Iranian) regimes after the 1973 oil-price increases, to have served as an idiom of protest against the failure of development policies. All of these explanations had a plausibility about them, but since most of the work lacked any comparative perspective with other religious revivals of the time ("Jewish fundamentalism" in Israel, for example, or even Christian fundamentalism in the United States), not to say secular protest movements, few were rigorously tested. Indeed, the topic of ideological change seemed to lend itself to a sort of meditative style, perhaps best exemplified by Fouad Ajami's *Arab Predicament,* rather than rigorous scientific methods. As a consequence, much of the political science was indistinguishable from sophisticated journalism, and in fact, some of the more accessible works actually were written by journalists: Malise Ruthven's *Islam in the Modern World,* for example, and Edward Mortimer's *Faith and Power.*[26]

Because of the fascination with Islam among area specialists, it was often used by social scientists who were not regional specialists and were reliant on the work of their American colleagues as a convenient explanation for virtually anything that happened—or didn't happen—in the region. Theda Skocpol, for example, whose structural theory of revolution had been very influential in the late 1970s, found herself forced "to deepen [her] understanding of the possible role of idea systems and cultural understandings in the shaping of political action" because she felt she could not explain the Iranian revolution without addressing "the historical and changing place of Shi'a Islamic religious organizations and belief in Iranian society and politics." Samuel Huntington's assessment of the region's prospects for democracy relied no less on political culture: "Islam," he said flatly, "has not been hospitable to democracy."[27]

The continued focus in Middle Eastern studies on the causes and consequences of attitudes—particularly those that are somehow opposed to what is (usually implicitly) thought to be modern—was not limited to the influence of formal religion. Numerous important studies examined the political impact of social cohesion on bases other than economic class interest, such as kinship and patron-client relations. From John Waterbury's *Commander of the Faithful*, published in 1970, to Robert Springborg's *Family, Power and Politics in Egypt*, published over a decade later, political scientists marveled at the strength, resilience, and political salience of family, friendship, and factionalism.[28]

The very influential textbook *Politics in the Middle East*, by James Bill and Carl Leiden, provides a summary and example of this approach. In the chapter on social structure, called "The Genes of Politics," the authors argue that "political associations that have been able to take effective action have been conspicuously absent in the social history of the Islamic Middle East." The factors that have "stunted the growth" of formal groups are numerous, and the result is clear: "The most crucial units of interest aggregation in the Middle East remain informal groups." In a striking and by no means exceptional illustration of the tenacious attachment of Middle Eastern political scientists to modernization theory, they conclude that "the social structure described above is a formidable obstacle to the processes of modernization and political development that are underway in the Middle East."[29] By the late 1970s, the political culture so dear to the modernization theorists of the 1950s had been given content in regionally specific traditions, but it was no less lacking in historical or comparative perspective. Indeed, the infrequent references to history, such as the one just cited, were often breathtakingly sweeping and equally often incorrect. Usually, however, history was irrelevant; social structure was portrayed as unchanging and uncaused, influenced, if at all, only by beliefs and attitudes.

Although many of the works on the influence of religion, kinship, and other expressions of cultural traditions in politics contained very useful description, few of them evinced much theoretical sophistication and some merely reiterated long-standing Western stereotypes, now clothed as "cultural explanation." The principal problem with reliance on political culture to explain Middle Eastern political behavior is a sort of circularity of argument that is both bad logic in its own right and poor protection from the biases of the investigator. If we stipulate that politics in the Middle East and North Africa is more often characterized by primordial, personalistic, informal relationships than is the case elsewhere—a proposition usually asserted rather than demonstrated—presumably, unless we are content to characterize rather than comprehend, we want to know why. Although a variety of hypotheses present themselves, including causal roles for patterns of state formation and for paths of insertion into the world economy, the usual answer is that this behavior reflects attitudes whose content is apparent in the behavior itself. In other words, the cause and effect are indistinguishable. Small wonder the political science of the Middle East did not have a wider audience in the rest of the discipline.

The 1980s—History and the State:
Area Studies and the Discipline Meet Again?

By the 1980s, the society-centered approaches that had dominated political science since World War II were under challenge. The pluralist bias built into unfettered empiricism had been apparent for some time, as had the rarity of pluralist politics in much of the world, including the Middle East. Among the earliest responses was a return to analysis of institutions, particularly those of the state. The study of international political economy had revealed the importance of the state in generating, controlling, and distributing economic resources, and it had become apparent that state institutions not only reflect but also shape the organization of socially based groups. The strength and structure of the state—as indicated in such features as the public bureaucracy, the use of force, the pattern of taxation—were once again deemed important variables in politics.

Simultaneously, a movement to take history seriously also appeared. What had been understood in the 1950s and 1960s as "culture," and therefore of interest only to students of exotica, had become "tradition," the provenance of area specialists, in the 1970s. As we have seen, both tradition and culture proved very ambiguous and difficult notions. By the 1980s, efforts to account for observable regional variation in political institutions and behavior turned to what had obviously and unambiguously varied from region to region: history. This trend converged with the renewed interest in the state to provide a new perspective on political change in the study of state formation.

For Middle Eastern political science, these intellectual developments seemed to bode well for more theoretically informed research. Not only did they introduce new analytical approaches, they also spoke to, and permitted analysis of, observable changes in the region. By and large the Middle East had seen the strengthening of the state in the thirty or forty years since the countries of the region won independence. Civilian administrations had grown more extensive, differentiated, and capable; military establishments had transferred control of the means of violence from private to public hands; central banks and other financial institutions had been established to monitor and control the flow of revenues to and from state coffers.

Although the bureaucracies of the region had until then been accorded relatively little attention by students of the Middle East—the principal exceptions, not surprisingly, being those of the relatively highly institutionalized states such as Turkey and Egypt[30]—the consequences of state strength and structure for public policy and private loyalties increasingly drew notice. The four-volume collective work, *Nation, State, and Integration in the Arab World,* published in 1987, reflected this new approach— addressing, for example, the origins of the Arab state system; conceptions of the state in Arab and Islamic philosophy; agricultural, industrial, and service sector development policies; and fiscal systems and budgeting in both oil-producing and non-oil-producing countries.[31]

The renewed recognition in political science that the structure of the state is far from a neutral factor in politics revived interest in how policy is made and what influence it may exert on social and economic organization. Until that point in the political science on the Middle East, policy analysis had been the almost exclusive preserve of academics who also served as practitioners: officials in and consultants to governments. How policy is made, what information is available to policy-makers, how effectively feedback is incorporated into subsequent decision-making are always questions of immediate interest to practitioners, whatever the academic fashions. The relative neglect by academic political scientists had meant, however, that surprisingly little had been done on the finance, tax, and credit structures of the region, and, by the standards of other area studies, examination of the constituencies and constraints of the budget-making process or of economic development in specific sectors— agriculture, construction, industry, trade, and so forth—remained in its infancy.[32]

Among the works that brought together some of the newer approaches to political studies in the region was Robert Bianchi's examination of pluralist and corporatist patterns of policy-making in his *Interest Groups and Political Development in Turkey,* published in 1984. Distinctly more ambitious than the regionalists of a decade earlier, Bianchi describes his book as an effort "to use certain social science concepts to learn about politics in Turkey and then, in turn, to use evidence from Turkey and other systems to improve the concepts themselves." Like many political scientists working on the Middle East, Bianchi was concerned to understand the dynamics of group formation and interaction; unlike those of his predecessors who viewed virtually timeless cultural traditions as the principal causal or explanatory variable, however, Bianchi looked at public policy. As he put it:

> Much of what has been presented [in the book] can be understood as an investigation into an ongoing experiment in political manipulation involving a series of recent state initiatives toward establishing and strengthening stable clientelistic relationships with Turkey's most important associational leaders.[33]

Political culture was not absent from Bianchi's approach, but it was treated as one of several influences. Moreover, it was not a residual independent variable but an aspect of state policy that reflected "premodern Ottoman social organization and certain recurrent attitudes and practices of ruling elites regarding legitimate interest representation." His conclusion that pluralist and corporatist patterns of interest representation are not mutually exclusive, but rather may coexist as tendencies between which political elites oscillate, certainly merits examination by theorists of interest representation outside the Middle East.

Bianchi's use of history to reveal the sources and patterns of recurrent political attitudes characterized other efforts to trace change and continuity in state-society relations through public policy. Of the early postindependence development policies, the land reforms of the 1950s and 1960s had been among the best studied, and the role of the rural sector in politics in Egypt, Syria, and Iraq drew relatively sustained attention, as did the unintended contribution of the Shah's White Revolution to the subsequent Islamic revolution in Iran. Political scientists and political sociologists began explicitly to link their work on the political implications of agrarian policies to hypotheses about the historical role of rural power holders in politics and political transformations in Europe. Haim Gerber's *The Origins of the Modern Middle East,* for example, draws on the approach of Barrington Moore to elaborate a series of provocative hypotheses about the significance of Ottoman rural social structures, particularly the absence of a major landed aristocracy, for the nature of modern states and revolutions in the region. Similarly, my own *The State and Social Transformation in Tunisia and Libya* attributes the distinctive patterns of rural social-structural and political organization in Tunisia and Libya to historical variations in the experience of modern state formation.[34]

Renewed recognition that political elites as holders of state power play an important role in extracting and distributing economic resources and in determining the shape and direction of economic development prompted reexamination of the relationship between economic organization and regime type. Changes in the direction of economic policy—from "state capitalist" to a more "mixed economy," for example—may herald or accompany changes in political organization or regime type. In many of the countries of the Middle East, particularly those whose economies could be characterized as "state capitalist" (such as Egypt, Tunisia, and, to some extent, Iran in the 1960s and Iraq, Syria, and Algeria through the 1970s) the state initially had acted as the engine of growth because of the presumed weakness of the private sector. The regimes were authoritarian, often mobilizational. Beginning in the early 1970s in Tunisia and Egypt—more recently in Algeria, Iraq, and some of the major oil producers—government policy was marked by a distinct shift toward what is known as economic "liberalization" or "privatization." State involvement in the economy was scaled back and private foreign and domestic investment encouraged in an effort to spur local productive activity that might provide, among other things, a stronger tax base. These liberalizations were neither notably popular nor particularly successful where they had the longest trial, but they did seem linked with greater demands for, or concession of, political liberties and political participation.[35]

There was much discussion in Middle East Studies Association workshops and Social Science Research Council-sponsored seminars of the opportunity provided by such shifts to examine the relationship between the organization of political and that of economic power during the 1980s. As before, however, most political scientists in Middle Eastern studies contented themselves in print with single-country snapshot descriptions of regimes. Indeed, in a review of the state of political science of the Middle East in the mid-1970s, I. W. Zartman had noted this phenomenon:

> Despite the area isolation within the discipline, there is no "political science of the Middle East." Each polity is seen as an example of its particular characteristic, for example, Tunisia as the single-party regime, Pakistan as religious politics, Algeria as revolution, Turkey as multiparty dynamics, Lebanon as ethnic accommodation, and Egypt as a military and class polity; but there has been little attempt to examine the same characteristic in other states or to develop a comparative cross-national analysis.[36]

Fifteen years later this general observation still obtained in large measure, although the types of regime in favor—both in the region and among social scientists—had changed.

For many of the states in the Middle East, domestic appropriation was a negligible part of government revenues and privatization to increase a tax base was unnecessary. The availability of revenues generated outside the domestic economy—from petroleum rents to foreign aid to government borrowing abroad—substantially lessened the reliance of governments on their own populations. Political scientists came to realize that such revenues released many of the regimes of the Middle East from the accountability ordinarily exacted by domestic appropriation of surplus. In a sadly neglected essay, Jacques Delacroix argued that in rentier states, such as oil-producing Kuwait and Libya, the government ensures popular acquiescence through distribution rather than representation; demands for political rights and responsibilities are therefore unlikely to reflect economic interests so much as noneconomic "traditional" bases of social cohesion and political activism. Here again, we find an effort to account for the apparent importance of the traditional social organization of the Middle East, but rather than being characterized as a timeless reflection of local culture, it is attributed to the singular character of the modern state and economy of the region.[37] This perspective suggested possible causes of the relative strength of monarchy in the Middle East, but there was a surprising lack of systematic comparative research on the institution of hereditary rule, despite its importance in the region and the vast historical literature on monarchy in Europe.

Democracy was also given short shrift, presumably because of its rarity and apparent fragility. The existence of contested elections for national parliaments at various times in a number of countries from Morocco, Egypt, and Kuwait to Turkey and, until the mid-1970s, Lebanon suggested that although democratic norms are not the sole or even primary ideological standard of the region, they have been by no means absent. Nonetheless, the literature on electoral politics and competitive parties was scant and, ironically, much of the empirical work had been done by anthropologists.[38]

If institutionalized political succession through heredity or electoral competition was relatively rare in the Middle East—and even more rarely studied—revolutionary change was far more frequently claimed by regimes and studied by academics. Virtually all military governments in the Middle East described the *coup d'état* that inaugurated the regime as a "revolution," and while few could be taken seriously by most conventional definitions of revolution (Algeria is an obvious exception), the implication that these regimes sought to both symbolize and engineer profound transformations in their societies was usually conceded. One of the few cross-cultural studies to include Middle Eastern cases—Ellen Kay Trimberger's *Revolution from Above*—examined the potential and limitations of this sort of "revolution," but it has rarely been cited by Middle East area specialists.[39]

Obviously, it was the Iranian revolution that not only most dramatically changed the face of politics in the Middle East in the 1980s, but also introduced students of the region to the literature on social revolution and created a virtual industry of commentary and analysis in the United States. Among the more interesting of these were those by non-area specialists who emphasized the similarities and differences of the Iranian revolution in systematic comparison with other social revolutions. Regional studies scholars borrowed from the general literature on revolution to examine factors as various as land reform, the urban poor, Shi'a political theory, the United States, Khomeini's charisma, and the Shah's bad judgment in contributing to the revolution, while still others used the revolution as a backdrop for surveys of the predictive or explanatory utility of various theoretical approaches in favor among American political scientists during the last several decades. Whatever contribution the Iranian revolution proves to have made to Middle Eastern politics, it had—with the absence of peasant mobilization and the importance of religious leaders and symbols—already profoundly altered the social science understanding of social revolution.[40]

Yet, as the 1980s drew to a close, political scientists who worked on the Middle East seemed somewhat stymied. For many the deficiencies of the field were readily apparent, but remedies seemed to remain out of reach. The founders of the field were retiring; the temptations of policy-making and policy analysis—not to say academic administration!—seduced some of their potential successors away from theoretically informed research. Still others sought refuge outside the area, in Mexican and Indian studies. For younger scholars, the logistical problems of the area study were not compensated by active and lively debates in the field.

Research and Methods

And logistical problems there certainly were, for the problems in the American study of Middle Eastern politics discussed earlier are compounded by "technical" disputes in political science and by tension between the area study and the discipline. In the first place, American political scientists are divided on the question of methodology. Those who wish to make the study of politics as scientific as possible emphasize quantitative methods: polling, surveys, elaborate statistical manipulation of economic and political data. Those who view politics and its study as more akin to the arts and humanities rely on more routine methods of "establishing a database": interviews, particularly with political elites and "influentials"; government documents, both contemporary and archival; the media, especially newspapers but increasingly radio and television as well.

By and large, foreign area scholars, particularly those who work on the Middle East, are of the latter persuasion. Although there has been survey research done in the Middle East,[41] it is dwarfed by the literature that does not use quantitative methods systematically. The reasons for this are various. As we have seen, approaches to Middle Eastern politics that emphasize the cultural specificity of the area are popular, and many of the proponents of such perspectives fear that surveys and questionnaires may introduce cultural biases, in both the wording and the asking of the questions. Official data collection is uneven and sometimes unreliable, and foreign researchers are often discouraged by sensitive governments from conducting surveys or collecting large amounts of undigested data. Finally, few of the American political scientists who have devoted precious time and training to mastery of a Middle Eastern language are equally well equipped to use quantitative methods. Whatever the reasons, the marked disinclination to use quantitative reasoning and methods has contributed to the isolation of Middle Eastern studies in political science.

Unfortunately, mathematical illiteracy is not always redeemed by intimate knowledge of the region, for not all American scholars of the Middle East are convinced of the necessity of long or frequent visits to the area. The wide dissemination of the reports of governments and international organizations, of regional newspapers and broadcast transcripts—indeed, their translation into English in services like FBIS and JPRS—makes visiting the area (or even knowing the relevant languages) unnecessary for certain kinds of projects.[42]

Most foreign area scholars protest that immersion in the local language and culture, to say nothing of exposure to the people and scholarship that never reach the United States, is inherently useful and desirable. This, they say, is where students' time and money should be spent rather than in learning statistical methodology. What gives importance to this otherwise moot question are the limited sources of funds for travel to the Middle East and the restrictions on research by American citizens in a number of the countries of the region. At the moment, American political scientists cannot pursue research at all in Libya, Iran, or South Yemen and face substantial obstacles of various bureaucratic and political origins in Algeria, Saudi Arabia, and a number of the other Arab Gulf states—Iraq, Syria, and Lebanon. Political scientists are particularly suspect because of the field's long-standing linkage of academic and policy concerns: this suspicion often translates into the assumption on the part of potential host governments and nongovernmental informants that

American political scientists are merely thinly disguised intelligence oper-
atives. Whatever the reasons, the consequences may be quite serious; as
Bayley Winder recently lamented:

> A generation of young scholars has now moved into the academy
> without ever walking on the campus of the American University of
> Beirut, eating *masguf* on the banks of the Tigris, marveling at Isfahan
> . . . They go to Cairo, Istanbul and Jerusalem but the scope of their
> view of the area has been egregiously narrowed. The blacking out of
> a few more countries would mean that our field might end up like
> Chinese studies were for a quarter century after World War II—with
> Israel as a kind of Taiwan.[43]

Agendas for Research

In a brief survey of the literature on the modern diplomatic history of
the Middle East, L. Carl Brown noted recently that no "scholarly consensus [has] emerged on just how to classify and study the international
relations of the post-Ottoman Middle East" and that, moreover, "the
strong Western bias for depicting the nation-state as the basic unit of
political history strengthens the tendency to avoid the region-wide approach."[44] It is difficult to dispute the observation that for too long biases,
predispositions, and enthusiasms have served instead of theory or even
classification to guide research on the politics of the Middle East. Some
of the new or revived theoretical perspectives in political science might
contribute to rectification of this inadequacy, however, if the study of
politics in the Middle East is understood to entail a commitment to theory
building as well as data collection or policy analysis.

As "society-centered" approaches to the study of politics have been
supplemented in political science, it has become a commonplace that the
state is neither a "natural" or "necessary" form of political organization
nor a neutral arbiter of conflict that originates in society. This recognition
has a number of implications for the study of the Middle East. In the
first place, it is more apparent than ever that the origins of the contemporary state system need to be established, not simply stipulated. How the
states of the modern era came into being profoundly influences their
relations with one another and with their subjects and citizens.

From the point of view of regional politics, the focus on the state and
the history of state formation illuminates unique aspects of the region's
politics. The existence of several important nonstate actors—notably the
Palestine Liberation Organization but also, for example, the Polisario in
the Western Sahara—not only distinguishes this region from others,
such as Latin America, where insurgency is more often ideological than

irredentist, but also suggests the importance of demonstrating rather than postulating the primacy of states and their foreign policies as appropriate analytical units. This would contribute significantly to correcting one of the most surprising lacunae in the American study of international relations in the Middle East: the virtual absence of theoretically informed analysis of the myriad conflicts among the states of the region.

Too often the region is still viewed as it was at the height of the Cold War in the 1950s—not to say the nineteenth century, when the whole region was encompassed by the term "the Eastern Question"—as little more than a battlefield between the world powers of the day. Although some preliminary work has been done on the role of perceptions and misperceptions in contributing to the Arab-Israeli conflict and on the role of military spending in distorting the economies of the region, the field is otherwise barren, left to the compilers of grisly technical statistics.[45] The recent work on state formation in Europe that suggests that violence is a natural, perhaps necessary, concomitant to state formation and nation building merits serious attention from scholars of regional politics in the Middle East.

Since neither comparativists nor international-relations specialists can afford to take the state as a basic and irreducible unit of analysis, neither can they assume that the boundaries of the state and the national economy are congruent. The state system did develop in Europe simultaneously with, and largely as the political expression of, the capitalist industrial order, but this relationship cannot be assumed to hold today. We must explore the implications of the imposition of state institutions and state policies on local and regional economic and political organization to understand how the state and society influence each other. State policy is not simply imposed on a societal *tabula rasa*; it shapes and reshapes preexisting social organization, just as it is shaped in novel ways by those same local economic and social formations.

This kind of research agenda requires pursuing historical studies seriously. The relationship between prior or simultaneous nonstate forms of political authority and the state must be explored systematically. Comparativists must inquire about the relation between historical conceptions of community and contemporary appeals for legitimacy, for example, and about the ties and tensions between state institutions and forms of nonstate political authority based on kinship or religion. We can be assisted in this by the textual analysis of scholars of the normative political theory of Islam, but we must bear in mind that what we wish to understand is political practice, in the past as in the present. Only armed with a much better sense than we now have of the nature of political life in the past can we explore whether the notion of civil society is a useful one in this region, for example, and what the answer may say both about govern-

ment efforts at privatization and encouragement of the private sector
and about the existing political theory of state-society relations.

As this perspective should suggest, the contemporary interest of political science in the state has been accompanied by a salutary revival of
political economy and history in both international relations and comparative studies, and it behooves students of Middle Eastern politics to
capitalize on this movement to understand their area and reintegrate its
study into their discipline. But perhaps the most important consequence
of these new approaches is to direct attention from crisis management
to routine policy-making, thereby revealing trends and patterns obscured
in the crisis-driven concentration on the high drama of politics—military
coups, outbreaks of war, succession crises, and the like.

Attention to the level of mundane politics where the exercise of power
actually takes place and where conceptions of accountability and responsibility are defined and realized is particularly important in political science
of the Middle East because of the discipline's close links with policy and
policy-making. As we have seen, American policy in the Middle East is
unusually prone to responding to crises, and this tendency has infected
the political science of the region. We have now hardly begun to examine
the ordinary day-to-day politics of survival and development, to look at
who wins and loses when new wells are dug, new airplanes bought, new
police assigned or political parties recognized. Only when we have a
much better sense of the structures, tempos, and biases of mundane
politics will we know the real political meaning of the crises that we chart
so enthusiastically and the real significance of the cultural variations we
area specialists hold so dear. The introduction of the critical perspectives
of history, political economy, and state-centered approaches should have
a salutary effect in its own right and serve, as well, as a counterweight to
easy, and often lazy, reliance on cultural explanation.

Notes

1. Throughout this discussion, the term "the Middle East" refers to the predominantly
   Muslim region between Iran and Morocco, Turkey and the Sudan. The term "American political science" refers to the body of literature written by or for American political
   scientists. The discussion is limited to works in English, but I refer to books and articles
   by individuals who are neither Americans nor political scientists when they bear on the
   field. I would like to thank Richard Bulliet, Gregory Gause, Bradford Dillman, Kamall
   Shehadi, and the members of the Study Group sponsored by the Center for Contemporary Arab Studies, particularly Louis Cantori, for their comments on an earlier draft.

2. To cite but one recent example: the influential volume, *Bringing the State Back In*,
   sponsored by the Social Science Research Council and edited by Peter B. Evans, Dietrich
   Rueschemeyer, and Theda Skocpol (New York: Cambridge University Press, 1985)
   includes contributions representing every major region of the world save one: the
   Middle East.

3. The importance of policy-makers and former policy-makers in establishing the academic study of Middle Eastern politics in the United States has been amply demonstrated. See Peter Johnson and Judith Tucker, "Middle East Studies Network in the United States," *MERIP Reports* 38 (1975).

4. Kenneth Stein, "The Study of Middle Eastern History in the United States," *Jerusalem Quarterly* 46 (1988), p. 57.

5. The term is Theda Skocpol's. See her introduction to *Bringing the State Back In*.

6. Most of the criticism of modernization theory is summarized, and an excellent bibliography of the theory and its critiques is provided, in Irene L. Gendzier, *Managing Political Change: Social Scientists and the Third World* (Boulder, CO: Westview Press, 1985).

7. For examples, see the relevant chapters, particularly "The Politics of Patrimonial Leadership," in James A. Bill and Carl Leiden, *Politics in the Middle East* (Boston: Little, Brown, 1984). A recent—and unusually elegant—use of political cultural explanation is to be found in Fouad Ajami, *The Vanished Imam: Musa al-Sadr and the Shia of Lebanon* (Ithaca, NY: Cornell University Press, 1986), while the dangers of this approach have been persuasively outlined by Edward W. Said in *Orientalism* (New York: Vintage Books, 1978) and *Covering Islam* (New York: Pantheon, 1981). One of the few regionally focused works to use a political cultural approach and nonetheless gain attention among political scientists outside Middle East studies is Michael Hudson, *Arab Politics: Search for Legitimacy* (New Haven: Yale University Press, 1977); not surprisingly, it constitutes a conscious effort to address general questions about the nature of authority, legitimacy, and loyalty. The same characteristics of the region that contribute to the strength of anthropology of the Middle East appear to have overawed and frustrated political scientists.

8. Daniel Lerner, *The Passing of Traditional Society: Modernizing the Middle East* (New York: Free Press, 1958), p. 45.

9. See Scott D. Johnston, "The Study of Parties in the Political Development of the Middle East and North Africa," *Middle East Studies Association Bulletin* 3, no. 2 (1969) for a survey; on specific single parties, see Clement Henry Moore, *Tunisia Since Independence* (Berkeley, CA: University of California Press, 1965); John Devlin, *The Ba'th Party* (Stanford, CA: Hoover Institution Press, 1976), and, more recently, the relevant sections of Christine Moss Helms, *Iraq: Eastern Flank of the Arab World* (Washington, DC: Brookings Institution, 1984).

10. Moore, *op. cit.*, p. 8.

11. Manfred Halpern, *The Politics of Social Change in the Middle East and North Africa* (Princeton: Princeton University Press, 1963), pp. 51–52. The nature of political elites and leaders in the region has been a consistent preoccupation; see Fredrick W. Frey, *The Turkish Political Elite* (Cambridge, MA: MIT Press, 1965); William Quandt, *Revolution and Political Leadership: Algeria, 1954–1968* (Cambridge, MA: MIT Press, 1969); Richard Hrair Dekmejian, *Egypt Under Nasir* (Albany: SUNY Press, 1971) and *Patterns of Political Leadership: Egypt, Israel, Lebanon* (Albany: SUNY Press, 1975); George Lencowski, ed., *Political Elites in the Middle East* (Washington, DC: American Enterprise Institute, 1975); and I. William Zartman, *Political Elites in Arab North Africa* (New York: Longman, 1982).

12. See J. C. Hurewitz, *Middle East Politics: The Military Dimension* (New York: Praeger, 1969); Nikolaos van Dam, *The Struggle for Power in Syria: Sectarianism, Regionalism, and Tribalism in Politics, 1961–1978* (London: Croom Helm, 1979); Hanna Batatu, "Some Observations on the Social Roots of Syria's Ruling Military Group and the Causes for Its Dominance," *Middle East Journal* 35, no. 3 (1981).

13. Among other examples, see Nadav Safran, *Egypt in Search of Political Community* (Cambridge: Harvard University Press, 1961); Hisham Sharabi, *Nationalism and Revolution in the Arab World* (Princeton, NJ: Van Nostrand, 1966); Clement Henry Moore, *Politics in North Africa* (Boston: Little, Brown, 1970); Richard Cottam, *Nationalism in Iran* (Pittsburgh: University of Pittsburgh Press, 1979); and William Quandt *et al.*, *The Politics of Palestinian Nationalism* (Berkeley, CA: University of California Press, 1973).

14. The classic discussion of Middle East regional politics is Leonard Binder, "The Middle East as a Subordinate International System," *World Politics* 10, no. 3 (1958), updated by Tareq Y. Ismael in *The Middle East in World Politics* (Syracuse, NY: Syracuse University Press, 1974) and by Paul Noble in his contribution to Bahgat Korany and Ali E. Hillal Dessouki, *The Foreign Policies of Arab States* (Boulder, CO: Westview Press, 1984).

15. See Fouad Ajami, *The Arab Predicament: Arab Political Thought and Practice Since 1967* (New York: Cambridge University Press, 1982); Adeed Dawisha, *Islam and Foreign Policy* (Cambridge: Cambridge University Press, 1983); Jerrold D. Green, "Are Arab Politics Still Arab?" *World Politics* 38, no. 4 (1982); Korany and Dessouki, *op. cit.*

16. Binder, *op. cit.*; Malcolm H. Kerr, *The Arab Cold War* (London: Oxford University Press, 1971); also see Patrick Seale, *The Struggle for Syria* (London: Oxford University Press, 1965).

17. Leonard Binder, "The Natural History of Development Theory," *Comparative Studies in Society and History* 28, no. 1 (1986), p. 12.

18. Samuel P. Huntington, *Political Order in Changing Societies* (New Haven: Yale University Press, 1968).

19. Dependency theory is associated with Andre Gunder Frank—see his *Capitalism and Underdevelopment in Latin America* (New York: Monthly Review Press, 1969)—and Fernando H. Cardoso—see the book he coauthored with Enzo Faletto, *Dependency and Development in Latin America* (Berkeley, CA: University of California Press, 1979). On bureaucratic-authoritarianism, see the work of its original formulator, Guillermo O'Donnell, *Modernization and Bureaucratic-Authoritarianism: Studies in South American Politics* (Berkeley, CA: University of California Press, 1973), and David Collier, ed., *The New Authoritarianism in Latin America* (Princeton: Princeton University Press, 1979). John Waterbury's *Egypt of Nasser and Sadat* was published by Princeton University Press in 1983.

20. Leonard Binder, *In a Moment of Enthusiasm: Political Power and the Second Stratum in Egypt* (Chicago: University of Chicago Press, 1978), pp. xvii–xix; Waterbury, *op. cit.*, p. xvii.

21. For a sampling of the literature, see Malcolm Kerr and El Sayed Yassin, eds., *Rich States and Poor States in the Middle East: Egypt and the New Arab Order* (Boulder, CO: Westview Press, 1982); the special issues of *MERIP Reports* 117 (1983) on "Debt and Development" and 127 (1984) "Insurrection in North Africa"; the various works of J. P. Birks and C. A. Sinclair, including *International Migration and Development in the Arab Region* (Geneva: ILO, 1980); Saad Eddin Ibrahim, *The New Arab Social Order: A Study of the Social Impact of Oil Wealth* (Boulder, CO: Westview Press, 1982); John Waterbury and Ragaei El Mallakh, *The Middle East in the Coming Decade* (New York: McGraw-Hill, 1978); and Naiem Sherbiny and Mark Tessler, eds., *Arab Oil: Impact on Arab Countries and Global Implications* (New York: Praeger, 1976).

22. H. Mahdavy, "The Patterns and Problems of Economic Development in Rentier States: The Case of Iran," in M. A. Cook, ed., *Studies in the Economic History of the Middle East* (New York: Oxford University Press, 1970); J. A. Allan, *Libya: The Experience of Oil*

(Boulder, CO: Westview Press, 1981); Peter Nore and Terisa Turner, eds., *Oil and Class Struggle* (London: Zed Press, 1980).

23. For unusual exceptions, see the critical perspectives on oil-producing monarchies in Eric Davis, "The Political Economy of the Arab Oil-Producing Nations," *Studies in Comparative International Development*, 14 (1979); and Jacqueline S. Ismael, *Kuwait: Social Change in Historical Perspective* (Syracuse, NY: Syracuse University Press, 1982).

24. MERIP's linkage of theoretical analysis and policy prescription is more typical of other area studies in the United States. Among the critical works in the Marxist tradition of political economy that have been influential in American political science are those of Samir Amin, especially *The Arab Nation: Nationalism and Class Struggle* (London: Zed Press, 1978); of Caglar Keyder, particularly *State and Class in Turkey* (London: Verso, 1987); and of the pseudonymous Mahmoud Hussein, *Class Conflict in Egypt: 1945–1970* (New York: Monthly Review Press, 1973).

25. Michael C. Hudson, *The Precarious Republic: Political Modernization in Lebanon* (New York: Random House, 1968) and "The Palestinian Factor in the Lebanese Civil War" *Middle East Journal* 32, no. 3 (1978). Also see, on Lebanon, P. Edward Haley and Lewis Snider, eds., *Lebanon in Crisis* (Syracuse, NY: Syracuse University Press, 1979); Walid Khalidi, *Conflict and Violence in Lebanon* (Cambridge, MA: Harvard University, 1979); A. Richard Norton, *Amal and the Shi'a: Struggle for the Soul of Lebanon* (Austin: University of Texas Press, 1987); and on the Syrian role, Naomi Weinberger, *The Syrian Intervention in Lebanon* (New York: Oxford University Press, 1986); Yaacov Bar-Siman-Tov, *Linkage Politics in the Middle East: Syria between Domestic and External Conflict* (Boulder, CO: Westview Press, 1983); Adeed Dawisha, *Syria and the Lebanese Crisis* (New York: St. Martin's Press, 1980).

26. Fouad Ajami, *The Arab Predicament*; Malise Ruthven, *Islam in the Modern World* (New York: Oxford University Press, 1984); Edward Mortimer, *Faith and Power* (New York: Random House, 1982). In the vast academic literature on Islam and politics, see, among others, John L. Esposito, ed., *Islam and Development* (Syracuse, NY: Syracuse University Press, 1980); Michael Curtis, ed., *Religion and Politics in the Middle East* (Boulder, CO: Westview Press, 1981); Alexander Cudsi and Ali E. Hillal Dessouki, eds., *Islam and Power* (Baltimore: Johns Hopkins University Press, 1981); Hamid Enayat, *Modern Islamic Political Thought* (Austin: University of Texas Press, 1982); John Obert Voll, *Islam: Continuity and Change in the Modern World* (Boulder, CO: Westview Press, 1982); James Piscatori, *Islam in the Political Process* (New York: Cambridge University Press, 1983); Said Amir Arjomand, ed., *From Nationalism to Revolutionary Islam* (Albany: SUNY Press, 1984); Saad Eddin Ibrahim, "Anatomy of Egypt's Militant Groups," *International Journal of Middle East Studies* 12 (1984); Henry Munson, Jr., "The Social Base of Islamic Militancy in Morocco," *The Middle East Journal* 40, no. 2 (Spring 1986).

27. Theda Skocpol, "Rentier State and Shi'a Islam in the Iranian Revolution," *Theory and Society* 11, no. 3 (1982), pp. 268, 273; Samuel P. Huntington, "Will More Countries Become Democratic?" *Political Science Quarterly* 99, no. 2 (1984), p. 208.

28. John Waterbury, *The Commander of the Faithful: The Moroccan Political Elite* (New York: Columbia University Press, 1970); James A. Bill, *The Politics of Iran: Groups, Classes, and Modernization* (Columbus, OH: Merrill, 1972); Ernest Gellner and Charles Micaud, eds., *Arabs and Berbers: Tribe to Nation in North Africa* (London: Duckworth, 1977); Hanna Batatu, *The Old Social Classes and the Revolutionary Movements of Iraq* (Princeton: Princeton University Press, 1979); Robert Springborg, *Family, Power, and Politics in Egypt* (Philadelphia: University of Pennsylvania Press, 1982). Also see the often appropriately skeptical treatments in Ernest Gellner and John Waterbury, eds., *Patrons and Clients in Mediterranean Societies* (London: Duckworth, 1977).

29. Bill and Leiden, *op. cit.*, pp. 77, 83, 131.

30. On Egypt, see Morroe Berger, *Bureaucracy and Society in Modern Egypt* (New York: Russell and Russell, 1957), and Nazih N. M. Ayubi, *Bureaucracy and Politics in Contemporary Egypt* (London: Ithaca Press, 1980); on Turkey, see the work of Metin Heper, including "Patrimonialism in the Ottoman-Turkish Public Bureaucracy," *Asian and African Studies* 13 (1979), and Leslie L. Roos and Noralee P. Roos, *Managers of Modernization: Organization and Elites in Turkey, 1950–1969* (Cambridge, MA.: Harvard University Press, 1971).

31. Giacomo Luciani, ed., *Nation, State, and Integration in the Arab World* (London: Croom Helm, 1987). Earlier efforts in this direction include Fuad Khuri, *Tribe and State in Bahrain* (Chicago: University of Chicago Press, 1980); Elia Zureik, "Theoretical Considerations for a Sociological Study of the Arab State," *Arab Studies Quarterly* 3, no. 3 (1981); Gabriel Ben-Dor, *State and Conflict in the Middle East* (New York: Praeger, 1983).

32. Among the few treatments of the formal tax and banking systems are Hossein Askari, John T. Cummings, and Michael Glover, *Taxation and Tax Policies in the Middle East* (London: Butterworth, 1982), and Rodney Wilson, *Banking and Finance in the Arab Middle East* (New York: St. Martin's Press, 1983). For an example of a study in public administration that attempts to "cross over" into political science, see Omar I. El-Fathaly *et al.*, *Political Development and Bureaucracy in Libya* (Lexington, MA: Lexington Books, 1977).

33. Robert Bianchi, *Interest Groups and Political Development in Turkey* (Princeton: Princeton University Press, 1984), p. 338; also see his "The Corporatization of the Egyptian Labor Movement," *Middle East Journal* 40, no. 3 (1986).

34. Haim Gerber, *The Social Origins of the Modern Middle East* (Boulder, CO: Lynne Rienner Publishers, 1987); Lisa Anderson, *The State and Social Transformation in Tunisia and Libya, 1830–1980* (Princeton: Princeton University Press, 1986). Also see Hanna Batatu, *The Old Social Classes and the Revolutionary Movements of Iraq*; Robert Springborg, "Baathism in Practice: Agriculture, Politics, and Political Culture in Syria and Iraq," *Middle Eastern Studies* 176, no. 2 (1981); Eric J. Hoogland, *Land and Revolution in Iran* (Austin: University of Texas Press, 1982); Tarif Khalidi, ed., *Land Tenure and Social Transformation in the Middle East* (Beirut: American University of Beirut, 1984).

35. Most of the sustained work along this line has been done on Egypt. See John Waterbury's, *The Egypt of Nasser and Sadat: The Political Economy of Two Regimes*, and "The 'Soft State' and the Open Door: Egypt's Experience with Economic Liberalization, 1974–1984," *Comparative Politics* 18, no. 1 (1985); Mark Cooper, "Egyptian State Capitalism in Crisis: Economic Policies and Political Interests, 1967–1971," *International Journal of Middle East Studies* 10 (1979); Michel Chatelus and Yves Schemeil, "Towards a New Political Economy of State Industrialization in the Arab Middle East," *International Journal of Middle East Studies* 16 (1984).

36. I. W. Zartman, "Political Science," in Leonard Binder, ed., *The Study of the Middle East* (New York: Wiley Press, 1976), p. 295.

37. Jacques Delacroix, "The Distributive State in the World System," *Studies in Comparative International Development* 15, no. 3 (1980).

38. Linda L. Layne, ed., *Elections in the Middle East* (Boulder, CO: Westview Press, 1987); Dale Eickelman, "Royal Authority and Religious Legitimacy: Morocco's Elections, 1960–1984," in Myron Aronoff, ed., *The Frailty of Authority* (New Brunswick, NJ: Transaction Books, 1986); Ergun Ozbudun, *Social Change and Political Participation in*

Turkey (Princeton: Princeton University Press, 1976); Jacob Landau *et al.*, *Electoral Politics in the Middle East* (Stanford, CA: Hoover Institution Press, 1980)

39. Ellen Kay Trimberger, *Revolution from Above: Military Bureaucrats and Development in Japan, Turkey, Egypt, and Peru* (New Brunswick, NJ: Transaction Books, 1978).

40. See, among many other works on the causes and consequences of the Iranian revolution, this sampling: Skocpol, "Rentier State and Shi'a Islam"; Fred Halliday, *Iran: Dictatorship and Development* (New York: Penguin, 1979); Farhad Kazemi, *Poverty and Revolution in Iran: The Migrant Poor, Urban Marginality and Politics* (New York: New York University Press, 1980); Nikki Keddie, *Roots of Revolution* (New Haven: Yale University Press, 1981); Homa Katouzian, *The Political Economy of Modern Iran: Despotism and Pseudo-Modernism, 1926–1979* (New York: New York University Press, 1981); Ervand Abrahamian, *Iran Between Two Revolutions* (Princeton: Princeton University Press, 1982); Cheryl Bernard and Zalmay Khalilzad, *"The Government of God": Iran's Islamic Republic* (New York: Columbia University Press, 1984).

41. For a bibliography, see Monte Palmer *et al.*, *Survey Research in the Arab World* (London: MENAS Press, 1982); for examples, see Tawfic E. Farah and Yasumasa Kuroda, eds., *Political Socialization in the Arab States* (Boulder, CO: Lynne Reinner Publishers, 1987) and Tawfic Farah, ed., *Political Behavior in the Arab States* (Boulder, CO: Westview Press, 1983).

42. The Foreign Broadcast Information Service and the Joint Publications Research Service, both of which are services of U.S. Government translation bureaus, publish daily translations of selections from print and broadcast media throughout the world.

43. R. Bayley Winder, "Four Decades of Middle Eastern Study," *Middle East Journal* 41, no. 1 (1987), p. 63.

44. L. Carl Brown, *International Politics and the Middle East* (Princeton: Princeton University Press, 1984), pp. 289–90.

45. On the literature on conflict management and perceptions, see the discussion and references in Ben-Dor, *State and Conflict*; Janice Gross Stein, "Calculation, Miscalculation, and Deterrence, I & II: Views from Cairo and Jerusalem," in Robert Jervis, Ned Lebow, and Janice Gross Stein, eds., *Psychology and Deterrence* (Baltimore: Johns Hopkins University Press, 1985); on military spending, see Paul Jabber, *Not by War Alone: Security and Arms Control in the Middle East* (Los Angeles: University of California Press, 1981); Anthony H. Cordesman, "The Middle East and the Cost of the Politics of Force," *Middle East Journal* 40, no. 1 (1986); and *MERIP Reports* 112 (1983) on "The Arms Race in the Middle East." Ian Lustick's forthcoming comparative work on the nature of colonialism and occupation in French Algeria, Northern Ireland, and the territories is an important exception to the general neglect of the linkage of raison d'état with violence, and it points up the importance of state-focused perspectives; see his *State Building Failure in British Ireland and French Algeria* (University of California: Institute of International Studies, 1985).

3

Anthropology's Orient: The Boundaries of Theory on the Arab World

Lila Abu-Lughod

Introduction

It was January 1987. I had returned to visit the family in the Egyptian Bedouin community among which I had lived and done research from 1978 to 1980. The book I had written about them had just come out, and I had brought them my first copy. No one in the community knew English; not many were literate even in Arabic. Yet it was important to me to offer them this book, whose contents I briefly described. They enjoyed the photographs, which I had carefully selected with an eye to the way they would be "read" by this community, making certain that at least one member from each of the families I knew was included. And we discussed the book and its purpose.

The Haj, my host, said it was a pity I had published it in English. He wanted to know who in America was interested—who would read it? I explained that not many people in America were interested, but that I hoped people who wanted to understand the Arabs would read it, mostly students and scholars who specialized in understanding humanity as it existed all around the world.

I felt uncomfortable as I said this, suddenly aware of how ingenuous and odd anthropology's avowed purpose sounded. The Haj listened and remarked, "Yes, knowledge is power (*l-mi'rifa guwwa*). The Americans and the British know everything. They want to know everything about people, about us. Then if they come to a country, or come to rule it, they know what people need and they know how to rule."

His tone was accusatory, and there was a sense in which I felt defensive about being linked with foreigners, even though I knew that he did not think of me as an American but as an Arab who lived in and was unfortunately influenced by America. "Exactly!" I said, laughing, and told him that a well-known book written by a Palestinian professor in

America had said just that. My Bedouin host had brought up an issue about scholarship that we as Western or Western-oriented scholars have only recently begun to explore (in a somewhat more nuanced form): the relationship between knowledge and power. In Middle East studies, Edward Said's *Orientalism* opened up this domain of questioning, and it is with this issue that any discussion of theory and method must begin.[1]

What follows is to be seen not as a review of the literature in Middle East anthropology but as a tracing of the shapes and patterns of anthropological discourse on the Arab world. In keeping with the purpose of this volume, I pay particular attention to theoretical issues. To make my task manageable, I have confined my discussion to anthropological works published in or translated into English in the past decade. Throughout the essay I am concerned with the relationship of the anthropology of the Arab world to the study of the region, on the one hand, and to anthropological theory, on the other.

I begin with a consideration of those anthropologists whose work, although based on fieldwork in some part of the Arab world, has been primarily directed toward and taken up by anthropologists outside the circle of Middle East specialists. Their contributions to anthropological theory have been in two related areas: epistemology and the analysis of what used to be called the subjective aspects of human life—culture or ideology.

In the second half of the essay I turn to anthropological works that, while taking up or speaking to theoretical concerns, locate themselves more squarely within the study of the Arab Middle East. I show that the zones of theorizing within Middle East anthropology are few and begin to ask the questions raised by this observation: Why is theorizing distributed into these particular zones? Why do the zones have these particular boundaries? What fashions and forces channel this distribution? What limits, exclusions, and silences does this distribution entail?

Although the review is critical, I offer it in the spirit of another of the Haj's ways of understanding me and my project. As the years have gone by he has become increasingly concerned about my gray hairs and lack of children. But to indicate that he respects and understands what he perceives as my single-minded devotion to learning, he usually prefaces his well-meaning advice with the remark, "Of course, the Qur'an says that learning is illumination (*al-'ilm nuur*) and it is a good thing." I hope to illuminate, through this critical reflection on my work and the work of my colleagues, the ways in which our scholarship is part of a complex world, not just about (and outside) it. I have had to be selective and have been unable to do justice to the subtlety or range of argument and ethnography in many of the exemplary works I do cite.[2] This has caused me a few new gray hairs.

Orientalism and Anthropology

Anthropologists do not usually consider themselves Orientalists (and have often been looked down upon by traditional Orientalists) because their training within the discipline of anthropology has been stronger than their training in the languages, literatures, and history of the Middle East.[3] Yet they fall within Said's definition of an Orientalist as "anyone who teaches, writes about, or researches the Orient" (1978:2). Said, however, means something both more specific and more general than this simple definition suggests. He defines Orientalism as "a style of thought based upon an ontological and epistemological distinction made between 'the Orient' and (most of the time) 'the Occident,' " and also argues that Orientalism is "a corporate institution for dealing with the Orient— dealing with it by making statements about it, authorizing views of it, describing it, by teaching it, settling it, ruling over it" (1978:2–3). This Foucauldian approach to Orientalism as a "discursive formation" enables him to analyze a whole group of texts constituting a field of study for themes, correspondences, affiliations, and silences, and to show how these texts interpenetrate the political and economic project of colonizing "the East."

Is anthropology implicated? These days, the totalizing opposition between East and West does not have particular currency in anthropology, where other dichotomies such as primitive/modern, black/white, savage/ civilized, and now Self/Other are more salient. Some even argue that complex literate societies like those found in the Middle East or the Indian subcontinent do not fit easily within these dichotomies and have, for that reason, been second-class citizens when it comes to anthropological theorizing (cf. Appadurai 1986b).

Second, for Said one of the most striking characteristics of Orientalism is its textuality, especially the way the truths about a "real place" called the Orient are created out of texts that seem to refer only to other texts for their authority. This is what he calls the citationary nature of Orientalism.[4] Here again, anthropologists would seem at first to be reasonably innocent, since they pride themselves on working in communities no one else has visited and tend to gather their material from "the field," not the library. As recent critics of ethnographies-as-texts have noted, they are supposed to acquire *their* authority from such devices as quoting from field notes and telling stories that testify to their presence at the scenes of action, their "direct experience."[5]

However, insofar as the colonization of the Middle East is only one instance of European domination of the rest of the world, critiques of anthropology's links to colonialism might be expected to follow lines similar to Said's. There is a growing literature on this subject within anthropology, most of it going well beyond the simplistic and conspiratorial handmaiden-of-colonialism arguments such as those that accuse anthropology of being a justification for colonial rule. Arguments like these are easily rebutted with accounts of the ways particular anthropologists opposed colonial officials or tried to help "natives," or defenses that anthropologists are liberals who, like Franz Boas, were in the vanguard of the battle against ethnocentrism and racism.

What Said and the more sophisticated of the critics of anthropology's relationship to colonialism, like Asad (1973a, 1986a), Clifford (1983b), Fabian (1983), Maquet (1964), and Scholte (1974) are trying to get at is something far more subtle and pervasive—what Said calls "a *distribution* of geopolitical awareness into aesthetic, scholarly, economic, sociological, historical, and philological texts" (1978:12). This may work through individuals, as Said suggests in a passage noting the obvious point that:

> If it is true that no production of knowledge in the human sciences can ever ignore or disclaim its author's involvement as a human subject in his own circumstances, then it must also be true that for a European or American studying the Orient there can be no disclaiming the main circumstances of *his* actuality: that he comes up against the Orient as a European or an American first, as an individual second. And to be a European or an American in such a situation is by no means an inert fact. It meant and means being aware, however dimly, that one belongs to a power with definite interests in the Orient, and more important, that one belongs to a part of the earth with a definite history of involvement in the Orient almost since the time of Homer (1978:11).

Although it may work through individuals, the fundamental structural inequality between the worlds of Western scholars and their Third World subjects affects in complex and indirect ways the disciplines within which such individuals work. This is what needs to be explored.[6]

To say this, however, is not to deny that there are exceptional individuals,[7] that individual works are unique, or that there are contradictions and ambiguities within any discourse/world situation, contradictions that imply, as Asad notes (1973a:18), the potential for self-criticism and transcendence. Within anthropology and Middle East studies I think we can see clear signs of the latter.

It is crucial to keep in mind, however, that there are no easy solutions to the problems raised by such disciplinary critiques. Contrary to what naive attacks on Middle East studies or enthusiastic (pro and con) misreadings of Said have suggested, Said (1978:322) rightly argues that "the methodological failures of Orientalism cannot be accounted for either by saying that the *real* Orient is different from Orientalist portraits of it, or by saying that since Orientalists are Westerners for the most part, they cannot be expected to have an inner sense of what the Orient is all about." Such arguments, which apply equally to anthropology, would presume that discourses were not always "representations" or that knowledge could somehow be separated from power and position and made something pure, two presumptions Said refuses to make and takes great pains to refute (see 1978:10). It follows then that the claims of truth made by even an indigenous anthropologist who lives in and identifies with the society he or she writes about would have to be subjected to the same sorts of questions.[8] I will return to these questions of what could be called "the politics of place" when I consider more specifically the relationship between Orientalism and anthropological theorizing about the Arab world. Before that, however, I want to take up the work of those anthropologists whose theorizing seems to raise more general issues in anthropology and whose contributions are worth presenting to non-anthropologists.

Analyzing Human Action: Culture, Ideology, and Discourse

In 1975, the parochialism of Middle East anthropology was such that it could still be said in a major review of the field that "anthropological studies in MENA (Middle East and North Africa) have largely failed to attract an audience of scholars beyond those devoted to undertaking such studies themselves" and that "with few exceptions, contributions to anthropological literature based on Middle Eastern research have failed to have an important impact upon theoretical concerns in the field of ethnology" (Fernea and Malarkey 1975:183). This is no longer the case. Middle East anthropology can now claim two (highly) influential thinkers in current anthropology, Clifford Geertz and Pierre Bourdieu, as well as some of the key figures in what is often called "reflexive anthropology," including Vincent Crapanzano, Paul Rabinow, and Kevin Dwyer. At least a brief discussion of the theoretical import of their work is essential to any assessment of anthropology's contributions to theory and method in Middle East studies.[9] This is a different matter from that of anthropology's contributions to our understanding of the Middle East, a question that will take up the second half of this essay.

It seems to have become fashionable to criticize and even dismiss Geertz for what amounts to the sin of writing well. He is accused, often with a peculiar animus, of wielding his magical pen to conjure phantoms capable of taking in his poor unsuspecting readers. These strange charges must be taken as a tribute to his stature, since they overestimate any writer's powers and the gullibility of readers. There are criticisms to be made of

Geertz's approach, but they must begin with a recognition of the nature of his theoretical contribution.

Although his work covers a wide range of topics, is distributed throughout a large number of books and essays written over a long period, and is based ethnographically on fieldwork in Indonesia (Java and Bali) as well as Morocco (and is often comparative), I will pick out only a few of its most influential general aspects. Considered by many the key figure in what has come to be called interpretive anthropology, Geertz reintroduced into an anthropology influenced by either Emile Durkheim or Franz Boas a Weberian concern with "meaning" or "culture." One of the more celebrated statements in his seminal essay, "Thick Description: Toward an Interpretive Theory of Culture," sums up the approach: "Believing, with Max Weber, that man is an animal suspended in webs of significance he himself has spun, I take culture to be those webs, and the analysis of it to be therefore not an experimental science in search of law but an interpretive one in search of meaning" (1973c:5). This links him immediately to literary criticism, and he does indeed play richly with the metaphor of cultures as texts to be read.[10]

Which brings us to the question of method. According to Geertz what is to be read is social action. Because it is important to get at "the native's point of view"—a phrase Geertz borrows from Malinowski's 1922 pronouncement about anthropology's goals[11]—the anthropologist cannot simply observe behavior but must try to figure out what peoples' actions mean, to themselves and to others. To designate this process he borrows the notion of "thick description" from the philosopher Gilbert Ryle. Borrowing Ryle's example of how important it is to know the difference between a twitch of an eyelid and a wink, even though they may appear identical, he goes on to state that the object of ethnography is "a stratified hierarchy of meaningful structures in terms of which twitches, winks, fake-winks, parodies, rehearsals of parodies are produced, perceived, and interpreted, and without which they would not . . . in fact exist, no matter what anyone did or didn't do with his eyelids" (1973c:7).

Geertz's approach is also sometimes labeled "symbolic anthropology" because he took symbols to be the vehicles of the meanings he was interested in getting at. As Ortner (1984:129) puts it, "Geertz's most radical theoretical move (1973b) was to argue that culture is not something locked inside people's heads, but rather is embodied in public symbols, symbols through which the members of a society communicate their worldview, value-orientations, ethos, and all the rest to one another, to future generations—and to anthropologists." What anthropologists should do is to interpret peoples' actions, even the most minute, in terms of systems of publicly shared symbols and to seek to understand how these symbols shape people's understandings and feelings. His article on the Moroccan "bazaar" as a cultural system (1979) is his most recent and extended analysis of a Middle Eastern society in these terms.

Geertz's arguments have influenced the direction American anthropology has taken over the last two decades. He mediated the debate between the behaviorists and idealists by arguing for a view of humans as essentially cultural and their actions always meaningful or symbolic, and he balanced the British anthropological concern with social structure (which had dominated Middle East anthropology) with a stress on cultural analysis and interpretation.[12] His notion of cultures as texts and his recognition of the textual nature of ethnography ("writing fictions" [1973c:15]) laid the groundwork for what has now become a major issue in anthropology, the relationship between fieldwork and the writing of ethnographies, a topic that several other Middle East anthropologists have explored further.[13]

Pierre Bourdieu, the other major theorist with ethnographic experience in the Middle East (among the Kabyles in Algeria), shares with Geertz two central concerns: the relationship between social actors and the ideas they work with and the relationship between objectivity and subjectivity in modes of social analysis. Drawing on and thus reacting against different intellectual traditions, however, they have ended up representing radically different theoretical turns in anthropology. Bourdieu, whose own approach has weaknesses that will be discussed, can profitably be used to highlight the assumptions and lacunae in the Geertzian approach.

Bourdieu begins his book, *Outline of a Theory of Practice*, by arguing that "the anthropologist's particular relation to the object of his study contains the makings of a theoretical distortion." This distortion is due, he says, to the anthropologist's very position—however "direct" his or her experience—as an observer, one who is "excluded from the real play of social activities by the fact that he has no place . . . in the system observed and has no need to make a place for himself there." This exclusion "inclines him to a hermeneutic representation of practices, leading him to reduce all social relations to communicative relations."

> Condemned to adopt unwittingly for his own use the representation of action which is forced on agents or groups when they lack practical mastery of a highly valued competence and have to provide themselves with an explicit and at least semi-formalized substitute for it, [the anthropologist] in his preoccupation with *interpreting* practices, is inclined to introduce into the object the principles of his relation to the object (1977: 1–2).

Bourdieu thus argues that the unwary "outsider" anthropologist mistakes practical activity for a drama played out before a spectator, an object to be observed, a representation to be interpreted or read. Although primarily directed to the structuralists, whose formative influence is reflected in Bourdieu's own work, this critique could well be used to question Geertz's hermeneutic approach, his view of "culture" as text or map or model, and his assumption that social action has to do primarily with meaning.

If Bourdieu would question "reading" as the proper mode by which anthropologists should analyze social action, he would be equally suspicious of the Geertzian notion that the people we study are themselves reading one another. He considers "practice" the central object of study and his notion of human actors is that they are primarily engaged in regulated improvisations in the art of living. In answer to the question of why individuals in particular communities seem to act similarly, he prefers a concept called "habitus" to "culture." By habitus he means dispositions that generate and structure practices and representations but are themselves structured by such things as material conditions characteristic of a class condition (1977:72, 78). Unlike Geertz, he is especially concerned with those political and historical forces that create a particular habitus, that which generates what the anthropologist perceives as culture.

For method Bourdieu proposes a dialectical movement between, and in a sense beyond, a phenomenological approach and an objectivist approach. By "phenomenological" he means the experience people themselves have of their world. By "objectivist" he means the outsider's knowledge of the structures of the social world that shapes this experience and of the nature of this primary experience as that which is "denied *explicit* knowledge of those structures" (1977:3).

In what has been described thus far, and is more evident in his brilliant and detailed ethnography of Kabyle society, Bourdieu's affinities with Marx rather than Weber are clear. If Geertz can be faulted for viewing "culture" as overly unified and timeless and for passing too lightly over questions about the social, economic, historical determinations of "culture" and its role in power relations, Bourdieu must be confronted with ambiguities inherent in the Marxian concept of ideology as a mystifying tool of power. Implicit in this concept is a belief in the possibility of stepping outside the structures to know the "truths" that ideology masks (for example, the misrecognized strategies of domination), and an assumption that at bottom, as Bourdieu suggests in his analysis of "symbolic capital," these truths are economic.[14]

As anthropologists pursue analyses of sociocultural life made possible by their initial insights, some of the limitations of both Geertz's and Bourdieu's theoretical approaches are becoming more apparent. One type of phenomenon that resists analysis in terms either of a theory of culture or a theory of ideology is the coexistence of contradictory discourses in a single society, especially when one seems to subvert the other. For example, the central problematic in my work was how to account for the radical disjuncture, in the Egyptian Bedouin community in which I did research, between what individuals said in ordinary conversation and what they expressed in poetry.

Second, like most anthropologists, both Geertz and Bourdieu have been unable to find satisfactory ways of dealing with historical transformation. Other issues with which they grapple—in particular how to mediate the dualities of ideal versus material, subjective versus objective, representations versus practices, knowledge versus power—are far from resolved. Among those whose work addresses itself to dilemmas posed by these approaches is Michel Foucault, whose notions of discourses and discursive formations, always historically situated, always tied to and produced by power (whether from the center or the margins), provide us with a provocative and interesting way of thinking about issues of social actors and their ideas.[15] Although anthropologists are only beginning to explore theoretical pathways Foucault opens up, this is a direction that could (as *Orientalism* demonstrates and my discussions below of theorizing about women and about Islam suggest) be fruitful. Finally, one must ask what the consequences, if not determinations, are of social theorizing that concentrates on the internal dynamics of cultures treated as ahistorical social wholes detached from their global contexts—theorizing that does not seriously question the global and historical conditions of its own presence.

Fieldwork and Ethnographic Writing

Epistemological concerns like those explored by Geertz and Bourdieu have come to the fore in theorizing within anthropology over the past decade. At issue is anthropology's method, participant observation. Three anthropologists who worked in Morocco in the late 1960s and early 1970s—Paul Rabinow, Vincent Crapanzano, and Kevin Dwyer—have been central figures in this discussion, which involves a questioning both of the fieldwork encounter and of the relationship between the encounter and the production of ethnographic texts. Some associate this scrutiny with a despair over the fragmentation of anthropology as a discipline. Others associate it with an exhilaration born of the disintegration of positivistic paradigms.[16]

All three writers are concerned about the tendency to ignore the process by which knowledge about the Other (as they refer to their objects of study) is gained, hence the disengagement of the activity of fieldwork from its result in the written text. Rabinow, like Geertz, argues that anthropology is an interpretive enterprise and extends this hermeneutical approach to the actual situation of fieldwork. With Bourdieu, however, he asserts that anthropological "facts" are a hybrid product of the encounter between the anthropologist and the persons being studied, and must not be confused with the lived experience of the latter. In the process of being questioned by the anthropologist, "the informant must first learn to explicate his own culture . . . to begin to objectify his own life-world" (1977:152). Both are active in developing "a system of shared symbols" (1977:153). In other words, Rabinow sees fieldwork primarily as a (halting and imperfect) process of communication and the creation of intersubjective meaning.

His essay is a mix of theoretical reflection and brief accounts of his attempts to communicate and develop relationships with a number of informants who were, as he puts it, his guides to various zones of Moroccan culture by virtue of their own differing social locations within Moroccan society (1977:156). He orders the informants by their increasing "otherness" proceeding from the French-speaking hotel owner to the orthodox paragon of a saintly lineage. This progression serves as the narrative drama of the book whose climax is his final confrontation with utter "otherness," a confrontation that makes him decide it is time to go home, hardly a year after he has begun fieldwork.

Crapanzano and Dwyer too are disturbed by the anthropological conventions of transmuting negotiated realities to objective ones attributed to the Other (Crapanzano 1980:x), but their accounts take more seriously than Rabinow's the consequent need to reveal the nature of actual encounters. Where Rabinow admits he sometimes "collapsed" individuals to make composites, Crapanzano (1980) and Dwyer (1982) each structure their books in an experimental fashion around their relationship with a single individual, interspersing interview material with commentary and theoretical reflection.

Crapanzano's book is a complex, evocative and highly self-conscious reflection, often within a psychoanalytic idiom, on what transpired within the space of his encounter (1980:xiii) with Tuhami, an unusual and troubled Moroccan tile-maker married to 'Aisha Qandisha, a she-demon. As Tuhami's interlocutor he "became an active participant in his life history" (1980:11), eventually succumbing to the temptation to take on the role of therapist. Crapanzano recognizes in this transformation of their relationship the reproduction of the familiar power dynamics of the colonial relationship, just as he recognizes in his role as writer and interpreter of the encounter a privileged position of final authority. Yet his central concern remains the dynamics of the interpersonal relationship.

Dwyer's more dedicated effort to expose what is hidden in what he calls the contemplative stance of anthropology adds a twist to Bourdieu's argument about the projection of the experience of the outsider onto the workings of the social worlds being studied. Dwyer reminds us that anthropologists do not really stand outside the societies they study; they stand in a definite historical and social relation to those societies. They come from dominant societies and they intrude just as colonials did before them (1982:274). The Self and Other are not isolated from each other, nor is their encounter isolated from the world-historical conditions that shape it (1982:270).

His book attempts to reformulate anthropology's project in line with a desire to let "the Other's voice . . . be heard . . . addressing and challenging the Self" (1982:xxii). Like Crapanzano, he focuses on the human encounter between anthropologist and informant, in his case one Moroccan villager with whom he tape-recorded a series of interviews (what he calls dialogues) about a number of events (broadly defined) over the course of one summer. Unlike Crapanzano, he chooses actually to reproduce the "dialogues" he had with this man, including all the questions the Moroccan was responding to. He preserves the sequence to make clear both his own role in the interactions and the incomplete, contingent, and always changing quality of the exchanges out of which anthropologists develop their knowledge of other societies.

Laudable in these works is the attempt to expose the complex character of the stuff out of which anthropological "facts" are made by showing the peculiarities and incompleteness of the personal encounters out of which knowledge comes. By exposing their own contributions to the encounters, Dwyer and Crapanzano also make themselves vulnerable in ways unusual for social scientists.[17] Crapanzano tells us that in addition to feeling ambivalence about the encounter with Tuhami and to structuring and limiting it, he fundamentally betrayed the relationship by suddenly abandoning Tuhami (which would have been an unpardonable mode of termination for a therapist). Dwyer allows us to see the intrusive nature of his questions and the way in which the dialogues were initiated by him and occasionally annoyed his informant.[18]

Yet it is as if this self-exposure obviates the need for critical analysis of the Self in the encounter, and thus some of the most interesting questions about the anthropological encounter are sidestepped. Ironically, these theorists who deplore the false distance of objectivity risk setting up the divide between Self and Other as more fundamental, fixed, and absolute. In all three works, one senses a distance at the core of the encounter. This is conveyed by the very abstractness of the designation "Other," by the revelation of a lack of mutuality in the relationships themselves, or by the refusal to fill in the context in such a way as to make an informant's comments seem sensible and ordinary. Crapanzano writes about a man who is a seriously maladjusted, unusually isolated and miserable person in his own society. Although his life history may bring certain cultural issues into relief, it may inadvertently highlight the "Otherness" of Moroccans. Dwyer's villager is more ordinary, but we know him only as the sometimes impatient answerer of Dwyer's questions. In labeling as a dialogue what is actually a series of questions and answers, Dwyer implicitly denies the possibilities for a real conversation. In stripping his villager of the context of his community, Dwyer makes it seem as if the two of them stand opposite each other as Western-style isolated individuals in a social void.

Rather than fetishizing the impossibility of empathy through this reification of the Self/Other distinction, one is tempted to go beyond this critique of the positivistic assumptions and conventions of anthropology by asking, too, how the Western Self might be shored up and given an identity by such oppositions. To recognize that the Self may not be so unitary and that the Other might actually consist of many *others* who may not be so "other" after all is to raise the theoretically interesting problem of how to build in ways of accepting or describing differences without denying similarities or turning these various differences into a single, frozen Difference.[19]

Geopolitics is one of the factors that both divide and unite Western anthropologists and the people they study. All three of the reflexive anthropologists whose language for Self and Other tend toward the existential or literary also remark that they are historical and social selves. But they hardly elaborate. For example, Dwyer, like Rabinow, refers to the colonial situation and the French in setting the terms of his encounter with a Moroccan; neither refers much to relations between Morocco (as an Arab country) and the United States or considers ways in which their relationships, as Americans, with Moroccans might have been colored (on both sides) by the polarization made vivid by the June 1967 war. There are other aspects of these anthropologists' selves that could have received more attention: gender, disciplinary constraint,[20] and ethnic background. All are elements that make up their selves and that interact in perhaps conflicting ways with aspects of "others" they have encountered.

The Politics of Place in Anthropological Theory

If, as I have just shown, it can no longer be said that there are no theorists in Middle East anthropology whose work is read outside the field, it still must be said that most theorizing in the anthropology of the Arab world is about more localized concerns. For the second half of this essay, I want to look at anthropological work specifically devoted to making sense of the Arab world. Because of the reliance on the "direct experience" of fieldwork (however problematized by the reflexive anthropologists) anthropological work may seem less citationary than Orientalism, less liable to conjure up a "real place" out of textual references. I want to argue, however, that anthropological writing shapes a Middle East of its own, fashioned out of conventions, standards of relevance, imaginative and political concerns, and zones of prestige.

I will be building on an argument made by Arjun Appadurai in a little gem of an article written in response to Ortner's (1984) major review of anthropological theory. He asks about the relationship between scholarship (in this case anthropological theorizing) and place (which he calls the "purloined letter of anthropology"). His thesis is that "what anthropologists find, in this or that place, far from being independent data for the construction and verification of theory, is in fact a very complicated compound of local realities and the contingencies of metropolitan theory" (1986b:360). One could call this the politics of place in anthropological theorizing, and it is with the politics of theorizing about the Arab world that I will be especially concerned.[21]

The *anthropology* of the Orient is a special blend that cannot be reduced to Orientalism or understood without reference to the context of general anthropological preferences whose imprint can be seen clearly in its contours. As Appadurai has noted, there are prestige zones of anthropological theorizing, mostly determined by anthropology's tendency (until recently) to concentrate on "the small, the simple, the elementary, the face-to-face" Other and to avoid the complex, literate, and historically deep (1986b:357). These tendencies are reproduced in Middle East anthropology in a number of ways, one of the most obvious of which is through geography.

Geographically, the prestige zones are Morocco and now North Yemen. These two countries have more in common than scenic mountains and governments friendly to American visitors and researchers. Exotic, colorful, on the peripheries of the Arab world (Geertz calls Morocco a "wild west sort of place"), they are ideal places for anthropologists. At least they are as ideal as anywhere could be in a region as miserably deficient in myth and "pagan" ritual and as abundant in clothing and historical complexity as the Middle East. These two countries also share the virtues of being away from the central war zones and the political and moral mine field of the conflict over Palestine.

This is not to say that anthropologists do not study other places in the Arab world. But as a rule, peripheries seem preferable to cores and sparsely populated deserts and mountains seem preferable to densely populated and well-watered regions that are centers of power.[22] One can see the foci of work in Middle East anthropology in part as the result of the interaction of the particularities of the Middle East situation with the general romanticism of anthropology and its uneasy sense that since most of its analytical tools were honed in simple societies they are unwieldy if not useless in different sorts of contexts.

Appadurai's most insightful remark is that especially in its studies of complex civilizations anthropology tends to develop "theoretical metonyms" or "gatekeeping concepts . . . concepts, that is, that seem to limit anthropological theorizing about the place in question, and that define the quintessential and dominant questions of interest in the region" (1986b:357). As someone who works on India, he is particularly disturbed by the predominance of theorizing about caste as the "surrogate" for Indian society (Appadurai 1986b;1988).

Is the same true of the Middle East? I think so. It seems to me that there are three central zones of theorizing within Middle East anthropology: segmentation, the harem, and Islam. These are the "theoretical metonyms" by which this vast and complex area is grasped, and I want to examine below the ways in which most theorizing about the Arab world falls within these three terms.[23]

How does it come to be that theorizing appears more or less restricted to these zones? Although the answers are various and will come out in my discussion of each zone, some general points can be made. The first is that paradigms popular within a discipline or a branch of a discipline always perpetuate discourse in certain veins. The second is that the exigencies of academic politics and careers must also play a part in restricting zones of theorizing in any field.[24] The standards (albeit changing and disputed) of anthropological competence against which work is judged contribute to shaping what is produced. All of us work in national intellectual milieus which shape how we work and on what. Also, unless one speaks to issues that concern others in the field, one is likely to be ignored and one's work to float ghostlike, seen but unseen, popping up suddenly in a lone reference only to disappear again. It also cannot be denied that one way to make a name for oneself is to say something new about an old debate, preferably in argument with a famous elder, dead or alive. But these are only the most general and superficial of the determinations of these zones. In what follows I will explore others.

Homo Segmentarius

Perhaps the most prestigious and enduring zone of anthropological theorizing about the Arab world is what is known as segmentation, segmentary lineage theory, or tribalism. The literature is vast, the genealogy long (some begin with Robertson Smith in 1885), the pedigree impeccable (a mostly British line with Evans-Pritchard prominent), and the theoretical distinctions fine. Tribal sociopolitical organization or ideology has indeed been a field where some of the best minds in Middle East anthropology were exercised, whether in working out the meaning and significance of segmentation or, more recently, denying it. I want to outline briefly the points of debate within this arena of social theorizing before considering why this issue takes up an inordinate amount of anthropological space.

Among those who see segmentation as something central to understanding Middle Eastern society, the main cleavage is between those who see it as a description of the sociopolitical organization of tribal groups and those who see it as an ideology, variously defined and attributed. Most early works fall into the former category, as do those of Cole (1975), Gellner (1969), and Hart (1981). The kinds of institutions examined in this structural-functional approach are those thought to bind and divide men[25]—the land, resources, and patrimony that unite and the feuds that divide, as well as the mediators (in North Africa the saintly lineages) who prevent total violence. The central problem for these theorists is how social order is maintained in acephalous (headless) societies like the tribal societies of the Middle East in which there is no central authority. The answer has to do with the segmentary lineage that balances opposed groups at varying levels of sociopolitical organization. The result, according to the conventional wisdom, is a system of "ordered anarchy."

The trend in recent ethnography has been to see segmentation, the segmenting genealogy or the paradigm of patrilineal kinship as ideological, describing not what groups do or do not do "on the ground" but how they think or talk about themselves and what they do.[26] A number of these theorists seek to demonstrate what other forces impinge on tribesmen to determine their social and political behavior. Behnke (1980), for example, posits ecology as the basic "constraint and incentive" in Cyrenaican Bedouin choice, interacting with the morally charged conceptual kinship system (1980:185). Peters (1967), also dealing with Cyrenaican Bedouins, was the first to make the argument that the system might be an ideology, a set of beliefs that the "natives" had about how their system worked that bore little relation to sociological reality or what actually happened at times of conflict. He argued for a material determination of social groupings based again on some sort of economic/ecological concerns. Lancaster (1981:35, 151) is concerned with how, among the Rwala Bedouins, genealogy is a manipulable means of explaining the present and generating the future. He sees most actions as pragmatically motivated economic and political efforts to balance assets and options. These are, however, "invariably couched in segmentary, genealogical terms."

Rather than just describe the ideology of segmentation or describe how it works, Meeker also tries to explain why it developed historically. He writes, "The question is not whether Near Eastern tribal people actually adhere to genealogical principles in their political behavior, but why they should have conceived of such a bizarrely formal paradigm of political relationships with such disturbing implications" (1979:14). For him "the politically segmenting genealogy is . . . a form of political language" suggesting "a play of relationships around a problem of political violence" (1979:15). Finding segmentary politics relatively absent in the tribes of North Arabia, he argues that it must be understood as a peculiar adaptation to the circumstances of a pastoral nomadic tradition and politics tempered by the interests arising from sedentary agriculture (as in North Africa and Yemen). The central and more pervasive Near Eastern problem is the threat of violence posed by the possession of aggressive instruments (mounts and weapons), a problem Meeker regards as the implicit subject of the Rwala poetry he analyzes.

Caton (1984,1986,1987) is also concerned with segmentation as a form of political rhetoric in tribal societies and explores the implications of the notion "that political rhetoric is a communicative act of *persuasion* which is made in response to conflict in the segmentary social order" (1984:405). He is especially concerned with how conflict is mediated in such tribal societies, where order seems so fragile because central authority, by definition, is not only lacking but actively resisted as antithetical to tribesmen's ultimate values of voluntaristic action and political autonomy (1987). This leads him to a rich understanding of the role of tribal poetry as political rhetoric essential to dispute and its mediation (1990).[27]

This is only a partial list of theoretical elaborations on segmentation as ideology. It does not include, for example, either the recent discussions of political discourse in a tribal idiom in the context of modern states like Jordan (Layne 1986; 1987) and Libya (J. Davis 1985; 1988) or the radically structural interpretation to be presented below. In addition, the structural-functional version of segmentary theory has elicited one other type of response: rejection. This position is represented by Rosen (1984, 1979) and H. Geertz (1979) whose reaction against the vision of Moroccan society as segmentary corresponds to a theoretical rejection of the premises and emphases of the social structural approach in anthropological theorizing in favor of a cultural or interpretive approach.

Hildred Geertz (1979:377) argues that "the literature on kinship and family relationships in North Africa and the Middle East has been unnecessarily burdened with a model of opposing descent groups whose internal segments are structured genealogically" and hopes to show that this model is inadequate. Even if Moroccans occasionally use segmentation as an idiom, "their more fundamental concepts of intergroup and interpersonal relationships are really quite otherwise" (*ibid.*). Rosen has developed most fully this notion of fundamental concepts of social attachment. In the Moroccan case, he proposed origin, locality, and relatedness as "the fundamental bases to which individuals can look for possible relationships as they set about constructing a network of personal ties" (1979:101).

Both Combs-Schilling (1981; 1985) and Dresch (1986), although for different reasons, have argued that this debate between the segmentary and dyadic models of Moroccan social relations presents a false dichotomy. Combs-Schilling, somewhat like Salzman (1978), argues that both are idioms available to Moroccans in different contexts. Dresch, in a more theoretical vein, argues that both partake of a falsely mechanical type of social analysis with a misplaced focus on the interactions of solid bodies, either corporate groups or individuals, rather than on structural principles. To understand what he proposes as an alternative that both remains true to the interpretive project of delineating "the implicit assumptions which people themselves make" (Eickelman [1984:286] as cited in Dresch [1986:321]) and rescues segmentary theory, we must take up his attack on Gellner, who sparked much of the recent discussion of Middle East segmentation.

Before taking up Dresch's attack on Gellner, I shall mention one other sort of argument besides the interpretivists' leveled against a Gellnerian view of the total fit between segmentary theory and segmentary society. Hammoudi (1980)—who, unlike Dresch, accepts Gellner's claim to be heir to Evans-Pritchard—denies the validity of his extreme segmentary model. He shows, mostly through historical evidence, that the very tribes Gellner studied in Morocco do not conform to the model and that the segmentary genealogical principle provides the basis for hierarchy as well as the proverbial equality of tribesmen. Hammoudi argues that Gellner has imposed his simple theory on a complex situation, "brushing aside all history" (including fifty years of colonial administration). This is easy to do, he adds, in situations where the people in the society being studied themselves hold this ideology. But for Hammoudi it is clear that neither the tribesmen's ideology nor the corresponding anthropological theory describe Moroccan realities.

Dresch (1986), who disputes Gellner's claim to Evans-Pritchard's legacy, argues that what actually happens in any particular instance is not relevant to the validity of segmentary theory. He accuses theorists of having misread Evans-Pritchard's structuralist message and rendered it a structural-functionalist theory of corporate groups; actually, he maintains, it is a theory of segmentation or balanced opposition as a structural principle with the same sort of exteriority Louis Dumont attributes to the principle of hierarchy (based on the opposition between pure and impure) in Indian (caste) society. He argues, "the actor is constituted in accord with the same structural principle as the categories with which he works and the forms of action available to him" (1986:319). For Dresch, like Dumont, calling segmentation, like hierarchy, an ideology downgrades it (1986:318) and denies the intimacy of the relation of action to the notion of segmentation (319).

In Dresch's work, segmentary theory thus reaches its apogee and Middle Eastern tribal man becomes *homo segmentarius*. There are two problems with this. In recapitulating through the medium of Middle East segmentary theory the movement within British social anthropology to claim Evans-Pritchard as a homegrown precurser of structuralism, Dresch stops theoretical time in the early 1970s. Structuralism has in the past decade and a half been subjected to a range of quite serious critiques, the most trenchant of which have emerged in France. Even if he prefers not to consider the more philosophical poststructuralist arguments of Foucault or Derrida, Dresch must at least take into account Bourdieu's powerful critiques of the idealism of structuralism. Specifically relevant are Bourdieu's sophisticated analysis of the relationship between official representations and practical strategies and even a similar concern in Eickelman with implicit and explicit practical notions (1981:97) and "the political economy of meaning" (Eickelman 1985a).

Second, one must ask about segmentation the same question Appadurai (1986a;1986b;1988) has asked about caste (and particularly the Dumontian structuralist version of caste): Why privilege this aspect of society and say it accounts for the whole? To be fair, Dresch says segmentation is not the only principle at work in tribal society. But he mentions no other. On the contrary, he remarks (1986:313) that "segmentation in the Yemeni case has an oddly inclusive power. What is put into the system emerges looking like tribalism." I find more striking the oddly inclusive power of theories of segmentation in the anthropology of the Arab world.

In general, the question that must be raised about theorizing about segmentation is: Why has there been so much of it? Even if one grants that some agricultural societies in the Arab Middle East are tribal, and that therefore the analytical issues are relevant to understanding more than the approximately 1 percent of the Middle Eastern population who are pastoral nomads or transhumants, the ratio of anthropologists, articles, and books to population remains staggering.[28] If in defense anthropologists want to argue that segmentary opposition is a widespread principle of Arab social life, they will have to show its relevance in nontribal contexts. Such studies have not been done.

That anthropologists are beginning to sense this excess seems apparent from the justificatory statements which now regularly preface discussions of segmentation. For example, Meeker (1979:14) writes:

There are now many Near Eastern anthropologists who believe that the entire question of political segmentation and tribal genealogies should be set aside as an exhausted area of research. So long as segmentary theory is conceived as a problem of describing political alliances, they are no doubt correct. Yet the segmentary theorists in general, and Evans-Pritchard in particular, have touched upon a distinctive feature of Near Eastern tribal societies.

Dresch (1986:309) reiterates, "Segmentary lineage theory . . . has had its day in studies of Middle Eastern tribalism. Nothing satisfactory has replaced it. In the present paper I wish to suggest that although lineage theory is best discarded, the simpler idea of segmentation which underlay it is less easily dispensed with and remains useful." These statements could be read as symptomatic of the increasingly defensive tenacity with which Middle East anthropologists are clinging to this theoretical metonym.

Certainly no one—not even the interpretivists—would deny that tribalism or segmentation has some relevance for understanding some Middle Eastern societies. But I think we need to stand back from the internal debates about segmentation to ask why it has dominated anthropological discourse on the Middle East. Some of the volume of this work can be dismissed as an artifact of the previously noted anthropological proclivity for working in "simple" societies in remote places. In the Arab world, Yemen and Morocco are such places, and tribal groups, especially pastoral nomads constitute such "simple" societies. Some of it can be attributed to the stress in social anthropology on social and political organization and the concern with formal systems of classification.[29] Yet other Middle Eastern problems, notably patrilateral parallel cousin marriage, which were both appropriate to social anthropological theorizing and arenas of tremendous concern in the 1950s and 1960s, have practically faded from attention in the last decade.[30] The concern with segmentation has been central to political anthropology since the 1940s, and there is little doubt that political anthropological paradigms can be related in a variety of ways to both concerns of colonial administration and liberal paradigms in social science. Segmentation may seem to be the only issue in the anthropology of the Arab world that relates to a classical anthropological debate actually transcending the region, as Dresch (1988) masterfully points out. But any answer to the question of why segmentary theory is a prestige zone in the anthropology of the Arab world in the 1970s and 1980s, I want to suggest, also depends on considering the themes or referents of segmentary theory: men, politics, and violence.

I have argued elsewhere (1986:30;1988) that the primacy of the theme of segmentary lineages in the literature on Arab tribal societies is due in part to the association of men with politics in modern Western societies. Without denying the existence of segmentary concerns in Middle Eastern societies, I posited that "a felicitous correspondence between the views of Arab tribesmen and those of European men has led each to reinforce particular interests of the other and to slight other aspects of experience and concern" (1986:30).

One important clue to the fact that this is a masculine discourse is the way a variety of thinkers link the concept of honor to segmentary politics. The literature on honor is substantial, for both the Middle East and the northern shore of the Mediterranean; it could easily have formed a separate section of this review.[31] But it can be subsumed, at least for the anthropology of the Arab world, under the heading of segmentation because, from the early discussion by Abou-Zeid (1966) on to the more recent ones—including those of Caton (1984, 1985), Dresch (1986), Marcus (1987), Meeker (1976,1979), Bourdieu (1977,1979), and Jamous (1981)—one thing remains constant: the interpretation of honor as an attribute or ideal exclusively of men. Either women are not considered at all, or they are viewed as that which men must protect or defend to maintain their own honor.

I have questioned this association of men with honor and explored, for the Awlad 'Ali Bedouins, the ways in which honor is the moral ideal of both men and women.[32] I have argued that modesty, usually interpreted negatively as shame, is rather the form that honor takes for the weak or socially dependent. In making this argument about the dialectical relationship between honor and modesty in the Bedouin moral system, I show that both men and women are included within a single social system and that any social analysis therefore must be able to account for both men and women and for their relationships. One implication of my analysis is that conventional definitions of politics, as the system of relations among men about external affairs, are too narrow. The politics of personal life and the system of domination in the "domestic" domain of the family and lineage intersect with the segmentary politics of tribal life; they are part of politics.

To notice that segmentation theory is also a discourse on masculinity, all we need to do is consider the way that, for many theorists, honor and segmentation are also tied to violence. Violence is implicit in works that posit social order as the central problematic. It is explicitly discussed in all works that take up the subjects of raids, feuds, and disputes. It could even be argued that a concern with politics is always to some degree a concern with potential or actual conflict and hence violence.

The first point to be made about this is that there is scattered evidence that the emphasis on politics (narrowly defined) or the threat of violence may be less pronounced in the societies than in the relevant studies of them. Gilsenan (1976) shows in his article on "lying" how Lebanese villagers circumvent in their social action the seemingly rigid rules of violence associated with a concern about honor. My own work (1985b) in a tribal community uncovers the coexistence of a highly valued discourse of vulnerability and attachment counterposed to the official discourse of honor. Eickelman's (1976) emphasis on "closeness" as a fundamental concept of relatedness among Moroccan tribesmen suggests affiliative rather than agonistic concerns.

More interesting to reflect on is what meaning this violence thought to lie at the heart of segmentary societies has for anthropologists. Violence seems to have two sides and anthropologists a corresponding ambivalence toward it.

On the one hand, in many cultures, including several Western ones, agonistic encounters are signs of virile masculinity.[33] A certain admiration tinges descriptions of the fierce independence attributed to those in segmentary societies, including Middle Eastern tribesmen. These are real men, free from the emasculating authority of the state and polite society. Furthermore, for many writers, these tribesmen represent romantic political ideals of freedom from authority and loyalty to democracy. But as Rosaldo (1986:96–7) has argued in an intriguing rumination on the rhetoric of Evans-Pritchard's celebrated study of the Nuer (1940), the anthropologist's grudging admiration of the Nuer's indominability coincides with his own anthropological project of interrogating and observing within the context of the British colonial political project in the Sudan. Rosaldo suggests that a fascination with the freedom of pastoral nomads is in part a rhetorical assertion of anthropologists' freedom from the projects of domination in which they participate, directly or indirectly.

On the other hand, violence must be condemned as dangerous by anyone who does not believe that individuals or local groups have the right to bear arms or engage in self-help politics. That includes just about everyone living in modern nation-states as well as many others. The barbarism of those who live without government is considered apparent from the raiding and feuding thought to be central activities in their societies. The nightmare is that there might be never-ending violence and counterviolence. In a telling abuse of this type of theory, tribalism and Middle East "terrorism" have on occasion been explicitly linked, a step which suggests that the insistence on the essential segmentariness of Arab societies may facilitate their representation as especially divisive and violent.[34]

In comparing the Orientalists' descriptions of Middle Eastern despotic rule and the functional anthropologists' descriptions of African tribal rule, Asad (1973b) has shown that images of the politics of other societies are linked in complex ways to political relations between the societies being studied and those doing the studying. He has also shown the importance of considering the political interests of the observers' societies at particular historical moments. A full analysis of the discourse on segmentation would have to place it historically in the context of a changing world political situation. This effort, beyond the scope of this paper, would have to include some consideration of the timing of interest in Middle East segmentation long after its eclipse in African studies. Although these reflections on masculinity and violence do not constitute a full answer to the question of why segmentary theory is such a prominent part of the anthropological discourse on the Middle East, I hope at least to have suggested how theorizing about one Middle Eastern subject is caught up in and shaped by the extraordinarily complex confluence of academic, political, and imaginative streams.

Harem Theory

In the past decade or so, theorizing about women, gender, and sexuality has begun to challenge in both quantity and significance, though not in prestige, that on segmentation. Yet in this zone of theorizing the ironic way that scholarship occasionally corresponds to its object is manifest. If Arab society is popularly known for its sharp sexual division of labor and its high degree of sexual segregation related to an extreme distinction between public and private, a look at the anthropological literature suggests that such patterns are not confined to the society being studied. Nearly all the segmentation theorists are men, while nearly all those who theorize about women are women. The former work mostly among pastoralists or in semiagricultural tribal societies; most of the latter work in agricultural villages, in towns, and in cities. The former have long genealogies, the latter short ones. In the former the theoretical distinctions are fine, in the latter theoretical debate is muted. And if the segmentation theorists are concerned exclusively with politics, narrowly defined to refer only to the public world of men, the scholars working on women begin with (but, as I will argue, successfully move out of) the study of the women's sphere, the harem. I use the word provocatively, both to denote the women's world and women's activities and to connote an older, Orientalist, imaginative world of Middle Eastern women which, I will argue, shapes anthropological discourse by providing a negative foil.

Like theorizing about segmentation, theorizing about women follows disciplinary trends, as Nelson (n.d.) describes in her excellent current review of "women in Middle Eastern studies." She situates anthropological scholarship about Arab women within the larger historical context of major changes in the relationship between Europe and the Third World, the Middle East in particular, as linked to changes in the paradigms of social science. The first two phases she outlines take us from work done up to the 1950s, in which one saw an "awakening" of interest in women, to that done up to the late 1960s, in what she calls "the period of the empirical gaze." During this second period women were increasingly brought into public view through scholarship on Middle Eastern women that stayed well within the positivistic paradigm of structural functionalism. The literature centered on issues of the changing status, position, and role of women.

The next two periods are roughly those covered in the present essay. Divided by Nelson into the period in the early seventies of the "critical response" and that in the mid-eighties of an emergent "indigenous response," they are in my view more of a piece. Nelson writes of the relationship between theorizing and the historical situation at this juncture:

> The old paradigms did not provide any resonance for the new structure of sentiments that was emerging—neither in the west where, among other challenges, the feminist re-awakening was forcing a reexamination of ideas about gender, female sexuality and women's appropriate social roles; nor in the Middle East where the 1967 defeat was forcing Arab intellectuals to re-think the foundations of their own knowledge about themselves and their society and its relation to the western world (Nelson n.d.).

She sees the development during this period of a new anthropological discourse on women mostly by women, many of them from the region, critical of standard analytical categories and social scientific paradigms,[35] critical of Islamic Arab "patriarchy," and critical of previous scholarship on women.

Nelson argues quite persuasively that the three most productive spheres of rethinking and research were the definition and understanding of power, the analysis of patriarchy (defined as "institutionalized forms of male dominance and female subordination"), and women and production. Work in these areas continues to the present, but due in part to the politicization of the issue of women as "a new wind of cultural decolonization blows through the Middle East," a new period and type of theorizing Nelson labels "the indigenous quest" has begun to take form alongside it. The question of indigenizing research is one of "who participates in the construction of knowledge about women in the Middle East and who controls the process" (Nelson n.d.), a type of questioning related to the epistemological concerns explored by the reflexive anthropologists.

Although Nelson's outline of developments is compelling, I feel less sanguine about the field with regard to its contributions to anthropological theory. Before going on to detail what I see as harem theory's most significant contributions and to outline the theoretical and methodological potential of feminist anthropology, I must express some reservations. Like its Middle Eastern counterparts in some other zones of anthropological theorizing, the anthropology of Middle Eastern women is theoretically underdeveloped relative to anthropology as a whole.[36] More disturbing is its theoretical underdevelopment relative to feminist anthropology, which itself, for reasons explored cogently by Marilyn Strathern (1985), has not kept pace with feminist theory or scholarship in other disciplines.

In reflecting on why this might be so, I considered the wider world into which books enter. Why (if my impression is correct) do we seem to have a larger than usual number of monographs only minimally concerned with contributing to or engaging with anthropological theory?[37] This phenomenon must be attributed in part to the apparently large and insatiable market for books on Middle Eastern women.[38] The market has changed over the past two decades, reflecting changes in the academy. Women's studies has now come into its own as one of the most intellectually exciting areas of scholarship and a growth field in the book industry. Yet there is still a sense, with regard to women in the Middle East, that what people want is a glimpse into a hidden life, "behind the veil." Books that offer this unwittingly partake in a colonial discourse on Oriental women, a discourse whose elements are incisively analyzed in Malek Alloula's (1986) *The Colonial Harem.*

The irony is that nearly every anthropological study of Arab women is intended, with varying degrees of self-consciousness, to undermine stereotypes of the Middle Eastern woman. This oppositional stance is, I think, a source both of the strengths of the field (to be discussed below) and the weakness of its theoretical development. How many books and articles begin with the same trope which opened my early article (1985) on Bedouin women: the grossly misleading conceptions of the harem and the idle or submissive veiled Arab women. This rhetorical ploy of conjuring up an imagined or intended audience of those who hold such views which are then going to be corrected risks degenerating into the sole raison d'être for the study. The danger is that the scholar will take the less theoretically rigorous path of arguing against a vague but unchanging stereotype. This is no way to sharpen one's thoughts, nor is it a way to develop theoretical sophistication. That requires debating one another and building on one another's work, a process that need not be adversarial.

This battle against shadow stereotypes has contributed as well to a certain parochialism vis-à-vis feminist anthropology. Here our failure to engage with theory is especially disappointing because, unlike many other zones of theorizing that seem to be tied to place, the comparative potential of theorizing about gender is great. Within feminist anthropology there has been a disaffection with the earlier attempts to universalize and to find analytical frameworks (like M. Z. Rosaldo's (1974) public/domestic distinction or Ortner's male:female::culture:nature (1974) or even the Marxian production/reproduction) that could encompass gender relations and women's experience in all societies. The recognition of the irreducibility of historical and cultural specificities has been the starting point of more recent work.[39] The best approach would probably respect and work with the specificities while being informed by research and theorizing about women in other ethnographic areas.

Despite its shortcomings (and I have been especially critical because I care so much about this enterprise of which I am a part), work on Arab women, motivated as it has been by this oppositional stance, has been impressive. There is a good deal of fine work and theoretical development in at least five areas. First, by taking seriously women and their activities, these anthropologists have indeed transformed our understanding of the harem, or women's world. From the work of most anthropologists in the field—but especially Altorki (1986), S. Davis (1983), Dorsky (1986), C. Eickelman (1984), Makhlouf (1979), and Wikan (1982)—the rich and varied character of women's relationships to each other, to their children, and to the men with whom they interact is unmistakable. Also apparent from these ethnographic studies based on fieldwork primarily within the world of women is the varied nature of women's activities. These range from the predictable ones of socializing children and caring for them and for men within the home to activities that take them outside the home, like visiting and politicking about marriages and the fates of relatives, participating in religious activities, and engaging in a range of productive activities. The importance of community and the sense in which women form part of a network, whether of kin, affines, or neighbors, has been brought out.

A second significant, and related, contribution has been the insistence of these anthropologists—as well as others including Abu-Lughod (1985), D. Dwyer (1978), and Nelson (1974)—that women are actors in their social worlds. This debunking of the myth of their passive subordination is repeated in nearly every account that presents evidence of the ways women strategize, manipulate, gain influence, and resist. Many have also shown how sexual segregation creates a space of greater independence of action in everyday life than women have in less sex-segregated societies.

The third crucial area has been the deconstruction of the harem itself. Proceeding from a focus on the women's world, most ethnographers have been led to recognize the dialectical relationship between the men's and women's worlds and the impossibility of talking about women's lives without talking about men's. The theoretical implications of this are serious, for if women are not really part of a separate sphere, then how can analyses of the men's domains of politics and economics and religion proceed without reference to women?

This development in thinking about the harem and its inhabitants, like the two earlier ones, was facilitated by and contributed to theoretical suspicions about the categories by which society had previously been analyzed. Nelson's (1974) ground-breaking "Public and Private Politics" showed how conventional Western cultural notions of power which previously informed our understandings of politics blinded us to the ways women participate in decision-making and the workings of society. Altorki (1986) argued that in societies organized by kinship, marriage arrangement is a political matter, and one in which women have a crucial role. The play of the formal and informal, the public and private, and the official and unofficial were brought to light (S. Davis 1983:169). The most important contribution of this theorizing has been the way it has revealed that analytical categories often conceal Western cultural notions.

The best theorizing has been about ideology, specifically about the relationship between meaning and power.[40] In her review, Nelson takes most of this work to be a contribution to the analysis of "patriarchy," but what I find interesting about it is the way it problematizes the notion of patriarchy by asking a set of interconnected questions which the extreme situation of Middle Eastern women starkly forces: How do women experience and maintain sexual segregation? How and why do they seem to cooperate in this system that is patently unequal (even if the work discussed above has shown that it is not as bad as it looks from the outside)? How do they contribute to reproducing the system, and how do they resist or subvert it?

Such questions have produced a body of rich and complex descriptions of ideology about male-female relations in the Arab world.[41] This work makes use of a range of interpretive devices and takes as its object an imaginative array of discourses and practices including ordinary talk and action, folktales (D. Dwyer 1978), poetry (Abu-Lughod 1986), the order of houses (Bourdieu 1979a), sacred, erotic, and legal texts (Sabbah 1984), symbolic elaborations of rituals such as clitoridectomy (Boddy 1980), the zar (Nelson 1971; Boddy 1988), folk illness (Morsey 1978), visits to saints' tombs (Mernissi 1983) or other rituals of spirit possession (Crapanzano 1977a; Maher 1984), and most recently, even everyday practices such as weaving (Messick 1987) and the milling of grain (Pandolfo 1989).

Even those cultural studies that do not specifically look at male/female relations in terms of power suggest that women dissent in various ways from the official or male collective representation of social reality and human nature. For example, Rosen (1978) argues that men and women in Sefrou begin with different assumptions about themselves and each other, and Wikan (1982) argues that Sohari women judge each other in different terms than men judge them, bringing into question the concept of honor. El-Messiri (1978) shows how traditional urban women in Cairo have self-images not in accord with images of them held by those in other classes.

Arguments like Messick's (1987) about the "subordinate discourse" of North African women's weaving bring out the importance of looking at power, however. Although he posits that weaving in precolonial North Africa embodied a vision of the role of women and their relations to men alternative to that presented in the legal and sacred texts and the official ideology corresponding to it, he recognizes the subordinate and fragile character of this alternative ideology. The subordination of the weaving discourse is related to the social and political subordination of the group that practices it: lower-class nonliterate women. He goes on, in a historical move rare in Middle East anthropology, to show how the discourse dissolved with the progressive incorporation of domestic weaving into capitalist production.

Practices like veiling and seclusion and the moral ideology in which they participate, specifically the discourse on sexual modesty, have provided the most fruitful area for theorizing about the relationship between ideology and power relations. Varying weights are given to Islam as an ideological system providing concepts that influence women's experience of subordination, an issue brilliantly considered by Kandiyoti (1987). In these studies, unlike the more general ones cited above, the variety of arguments does not just reflect the different situations of women within the Arab world, whether distinguished by class, mode of livelihood, or location in town or country, but relates to important theoretical differences.

D. Dwyer's work addresses debates within feminist anthropology about the universality of sexual systems of inequality and argues strongly for "the role of belief in sexual politics" (1978:179). She analyzes Moroccan sexual ideology, in the images of male and female conveyed primarily in folktales, to show how it differs from Western ideologies, particularly in its developmental thrust (men and women change over their lifetimes in opposite directions), and what implications this has for women's support of a system of sexual inequality. Maher (1984) uses the Marxian and Freudian language of repression, catharsis, and false consciousness to account for the surprising (to her, given the tension in marital relationships) absence of antagonism toward men in three women's rituals she witnessed in Morocco.

I have questioned the value of the latter sorts of arguments in trying to make sense of the apparently contradictory discourses Bedouin women participate in: the discourses of modesty and of love poetry. In analyzing the relationship of these discourses I was led to explore the interpenetration of power and ideology. I argued for the existence of multiple ideologies which structure subjective experiences and which individuals use to assert a variety of claims. I also argued for a theory of ideology and power that respects, in this case, the way Awlad 'Ali women can simultaneously reproduce the structures of domination through their commitment to morality and resist them through, among other things, their poetry (Abu-Lughod 1986, 1987, 1990).

The fifth and final area in which harem theorists have made a contribution has been, as Nelson (1988) suggested, methodological. The epistemological and political issues raised by the reflexive theorists discussed above are very much alive in this zone of theorizing.[42] Instead of the tortured discussions of the impossibility of knowing the Other, however, there has been an attempt to listen to the voices of the Other. The existence of collections that have sought out Arab women's voices or attempted to let individual women tell their stories is significant (Atiya 1982, Fernea and Bezirgan 1977, Fernea 1985).

More intriguing perhaps is how, despite problems, more than in any other branch of feminist anthropology, there has been respect for and concern with the messages of both "indigenous" and foreign voices. The number of Arab or Arab-American women scholars who write on the topic is high (e.g., Abu-Lughod, Abu-Zahra, Altorki, Chatty, Joseph, Rassam, Mernissi, el-Messiri, Mohsen, Morsey). There is beginning to be a reflexive reflection on the meaning of this "indigenization" of scholarship (cf. Altorki and El-Solh 1988). Anthropologists are increasingly involved in a three-way conversation which includes themselves, the ordinary women they study (generally nonfeminist and not formally educated), and Arab feminists and scholars (most influential in the West are El Sa'dawi and Mernissi). Although I occasionally look enviously at the Melanesianists, who seem to have such an extraordinary development of gender theory, I then wonder how this is related to the muted anticolonial discourse in the region, the absence of natives' voices interrupting, questioning, challenging, and subverting the anthropological enterprise so dependent on the us/them distinction.[43] What is lost there that remains highly visible in harem theory is the issue of the political implications of knowledge and theorizing.

Yet despite these considerable contributions to theory, it strikes me that here is a case in which academic scholarship (Middle East anthropology) seems to reproduce a structure of knowledge I have described for the Awlad 'Ali: the asymmetry of men's and women's knowledge about each other's worlds (Abu-Lughod 1985). Women know more about the men's world and its activities than the reverse. Although I have seen in this asymmetry a source of community (based on secrets) for women, it must be recalled that it is ultimately a function of unequal power. Men can get by with less knowledge about the doings of women; women need to know what goes on in the men's world, not only because it is culturally privileged but because it affects their lives. And yet the ideology maintains that women are in a separate sphere, secluded from male activity.

Women in the societies we study deny this vision. Numerous studies show how women have a different understanding of themselves and their roles than the official male vision. Feminist scholars also deny this vision, seeing their work not as an appendage to "mainstream" work but as radically undermining its basic assumptions and findings in disciplines from literary criticism to biology. Feminist theorizing about the social world, inside or outside of the Middle East, has shown how analysis that takes account of gender fundamentally alters the understanding of the social world being described and the way social worlds must be understood. Yet in Middle Eastern anthropology, even more than anthropology in general, the study of men (represented most clearly in the study of segmentation) is still the unmarked set and the anthropology of women (harem theory) the marked set, the addition.

Islam

Islam is the third "theoretical metonym" for the Arab world. My discussion of this zone of theorizing will be far briefer than of *homo segmentarius* or the harem—not because it is smaller or less important: quite the contrary. The Islam industry (mostly outside rather than inside anthropology), for obvious political reasons, has been producing texts at an ever-increasing pace. Rather, the issues are too complex to treat adequately in such a short review. Furthermore, many of the issues I would want to raise have been eloquently discussed by Talal Asad in his 1986 review of the subject, *The Idea of an Anthropology of Islam*.[44] In this section, therefore, I will only summarize some of Asad's points, quibble with a few, and discuss a few new and important works that he did not include to show why anthropological theorizing about Islam strikes me both as more promising than other sorts of theorizing about Islam and as potentially contributive to the general development of anthropological theory. It must be remembered, finally, that, however sophisticated, the anthropology of Islam cannot be made to stand for the anthropology of the Arab world. Not just because not all Arabs are Muslims, nor all Muslims Arabs, but because not all practices and discourses in Arab societies refer or relate to an Islamic tradition.

Asad begins his essay by asking what various theorists have taken to be the object of investigation in the anthropology of Islam. Three answers have been given to this question: "(1) that in the final analysis there is no such theoretical object as Islam; (2) that Islam is the anthropologist's label for a heterogeneous collection of items, each of which has been designated Islamic by informants; (3) that Islam is a distinctive historical totality which organizes various aspects of social life" (1986:1). Dismissing the first two in a couple of paragraphs, he goes on to explore perceptively and in devastating detail an example of the third type, Gellner's *Muslim Society* (1981). Asad wants from this exercise in close reading and thinking "to extract theoretical problems that must be examined by anyone who wishes to write an anthropology of Islam" (1986:3).

His main argument against Gellner and others is that there is no such thing as an essential Islamic social structure. He builds his argument out of a number of pieces, beginning with the point that to equate Islam with the Middle East and to define Muslim history as a mirror image of Christian history is problematic. Then he critiques approaches that seek to account for diversity by adapting the Orientalists' polarities of ortho-dox/nonorthodox or Great/Little Traditions in the form of a dualism of puritanical town faith versus saint-worshipping countryside faith, the latter two correlated with two types of social structure, one urban and centralized, the other rural and segmentary.

Asad points out that Gellner elaborated these notions with the help of segmentary lineage theory (as described above) and then argued that they covered most of the Middle East and nearly all of Muslim history. He then criticizes the forms Gellner uses to represent the social and political structures of classic Muslim society: dramatic narratives that mistake tribes for social actors. He finally shows the inadequacy of the ways these theorists analyze both society and religion (Asad 1986:2–14). As an alternative he argues that the object of study must be recognized to be a "discursive tradition," and he goes on to outline what he means by this.

My quibbles with Asad are not about his basic points but about the way he slights some recent work, most particularly Gilsenan's, which he sees as exemplifying the second approach to the anthropology of Islam. To fault Gilsenan (1982) for failing to come to terms with the fact that communities of Muslims believe that other Muslims' beliefs or practices are not Islamic may be fair. But to reduce his position to a relativistic acceptance of the idea that Islam is whatever Muslim informants say it is does not do justice to Gilsenan's considerable contribution to anthropological theorizing about Islam. Not only is this fundamental respect for the ordinary people through whom he comes to recognize Islam impor-tant in itself, but Gilsenan's linking of these "different and sometimes mutually exclusive apprehensions and practices of Islam" (1982:265) to social forces that range from colonialism to the emergence of new class divisions is a breakthrough for anthropology. Asad undervalues the creativity involved in the variety of domains to which Gilsenan turns in his search for Islam—the Lebanese salon, the colonial city, the passion play, the miracle of peanuts. Finally, he does not appreciate Gilsenan's sensitivity to issues of the reflexivity and method in ethnographic fieldwork and writing, embodied in the personal voice which weaves the thoughts and observations together in his text.

Others not cited in Asad's review are also contributing to this enterprise in interesting ways. Munson (1984) allows us to glimpse how the forces Gilsenan outlines have been and are being lived by a number of individuals in one extended family in Morocco. His "oral history of a Moroccan family" vividly brings to light the complex ways that Islam as a discursive tradition is interpreted and deployed in people's lives in a push and pull that involves political, rhetorical, and socioeconomic factors. Fischer (1980;1982) breaks with anthropological conventions by systematically looking across national boundaries to analyze the dynamic interactions between religious and political ideologies and their class bases in the Arab and non-Arab Muslim Middle East. El-Guindi's (1981) work on modest dress and the veil among the Egyptian women participating in the new Islamic movements blends exploration of ideology with sociopolitical and economic analysis to undercut any simple understandings of Islamic militancy as a "back" to Islam problem. Antoun (1989) considers the social organization of a tradition through the Friday sermons of a single Muslim preacher in Jordan.

Eickelman's (1985) social biography of a "traditional" Moroccan intellectual, "focusing upon the training, career, and moral imagination of a rural *qadi* [judge]" (1985:14) opens up to view a world of learning, a discursive tradition, rarely examined by anthropologists. Like the people they have commonly studied, anthropologists have tended to be nonliterate. This means they have neither access to archives and texts that might illuminate what they are seeing nor interest in the complex roles of texts in the communities they study. The advantages of such literacy and concern with literacy for an understanding of Islam are apparent in the work just cited and that of Messick (1986).

The theoretical approach that seems to be emerging, as these diverse elements are brought together in ways that resist classifying Islam as a monolithic system of beliefs or an all-determining structure, might well follow lines set by Bourdieu and Foucault. Notions like Bourdieu's "bodily hexis," which suggests ways individuals come to live as natural, through their very body movements, the basic principles of an "ideology" could be helpful if one thinks about the organization of space in Muslim societies or the meaning of prayer and pilgrimage. Notions like "practice," which examines the individual as not simply a cognitive being but an actor, whose improvisations in life are constrained by a set of already determined forces but whose actions create the patterned realities the analyst sees, might allow us to take into account traditions, texts, and socioeconomic formations in such a way as to be able to understand change and the current politics of Islam.

In a sense, this is a way of saying what Asad is saying, but in a Foucaultian language of discourse: "If one wants to write an anthropology of Islam one should begin, as Muslims do, from the concept of a discursive tradition that includes and relates itself to the founding texts of the Qur'an and the Hadith. Islam is neither a distinctive social structure nor a heterogeneous collection of beliefs, artifacts, customs, and morals. It is a tradition. . . . The most urgent theoretical need for an anthropology of Islam is a matter not so much of finding the right scale but of formulating the right concepts. 'A discursive tradition' is just such a concept" (1986:14).

Perhaps Asad's most significant point, though, and one that resonates with the issues I have been raising generally in this review, is found in his concluding remarks on the positioning of scholars of Islam in relation to the tradition which is their object. Recognizing that "to write about a tradition is to be in a certain narrative relation to it, a relation that will vary according to whether one supports or opposes the tradition, or regards it as morally neutral," he goes on to suggest that contests about how to represent the tradition "will be determined not only by the powers and knowledges each side deploys, but the collective life they aspire to— or to whose survival they are quite indifferent" (1986:17).[45]

Whatever shortcomings Asad has uncovered in the anthropology of Islam, the fact remains that the strengths of the anthropological study of Islam relative to other disciplinary approaches are, I would argue, considerable. Within anthropology, the tendency to explain societies in terms of a single totalizing concept is nearly always countered by attention to cross-cultural differences and to the relevance of a variety of domains, from political economy to gender relations. More importantly, this tendency is tempered by the fieldwork encounter, which can introduce anthropologists to a variety of ordinary individuals whose statements and actions are neither internally consistent nor consistent among individuals or social groups. They are certainly not consistent in any straightforward way with learned or scriptural statements. Since the anthropology of religion developed, like most anthropology, in the study of nonliterate societies, there remains a healthy bias toward looking for religion in what people say and do, whether in the rituals of everyday living or the symbolically elaborate communal activities usually defined as religious ritual.

If Asad's notion of Islam as a discursive tradition in addition suggests that more attention must be paid to the interplay between these everyday practices and discourses and the texts to which they are referred, the histories of which they are a part, and the political enterprises of which they partake, this is a theoretical enterprise that links Middle East anthropologists to those exploring similar problems with regard to other complex civilizations, including China and India. Even more importantly, this zone of theorizing links Middle East anthropologists to others concerned with developing methods and theories appropriate to analyzing the heterogenous and complex types of situations in which most of the world's people now live.

Conclusion

To conclude, I want to return to the Haj, my Bedouin host who introduced some of the themes I explored in this essay. I think that he, especially in his relationship to his senior wife Gatiifa (a pseudonym), can once again make vivid a problem in anthropology. This time it is the inadequacy of its three-zone character. In a sense, the following fragments of an account of this marriage between two people living in the Egyptian Western Desert highlights the inadequacy of all anthropological theories in the face of the rich complexities of individuals' lives.

On a hot day in June (1987), when there was an unexpected respite from the constant flow of guests coming through his household, the Haj and I sat together talking. He began telling me a story replete with poetry about a poor young man rebuffed by his paternal cousin whom he wished to wed. In the final scene, the young man returns to his camp having made his fortune elsewhere. His cousin, still unmarried, begs him to marry her. He agrees, but after a lavish wedding and a large bride price he refuses to touch her. On the wedding night he recites her a poem that answers the one she had recited when she rejected him and he tells her to pack her belongings on a camel and get lost. The next morning the man holds another wedding and marries someone else.

Just as he was finishing this story, the Haj's wife Gatiifa came in to tell us that lunch was almost ready. He ignored her to continue the story, his final admiring comment about the young man's response being, "He really burned her!" At this Gatiifa answered sharply, "He only felt the ways that she hurt him. He didn't feel what he did to her." The Haj fell silent at this surprisingly pointed remark and she left the room.

When I joined Gatiifa a bit later, I asked why she had said that. She repeated the comment and this time there was no doubt that she had, as the Haj and I had both sensed, meant that comment for him. She was accusing her husband of being insensitive to the pain he caused others (her) at the same time that she was indicating some general sympathy for the plight of women mistreated by men.

The personal reference, as far as I knew, was to something that had happened a couple of days earlier. We had all just driven back from their nephew's wedding. The Haj joked, in front of his two wives, that he had seen all these beautiful women at the wedding (when he had entered the women's tent to shake hands with his aunts and other relatives) and that he didn't understand why all these men who were nobodies should have more beautiful wives than he. Neither of his wives smiled (nor did I). Tears began to form in their eyes, but they said nothing. I protested and looked disapproving, not wanting him (or them) to think he had an ally.

In light of this, Gatiifa certainly seemed justified in her anger. But the twenty-five-year-old marriage was—like all marriages perhaps—much more complex. Later in my conversation with Gatiifa she had pointed out that what her husband seemed not to have grasped was that all these other women looked beautiful because they were at ease; their husbands didn't impose troubles and worry on them. But she was forced to deal with Azza, her co-wife.

Azza, who lived in the same household and had been there off and on for twelve years, was indeed a difficult person, very different in style, comportment, and values from Gatiifa and was made more troublesome by her unhappiness. She had a stormy relationship with her short-tempered and equally stubborn husband, adjustment troubles caused by differences between the more Egyptianized ways of her town-living relatives and conditions in her more rural and conservatively Bedouin marital household, and the disadvantages of being a junior and "outsider" (noncousin) wife now not favored by her husband.

A few days later, I joined Gatiifa and the Haj as they sat together in her room, where he usually went if he didn't have guests. He began teasing her about something that had happened the day before. I had found them sitting outdoors at sunset, side by side but not talking to each other. The Haj had joked that she was useless company because she refused to talk to him. With a twinkle he repeated this accusation, that she always held back. She has never forgiven me, he remarked, for taking other wives. She laughed and winked at me, retorting, well, who told you to do it?

This prompted him to recount to me the story of how it was that he had come to marry two wives (Gatiifa and the wife he took before Azza) within the space of a few months. He also went into much detail about the story I had heard from others, of how young Gatiifa had been—that she was still playing with dolls and had no idea what marriage was about (i.e., sex). For several years after marrying him she continued to sleep with her grandmother (also his) or another older woman in the camp who also did not have a man. He had respected this and treated her, as in some ways he still did, as a protected sister. She was the only child of one of his father's two brothers, who had been killed at an early age by an exploding mine left over from World War II.

The Haj on another occasion confided his regret that Gatiifa held back in all sorts of ways. He admitted that he had been difficult when young, and that he had not always been able to treat her as well as he should, but he thought that in some ways (I was dubious) his other marriages had been forced on him. He had also, on that same day I had joined them as they sat silently, remarked that Gatiifa was a gazelle (beautiful) as we looked at the photos of her in the *Natural History* article I had just published.

Gatiifa is aware of the ways he honors her. Her anger is mixed with a deep understanding and respect for what he goes through and what he cares about. She shares his values. And she depends on him to back her in conflicts with other women and men in the community.

They had both told me versions of the story of the fight she and her co-wife had had just before I arrived. Her co-wife Azza had insulted her by calling her an orphan with no family in the community. Gatiifa had hit her. Azza had gone off "angry," complaining to her mother-in-law. When the Haj came back, he took no notice of Azza's loud complaints about the "beating." He made her come home and apologize to Gatiifa and ask her forgiveness. There was some truth to the co-wife's insult. Gatiifa really was isolated in the women's community, despite being a member of the lineage. Her mother-in-law had always favored the other wives, perhaps because she did not like Gatiifa's mother. Most of the other women in the camp were sisters and stuck together. Some of the outsider wives also formed coalitions. Gatiifa somehow was left on her own, relying on her husband for more than most women. That was what made the remark so hurtful and the Haj's response so protective.

Two days before I left the field, Gatiifa gave birth to her ninth daughter, who they swore would be her last child given the difficulty of pregnancy at her age. A calamity by most Bedouin standards, this birth of yet another girl instead of a boy was taken in stride. Gatiifa, as ever, expressed nothing but gratitude to God for delivering her safely. I did not hear what the Haj had to say, but I know that he went in the next morning to see her, breaking the convention that stipulates a forty-day post-partum avoidance of wife by husband.

The following day, when Gatiifa had some women visitors from the community, he came in with his cassette player to share with her a tape he had just received from an old friend of theirs who had gone to Libya. The young women present all got up to leave, modesty making them too uncomfortable to be able to sit with (no less listen to a tape in the presence of) a man of his stature. An older cousin of theirs stayed and witnessed the Haj offering his wife a cigarette. She later commented to a number of women on how impressed (surprised/pleased) she was to see this. The familiarity and affection this gesture betrayed is hard for us to grasp, but one of the signs of deference for women and young men is not to smoke in front of elder or high-status men. Most women who smoke do so secretly.

Although I left the field the next day, I am sure that the Haj continued to spend time with Gatiifa in her confinement. His eldest daughter had commented to me on how impossible he was when Gatiifa was away for even a few hours, not to mention when she went away for days at a time to visit her mother or attend weddings or funerals. She said he just wandered around and didn't know what to do with himself. That was why he always brought Gatiifa back from these visits sooner than most other women were brought back, and sooner than he would pick up his other wives. And it seemed to me that he did not feel truly comfortable anywhere but in her company. The same could not be said about her, but perhaps in front of me she always felt some modesty about this relationship.

There is much more I could say about this marriage, but I think this is enough to demonstrate my point. It is obvious to me, and could be supported with evidence were there space, that as individuals who not only talk of tribes and politics in the ways segmentary theorists would predict, but are also especially deeply enmeshed in tribal politics and kin relations through their respective roles as a tribal mediator and important member of this lineage's women's community, the Haj and Gatiifa are quintessential Bedouins. Both are conservative upholders of Bedouin tribal ways and they are also paternal first cousins, the ideal match in this social order. This is material for segmentary theory. In their daily lives and their sexual morality they embody and defend the male/female patterns analyzed by the harem theorists. They are also both enthusiastically faithful Muslims who do not think there is any other way to be a good human being. And yet, to have said this about them is hardly to have begun to grasp who these extraordinary individuals are and what their marriage, even as indicated by these small fragments I have presented, is about.

My point about the three-zone character of anthropological theorizing in this region is not that it takes up issues that are not significant, perhaps crucial, for understanding life in Arab societies, just as it is not Appadurai's intention to deny the existence of caste in India or to suggest that caste is irrelevant to an understanding of Indian society. It is also not to denigrate the quality of the work done in these areas. As should be clear from my discussion, I think much of the work is very good. It is to suggest that it is inadequate for understanding the richly complex and often contradictory qualities of people's lives in the Arab world. The question that haunts is, why are such theoretical metonyms privileged—and, more important, what do they exclude?

Someone steeped in Middle East anthropology might ask, well, what else could one talk about? In answer one can turn first to what else has been done. Scattered individuals have asked different questions of the Arab world or looked into different matters. Some of the questions and subjects have come from an acquaintance with the literature of Orientalism, but not all. Examples of different issues taken up are markets (Geertz 1979; Larsen 1985), cultural pluralism (Barth 1983), narratives or the verbal arts in a society known for the richness of its play of language and its own appreciation of that richness (Abu-Lughod 1986; Caton 1984, 1985; Early 1985; Meeker 1979; Slyomovics 1987), concepts of the person or emotions (Abu-Lughod 1986; Bourdieu 1979b; Crapanzano 1977a; Rosen 1984), and agrarian life (Hopkins 1987; Seddon 1981).

The relative absence of theorizing within Middle East anthropology about such subjects is glaring in at least two cases. In a recent review article on the anthropological study of emotion, the references to literature on the Pacific were legion; those to that on the Middle East were few (Lutz and White 1986). More telling is the fact that in his recent book on agricultural transformation in rural Egypt, the only references Hopkins makes to theoretical works by anthropologists are to books and articles written by Africanists. There is little indication that farmers form a less substantial part of the population or are less important in the Arab world than in many African countries.[46] And anthropologists—who, after all, can do fieldwork in villages—are in a privileged position to comment on a set of questions that have recently begun to interest South and Southeast Asian scholars: the relationship between peasants and the state as lived on the local level, and especially the coexistence of resistance and cooperation. Are there household economies only in Africa? Is there peasant resistance only in Asia? And to return to the topic of emotions, if all it took for me to come to think about sentiment and to drive a wedge between honor and segmentary politics was an appreciation for the personal poetry of everyday life rather than the male heroic poetry usually studied, then beginning to break out of the three zones would seem not so difficult.

There are at least two good sources for new kinds of questions to bring to the anthropology of the Arab world. One is anthropological theorizing and ethnography from other parts of the world. This would require that Middle East anthropologists be less parochial in their reading. Harem theory has, I think, benefited from its relationship to feminist anthropology. An even better source, although one that is far more difficult to tap (as all of our self-critical reflections on scholarship, and even the most rudimentary formulations of the problems of "objectivity" have suggested), is to be found in the Arab world. I maintain faith in the possibility that questions can come from the statements and lives of those with whom we work. Here I would include both intellectuals from the region and the kinds of ordinary individuals with whom we spend most of our time in the field, few of whom have much interest in metropolitan anthropological theory. Some courage will be required in this listening, since we will have to go to the cores as well as the peripheries of the Arab world and we will have to face some painful but pressing issues that people live with: state violence and repression, military occupation, poverty, migration, and cultural imperialism, to name just a few. We will also have to break with the anthropological predisposition to ignore the history of interactions between this part of the world and others (Wolf 1982).

The only way to open up anthropological discourse on the Arab world is to combine a self-critical stance with a willingness to let others tell us things we did not already know. The value of works such as Said's (1978) analysis of scholarship on "the Orient" and Alloula's (1986) analysis of colonial postcards from Algeria is in the way they turn back the gaze to which Arabs have been subjected by revealing the patterns and politics of the cultural productions of the West. Anthropologists can do something similar. In addition to analyzing, as I have just done, their scholarly productions, they can turn back the gaze on themselves and the society that produced them by letting the worlds they come to know bring their assumptions and analytical categories, not to mention their whole enterprise, into question.[47] Rabinow (1986) calls this the project of "anthropologizing the West," something Mitchell (1988) has done in a systematic way through a study of Egypt, but others have also done in various ways. Such an anthropologizing would include among other things recognizing the ways in which the Western Self and sense of identity is formed through an opposition to the non-Western Other as well as exploring further the ways that theorizing and its categories may be culture-bound, historically specific and politically charged.

All of these efforts depend, above all, on a different relationship than the semihostile distance of the Self studying Other that has characterized much of Middle East studies. Without having illusions about the power of texts to change the world,[48] one can advocate a self-critical reflection on the fieldwork encounter, the process of writing ethnography, and theorizing and a sharply self-critical analysis of the relations between the societies that study and those that are studied. That effort has gone farther in anthropology than in other disciplines, which is why, despite reservations, I do anthropology.

To understand this ambivalence and its value, I want to invoke in a different context Asad's remarks about the situated character of narratives of Islamic tradition. My narrative has been about the tradition of Middle East anthropology. I doubt that anyone else would have narrated it just as I have, and I am sure that this narrative is not precisely the one I would have told a few years ago. I am also certain I would not tell the same tale in a few years. In ways obvious to those who know me and my work, it is a reading and writing from a particular place, from an individual who is personally, intellectually, politically, and historically situated. I hope that I have made clear through this essay that it could not be otherwise. One can be aware of it, or deny it. But what Asad said regarding writers' relationships to the tradition about which they are writing applies equally to me, in both my relationship to the Arab world and my relationship to anthropology. I write from within and without both communities, and I have an interest in the survival of both.[49]

Notes

This paper was written while I was a member of the Institute for Advanced Study in Princeton, to which I am very grateful for support. Many people kindly took the time to read carefully and comment incisively on earlier drafts, reacting with varying degrees of enthusiasm or dismay. Arjun Appadurai, Talal Asad, Michael M. J. Fischer, Robert Fernea, Clifford Geertz, Michael Gilsenan, Nicholas Hopkins, Linda Layne, Brinkley Messick, Timothy Mitchell, Lucie Wood Saunders, and the participants in the Faculty Study Group at the Center for Contemporary Arab Studies at Georgetown University (where it was first presented) all helped improve the paper; none should be held responsible for its remaining flaws.

1. Although, as Brynen (1986:415) notes wryly in his comparative study of Middle Eastern, Latin American, and African studies, "the Orientalist/post-Orientalist conflict—while real enough in the *New York Review of Books*—appears remarkably absent from the journal literature [in Middle East studies], which devotes scant attention to this or any other epistemological debate." This is less true in anthropology, although it is my impression that Said's project is taken up less (and with more hostility) by anthropologists working in the Middle East than those working elsewhere in the world.

2. For fuller references and far more careful considerations of the anthropological literature on the Middle East, see Dale Eickelman's textbook/essay (1981). Other important review articles are cited throughout the paper.

3. For a thoughtful and much more thorough discussion of *Orientalism*'s relevance to anthropology and *its* problematics, see Clifford (1980).

4. For further elaboration of this citationary quality, see Mitchell (1988).

5. See Clifford (1983a), Marcus and Cushman (1982), and Marcus and Fischer (1986) for discussions of the conventions of authority in ethnographies.

6. Some of the obvious issues are: Who is writing about whom, whose terms define the discourse, and even, as Asad (1986) argues, who translates whose concepts and whose language bends to the other. The ways anthropology's colonial and bourgeois origins

affect the writing of ethnographies has begun to be taken up by a number of anthropologists other than Asad.

7. Said argues there are some.

8. For a critical review of the issues involved in indigenizing anthropology in the Arab world, see Morsy *et al.* (n.d.). Some of the problems involved in this notion were raised poignantly in Duvignaud's (1970) work in Tunisia nearly twenty years ago. The encounter between Tunisian university students doing the research and villagers in Shebika was even more complex than that between total outsiders and the villagers. Yet many are exploring this possibility in the Middle East, some advocating (Fahim 1982) and some questioning (Altorki 1982; Altorki and El-Solh 1988). In pointing to the dangers of the enterprise, they fail to take sufficiently into account the special place of Arabs in American consciousness. A person who does not share the general antipathy toward them and is not perceived with corresponding ambivalence can have a different sort of fieldwork encounter. This is no guarantee of a new kind of ethnography, as Nelson (n.d.) points out, but—as those concerned with epistemological issues (to be discussed below) have shown us—it could be relevant. That even insider-outsiders—such as an Arab-American like myself, a Japanese-American like Dorinne Kondo working in Japan, a Tamil Sri Lankan working with Tamils in South India, or an American-schooled woman with an Indian father working in India—have a different sort of fieldwork process is clear from the accounts (Abu-Lughod 1988; Daniel 1984; Kondo 1986; Narayan 1989).

9. The discussion of these theorists' work that follows is extremely basic and truncated. Anyone unfamiliar with their work would do well to consult the texts.

10. This is most sharply developed in his essay, "Deep Play: Notes on the Balinese Cock-fight" (Geertz 1973a).

11. The phrase is to be found in Malinowski's introduction to *Argonauts of the Western Pacific*. The publication of Malinowski's diaries has cast a shadow on his statements, and the unfashionableness of the colonial word "native"—if not the attitudes that went with it—make the statement even more suspect.

12. Although see Asad (1983) for a critique of the idealism of his approach.

13. He has developed these ideas about anthropologists as writers in Geertz (1987).

14. Analyzing cultural practices as methods of maximizing "symbolic capital" allows Bourdieu "to abandon the dichotomy of the economic and the noneconomic," while insisting that "symbolic capital, a transformed and thereby *disguised* form of physical 'economic' capital, produces its proper effect inasmuch, and only inasmuch, as it conceals the fact that it originates in 'material' forms of capital which are also, in the last analysis, the source of its effects" (Bourdieu 1977:183).

15. See especially Foucault (1980) for a critique of the notion of ideology, Foucault (1972) for an early formulation of discourse, and Foucault (1978, 1980) on power and discourse.

16. For a thorough discussion of this trend, see Marcus and Fischer (1986) and for other thinking along these lines, see Clifford and Marcus (1986).

17. One of Dwyer's explicit goals is to embrace his own vulnerability (1982:285).

18. Dwyer (1982:15) reports that the Faqir says to him, "What do you want to make noise about now?"

19. Appadurai (1988) takes up related issues of comparison and of freezing in his discussion of the anthropological construction of "natives."

20. Crapanzano (1977a) does talk about some of the ways this disciplinary anthropological Self affects the process of writing ethnography.

21. Separate treatment is required for the sorts of political issues raised by the silences and subjects of Israeli or Israel-based anthropological work on Arabs. For a sense of what these are, see Asad (1975), Escribano (1987) and Morsy (1983).

22. That this set of preferences is general to anthropology is apparent from such things as the preponderance in Melanesian studies of New Guinea highland societies despite the greater population of the lowland coastal or island areas (Steven Feld, personal communication).

23. Had this review not been restricted to studies of the Arab Middle East, the themes might have been different. My sense is that anthropological work in Iran and Turkey is more agrarian- and urban-centered and deeply concerned with stratification, including "despotism."

24. Rabinow's (1986) reminder about the importance of academic politics in the production of texts is a crucial point.

25. In this section I use only the masculine since most of the works I am discussing speak only of men.

26. I discuss below, in the context of the related concept of honor, my own work on this issue.

27. For a comparison of Meeker and Caton on tribal poetry, see Abu-Lughod (1986:28–29).

28. The written work on the subject includes not just the mostly published works discussed above, but a rapidly growing number of unpublished dissertations and a host of published and unpublished papers. For example, Daniel Varisco takes up some of the same issues in his unpublished paper, "The Bedouin Mystique."

29. The fact that segmentation theory has been discussed by both Africanists and Melanesianists is evidence for this.

30. For discussion of this issue, see Eickelman (1981:129–31), Bourdieu (1977:30–71); McCabe (1983); Abu-Lughod (1986:56–58, 145–148); Jamous (1981).

31. Herzfeld (1980;1984) discusses this issue cogently. Also see Gilmore (1987) for the most recent collection of essays, including bibliographical material.

32. Adra (1985:280) also mentions that "it is important to emphasize that despite the male presentation of *qabyala* [tribalism], women are not considered any less tribal than men" and that "tribal women are expected to adhere to tribal standards of honor, generosity, and industry." She is practically alone in noting this.

33. With Rosen's portrayal of Moroccans as individualistic bargainers in the bazaar of social life, the overt violence disappears, but along with it the positive qualities associated with masculine warrior-nomads. If for segmentary lineage theorists Arab social systems were those of ordered anarchy, for Rosen they are "labyrinthian" worlds threatened by chaos and disorder.

34. In an Op-Ed piece in the July 7, 1985, *New York Times*, an Israeli academic named Clinton Bailey, denouncing the Syrian backing of the Lebanese "tribal barbarians" who hijacked the TWA plane, asserted that "much Middle Eastern terrorism . . . can be traced to the tribalism that still colors the politics of that region. Tribalism was the natural state of the desert-dwelling nomadic Arabs before they settled more permanently in the early years of Islam, and it has never disappeared. The nomadic Arab's fierce independence and ruthless concern for narrow interests are still apparent—and

have meant that Middle Eastern governments are rarely able to function as ultimate authorities." In a letter to the editor on July 17, anthropologist E. Traube brilliantly deconstructs Bailey's text and tropes to expose the way he uses antiquated anthropological concepts which are "self-authenticating devices that have operated historically to confirm the value of their conceptual opposites." She then deplores the racist implications of Bailey's use of language.

35. Although see Strathern (1985) for an intriguing argument against applying the Kuhnian notion of paradigms to social science.

36. Brynen (1986) uses this concept of theoretical underdevelopment in his comparative review of Middle Eastern, Latin American, and African studies.

37. It is possible that my impression is due to my own involvement in the field and the high standards I therefore set for it. It may also be due to my relatively complete knowledge of the field as compared with that of work in other ethnographic areas. One usually reads only the best of other fields; one reads everything in one's own. I still maintain that even if these distortions were factored in, my impression would still be correct. I suspect that the only other field in women's studies that may have some of the same problems, and for the same reasons, is the study of "Asian women."

38. My evidence for this, although anecdotal, is suggestive. Elizabeth Fernea describes how Doubleday's promotion department initially gave her first book, *Guests of the Sheik*, the jazzy subtitle "An Invitation to Visit a Harem" with the hope that the exotic harem would attract readers. When the book disappointed those looking for sex and violence and appealed to those teaching about women in the Middle East, it was reissued in paperback with a serious academic subtitle, "An Ethnography of an Iraqi Village" (Fernea 1987:2–3). Two decades later, my own publisher's marketing department requested that I put "women" in the title of my book—a request I refused, although I compromised by using "veiled." The director of the press which later enthusiastically agreed to issue a Middle East edition of the book initially expressed the reservation that "women" was not in the title.

39. The key reference for this trend among those in non-Marxist-feminist circles is M. Z. Rosaldo's (1980) often cited "recantation." For a sophisticated overview of feminist anthropology, see Yanagisako and Collier (1987).

40. This is the helpful way Messick (1987) puts it.

41. The grammatical ambiguity here is deliberate since I think the difficulties of separating Arab ideologies from foreign ideologies about Arab ideology are formidable.

42. Perhaps harem theory is more in touch than segmentation theory with recent currents in anthropological theorizing because its genealogy is not so long.

43. Strathern (1987) sees a tension between this fundamental cultural us/them divide which structures anthropological discourse and the fundamental divide in feminist discourse, between women and men.

44. This was presented originally at the Center for Contemporary Arab Studies at Georgetown University.

45. The positive effect of a sense of community on accounts of a tradition may be felt in the sensitive and loving portrait of an Arab community Udovitch and Valensi (1984) present in *The Last Arab Jews*.

46. Yet economic anthropology is only beginning to receive attention in anthropology of the Arab world. See Larsen (1985) and Hopkins (1978). It is testimony to the dearth of recent work on peasants that, as Mitchell (1990) shows, practically the only monograph on an Arab peasant group that is in print and popular for classroom use,

reviewed in major anthropological journals and carrying a foreword by a noted anthropologist, is a journalistic account (Critchfield 1978) that contains long passages lifted from Ayrout's (1938) prewar classic on the Egyptian peasant. It reproduces, therefore, the ahistoricism and colonial stereotypes of that period.

47. In a sense, as Marcus and Fischer (1986) point out, this has always been a part of anthropology's project.

48. I am sympathetic to suspicions voiced by Asad (1986b) regarding the textual experimentation advocated by a number of anthropologists whose essays appear in Clifford and Marcus (1986).

49. Fischer's (1986) interest in biculturalism and bifocality in writing led him to reflect on my work in such terms. He argues that my book represents an "honest love-critique that goes with (insecure) roots" (1987:435). Perhaps this review should be understood in similar terms.

Bibliography

Abou-Zeid, Ahmed. "Honour and Shame among the Bedouins of Egypt," in J. G. Peristiany, ed. *Honour and Shame.* Chicago: University of Chicago Press, 1966:243–59.

Abu-Lughod, Lila. "A Community of Secrets: The Separate World of Bedouin Women." *Signs: Journal of Women in Culture and Society* 10, no. 4 (1985a):637–57.

———. "Honor and the Sentiments of Loss in a Bedouin Society." *American Ethnologist* 12 (1985b):245–61.

———. *Veiled Sentiments: Honor and Poetry in a Bedouin Society.* Berkeley: University of California Press, 1986.

———. "Modest Women, Subversive Poems: The Politics of Love in an Egyptian Bedouin Society." *Bulletin of the British Society for Middle East Studies* 13, no. 2 (1987): 159–68.

———. "The Romance of Resistance: Tracing Power Through Bedouin Women." Unpublished ms., n.d.

Abu-Zahra, Nadia. "On the Modesty of Women in Arab Muslim Villages: A Reply." *American Anthropologist* 72 (1970):1079–87.

———. "Material Power, Honour, Friendship, and the Etiquette of Visiting." *Anthropological Quarterly* 47 (1974):120–38.

———. "Baraka, Material Power, Honour, and Women in Tunisia." *Revue d'Histoire Maghrebine* 10–11 (1978):5–24.

Adra, Najwa. "The Tribal Concept in the Central Highlands of the Yemen Arab Republic," in Nicholas Hopkins and Saad Eddin Ibrahim, eds. *Arab Society.* Cairo: The American University in Cairo Press, 1985. 275–85.

Alloula, Malek. *The Colonial Harem.* Minneapolis: University of Minnesota Press, 1986.

Altorki, Soraya. "The Anthropologist in the Field: A Case of 'Indigenous Anthropology' from Saudi Arabia," in Hussein Fahim, ed. *Indigenous Anthropology in Non-Western Countries.* Durham: Carolina Academic Press, 1982.

———. *Women in Saudi Arabia: Ideology and Behavior Among the Elite.* New York: Columbia University Press, 1986.

Altorki, Soraya, and Camillia F. El-Solh, eds. *Studying Your Own Society: Arab Women in the Field.* Syracuse: Syracuse University Press, 1988.

Antoun, Richard. *Muslim Preacher in the Modern World: A Jordanian Case Study in Comparative Perspective.* Princeton: Princeton University Press, 1988.

Appadurai, Arjun. "Is Homo Hierarchicus?" *American Ethnologist* 13, no. 3 (1986a):745–61.

————. "Theory in Anthropology: Center and Periphery." *Comparative Studies in Society and History* 28, no. 2 (1986b):356–61.

————. "Putting Hierarchy in its Place." *Cultural Anthropology* 3, no. 1 (1988):36–49.

Asad, Talal, ed. *Anthropology and the Colonial Encounter.* New York: Ithaca Press, 1973a.

————. "Two European Images of Non-European Rule," in Talal Asad, ed. *Anthropology and the Colonial Encounter.* New York: Ithaca Press, 1973b. 103–18.

————. "Anthropological Texts and Ideological Problems: An Analysis of Cohen on Arab Villages in Israel." *Review of Middle East Studies* 1 (1975):1–40.

————. "Anthropological Conceptions of Religion: Reflections on Geertz." *Man* (n.s.) 18 (1983):237–59.

————. "The Concept of Cultural Translation in British Social Anthropology." In James Clifford and George Marcus, eds. *Writing Culture: The Politics and Poetics of Ethnography.* Berkeley: University of California Press, 1986a. 141–64.

————. *The Idea of an Anthropology of Islam.* Occasional Papers Series, Center for Contemporary Arab Studies. Washington DC: Georgetown University Press, 1968b.

Atiya, Nayra. *Khul Khaal: Five Egyptian Women Tell Their Stories.* Syracuse: Syracuse University Press, 1982.

Ayrout, Henry. *The Egyptian Peasant.* Boston: Beacon Press, 1963 (1938).

Barth, Fredrik. *Sohar.* Baltimore: Johns Hopkins University Press, 1983.

Beck, Lois, and Nikki Keddie, eds. *Women in the Muslim World.* Cambridge: Harvard University Press, 1978.

Behnke, Roy. *The Herders of Cyrenaica.* Urbana: University of Illinois Press, 1980.

Boddy, Janice. "Womb as Oasis: The Symbolic Context of Pharaonic Circumcision in Rural Northern Sudan." *American Ethnologist* 9, no. 4 (1982):682–98.

————. "Spirits and Selves in Northern Sudan: The Cultural Therapeutics of Possession and Trance." *American Ethnologist* 15, no. 1 (1988):4–27.

Bourdieu, Pierre. *Outline of a Theory of Practice.* Cambridge: Cambridge University Press, 1977.

————. *Algeria 1960.* Cambridge: Cambridge University Press and Maison des Sciences de l'Homme, 1979.

————. "The Kabyle House," in *Algeria 1960,* 133–52. Cambridge: Cambridge University Press, 1979a.

————. "The Sense of Honour," in *Algeria 1960,* 95–132. Cambridge: Cambridge University Press, 1979b.

Brynen, Rex. "The State of the Art in Middle Eastern Studies: A Research Note on Inquiry and the American Empire." *Arab Studies Quarterly* 8, no. 4 (1986):404–19.

Caton, Steven. "Tribal Poetry as Political Rhetoric from *Khawlān Aṭ-Ṭiyāl, Yemen Arab Republic.*" Ph.D. dissertation, University of Chicago, 1984.

————. "The Poetic Construction of Self." *Anthropological Quarterly* 58, no. 4 (1985):141–51.

————. *"Salām Taḥiyah:* Greetings from the Highlands of Yemen." *American Ethnologist* 13, no. 2 (1986):290–308.

————. "Power, Persuasion, and Language: A Critique of the Segmentary Model in the Middle East." *International Journal of Middle East Studies* 19, no. 1 (1987):77–102.

————. *Peaks of Yemen I Summon.* Berkeley: University of California, 1990.

Chatty, Dawn. "Changing Sex Roles in a Bedouin Society in Syria and Lebanon," in Lois Beck and Nikki Keddie, eds. *Women in the Muslim World.* Cambridge: Harvard University Press, 1978. 399–415.

————. *From Camel to Truck.* New York: Vantage Press, 1986.

Clifford, James. "Review Essay of *Orientalism* by Edward Said." *History and Theory* 19 (1980):204–23. Reprinted in Clifford, *The Predicament of Culture.*

————. "On Ethnographic Authority." *Representations* 1, no. 2 (1983a):118–46. Reprinted in Clifford, *The Predicament of Culture.*

————. "Power and Dialogue in Ethnography," in George W. Stocking, Jr., ed. *Observers Observed: Essays on Ethnographic Fieldwork.* Madison: University of Wisconsin Press, 1983b. 121–56. Reprinted in Clifford, *The Predicament of Culture.*

————. *The Predicament of Culture: Twentieth Century Ethnography, Literature, and Art.* Cambridge: Harvard University Press, 1988.

Clifford, James, and George Marcus, eds. *Writing Culture: The Politics and Poetics of Ethnography.* Berkeley: University of California Press, 1986.

Cole, Donald P. *Nomads of the Nomads: The Al-Murrah Bedouin of the Empty Quarter.* Chicago: Aldine, 1975.

Combs-Schilling, M. Elaine. "The Segmentary Model versus Dyadic Ties: The False Dichotomy." *MERA Forum* 5, no. 3 (1981):15–18.

————. "Family and Friend in a Moroccan Boom Town: The Segmentary Debate Reconsidered." *American Ethnologist* 12, no. 4 (1985):659–75.

Crapanzano, Vincent. "Mohammed and Dawia: Possession in Morocco," in Vincent Crapanzano and Vivian Garrison, eds. *Case Studies in Spirit Possession.* New York: Wiley and Sons, 1977a.

————. "On the Writing of Ethnography." *Dialectical Anthropology* 2 (1977b):69–73.

————. *Tuhami: Portrait of a Moroccan.* Chicago: University of Chicago Press, 1980.

Critchfield, Richard. *Shahhat: An Egyptian.* Syracuse: Syracuse University Press, 1978.

Daniel, E. Valentine. *Fluid Signs.* Berkeley: University of California Press, 1984.

Davis, John. "Qaddafi's Theory and Practice of Non-Representational Government," in Nicholas Hopkins and Saad Eddin Ibrahim, eds. *Arab Society.* Cairo: American University in Cairo Press, 1985. 365–78.

————. *Libyan Politics: Tribe and Revolution.* Berkeley: University of California Press, 1988.

Davis, Susan. *Patience and Power: Women's Lives in a Moroccan Village.* Cambridge, MA: Schenkman, 1983.

Dorsky, Susan. *Women of 'Amran: A Middle Eastern Ethnographic Study.* Salt Lake City: University of Utah Press, 1986.

Dresch, Paul. "The Significance of the Course Events Take in Segmentary Systems." *American Ethnologist* 13, no. 2 (1986):309–24.

————. "Segmentation: Its Roots in Arabia and its Flowering Elsewhere." *Cultural Anthropology* 3, no. 1 (1988):50–67.

Dumont, Louis. *Homo Hierarchicus: An Essay on the Caste System.* Chicago: University of Chicago Press, 1970.

Duvignaud, Jean. *Change at Shebika.* New York: Pantheon Books, 1970.

Dwyer, Daisy H. *Images and Self-Images: Male and Female in Morocco.* New York: Columbia University Press, 1978.

Dwyer, Kevin. *Moroccan Dialogues.* Baltimore: Johns Hopkins University Press, 1982.

Early, Evelyn. "Catharsis and Creation in Informal Narratives of Baladi Women of Cairo." *Anthropological Quarterly* 58, no. 4 (1985):172–81.

Eickelman, Christine. *Women and Community in Oman.* New York: New York University Press, 1984.

Eickelman, Dale. *Moroccan Islam: Tradition and Society in a Pilgrimage Center.* Austin: University of Texas Press, 1976.

————. *The Middle East: An Anthropological Approach.* Englewood Cliffs, N.J.: Prentice-Hall, 1981 (2nd ed. 1989).

————. "Introduction: Self and Community in Middle Eastern Societies." In *Self and Society in the Middle East* edited by Jon Anderson and Dale Eickelman. *Anthropological Quarterly* 58, no. 4 (1985a):135–40.

————. *Knowledge and Power.* Princeton: Princeton University Press, 1985b.

El-Guindi, Fadwa. "Veiling *Infitah* with Muslim Ethic: Egypt's Contemporary Islamic Movement." *Social Problems* 28 (1981):465–83.

Escribano, Marisa. "The Endurance of the Olive Tree: Tradition and Identity in Two West Bank Palestinian Villages." Ph.D. dissertation, Harvard University, 1987.

Evans-Pritchard, E. E. *The Nuer.* Oxford: Clarendon Press, 1940.

————. *The Sanusi of Cyrenaica.* Oxford: Clarendon Press, 1949.

Fabian, Johannes. *Time and the Other: How Anthropology Makes Its Object.* New York: Columbia University Press, 1983.

Fahim, Hussein. *Indigenous Anthropology in Non-Western Countries.* Durham, NC: Carolina Academic Press, 1982.

Fernea, Elizabeth W., ed. *Women and Family in the Middle East: New Voices of Change.* Austin: University of Texas Press, 1985.

————. "Presidential Address, 1986." *Middle East Studies Association Bulletin* 21, no. 1 (1987):1–7.

Fernea, Elizabeth W., and Basima Bezirgan. *Middle Eastern Muslim Women Speak.* Austin: University of Texas Press, 1977.

Fernea, Robert, and James Malarkey. "Anthropology of the Middle East and North Africa: A Critical Assessment." *Annual Review of Anthropology* 4 (1975):183–206.

Fischer, Michael M. J. "Competing Ideologies and Social Structures in the Persian Gulf," in A. J. Cottrell, ed. *The Persian Gulf States.* Baltimore: Johns Hopkins University Press, 1980.

————. "Islam and the Revolt of the Petit Bourgeoisie." *Daedalus* (1982):101–25.

————. "Ethnicity and the Post-Modern Arts of Memory," in J. Clifford and G. Marcus, eds. *Writing Culture.* Berkeley: University of California Press, 1986. 194–233.

———. "Aestheticized Emotions and Critical Hermeneutics." *Culture, Medicine and Psychiatry* 11 (1987):425–36.

Foucault, Michel. *The Archaeology of Knowledge*. New York: Pantheon Books, 1972.

———. *The History of Sexuality, Volume 1: An Introduction*. New York: Random House, 1978.

———. *Power/Knowledge*. Edited by Colin Gordon. New York: Pantheon Books, 1980.

Geertz, Clifford. *The Interpretation of Cultures*. New York: Basic Books, 1973.

———. "Deep Play: Notes on the Balinese Cockfight," in *The Interpretation of Cultures*. New York: Basic Books, 1973a. 412–53.

———. "Religion as a Cultural System," in *The Interpretation of Cultures*. New York: Basic Books, 1973b. 87–125.

———. "Thick Description: Toward an Interpretive Theory of Culture," in *The Interpretation of Cultures*. New York: Basic Books, 1973c. 3–30.

———. *Works and Lives*. Stanford: Stanford University Press, 1987.

Geertz, Clifford, Hildred Geertz, and Lawrence Rosen. *Meaning and Order in Moroccan Society*. Cambridge: Cambridge University Press, 1979.

Geertz, Hildred. "The Meanings of Family Ties," in Clifford Geertz, Hildred Geertz, and Lawrence Rosen. *Meaning and Order in Moroccan Society*. Cambridge: Cambridge University Press, 1979. 315–91.

Gellner, Ernest. *Saints of the Atlas*. Chicago: University of Chicago Press, 1969.

———. *Muslim Society*. Cambridge: Cambridge University Press, 1981.

Gilmore, David, ed. *Honor and Shame and the Unity of the Mediterranean*. Washington DC: American Anthropological Association, 1987.

Gilsenan, Michael. "Lying, Honor, and Contradiction," in B. Kapferer, ed. *Transaction and Meaning*. Philadelphia: Institute for the Study of Human Issues, 1976. 191–219.

———. *Recognizing Islam: Religion and Society in the Modern Arab World*. New York: Pantheon Books, 1982.

Hammoudi, Abdellah. "Segmentarity, Social Stratification, Political Power and Sainthood: Reflections on Gellner's Theses." *Economy and Society* 9, no. 3 (1980):279–303.

Hart, David. *Dadda 'Atta and his Forty Grandsons: The Socio-Political Organisation of the Ait 'Atta of Southern Morocco*. Cambridge: MENAS Press, 1981.

Herzfeld, Michael. "Honor and Shame: Some Problems in the Comparative Analysis of Moral Systems." *Man* (n.s.) 15 (1980):339–51.

———. "The Horns of the Mediterraneanist Dilemma." *American Ethnologist* 11 (1984):439–54.

Hopkins, Nicholas. "The Articulation of the Modes of Production: Tailoring in Tunisia." *American Ethnologist* 5, no. 3 (1978):468–83.

———. *Agrarian Transformation in Egypt*. Boulder and London: Westview Press, 1987.

Hopkins, Nicholas, and Saad Eddin Ibrahim, eds. *Arab Society*. Cairo: American University in Cairo Press, 1985.

Jamous, Raymond. *Honneur et Baraka: Les Structures sociales traditionnelles dans le Rif*. Cambridge and Paris: Cambridge University Press and Maison des Sciences de l'Homme, 1981.

Joseph, Suad. "Working-Class Women's Networks in a Sectarian State: A Political Paradox." *American Ethnologist* 10, no. 1 (1983):1–22.

Joseph, Terri Brint. "Poetry as a Strategy of Power: The Case of Riffian Berber Women." *Signs: Journal of Women in Culture and Society* 5 (1980):418–34.

Kandiyoti, Deniz. "Emancipated but Unliberated? Reflections on the Turkish Case." *Feminist Studies* 13, no. 2 (1987):317–38.

Kondo, Dorinne. "Dissolution and Reconstitution of Self: Implications for Anthropological Epistemology." *Cultural Anthropology* 1 (1985):74–88.

Lancaster, William. *The Rwala Bedouin Today*. Cambridge: Cambridge University Press, 1981.

Larson, Barbara. "The Rural Marketing System of Egypt over the Last Three Hundred Years." *Comparative Studies in Society and History* 27 (1985):494–530.

Layne, Linda. "The Production and Reproduction of Tribal Identity in Jordan." Ph.D. dissertation, Princeton University, 1986.

———. " 'Tribalism': National Representations of Tribal Life in Jordan." *Urban Anthropology and Studies of Cultural Systems and World Economic Development* 16, no. 2 (1987):183–203.

Lutz, Catherine, and Geoffrey White. "The Anthropology of Emotions." *Annual Review of Anthropology* 15 (1986):405–36.

McCabe, Justine. "FBD Marriage: Further Support for the Westermarck Hypothesis of the Incest Taboo?" *American Anthropologist* 85 (1983):50–69.

Maher, Vanessa. "Possession and Dispossession: Maternity and Mortality in Morocco," in Hans Medick and David W. Sabean, eds. *Interest and Emotion: Essays on the Study of Family and Kinship*. Cambridge: Cambridge University Press, 1984.

Makhlouf, Carla. *Changing Veils: Women and Modernisation in North Yemen*. London :Croom Helm, 1979.

Malinowski, Bronislaw. *Argonauts of the Western Pacific*. New York: E. P. Dutton, 1961 (1922).

Maquet, Jacques. "Objectivity in Anthropology." *Current Anthropology* 5 (1964):47–55.

Marcus, George, and Dick Cushman. "Ethnographies as Texts." *Annual Review of Anthropology* 11 (1982):25–69.

Marcus, George, and Michael Fischer. *Anthropology as Cultural Critique: An Experimental Moment in the Human Sciences*. Chicago: University of Chicago Press, 1986.

Marcus, Michael. "History on the Moroccan Periphery: Moral Imagination, Poetry and Islam." *Anthropological Quarterly* 58, no. 4 (1987):152–60.

Meeker, Michael. "Meaning and Society in the Near East: Examples from the Black Sea Turks and the Levantine Arabs." *International Journal of Middle East Studies* 7 (1976):243–70 and 383–422.

———. *Literature and Violence in North Arabia*. Cambridge: Cambridge University Press, 1979.

Mernissi, Fatima. *Beyond the Veil: Male-Female Dynamics in a Modern Muslim Society*. Cambridge, MA: Schenkman, 1975.

———. "Women, Saints, and Sanctuaries," in Elizabeth Abel and Emily Abel, eds. *The SIGNS Reader: Women, Gender and Scholarship*. Chicago: University of Chicago Press, 1983 (1977). 57–68.

Messick, Brinkley. "The Mufti, the Text and the World: Legal Interpretation in Yemen." *Man* (n.s.) 21 (1986):102–19.

———. "Subordinate Discourse: Women, Weaving and Gender Relations in North Africa." *American Ethnologist* 14, no. 2 (1987):210–25.

El-Messiri, Sawsan. "Self-Images of Traditional Urban Women in Cairo," in Lois Beck and Nikki Keddie, eds. *Women in the Muslim World.* Cambridge: Harvard University Press, 1978.

Mitchell, Timothy. *Colonising Egypt.* Cambridge: Cambridge University Press, 1988.

———. "Inventing and Reinventing the Egyptian Peasant." *International Journal of Middle East Studies* (forthcoming, 1990).

Morsy, Soheir. "Sex Differences and Folk Illness in an Egyptian Village," in Lois Beck and Nikki Keddie, eds. *Women in the Muslim World.* Cambridge: Harvard University Press, 1978.

———. "Zionist Ideology as Anthropology: An Analysis of Joseph Ginat's *Women in Muslim Rural Society.*" *Arab Studies Quarterly* 5, no. 4 (1983):362–79.

Morsy, Soheir, Cynthia Nelson, Reem Saad, and Hania Sholkamy. "Anthropology and the Call for Indigenization of Social Science in the Arab World," in Earl Sullivan and Tareq Ismael, eds. *The Contemporary Study of the Arab World.* Alberta: Alberta University Press, forthcoming, n.d.

Munson, Jr., Henry. *The House of Si Abd Allah.* New Haven: Yale University Press, 1984.

Narayan, Kirin. *Saints, Scoundrels and Storytellers.* Philadelphia: University of Pennsylvania Press, 1989.

Nelson, Cynthia. "Self, Spirit Possession and World View: An Illustration from Egypt." *International Journal of Social Psychiatry* 17 (1971):194–209.

———. "Public and Private Politics: Women in the Middle Eastern World." *American Ethnologist* 1, no. 3 (1974):551–63.

———. "Old Wine, New Bottles: Reflections and Projections Concerning Research on 'Women in Middle Eastern Studies.'" in Earl Sullivan and Tareq Ismael, eds. *The Contemporary Study of the Arab World.* Alberta: Alberta University Press, forthcoming, n.d.

Ortner, Sherry. "Is Female to Male as Nature Is to Culture?" in M. Z. Rosaldo and L. Lamphere, eds. *Woman, Culture and Society,* Stanford: Stanford University Press, 1974. 67–87.

———. "Theory in Anthropology since the Sixties." *Comparative Studies in Society and History* 26, no. 1 (1984):126–66.

Pandolfo, Stefania. "Detours of Life: Space and Bodies in a Moroccan Village." *American Ethnologist* 16 (1989): 3–23.

Peristiany, Jean G., ed. *Honour and Shame: The Values of Mediterranean Society.* Chicago: University of Chicago Press, 1966.

Peters, Emrys L. "The Proliferation of Segments in the Lineage of the Bedouin of Cyrenaica." *Journal of the Royal Anthropological Institute of Great Britain* 90 (1960):29–53.

———. "Aspects of the Family Among the Bedouin of Cyrenaica," in M. F. Nimkoff, ed. *Comparative Family Systems.* Boston: Houghton Mifflin, 1965. 121–46.

———. "Some Structural Aspects of the Feud among the Camel-Herding Bedouin of Cyrenaica." *Africa* 37 (1967):261–82.

Rabinow, Paul. *Reflections on Fieldwork in Morocco.* Berkeley: University of California Press, 1977.

————. "Representations Are Social Facts: Modernity and Post-Modernity in Anthropology," in James Clifford and George Marcus, eds. *Writing Culture: The Poetics and Politics of Ethnography.* Berkeley: University of California Press, 1986. 234–61.

Rassam, Amal. "Women and Domestic Power in Morocco." *International Journal of Middle East Studies* 12 (1980):171–79.

Robertson Smith, W. *Kinship and Marriage in Early Arabia.* Boston: Beacon Press, 1903.

Rosaldo, Michelle Z. "Woman, Culture, and Society: A Theoretical Overview," in M. Z. Rosaldo and L. Lamphere, eds. *Woman, Culture, and Society.* Stanford: Stanford University Press, 1974. 17–42.

————. "The Uses and Abuses of Anthropology: Reflections on Feminism and Cross-Cultural Understanding." *Signs: Journal of Women in Culture and Society* 5, no. 3 (1980):389–417.

Rosaldo, Renato. "From the Door of his Tent: The Fieldworker and the Inquisitor," in James Clifford and George Marcus, eds. *Writing Culture: The Poetics and Politics of Ethnography.* Berkeley: University of California Press, 1986. 77–97.

Rosen, Lawrence. "The Negotiation of Reality: Male-Female Relations in Sefrou, Morocco," in Lois Beck and Nikki Keddie, eds. *Women in the Muslim World.* Cambridge: Harvard University Press, 1978.

————. "Social Identity and Points of Attachment: Approaches to Social Organization," in Clifford Geertz, Hildred Geertz, and Lawrence Rosen. *Meaning and Order in Moroccan Society.* Cambridge: Cambridge University Press, 1979. 19–111.

————. *Bargaining for Reality: The Construction of Social Relations in a Muslim Community.* Chicago: University of Chicago Press, 1984.

El Sa'dawi, Nawal. *The Hidden Face of Eve: Women in the Arab World.* London: Zed Press, 1979.

Sabbah, Fatna. *Woman in the Muslim Unconscious.* New York: Pergamon Press, 1984.

Said, Edward. *Orientalism.* New York: Pantheon Books, 1978.

Salzman, Philip Carl. "Does Complementary Opposition Exist?" *American Anthropologist* 80 (1978):53–70.

Scholte, Robert. "Toward a Reflexive and Critical Anthropology," in Dell Hymes, ed. *Reinventing Anthropology.* New York: Vintage Books, 1974. 430–57.

Seddon, David. *Moroccan Peasants: A Century of Change in the Eastern Rif 1870–1970.* Folkestone, England: Wm Dawson & Sons, 1981.

Slyomovics, Susan. "Arabic Folk Literature and Political Expression." *Arab Studies Quarterly* 8, no. 2 (1986):178–85.

————. *The Merchant of Art.* Berkeley: University of California Press, 1987.

Strathern, Marilyn. "Dislodging a Worldview: Challenge and Counter-Challenge in the Relationship between Feminism and Anthropology." *Australian Feminist Studies* 1 (1985):1–25.

————. "An Awkward Relationship: The Case of Feminism and Anthropology." *SIGNS: Journal of Women in Culture and Society* 12, no. 2 (1987a):276–92.

————, ed. *Dealing with Inequality: Analyzing Gender Relations in Melanesia and Beyond.* Cambridge: Cambridge University Press, 1987b.

Udovitch, Abraham, and Lucette Valensi. *The Last Arab Jews: The Communities of Jerba, Tunisia.* New York: Harwood Academic Publishers, 1984.

Varisco, Daniel. "The Bedouin Mystique." Paper presented at the Twentieth Annual Meeting of the Middle East Studies Association, Boston, November 1986.

Wikan, Unni. *Behind the Veil in Arabia: Women in Oman*. Baltimore: Johns Hopkins University Press, 1982.

Wolf, Eric. *Europe and the People Without History*. Berkeley: University of California Press, 1982.

Yanagisako, Sylvia, and Jane Collier. "Toward a Unified Analysis of Gender and Kinship," in J. Collier and S. Yanagisako, eds. *Gender and Kinship*. Stanford: Stanford University Press, 1987. 14–50.

4

Beyond the Always and the Never: A Critique of Social Psychological Interpretations of Arab Society and Culture

Halim Barakat

Even more than other areas of cultural and sociological study, the field of social psychology requires a dual process of unlearning static and oversimplified interpretations of Arab society, and learning or relearning a dynamic approach to a highly complex and contradictory reality. Social psychological writing on Arab society is quite limited in quantity as well as in its development and approaches. Yet a wide variety of Western and Arab scholars have used some of the basic categories of social psychological analysis in examining the structure and dynamics of Arab and other Middle Eastern societies. Central concerns of Middle East studies have included the issues of national character and identity or personality, patterns of socialization, group and intergroup dynamics, attitudes and attitudinal change, interpersonal relations and social interaction, language and communication, processes of alienation and integration, violence and aggression, norms and value orientations, spontaneity and expressive behavior, and several others.

In order to delineate the scope of the present critical study on theory and method in the social psychological study of the Arab society, I will focus on some of the applications of social psychological categories of analysis. A comparison will be made of the different conceptions and approaches, in which special emphasis will be placed on the distinction between Western and Arab scholarship. While both may express similar criticisms of Arab culture and Arab national character, their views have totally different perspectives as their starting points. Unlike mainstream Western scholarship, Arab critical approaches are deeply imbedded in a sense of Arab belonging and commitment to transformation and transcendence of the prevailing order, and the ongoing struggle to achieve the *nahda* (awakening). Arab critical thought rejects the static view of Western Orientalist scholarship, which emphasizes the constancy of Arab culture and the "oneness" of what is referred to as the "Arab mind."

The critical approach argues, instead, that the Arab national identity is undergoing continuous change. The transitional nature of Arab culture and identity reflects a process of constant flux and becoming as a result of contradictions, new needs and circumstances, and challenging encounters with other cultures.

Specifically, and in contrast to Orientalist Western scholarship, Arab critical analysis is guided by the following analytical principles as it undertakes to explore social psychological phenomena in Arab society:

1. The phenomena under study are examined in social and historical contexts. The starting point is society in history rather than polity or religion per se.

2. Forces for change are explained in terms of internal and external contradictions, not merely of encounters with the West.

3. Behavior is examined in a complex network of interrelationships.

4. The prevailing conditions in Arab society are seen as making Arabs highly alienated. Hence the constant search for deliverance and struggle to transform their reality.

A critical approach guided by these principles may be described as dynamic, because of its emphasis on change; as analytical, because of its preoccupation with explanation; and as dialectical, because of its emphasis on contradictions and struggle. On a more general level, it opposes Western analyses rooted in relations of domination and presents reality from an Arab perspective. Hence the dual task of unlearning and relearning referred to at the beginning of this paper.[1]

I. The Question of National Character

Several Western and Arab scholars have attempted to use concepts of national personality, basic personality, national mind, social character, or modal personality, despite the challenges to their validity that have often been made. Some of these writings, such as those of Raphael Patai,[2] take a static approach and seem to reflect antagonistic political attitudes. Others, such as Sania Hamady's book *Temperament and Character of the Arabs*,[3] engage in oversimplifications reflecting a Westernized perspective. Among Arab writings in this area, some tend to be defensive, such as Fuad Moughrabi's critical survey of the literature on the Arab "basic personality."[4] Other Arab writings, such as El-Sayyid Yassin's book on Arab personality, depart from an Arab nationalistic framework and claim to follow a dialectical approach.[5]

A clear example of the misuses of the concept of national character is

Raphael Patai's *The Arab Mind.* In the first preface to the work Patai informs readers that his "interest in, and sympathy for, the Arabs never flagged," and speaks at length of his friendship for Ahmad Fakhr al-Din al-Kinani al-Khatib, "a shaykh of the famous al-Azhar of Cairo and a scion of one of the great Arab families of Jerusalem."[6] The preface to the paperback edition prepares the readers for a harsh process of stereotyping as Patai clarifies one of his contentions in the light of the October 1973 Arab-Israeli war. In response to a criticism that the war invalidates his previous contentions that "it is part of the Arab mentality to threaten without carrying out the threat" and that "in the Arab mentality words often can and do serve as substitutes for acts," Patai offers an even more oversimplified explanation. A counter-motivation in Arab personality, he points out, is "the drive to restore damaged honor," for "any injury done to a man's honor must be revenged, or else he becomes permanently dishonored."[7] Accordingly, in Patai's perspective, for Arabs war is a matter of satisfying the psychological need to avenge honor rather than an attempt to achieve concrete goals such as ending occupation and achieving self-determination.

Patai legitimizes his stereotyping by calling it an abstraction reached by processes of generalization about the Arab mentality, Arab mind, or mental characteristics of Arabs as a population and human group. By defining national character, he means "the sum total of the motives, traits, beliefs, and values shared by the plurality in a national population."[8] He assumes that Arabs are fairly homogeneous and that the Middle East, though inhabited by a mosaic of peoples "speaking many different tongues and exhibiting many different physical features," is nevertheless "the domain of one basically identical culture."[9] Conceptualizing Arab culture as characterized by "coherence, balance and inner consistency,"[10] Patai sets himself free of any restraints to qualify his statements about Arabs and Islam. Patai's oversimplified generalizations include:

- "To the Arab mind, eloquence is related to exaggeration" (p. 49).

- "In contrast to the West, the Arab world still sees the universe running its predestined course" (p. 147).

- "For the tradition-bound Arab mind, there is even something sinful in engaging in long-range planning, because it seems to imply that one does not put one's trust in divine providence" (p. 150).

- "In general the Arab mind, dominated by Islam, has been bent more on preserving rather than innovating, or maintaining than improving, or continuing than initiating" (p. 154).

- "Eloquence is to the Arab an achievement akin to the attainment of masculinity" (p. 49).

How does Patai reach these definitive conclusions and many similar others? In the first place, he overlooks notions of plurality of culture, cultural variations, and cultural struggle, dismissing the effects of social diversity and social class differences (though he discusses these matters in different contexts). Second, he perceives Islam as an external force shaping society—and not shaped by it. A statement attributed by the Mamluk historian al-Maqrizi (1364–1442) to Ka'b al-Ahbar, one of the companions of the Prophet Muhammad, is thus presumed to apply to contemporary Muslims.

Third, his quotations are often taken out of context from non-Arab secondary sources. In fact, when Patai refers to an Arab source, the quotation often turns out to be taken from a Western source. For instance, he quotes Bernard Lewis, who quotes Abdel Aziz al-Duri, who quotes al-Tha'alibi (d. 1038) to prove that "throughout the vast Arabic language area, people hold with relative uniformity that Arabic is superior to other languages" (p. 44). He also quotes Taha Hussein in reference to the unchangeable character of Egypt and its lack of fear of Westernization—as summarized by von Grunebaum. Similarly, Patai quotes my novel *'Awdat al-Ta'ir ila al-Bahr* as analyzed by Trevor Le Gassick in an article published in the *Middle East Journal* to demonstrate Arab ambivalence (see pp. 199, 203, and 350–51).

Fourth, several of Patai's oversimplified generalizations are based on selected proverbs which he believes "yield a fascinating folk view of the Arab character" (p. 22), failing to realize that proverbs convey only specific meanings in specific situations under certain circumstances. Hence the presence (a matter he does not seem to realize) of conflicting proverbs as well as conflicting implications. On the basis of the frequently quoted proverb "I and my brothers against my cousin; I and my cousins against the stranger," Patai theorizes about Arab "in-group loyalty and out-group enmity,"[11] jokes about the absence of a female counterpart proverb which would say "I and my sister against my female cousins; I against my sister" (p. 36) and views the "Arab nation as an Arab family" (p. 42). What Patai fails to realize is that Arabs quite often repeat this particular proverb in the context of criticizing tribalism. He also fails to realize that Arabs frequently repeat proverbs to the opposite effect, such as the following: *Al-jar qabl al-dar* (the neighbor has the priority over members of the house); *jarak al-qarib wala khayak al-ba'id* (your close neighbor rather than your distant brother). Furthermore, Arabs consider these proverbs more normatively positive than the first one.

Fifth, Patai cites several stereotypes and counterstereotypes in Arab culture, taking them at face value as accurate descriptions instead of signs of tensions and conflicts in the area. He tells us that astute Arab observers had remarked on differences in national character between one Arab country and another many centuries before the concept of national character was formulated in the West. After quoting Maqrizi to this effect, Patai concludes that educated Arabs in the fourteenth and fifteenth century were well aware, not only of the existence of an Arab national character, but also of character differences between the Arab peoples inhabiting various countries (p. 23). If such character differences between Arab countries are so great, what becomes of Patai's notion of the Arab mind?

The same sort of Arab stereotyping is reflected in Morroe Berger's book on *The Arab World Today*. In a separate chapter on personality and values, he attempts to "delineate a group of traits encompassing the Arabs in their variety, a kind of modal point which they approximate in varying degrees."[12] Realizing that the idea of an "Arab personality" is a "formidable abstraction" to which he must resort in order to say what "kind of person" the Arab is, he makes several sweeping generalizations.

For Berger, the following generalizations combine to produce the Arab personality or general outlook, i.e., what kind of person the Arab is:

- "The Arabs display the double effect of wounded pride—self-exaltation and self-condemnation" (p. 136).

- "The Arab seems to harbor two major contradicting impulses: Egotism and conformity. The first takes the forms of extreme self-assertion before others, pride, and sensitivity to criticism. The second is reflected in obedience to certain group norms which are resented, and an inability to assert independence as an individual with confidence or finality" (p. 136).

- "By providing ready-made phrases, it [speech] obviates the need for thought and originality" (p. 155).

- "There is a high degree of authoritarianism in the personal make-up of Arabs" (p. 157).

- "Arab views of the external world of nature and of the arts display a similar rigidity, formalism, and disinclination to look into the unknown" (p. 158).

- "One aspect of the cultural outlook . . . is the Arab's infatuation with ideal forms; he clings to them emotionally even while he knows they are contradicted by reality" (p. 160).

These are only a few of the many generalizations. In contrast, not one positive value is mentioned in the chapter. Berger does not even wonder how a human society can function and survive without any positive values. For him, it does not seem that there is much of a need for explanations beyond merely naming in one paragraph what he believes to be the sources of the above Arab personality. These sources, according to Berger, are: "The nomadic bedouin values that permeated Arab society and Islam, the claims of the religious system itself, the long history of subordination, crushing poverty, and patterns of child rearing which stem in part from these sources and reinforce them in generation after generation."[13]

Again we ask, what is the basis for such conclusions? It would be expected that sociologists and anthropologists should base their views on field research and empirical data. Instead, they rely on a selected number of sayings, anecdotes, proverbs, quotes, readings, and Orientalist scholarship.

Janet Abu-Lughod makes a very interesting remark on the methodology of Western historiography of what has been called "the Islamic city." She observes that in some ways this historiography

> takes the same form as the traditions of the Prophet. The authenticity of any proposition is judged by the *isnad* or "chain" by which it descended from the past. Certain claims are deemed more trustworthy than others. . . . The idea of the Islamic city was constructed by a series of Western authorities who drew upon a small and eccentric sample of pre-modern Arab cities, . . . but more than that, drew upon one another in an *isnad* of authority.[14]

Thus Raphael Patai draws on Morroe Berger or Bernard Lewis or Sir Hamilton Gibb or von Grunebaum—who may have quoted Hassan al-Basri (d. 728) or Ibn Taimiyya (d. 1328) or al-Maqrizi (d. 1442) to make a strong generalization about contemporary Arab value systems. This sort of *isnad* may, at least partly, account for what Edward Said described as "the internal consistency of orientalism and its ideas about the Orient . . . despite or beyond any correspondence, or lack thereof, with a 'real Orient.' "[15] After all, Orientalism has served as a system for citing works and authors out of social and historical context, hence the dominant view of Arab society as being constantly the same and uniquely uniform or uniformly unique.

In a few instances, scholars refer to some field or empirical studies such as those conducted by E. Terry Prothro, Levon Melikian, and Hamed Ammar. In an attempt to discover whether "residence in an authoritarian culture" leads to greater acceptance of some items of the California Public Opinion Scale, Prothro and Melikian administered a thirty-three–item questionnaire to 130 Arab freshman students at the American University of Beirut (AUB). The results tended to confirm claims for the validity of the *F* scale but do not show a positive correlation between authoritarianism and politico-economic conservatism. This questionnaire was administered (we are not told how the sample was chosen) in the early 1950s.

The students were mostly Lebanese (77 out of 130) and Christian (70 out of 130). The authors base their study "upon the assumption that the culture of 'Greater Syria'. . . is authoritarian, and that authoritarianism is in general somewhat stronger in the Moslem than in the Christian communities."[16] This authoritarianism, they point out, "begins in Syrian family life, where the father is the absolute head of the household, and both wife and children obey him."[17] A comparison of Near Eastern and U.S. students showed that the mean score of AUB students on the thirty-three–item abbreviated *F* scale was 5.03, while that of a sample of California and Oregon students was 3.56, and that of Oklahoma students was 4.1. The authors deem these results significant in spite of the facts that the *F* scale items are culturally loaded and that they made no attempt to control for any other variables, such as social class, social background (e.g., rural-urban background), and conditions prevailing at the time of conducting the research. The researchers admit that the *F* scale was constructed in such a way that in "some instances the 'everyday phrases' of American life are unfamiliar to Arabs."[18] Furthermore, a more detailed comparison between Christian and Muslim students showed some inconsistencies in regard to scores on certain specific items. The mean score of Muslims on items connected with "insult to honor," punishment of "sex crimes," and attitudes toward homosexuals was much higher than the mean score of Christians. On the other hand, the "Muslims were as liberal as or even more liberal than Christians"[19] on those items connected with the responsibility of society to guarantee everyone adequate social services, increases in taxes on large companies, and solutions to social problems.

In a similar paper, Levon Melikian examines the correlations of authoritarianism with exposure to modernization in what he describes as "the relatively authoritarian culture of the Arab Middle East and in the relatively non-authoritarian culture of the United States."[20] He does so—though he admits that "no measure of cultural authoritarianism is available"—on the basis of the sweeping assumption that "there is enough anthropological evidence to substantiate the claim made about the two [Arab Middle East and U.S.] cultures."[21] In exactly the same fashion, anthropologists themselves (particularly Raphael Patai) have tended to base their arguments about Arab cultural authoritarianism on the assumption that there is enough social psychological evidence to substantiate this claim.

A more comprehensive and balanced interpretation is given by George H. Gardner in the same issue of *Journal of Social Issues*. Though he continues to hold some of the traditional Orientalist notions of mosaic composition and the "ways of life which have remained nearly unchanged during some seven or eight thousand years,"[22] he attempts to place issues in some historical perspective.

Another source of speculation about problems of Arab national personality and culture is Hamed Ammar's book *Growing Up in an Egyptian Village*. Some of his observations are overgeneralized to the Arab world or the Middle East as a whole, even though he himself clearly warns readers that he cannot claim that the village of Silwa, where he conducted his field research, was typical of rural Egypt. He plainly states that "it is extremely difficult to show the extent to which Silwa is a typical Egyptian village."[23] Since some of these generalizations pertain more to socialization of the individual than to natural personalities, I reserve comments to another section of the present paper. Here, I wish to address myself to a later work in which Ammar developed the concept of the Egyptian Fahlawi personality. This has proven useful to several other scholars in their portrayal of certain basic aspects of Arab national character and culture. For Ammar himself, the attributes of the Fahlawi modal character are rooted in the prevailing socioeconomic conditions and social organization in Egyptian society. These basically negative attributes of "the present social mode of Egyptian personality" and typical responses that occur in certain specific situations include the following:

- Quick adaptability to various new situations, reflecting both genuine flexibility and insincere agreement to avoid severe punishment.

- Quick wit (*nukta*), giving way to anger and resentment in confronting overwhelming misfortunes.

- Self-assertion, or a tendency to exaggerate in demonstrating one's superior power, as a result of lack of confidence.

- A romantic view of equality as a result of the prevailing conditions, which generate inequality and discrimination. Hence the tendency to reject authority and leadership as well as to decline responsibility, shifting it to an external agent in order to justify embarrassing situations.

- The psychological security derived from preference for individual rather than group activities.

- Attempts to achieve goals by the shortest and quickest means.

In presenting these attributes of the Fahlawi personality, Ammar insists on examining them in their social context, arguing that they change with changing conditions. He also explains that he focuses on "the weak points rather than the strong ones" in the Egyptian character out of a strong belief in self-criticism as "an indispensable necessity and a basic step in the building of the society."[24]

It is within this process of self-criticism—but much more highly intensified by the defeat of 1967—that Sadiq al-'Azm restates the attributes of the Fahlawi personality. This mode of behavior, al-'Azm points out, is an integral part of the structure of traditional Arab society, and inseparable from the characteristics of the social personality into which Arabs are socialized, under specific circumstances and situations. In confronting and responding to the June war of 1967, Arabs exhibited many of the above inclinations, including using shortcuts to achieve their goals, attempting to make favorable impressions, covering up failures out of fear of disgrace, disclaiming responsibilities, and blaming external forces for the disaster.[25]

Fuad Moughrabi argues against the validity of social psychological studies dealing with such constructs as "Arab basic personality" or "Arab mind." Methodologically, the problem is one of representation or generalization based on anecdotal reports and research studies either of village populations or of highly educated subjects. Such generalizations, he points out, tend to ignore the richness and diversity of Arab society.[26] It might be added that they also fail to take account of the diversity and transitional nature of Arab society. Moughrabi is also correct in criticizing the psychological reductionism and the ahistorical nature of the majority of such studies.

The defects of Moughrabi's argument lie in his lack of differentiation and distinction between Western and Arab scholarship in this area. Though he recognizes that Arab intellectuals are "irritated by the weaknesses that plague their respective societies," he nevertheless dismisses the process of self-criticism by Arab social scientists, suggesting that they see themselves in a Western perspective and "mistakenly accept this pattern of analysis and the model of development."[27] Yet self-criticism by Hamed Ammar, Sadiq al-'Azm, and myself (to mention a few of those criticized by Moughrabi) comes about not as a result of irritation with the weaknesses of Arab society but out of deep concern for the achievement of the *nahda* (awakening). Besides recognizing the complexity and the constantly changing nature of contemporary Arab society, such studies examine controversial issues from a non-Western perspective.

It is El-Sayyid Yassin, rather than Moughrabi, who offers the most effective and comprehensive critique of Western social psychological studies on Arab national character.[28] He argues that negative characterizations of Arabs by Orientalistic and antagonistic Israeli scholars are part of an ongoing psychological warfare based on a distortion of the Arab image. His task thus becomes twofold: to trace the roots of "the historical antagonism against Arabs in Western thought" and to explore the true nature of "Arab national personality."

In addressing himself to the first part of his task, Yassin concludes that Western thought on Arab national characteristics has focused on the negative aspects and neglected the positive ones. In his attempt to explore the true nature of "Arab national personality," Yassin notes that it is normal for nations to raise questions about their identities at decisive historical moments. In the case of the Arabs, that is exactly what happened after the 1967 defeat and the 1973 October war. Many questions were raised then and continue to be raised about the Arab ability to confront historical challenges. The focus, Yassin says, should be on Arab national personality, the nature of Arab societal building, and the problems of modernization in the Arab world.

Yassin concludes that one may talk of the "Arab personality" to the extent that the "dominant mode of production" in the Arab world is nearly the same. Since there is a multiplicity of social formations in the Arab world, the validity of describing the characteristic features of Arab personality should not make us overlook the fact "that the social history of every Arab country is likely to result in distinctive national features which do not exist in other Arab societies."[29] By admitting this fact, Yassin faces the task of reconciling what he calls the primary and secondary characteristic features of the Arab society. "The true challenge confronting the Arab nation," he concludes, "is how to establish lively and creative harmony between the primary and secondary patterns, i.e. between the various sub-personalities and the Arab personality."[30]

The question remains unanswered. The difficulty is that of the validity of the concept of national personality itself. Is it possible for highly complex societies, with their dominant culture, subcultures, and counter-cultures, to have one national personality? If not, a prominent group of sociopsychological studies are based on a false premise.

II. Patterns of Socialization

An important concern of social psychological studies of the Arab world has been with its patterns of socialization. Borrowing selectively from a few field studies on Arab child-rearing practices (Prothro, Ammar, Granqvist, Miner),[31] Raphael Patai argues that "the basic similarity of child-rearing practices in all parts of the Arab world" is among "the most important factors contributing to the formation of the modal personality."[32] Such a "general all-Arab pattern of child-rearing," the argument goes, exerts a "lasting effect on the Arab personality formation" and "produces similar personality configurations."[33]

On the basis of McClelland's thesis of a positive relationship between the need for achievement and economic development and of Prothro's findings, Patai postulates a blatantly reductionist "three-phase causal relationship: child-rearing practices—need for achievement—economic development."[34] He further quotes one of Prothro's basic hypotheses that "differences in rate of economic development in different countries might be attributable not to natural resources, available investment capital, or technological skills alone, but also to the amount of achievement motive found in the inhabitants of that nation."[35]

Hamed Ammar's study on growing up in an Egyptian village also focuses strongly upon the social and psychological aspects of the training of children. Ammar notes, however, that the process of growing up is not identical for all children, even in a village that is rather homogeneous, isolated, and lacking in complex social subdivisions and class structure. Though reserved in his generalization, Ammar tends to emphasize the docile rather than the aggressive aspects of socialization. Instead of showing how parents and other agencies socialize the child to strive aggressively for survival in a harsh environment, he focuses on ways of disciplining the child to conform to prescribed standards and become polite (or *mu'addab*). Hence the inaccuracy of his definition of the process of socialization in terms of "the eagerness of the adults to create a docile attitude in their children."[36] In fact, a more thorough examination of the pattern of socialization in its totality would show that restraint and docility may be the keynotes of children's behavior toward their parents but not toward the environment and acquiring a living. In fact, as marginally indicated by Ammar himself in a different context, if a child "shows any submissiveness, if wronged by his 'pals,' he would be punished by his parents and would be asked to retaliate for himself."[37] In instances of this sort, the main objective of child training is not to cultivate a docile and yielding disposition, in spite of the emphasis on being *mu'addab*. The motives of courage and toughness rather than fear are cultivated in bedouin and rural as well as urban poor children. As far as I know, these aspects of socialization have not been explored by any social psychological studies.

The reason for this neglect, I assume, is Arab scholars' acceptance of a framework of analysis aiming at explaining Arab weakness and crisis in confronting historical challenges. This was the intention of Hisham Sharabi's *Introduction to the Study of Arab Society*. Written with Arab readers in mind and aimed at inducing critical thought following the defeat of 1967, the book examines the effect upon individual and collective personality of the ways children are socialized in the urban feudal bourgeois Arab family. Intending to enhance Arab society's self-understanding, Sharabi starts from questions such as: Why has Arab society failed to modernize? Why have the Arab countries failed to cope with some of their most basic social tasks? Why have the Arab people been unable to cooperate, to organize, to unify? Sharabi attempts to answer these questions by proposing that genuine knowledge of a society can only be the product of self-knowledge and that real change emanates from within that society. His search for Arab self-knowledge rests on a strong belief that the family is the chief mediating institution between the personality and culture, that personality is molded in the family, and that the values and behavioral patterns of society are significantly transmitted and reinforced through the family. One of the basic assumptions here is that the typical personality of a given society depends on the child-rearing customs of that society.[38]

To Sharabi, the typical urban, Muslim, middle- and lower-middle-class Arab family—i.e., feudal-bourgeois family—uses the principal techniques of shaming, physical punishment, and rote-learning (*talqin*) in socializing its children. Treated thus, the typical child develops negative tendencies of dependency, incapacity, and escapism.

In spite of the overemphasis on child-rearing practices, Sharabi realizes that "the transformation of the feudal-bourgeois personality, which is the product of a feudal-bourgeois society, can only be achieved by the transformation of that society and its class structure."[39] That is exactly what he set himself to demonstrate in his latest book, more than a decade later. One of the basic arguments of *Neopatriarchy: A Theory of Distorted Change in Arab Society* is that those tendencies and others can be understood only in their totality, i.e., in their social, economic, political, and cultural aspects as concrete historical formations shaped by internal and external forces. From this standpoint, it is dependent capitalism (introduced into the Arab world in the nineteenth and early twentieth centuries) which is responsible for the distortion of the process of modernization. Taking this perspective, Sharabi examines Arab problems in a concrete historico-social context.

Viewed in these terms, modernity becomes dialectical on the level of thought and revolutionary on the level of action. Though Sharabi takes it here as given that adult behavior reflects the dominant cultural modalities of socialization, it is essentially Marxist thought (rather than social psychology) that influences the framework of analysis. Sharabi also approaches neopatriarchy in terms of its inner structure, at the core of which is the patriarchal family in Arab society. The patriarchal family, in turn, is assessed in terms of relations of authority, domination, and dependency, which both reflect and are reflected in the general overall structure of social relations.[40]

The psychoanalysis of the Arab self has become almost the entire career of the Lebanese psychologist 'Ali Zayour. Within the circles of what he calls the family and the socioeconomic mode as well as Arab society as a whole, Zayour has focused on the production of human personality. The central thesis of his "encyclopedia of the psychoanalysis of Arab ego" (five volumes so far) pertains to problems of disequilibrium. The Arab personality, he says, is affected by anxiety and disequilibrium due to sudden changes in all aspects of life, and fears for the future.

Zayour approaches the Arab ego as a patient, and as a subject of merciless scrutiny. We are reminded that the family is relentless in its repression, that the young are brought up to be obedient, well-mannered, and subservient to those above them, that scientific thinking has not taken root in the collective consciousness, that religious and superstitious attitudes are still dominant, that traditional structures coexist alongside modern structures, that myth prevails at the expense of logical and systematic thinking, that frustration emanates from difficulties in adjustment to the culture of the strong, that solutions are sought in regression into the past and its legacies and heroes, etc.[41] Zayour does consider these and other negative tendencies to be caused by specific and historical and social conditions which need to be changed, but he rarely, if at all, addresses himself to the tasks of identifying these issues and the ways to transcend them. Implicitly, he may be counting on resocialization. It is certainly not clear how and by whom.

To conclude this section, the literature on socialization is seriously deficient. The emphasis has been on identifying the negative consequences of traditional socialization, almost exclusively within the circle of the family. Few attempts have been made to explain these negative tendencies in their social and historical contexts. No attempt whatsoever has been made to distinguish between the way Arabs are brought up to behave at home and the way they are taught to struggle for survival in society. Furthermore, this literature has viewed the process of socialization itself as limited to early childhood. In other words, there does not seem to be a conception of socialization as a process that continues throughout adolescent and adult life. The increasing need, in modern societies, for higher and higher education, for training and retraining, and the transformation of consciousness in times of societal crises are most indicative of the continuity of the process of socialization.

III.   Value Orientations: The Third Angle

We describe social psychological studies of Arab society as essentially triangular in terms of their areas of concern. If national character and socialization are the first two sides, value orientations can be considered the third. The distinctiveness of national character is often assessed in terms of the prevailing value orientations, while socialization is usually defined in terms of learning to subscribe to, and/or internalize, society's value systems and conforming to the norms derived from them.

Values are defined here as beliefs about desired or preferred objects, goals, and forms of human behavior. Specifically, there are instrumental values which state that certain forms of behavior are preferable to others (such as "love is preferable to hatred"), and terminal values which define ideal goals (such as happiness, national unity, social justice). Both sets of values are intended to guide, to regulate social relations, or to define the meaning of human existence. In many instances they are intended to justify certain acts and facilitate adjustment to a certain reality, or to expose and instigate.

Values, then, are relative, multifarious in their sources and functions, conflicting, dynamic, and in a state of constant becoming. They are particularly so in transitional societies.

Value orientations in Arab society differ particularly by the individual's social class, patterns of living, social affiliations, and isolation or exposure to the outside world; by the values' sources and functions; and by the prevailing order.

My research has found deprived classes to be more likely than others to value the immediate and tangible, to adhere uncritically to religious faith, to express the need for patience and to place a high esteem on the close family ties which offer them material and other means of support. Middle classes, on the other hand, are more likely to value ambition, success, self-reliance, achievement, individuality, freedom, and clever-ness. On the level of ideology, they are more likely to subscribe to liberal values and reform of the prevailing system. The privileged classes are more likely than others to value continuity, stability, distinctiveness, man-ners, power and influence, consumptive affluency, etc. Ideologically, they subscribe to conservatism or maintenance of the dominant order. Simply, theirs is a culture of dominance, stability, and perpetuation.[42]

Values in Arab society differ also according to patterns of living. Bed-ouin way of life has traditionally asserted (1) solidarity (*'asabiyya*) and its derivatives (such as respect for parents and ancestors, pride in origin, ascription, loyalty to blood relations, honor, the taking of revenge, etc.); (2) chivalry (*furussiyya*) and its derivatives (courage, gallantry, power, independence, pride, dignity, manhood, defiance, austerity, adherence to a knightly code, etc.); (3) hospitality and generosity (giving freely, helping others, giving protection, etc.); (4) freedom (individuality, etc.); and (5) simplicity of life.[43]

On the other hand, the peasant way of life has traditionally called for putting a high value on (1) qualities associated with land (i.e., fertility, hope, patience, spontaneity, rebirth, sacrifice, renewal of life and seasons, and love of nature); (2) family ties (i.e., motherhood, cooperation, respect for ancestors and the elderly, family honor, etc.); (3) nonofficial religiosity (faith, sainthood, being blessed, hope, contentment, etc.); and (4) awareness of time (seasonality, endurance, struggle with or against time).[44]

In contrast to both the bedouin and the peasant way of life, urbanism values success, profit making, affluence, worldly enjoyments, modern outlook, middle- or upper-class origins and distinctions, compromise, realism, self-reliance and discipline, efficacy, contractual relations, official laws and texts; and vertical or status-oriented values rather than horizontal values concerned with peer relations. Since urban communities are highly stratified, urban values also differ, of course, by class situation.[45]

Besides social class and patterns of living, values in Arab society can be traced directly to their origins in family and religion.

The basic values that derive directly and traditionally from the family structure include emphasis on (1) membership in, and identification with the family rather than individuality (i.e., sharing positive as well as negative outcomes or happiness and sadness within the family); (2) interdependency, obedience, and respect (particularly of the elderly); (3) motherhood and self-denial; (4) fatherhood as the center of responsibility and authority; (5) socialization by punishment or reward (*al-targhib wa al-tarhib*); (6) assertion of the ego or the "I" as a direct reaction to the assertion of the "we" and of membership at the expense of individuality; and (7) dominance of the male over the female.

The basic values that derive directly and traditionally from religion include emphasis on (1) absolutism rather than relativism; (2) *tanzil* (the idea that truth is derived from God) over *inbithaq* (the idea that truth comes from within society); (3) orientation to the past rather than the future; (4) conformity rather than creativity; (5) fatalism rather than free will; and (6) charity rather than justice.

The sources of the prevailing value orientations—social classes, patterns of living, family, and religion—are reinforced or undermined by acculturation, historical challenges and crises, and specific situations and conditions, as well as the discovery of new resources and inventions or adoptions of new technology. Once all that is taken into account and issues are treated in their totality and in their historical and social contexts, static social psychological studies of Arab society can clearly be seen to be oversimplified.

By following a static approach to the study of Arab value orientations, some Western and Arab scholars have tended to rely on texts, proverbs, and anecdotes rather than field studies of actual behavior; to focus on traditional culture, overlooking countertrends to it and cultural struggle within it; to examine texts outside their historical and social contexts; and to stick to the explicit and mechanical rather than the implicit and situational or symbolic meanings of cultural concepts.

A dynamic approach, on the other hand, would demonstrate that an intense struggle has been taking place within Arab culture itself. This struggle is not merely between the dominant culture, the subcultures, and countercultures. As a matter of fact, struggle and contradictions exist within each one of these three types of culture. A thorough and comprehensive examination will reveal opposite and conflicting value orientations in contemporary Arab culture: fatalism versus free will, past versus future orientations, creativity versus conformity, culture of the mind versus culture of the heart, form versus content, shame versus guilt, open- versus closed-mindedness, obedience versus rebellion, charity versus justice, collectivity versus individuality, vertical versus horizontal values, religion versus secularism, the in-group versus the out-group.

Fatalism versus Free Will

Western scholarship has reached a definitive and almost unanimous conclusion that the Arab world, in contrast to the West, sees the universe (including human life) as running a predestined course. Morroe Berger quotes Ammar, Hilma Granqvist, and Gibb to support the argument that Arabs accept their fate or lot in life. G. E. von Grunebaum sought elements of fatalism in Islam's "claim to the totality of the believer's life and thought" and in its comprehensiveness—for "there is nothing too slight, too personal, too intimate not to stand in need of being arranged by the divine will. This approach, while completely ritualizing life, imparts meaning to the most insignificant act and hallows it as a necessary affirmation of the eternal order . . . Such a system is bound to prize stability. God is above change and so is His order, revealed once and for all by His Messenger."[46] At one point, von Grunebaum almost verged on questioning the Western fondness for viewing "the Oriental as a fatalist . . . who resigns himself in all vicissitudes to the whims of destiny." He then, however, reaffirms the view that Islam, in its answer to the problem of free will, "inclines to a deterministic solution; it is equally true that it cherishes the concept of predestination. . . . All this is to say that the Muslim deeply feels man's insignificance, the uncertainty of his fate, and the omnipotence of the uncontrollable power above him. Therefore, perhaps, he is more readily prepared than the Westerner to accept the accomplished fact."[47]

Raphael Patai makes particularly sweeping generalizations about Arab fatalism, for which he seeks evidence in Islamic concepts and proverbs, and quotations from other works. Allah, he says, "not only guides the world at large, but also predestines the fate of each and every man individually."[48] To demonstrate this view, he repeats a number of quotations from the Qur'an, such as "Lo! We have created everything by measure" (54:49), "createth, then measureth, then guideth" (87:2–3), "Allah verily sendeth whom He will astray, and guideth whom He will" (35:8). Such a deterministic view, he says,

> had become an ancient Judeo-Christian heritage by the time Muhammad lived. However, in the course of their development, both Judaism and Christianity in the West have considerably modified their original determinism, allowing human will to play a more and more decisive role. Not so Islam, where absolute will is still considered as one of God's attributes operating in the manner of an inexorable law.[49]

Patai finds further evidence of fatalism in the occasional invocation of God's name in Arab culture such as *"bismi Allah"* (in the name of God), *"in sha'a Allah"* (if God wills), *"Allah Kareem"* (God is generous). A similar source of his evidence is such proverbs and concepts as *"kismet wa nasib,"* or *"bakht,"* or *"maktub,"* reflecting a belief in predestination. Finally, Patai quotes other scholars such as Edward W. Lane, Sania Hamady, and Maqrizi (d. 1442). He argues that Arab culture is characterized by other traits closely related to fatalism, such as improvidence. "For the tradition-bound Arab mind," he concludes, "there is even something sinful in engaging in long-range planning, because it seems to imply that one does not put one's trust in divine providence. . . . The improvidence of the fellah has been for centuries a contributing factor to their impoverishment."[50]

To counter these oversimplifications, I wish to make the following arguments:

First, opposite and conflicting orientations are easily detected in Arab culture. Thus, one can refer to the Qur'an, religious traditions, quotes, proverbs, anecdotes, expressions, etc., to demonstrate that Arabs also emphasize free will. One of the most popular expressions of the Algerian revolution was the Koranic statement, "God does not change what is in a people unless they change themselves" (*surat al-Rad*:11). In a similar vein are the common quotations "Thus does God make clear His signs to you in order that you may understand" (*surat al-Baqara*:242), "And know that God is strict in punishment" (*surat al-Baqara*:196), implying individual responsibility for one's acts, and "Let there be no compulsion in religion" (*surat al-Baqara*:256). Equally important is the fact that there are different interpretations of Islam. Abdul Rahman al-Kawakibi defined the concept of fate itself to mean "strife and work" (*Inna al-Qada' wa al-Qadar Human al-Sai wa al-Amal*).[51] Not unlike other religions and in spite of its specificity, Islam lends itself to different interpretations according to the needs and the situations of the believers.

In the realm of proverbs and daily expressions, the diversity and contradictions are even greater. An Arab can easily refer to several proverbs that assert human free will and responsibility. For mere illustration, the following may be mentioned:

- Whoever toils will achieve.
- Livelihood is management.
- He who does not sow does not harvest.
- Hope without effort is a tree without fruits.
- Only he who goes to the market will buy and sell.
- God says, "Help yourself so I may help you."
- Don't blame anyone but yourself.
- He who exposes himself to death has no one to blame but himself.
- Think things out first and then rely on God.

These are only a few of many of the popular sayings. Some others are most sarcastic of fatalistic attitudes:

- Sit on a beehive and say this is fate.
- They told Jeha to seek livelihood at God's gate, and he went and sat at the door of the bakery.

Arab poetry is another very rich source of expressions of fatalism as well as free will. Two of the most popular passages of Arab poetry are:

> We walked our predestined course,
> And whoever's course is written
> Will have to walk it.
> Not every human wish is fulfilled
> The wind may blow contrary to sailors' desire.

Equally popular lines of poetry express free human will:

> The greater the strife the greater the achievement,
> And whoever aspires at high aims
> Will have to toil day and night,
> And whoever demands glory without effort
> Wasted will be his life in asking for the impossible.
> If the people ever wanted life,
> Fate will inevitably have to respond.
> Inevitably, night will have to clear
> And the chain will have to break.

Second, explicit expressions of fatalism do not always imply submission, resignation, or rejection of personal responsibility. For early and present revolutionary Muslims, fate is understood to mean having to struggle to change reality. Many Arabs today consider it their fate to fight until they achieve liberation and build a new order. Upon hearing of the assassination of his comrade, the renowned Palestinian writer Ghassan Kanafani, George Habash reportedly said, "That is our fate." By this he meant that those who engage in struggle to liberate their country know beforehand that they risk death.

In this respect, statements indicating fatalism need to be interpreted in light of their social context or of the particular occasions on which they are made. In the novel *Midaq Alley* by Naguib Mahfuz, Hamida faces certain death when her fiancé finds her with a British soldier in a tavern. She manages to escape by arguing that though she wishes to be faithful to her fiancé, God must have chosen a different destiny for her. This fatalistic expression, used as a mechanism of avoiding death, should not be interpreted at face value as a rejection of personal responsibility. In another novel by the same author, a young woman asserts her strong will and defiance by refusing the advances of a powerful man, even though he threatens to destroy her future unless she surrenders to him. She badly needs his support, but she responds, "My future is not in your hand; it is in God's hands." Here, fatalism means self-assertion.

Proverbs or expressions indicating fatalism thus often serve as mechanisms of adjustment to specific situations. To interpret them in absolute terms or at their face value might give them the opposite meaning. To grasp their real rather than explicit significance, we will have to explain them in terms of the actual functions they serve under particular circumstances. They need to be examined as social psychological mechanisms of dealing with human reality.

Shame and Guilt

Western scholars have often claimed that one of the greatest distinctions between the Arab and the Western value orientations is the greater emphasis in Arab culture on shame than on guilt. The emphasis is considered so pronounced that Arab society has been referred to as the "shame society."[52] According to Patai's much quoted *Arab Mind,* "what pressures the Arab to behave in an honorable manner is not guilt but shame, or, more precisely, the psychological drive to escape or prevent negative judgment by others."[53] Harold W. Glidden (formerly of the Bureau of Intelligence of the U.S. Department of State) once tried to explain what he called "the hostility of the Arab collectivity toward Israel" by pointing out that this Arab attitude "is governed by two key emotions inherent in the Arab culture. Their defeat by Israel brought them shame, which can only be eliminated by revenge."[54] To further simplify the issue to the experts of the Department of State and his American readers, Glidden engaged in the following generalizations:

> Conformity brings honor and social prestige. . . . Failure to conform, however, brings shame. Shame is intensely feared among the Arabs, and this fear is so pervasive that Arab society has been labeled a shame-oriented one. This contrasts sharply with Judaism and with Western Christian societies, which are guilt-oriented. . . . Shame is eliminated by revenge. It is difficult to describe the depth of the Arab's emotional need for revenge, but suffice it to say that Islam itself found it necessary to sanction revenge. . . . Therefore all members of the Arab collectivity are bound to support the cause of their kinsmen, the Palestine Arabs. . . . This is the vengeance that the Arabs feel must be taken not only to restore to the Palestine Arabs what was wrongfully taken from them, but to eliminate the shame that had been visited on them and the other Arabs by their defeats by Israel. Many Westerners and Israelis think that since Israel has more than once demonstrated that it is objectively stronger than the Arabs, the only rational thing for the Arabs to do is to make peace. But for the Arabs the situation is not governed by this kind of logic, for objectivity is not a value in the Arab system. For the Arabs, defeat does not generate a desire for peace; instead, it produces an emotional need for revenge.[55]

Glidden seems to have totally forgotten the American reaction to the attack on Pearl Harbor, the "Day of Infamy" and the declaration of war against Japan. Moreover, Israel's harsh treatment of the Palestinian Arabs, and the refusal of both major Israeli political parties to offer restitution of rights and property of which the Palestinians have been dispossessed by Israel, is hardly compatible with his notion that Israel is a "guilt-oriented" society. Glidden also seems to have forgotten that the concept of other-directedness which he considers to be "characteristic of both the Arab tradition and of the outlook of Islam" (p. 98) was first developed by David Riesman in *The Lonely Crowd* to describe the most dominant cultural trend in American society, which Riesman contrasted to the tradition-oriented and the inner-oriented trends. To the extent these concepts are relevant to Arab and Islamic cultures, it would have been much more accurate to describe them as tradition oriented.

Maybe such self-explanatory oversimplifications and distortions do not deserve so much emphasis. On the other hand, there seems to be a need in American and Israeli societies to believe them. Besides being repeated so often by scholarly works, the guilt/shame dichotomy has forcefully invaded the media and popular literary writings. Erica Jong's uninhibited novel *Fear of Flying* offers one example:

> Arabs, I thought, goddamned Arabs. What a disproportionate sense
> of guilt I had over all my petty sexual transgressions! Yet there were
> people in the world, plenty of them, who did what they felt like and
> never had a moment's guilt over it—as long as they didn't get caught.
> Why had I been cursed with such a hypertrophied superego? Was it
> just being Jewish? . . . Is it any wonder that everyone hates the Jews for
> giving the world guilt?[56]

An objective assessment would show, in fact, that Arabs exhibit both
shame- and guilt-oriented behavior. Arabs do not necessarily feel guilty
for the same reasons Westerners may. They feel a great deal of guilt when
they violate internalized values and expectations—when for instance they
disappoint their parents, especially their mothers. They also feel guilty
if they neglect their friends, or harm innocent people, or promote themselves at the expense of others and the country. Many Arabs living abroad
(e.g., in the US) may experience great feelings of guilt for forsaking their
countries, particularly in times of distress.

The shame/guilt and fatalism/free will dichotomies have been described in such detail to underscore the need for a dynamic rather than
a static, mechanical approach, and the need for an Arab perspective of
the study of Arab culture. Since the scope and limitations of the present
paper do not allow for a detailed description of all the other value
orientations. I will be brief in presenting those that remain.

Conformity and Creativity

Von Grunebaum argues that originality is not so highly prized in the
Muslim world as in the West:

> The Arab's unimaginative mind and his sober realism, his powers of
> accurate observation, his exactitude . . . are all accommodated by the
> pattern of Islamic civilization. The formalism of the religious approach
> is repeated in literature, even in science. Throughout the great age of
> Arabic literature the critics placed verbal perfection above poetical
> originality. . . . Inherited forms were faithfully preserved.[57]

Similarly, Morroe Berger observes of conventional speech that by "providing ready made phrases, it obviates the need for thought and originality, and encourages the treatment of every situation in a traditional,
familiar manner."[58]
Such conclusions can be reached only by overlooking the ongoing
struggle in Arab culture between what Taha Hussein calls the old and
the new. This particular battle was explored by the poet-critic Adonis in
a monumental study of Arab-Islamic culture entitled *al-Thabit wa al-*

Mutahawwil (The Permanent and the Changing).[59] In this three-volume work, Adonis stresses the contradictions and conflicts between two basic cultural trends in Arab history—the creative and the conformist. These two opposed currents manifest themselves in the religious, political, ideological, and literary aspects of Arab culture. In most periods of Arab history, there has existed a modernist trend that rejects the prevailing traditions and the static values. The creative and the innovative trend aspire to change the world and create a new mode of thinking and literary expression.

Mainstream Western scholars of Arab society have ignored this struggle. By doing so, they take into account only the conventional values, which emphasize conformity over creativity and *naql* (traditional authoritative transmission) over *aql* (reasoning). Hence the monodimensionality of their thought.

Past-Oriented and Future-Oriented Values

The above observations on conformity and creativity clearly apply to this distinction between the past-oriented and future-oriented values. The same sort of debate has taken place with regard to the ongoing battles between *salafiyyah* (traditionalism), which sees the past as the most appropriate model transcending the prevailing conditions, and modernization, which calls for a new model based on present needs and shaped by aspirations for the future. The principle of modernization calls for liberal or revolutionary changes instead of regression into the past.

This sort of struggle is not merely cultural. On the contrary, it is an integral part of a more comprehensive socioeconomic and political crisis. For the purpose of overcoming problems of underdevelopment, for example, there are those who resort to the past, those who try to reconcile the old and the new, and those who reject the past and seek to establish a totally new order.

Form and Content

Arab culture is often characterized as emphasizing form rather than content, or words at the expense of meaning. This orientation, it is asserted, is particularly apparent in Arab attitudes and relationships to language. Assessments of these attitudes and relationships are made by such scholars as Albert Hourani and Jacques Berque. The latter observes that "the East is the home of the word," that "the Arab language scarcely belongs to the world of men; rather, it seems to be lent to them," and that Arabic writing is "more suggestive than informative."[60] The former began his *Arab Thought in the Liberal Age* with the statement that Arabs are "more conscious of their language than any people in the world."

Exaggerated or not, such statements and many others to the same effect depict the peculiar relationship between Arabs and their language. Like any other relationship, it may have negative or positive consequences, depending on specific conditions. In times of national crisis, Arabs themselves have been most critical. A character in my novel *Awdat al-Ta'ir ila al-Bahr* (translated as *Days of Dust*) says in a reflective, angry mood following the defeat of June 1967:

> Words are the only weapon we know how to use. Our houses are of words, our castles are of dreams, our dreams are of words. Words are what we export. And we have an odd relationship with them: We invent them, but in the long run they gain control over us and re-create us as they wish. The created becomes the creator, the creator the created . . . We eat words, we drink words. We live in words. We kill ourselves with words.[61]

Such a relationship is not constant. It is not part of the nature of the Arab language or of the nature of the Arab. What it truly reflects is impoverishment of Arab culture in a specific historical period. An overly static interpretation of this phenomenon can only distort the role of language in Arab culture.

E. Shouby, a psychologist with training in both clinical and social psychology, explores the influence that the Arabic language exerts upon the psychology of Arabs without making any attempt to specify the period or the historical conditions. Hence his absolute freedom to make oversimplified generalizations about some aspects of this influence on "the psychology of the literate Arab: general vagueness of thought, overemphasis on the psychological significance of the linguistic symbols at the expense of their meanings; stereotyped emotional responses, overassertion and exaggeration; and two levels of life."[62]

In addressing himself to each of these various aspects, Shouby makes the following sweeping statements:

> Naturally, Arabic that deals with simple or familiar questions creates no difficulties; but the more novel or abstract the content, the more difficult it is to understand Arabic with accuracy. Words and even sentences may be transmitted, not as units but as whole structures, from one context to an entirely different one without sufficient modification (or even without modification at all) (p. 291). A successful Arab writer, so long as he pays attention to the grammatical and the idiomatic aspects of his writing, has only to make it diffusely comprehensible . . . Instead of manipulating the linguistic tools to make them convey his thought

and ideas in an appropriate manner, he frees his thoughts to accommodate themselves to the ready-made linguistic structures which he borrows from general use (p. 293).
The tendency to fit the thought to the word . . . rather than the word
to the thought is a result of the psychological replacement of the
thoughts by words, the words becoming the substitutes for thoughts,
and not their representative (p. 295).

The Arabic language, in fact, lends itself to all sorts of styles of writing.
The more successful Arab writers accept the classical definition of eloquence as "what is brief and denotative" (*al-balagha hiya ma qalla wa dalla*).
The other sets of Arab value orientations (culture of the mind vs.
culture of the heart, open vs. closed mindedness, obedience vs. rebellion,
charity vs. justice, collectivity vs. individuality, vertical vs. horizontal values, religious vs. secular, in-group vs. out-group) need not be pursued
here. The intention in this paper has been to identify the shortcomings
and biases of the static view and to propose a dynamic approach which
examines Arab culture in its social and historical contexts. In all instances,
the static approach fails to take account of the transitional nature of
contemporary Arab culture. Hence its tendency to overlook cultural
contradictions, struggle, and change.

The question is not merely one of difference, variation, or pluralism.
Essentially, the intensity of the cultural struggle between opposed forces
requires a comprehensive rather than a one-dimensional analysis of Arab
reality in modern times. Such an examination would have to start with a
framework of analysis which recognizes rather than dismisses the contradictions between the dominant culture, the subcultures, and the counter-
cultures of a vibrant society seeking to transcend itself. What characterizes present Arab society is this very intense struggle between opposed
orientations rather than any one of them on its own, no matter how
dominant it may be at a particular moment of modern Arab history.

IV. Conclusion: Beyond the Always and the Never

Several areas other than national character, socialization, and cultural
value orientations need to be examined in future social psychological
studies of the Arab world. Issues of attitudes and attitudinal change,
group dynamics, social interaction and interpersonal relations, social
power, social roles, problem-solving, and social perception have received
less attention than they deserve from either Western or Arab scholars.
The few attempts to apply some of those social psychological concepts

and notions to the study of Arab society have remained faithful to the static approach I have outlined in this paper.

In the area of attitudes and attitudinal change, the emphasis of too many studies has been on resistance to rather than the struggle for change. According to Lerner, "modernity is primarily a state of mind— expectation of progress, propensity to growth, readiness to adapt oneself to change."[63] Central to the process of change in this view is "an inner mechanism" which makes it possible "to see oneself in the other fellow's situation." It is this "empathic capacity" as a "personal style" or "personality mechanism" that determines modernization.[64] The question for him thus becomes, how can change take place "in a land inflamed by Arab nationalism and primitive xenophobia?"[65]

The Orientalist static approach locates resistance to change in a conservative perspective which defines "Islamic history" as the "history of a community in the process of realizing a divinely ordained pattern of society."[66] A prominent scholar such as von Grunebaum could allow himself to use such nonqualifying terms as "never" and "always" in his statements that "Islam has always been . . ." so and so, that "the consciousness of being an epigone never left the Muslim intellectual," that "throughout the great age of Arab literature the critics placed verbal perfection above poetical originality," that "Islamic constitutional law never limited the power of the ruler," that "the Bedouin never considers himself inferior to his leader," and that "it was only with Napoleon's expedition to Egypt (in 1798) that . . . Muslim civilization regained willingness to change."[67]

A dynamic critical approach to the study of attitudes would focus on social relationships rather than fixed characteristics and would examine the process of change in its historical context. By focusing on socioeconomic and political structures, we would realize that modernization is essentially a state of the society and its institutions and groups rather than merely a state of mind. A change in attitudes requires a change in the substructures that give rise to these attitudes and the values from which they derive.

What has preoccupied Arabs in the last century and a half has not been a wish for continuity and perpetuation of the dominant order, but for the achievement of change. This is easily detected in attempts at Arab analytical self-understanding. The works of Adonis, Sharabi, Jabri, Khatibi, Laroui, Arkoun, al-'Alim, al-'Azm and several others emphasize dynamism and continuous struggle as a result of complex contradictions rather than inner consistency and coherence within Arab culture. Hence the need to go beyond the always and the never in order to explore a society undergoing a process of renewal and transcendence. This is surely not an impossible task.

Notes

1. Halim Barakat, *Al-Mujtama' al-'Arabi al-Mu'asir* (Contemporary Arab Society) (Beirut: Markaz Dirasat al-Wihdah al-'Arabiyyah, 1984).

2. Raphael Patai, *The Arab Mind* (New York: Charles Scribner's Sons, 1973).

3. Sania Hamady, *Temperament and Character of the Arabs* (New York: Twayne, 1960).

4. Fuad M. Moughrabi, "The Arab Basic Personality: A Critical Survey of the Literature," *International Journal of Middle East Studies* (1978):99–112.

5. El-Sayyid Yassin, *al-Shakhsiyyah al-'Arabiyyah* (Arab Personality) (Beirut: Dar al-Tanwir, 1981).

6. Raphael Patai, *op. cit.*, p. 3.

7. *Ibid.*, p. x.

8. *Ibid.*, p. 18.

9. Raphael Patai, *Society, Culture and Change in the Middle East* (Philadelphia: University of Pennsylvania Press, 1962), p. 3.

10. *Ibid.*, p. 381.

11. *Ibid.*, p. 359.

12. Morroe Berger, *The Arab World Today* (New York: Doubleday Anchor, 1964).

13. Morroe Berger, *op. cit.*, p. 136.

14. Janet Abu-Lughod, "The Islamic City—Historic Myth, Islamic Essence, and Contemporary Relevance," *International Journal of Middle East Studies* 19, no. 2 (May 1987), p. 155.

15. Edward Said, *Orientalism* (New York: Pantheon Books, 1978), p. 5.

16. E. Terry Prothro and Levon Melikian, "The California Public Opinion Scale in an Authoritarian Culture," *Public Opinion Quarterly* 17 (Fall 1953), p. 355.

17. *Ibid.*, p. 355.

18. *Ibid.*, p. 361.

19. *Ibid.*, p. 360.

20. Levon H. Melikian, "Authoritarianism and its Correlates in the Egyptian Culture and in the United States," *Journal of Social Issues* 15, no. 3 (1959), p. 58.

21. *Ibid.*, p. 58.

22. George H. Gardner, "The Arab Middle East: Some Background Interpretations," *Journal of Social Issues* 15, no. 3 (1959), p. 24.

23. Hamed Ammar, *Growing Up in an Egyptian Village* (London: Routledge and Kegan Paul, 1954), p. xi.

24. Hamed Ammar, *Fi Bina' al-Bashar: Dirasat fi al-Taghir al-Hadari wa al-Fikr al-Tarbayyi* (On the Building of Human Beings: Studies on Civilizational Change and Educational Thought) (Sirs Allayan Publication, 1964), pp. 79–91.

25. Sadiq Jalal al-'Azm, *al-Naqd al-Dhati Ba'd al-Hazimah* (Self-Criticism After the Defeat) (Beirut: Dar al-Tali'ah, 1968), pp. 69–89.

26. Fouad M. Moughrabi, *op. cit.*, p. 105.

27. *Ibid.*, p. 109.

28. Yassin, *op. cit.*, especially pp. 59–60.

29. *Ibid.*, p. 65.

30. *Ibid.*, p. 216.

31. T. E. Prothro, *Child-Rearing in Lebanon* (Cambridge: Harvard Middle Eastern Monograph Series VIII, 1961); Hilma Granqvist, *Birth and Childhood Among Arabs* (Helsingfors: Söderstrom, 1947); Hamed Ammar, *Growing Up in an Egyptian Village* ; Horace M. Miner and George de Vos, *Algerian Culture and Personality in Change* (Ann Arbor: University of Michigan, 1960).

32. Raphael Patai, *The Arab Mind*, p. 25.

33. *Ibid.*, pp. 17, 26, 59.

34. *Ibid.*, p. 37.

35. *Ibid.*, p. 37.

36. Hamed Ammar, *Growing Up in an Egyptian Village*, p. 127.

37. *Ibid.*, p. 129.

38. Hisham Sharabi, *Muqaddamah li-Dirasat al-Mujtama' al-'Arabi* (Introduction to the Study of Arab Society) (Jerusalem: Salah al-Din, 1975), pp. 31–33.

39. *Ibid.*, p. 59.

40. Hisham Sharabi, *Neopatriarchy: A Theory of Distorted Change in Arab Society* (New York: Oxford University Press, 1988).

41. 'Ali Zayour, *al-Tahlil al-Nafsi lil-Zat al-'Arabiyyah* (Psychoanalysis of Arab Ego) (Beirut: Dar al-Tali'ah, 1977); and *Qita' al-Butulah wa al-Narjusiyyah fi al-Zat al-'Arabiyyah* (Aspects of Heroism and Narcissism in the Arab Ego) (Beirut: Dar al-Tali'ah, 1982).

42. For an in-depth discussion of social classes in the Arab world see Halim Barakat, *op. cit.*, pp. 131–69.

43. *Ibid.*, pp. 66–78.

44. *Ibid.*, pp. 78–89.

45. *Ibid.*, pp. 89–102.

46. G. E. von Grunebaum, *Islam: Essays in the Nature and Growth of a Cultural Tradition* (New York: Barnes and Noble, 1961), p. 67.

47. *Ibid.*, p. 70.

48. Raphael Patai, *The Arab Mind*, p. 147.

49. *Ibid.*, p. 148.

50. *Ibid.*, pp. 150–51.

51. 'Abdul-Rahman al-Kawakibi, *Al-'Amal al-Kamila* (Complete Works) (Beirut: al-Mu'assissah al-'Arabiyyah lil-Dirasat, 1975), p. 68.

52. See Raphael Patai, *The Arab Mind*, pp. 106–7, 111–12; David P. Ausubel, "Relationship Between Shame and Guilt in the Socialization Process," *Psychological Review* 62, no. 5 (Sept. 1955); Sania Hamady, *op. cit.*, pp. 34–39; Jean G. Peristiany, ed., *Honour and Shame: The Values of Mediterranean Society* (London: Weidenfeld and Nicolson, 1965); Harold W. Glidden, "The Arab World," *American Journal of Psychiatry* 128, no. 8 (February 1973).

53. Raphael Patai, *The Arab Mind*, p. 106.

54. Harold W. Glidden, *op. cit.*, p. 98.

55. *Ibid.*, pp. 98–100.

56. Erica Jong, *Fear of Flying* (New York: Signet Books, 1973), p. 245.

57. G. E. von Grunebaum, *op. cit.*, p. 67.

58. Morroe Berger, *op. cit.*, p. 155.

59. Adonis, *Al-Thabit wa al-Mutahawwil: Bahth fi al-Itiba' wa-Ibda' 'ind al-'Arab* (The Permanent and the Changing: A Study of Arab Conformity and Creativity) (Beirut: Dar al-'Awdah, 1974–1978).

60. Jacques Berque, *The Arabs: Their History and Future*, trans. by Jean Stewart (London: Faber and Faber, 1964), pp. 25, 191, 51.

61. Halim Barakat, *Days of Dust* (Washington, DC: Three Continents Press, 1983), p. 126.

62. E. Shouby, "The Influence of the Arabic Language on the Psychology of the Arabs," *Middle East Journal* 5, no. 3 (1951), p. 291.

63. Daniel Lerner, *The Passing of Traditional Society: Modernizing in the Middle East* (Glencoe, Il.: Free Press, 1958), p. viii.

64. *Ibid.*, p. 49–50.

65. *Ibid.*, p. 77.

66. Manfred Halpern, *The Politics of Social Change in the Middle East and North Africa* (Princeton, N.J.: Princeton University Press, 1963), p. 119.

67. G. E. von Grunebaum, *op. cit.*, pp. 29, 67–71, 74–75.

5

The Contemporary Sociology of the Middle East: An Assessment

Samih K. Farsoun and Lisa Hajjar

I. Introduction: A Sociology of Middle East Sociology

The sociology of the Middle East can be characterized as both undeveloped and underdeveloped. The discipline shares this with the sociology of much of the non-Western world. Modern sociological applications to the Middle East suffer from the problems of adapting Western-specific intellectual constructs to non-Western societies. Modern sociology, which was developed to study the West's own unique sociohistorical transformation, has often been applied to the Middle East mechanically and ahistorically, creating greater mystification rather than understanding of the structure and dynamics of the region's societies.

The social sciences were developed by Europeans in the post-Enlightenment period to enable them better to understand their own societies and consequently the societies that fell under their imperial control. The theoretical and methodological approaches developed for European self-comprehension, as well as for colonial domination, were historically situated but were reified as scientific and universal. European military, political, and economic hegemony was so thoroughly translated into intellectual hegemony that even the post–World War II liberation of colonies in the political and economic spheres has not led to a comprehensive decolonization of the social sciences. The social sciences have certainly evolved, diversified, and been transformed. But the underlying theoretical premises remain, to varying degrees, Eurocentric and thus not readily universalizable for the study of all societies, particularly non-Western societies.

Western intellectual hegemony, like its political and economic counterparts, has been a totally pervasive and overwhelming fact, perhaps nowhere more strongly than in the study of the Middle East. Orientalism,

the discipline that was developed in the nineteenth century to comprehend the non-Occidental world, preceded the development of the modern social sciences and therefore has acted as a preconditioning "schema-
tizing and dehistoricizing"[1] factor in the study of the Middle East.
According to Edward Said, Orientalism is not merely an "objective" field
of study but also "a corporate institution for dealing with the Orient"[2] in
association with imperial power. Orientalism has been maintained in
part by virtue of the self-authenticating and self-legitimizing citationary
method used by Orientalist scholars.

While Orientalism has lost substantial ground in Chinese, Indian, and
other oriental and African studies, it has retained great force in Middle
East and Islamic studies. The fusion of Orientalism with modern social
science and history has allowed social scientists and historians to continue
to deploy many elements of Orientalism. This is all the more remarkable,
given the various intellectual upheavals across the disciplinary spectrum.
In the discipline of sociology, Orientalism has earned a new lease on life
in the guise of modern social science of the Middle East. Central to the
reproduction and strengthening of Orientalism is the ideologization of
Middle East studies due to the American thrust into the region and to
Western support for Israel in the Arab-Israeli conflict.[3]

The social sciences are part and parcel of the world order, through
which the developed nations and their institutional infrastructures continue to dominate and shape that order. Paradigms of social structure
and social change, of economic development and of associated values,
ideologies, and institutions have been exported to the Third World regions in the context of Western economic, political, military, and ideological penetration into those areas. Ideas and models of socioeconomic
change, no less than commodities and armaments, have been packaged
for export. Conceptions of social, economic, and political development
have been exported through institutional means. Besides the World Bank
and the International Monetary Fund, academic institutions aid in this
exportation process by training indigenous leaders, policymakers, and
intellectuals in the acceptance and use of the paradigms based upon
capitalist development, free trade, and privatization. These paradigms
have become the models by which many Third World (including Arab)
intellectuals and policymakers view and understand the nature of their
own societies and plan their development.[4]

We have categorized sociological approaches to the Middle East into
five major genres: (1) Orientalist idealist; (2) modernizationist functionalist; (3) eclectic; (4) dependency perspective; and (5) a critical approach
incorporating varieties of Marxist and other critical theoretical formulations. Marxism and dependency theory have often been combined in

materialist studies, yet theoretically they remain divergent. This paper will review and assess the theoretical and methodological contributions of selected examples of each tendency.

The number of professional sociologists practicing their craft in the field of Middle Eastern studies is quite small. Their output in both quantity and quality has been modest. Thus, much of what can be considered as sociological writing on the Middle East emanates from outside the discipline of sociology. This chapter will focus on studies relevant to understanding Middle Eastern society(ies), in a selective rather than comprehensive way, including works by scholars who are not considered professional sociologists, but whose studies incorporate analyses of Arab societies and culture.

The issues that sociology of the Middle East deals with derive directly from the concerns that inform the sociology of Western urban industrial societies. And yet while the sociology of the Occident emphasizes one aspect—the problem of order, of structure—the sociology of the (Middle Eastern) Orient focuses on the problem of social change. In the post–World War II era, change in the Third World became the watchword not only for the social science analysts and foreign-policy makers of the Western world, but also for the indigenous intelligentsia and political leadership of the Third World. The theme of social change permeated the analysis of all aspects of society and at all levels. But as we will see below, "social change" in the Third World had a special meaning and special direction: socioeconomic development along Western capitalist lines. The sociology of development in the sense of an analytical search for the factors obstructing and conditions facilitating the process became popular and central. This overarching theme of development (sometimes called modernization or even Westernization) yielded specific studies on industrialization and urbanization.[5] It also yielded some analysis of changes in the patterns of stratification, especially the rise of a new modernizing middle class—a key concept in this development-minded formulation pertaining to change and modernity.

Derivative of the theme of change were value and normative changes, including secularization and the demise of community, and therefore the crises of social identity and societal integration. Here again factors preserving primordial values and ties were contrasted to undeveloped and inefficient "modern" social institutions unable to integrate the individual into the national society. As important, finally, were the hypothesized decay of family structure and the kin-based idiom of social organization and change into an isolated nuclear unit. Commensurate with the analysis of the presumed "modernization" of family structure were studies of intra-family dynamics, especially gender relations and child-rearing practices. Child-rearing studies in particular, like many of the other social psychological analyses, were serious efforts to assess the relationship between the personality structure of Arabs and their socioeconomic development.[6] In short, the theme of change has dominated the discourse of sociology of the Middle East up to the present.

Middle East sociology reflected closely the research and methodological practices of the Western discipline. Despite the overwhelming problems of validity and reliability, a very large number of surveys on the attitudes and behavior of Middle Eastern individuals were conducted. The scales and techniques of analysis, while very sophisticated, often suffered from serious methodological shortcomings. These surveys also reflected the interest in the theme of change.

This theme of social change continues to inform contemporary sociology of the Middle East. However its foci have shifted so that macro-sociological issues have come to predominate, as do derivative issues of structural dislocations/transformation. Thus, the scope, function, and nature of the state and state-society relations—in this sense political sociology—have emerged as central concerns of the 1980s. This general macro-emphasis in part has been encouraged by the emergence of new macro-theoretical perspectives in the sociology of both the West and the Third World, including the Middle East. Accordingly, the focus of our chapter is the macro-sociological study of Middle Eastern society(ies) and the nature and direction of social change. In short, our concern is the study of how the social-science literature views the structure of Middle East society(ies) as a whole. This, we believe, will afford us the best method for evaluating the theoretical paradigms of the sociology of the Middle East.

II. From Orientalist Sociology to Sociology of Religion

Orientalism is a perspective of long standing. Its impact on the sociology of the Islamic Middle East has been a determining factor in the conceptualization of the social dynamics, institutions, and typologies of those societies. To begin with, Orientalism's special view of Islamic societies in the past and present is unique, in contrast to its perspective on other Oriental societies, not to mention the West. Unlike Confucian China, Hindu India, Christian Europe, and Catholic Latin America, the Islamic societies of the Middle East are conceptualized principally in terms of the dominant role of religion. The former's histories are not treated as the history of Hinduism, Confucianism, Catholicism, or Christianity in the way that Middle Eastern history is conventionally viewed as the history of Islam.

It is arguable that the reason for this emphasis on Islam is that the religious impulse in all the other monotheisms has been largely secularized, whereas Islam continues to be a powerful religious force. Regardless of whether or not Islam is more strongly relevant to the internal dynamics of Middle Eastern society(ies) than religion is in other societies, Middle East studies reflect the theoretical assumption that the role of religion in society differs uniquely between Islam and all the other religions. Consider, for example, Ernest Gellner's opening statement in his book *Muslim Society*: "Islam is the blueprint of a social order."[7] Two paragraphs later he writes: "Judaism and Christianity are also blueprints of a social order, but rather less so than Islam." While this may very well be true, societies that profess Christianity are not analyzed as Christian societies. Israel, for example, is usually analyzed as a secular society, albeit it is commonly referred to as "the Jewish state." The latter term merely identifies the religious profession of the majority of its population, not some specific Jewish theory or practice of rule or statehood.

In short, Islam, in contrast to all major world religions, is deemed to shape the structure and history of the societies of the people who profess it. Islam is seen as totalitarian in its scope, organizing all aspects of society. In other words, Orientalism explicitly proposes that an ideological factor (the Islamic religion) *determines* the sociopolitical and economic structure of Middle Eastern society(ies) historically and into the present. This idealist perspective of society and history is the essential foundation of Orientalist cosmology: its methodology, theoretical posture, and intellectual dilemmas. Consider as an example Reuben Levy's *The Social Structure of Islam*[8] (the first edition of which was titled *The Sociology of Islam*). He presents a picture of classical "Islamic society" based on a textual reading of the Qur'an and the hadith placed in the broad sweep of Islamic history. The thrust of this book is that Islamic law (the Qur'an) and practice (the *hadith*) *determine* social structure and that this causes the unchanging character of Islamic society.

Orientalism's reliance on textual reading as a method to construct the social structure of Islamic Middle Eastern society(ies) gives these structures an air of static, eternal permanence uninfluenced by historical change, except, perhaps, the consequence of external factors, such as contact with the West. This is what Talal Asad calls the essentialist conception of Islam. It is as if historical Middle Eastern societies were self-contained, isolated from external relations, frozen in an immobile dynamic, and unchanging before their incorporation into the modern world system.

This essentialist conception of the stasis and permanence of Islamic social structures is expressed in various ways. For example, the "Islamic family" is analyzed by Arthur Jeffrey[9] in terms of the Qur'anic-hadith textual prescriptions without any reference to empirical variations of the family structure according to country, class, ethnicity, etc., or to historical period or context. Other more unsavory social features are also seen as essential and eternal attributes of Islamic society. Ralph Coury notes:

> One of the most pernicious and long-lived thematics of Western Orientalism has centered on the conviction that Islam and Islamic society are by nature totalitarian . . . a closed society in which force and violence and those who wield them are sanctified by religious and political traditions . . . [or] that Islam would not allow rational argument.[10]

Coury then proceeds to show the recurrence of these themes in the works of W. C. Smith, Kenneth Cragg, Stanley Diamond, Shlomo Avineri, and Mattityahu Peled.[11] This theme of centuries of stagnation underpins historical writings on specific "Islamic societies." P. Glavanis's critique of P. J. Vatikiotis's *Modern History of Egypt* shows how Vatikiotis "reproduces the view that the essential characteristics of the [Egyptian] Islamic political community are fundamentally unchangeable . . . [in the context of] the distinctive and enduring character of Egyptian society":[12] Not only is Egyptian society and polity static, "it is the *consciousness* of the Egyptian, which is overwhelmingly Muslim, that *determines* the nature of the political community in Egypt."[13]

Another essentialist view of Islamic society in Orientalist cosmology is the segmentary model of "mosaic or patchwork structures of tribes, religious minorities, social groups and associations."[14] According to this paradigm, these social elements are typically isolated from one another and are self-contained. Hence Islamic society is viewed as a complex structure of social groupings divided vertically along religious, sectarian, ethnic, occupational (guild), and tribal lines, but not horizontally along class lines. The mosaic is held together and integrated from above by a despotic state (Oriental despotism) which arbitrates, balances, and harmonizes the differing interests of the subparts of the social mosaic. This structure is not only writ large in society but also expressed in the ecological patterns of the Muslim city.[15] Examples of this view include H. A. R. Gibb and H. Bowen's *Islamic Society and the West*,[16] and Gabriel Baer's *Population and Society in the Arab East.*[17] This dualistic conceptualization of Islamic society (mosaic social structure and Oriental despotism), supposed to constitute the root of stagnation, is seen by Bryan Turner as the foundation of Marx's conception of the non-Western societies: the Asiatic mode of production.[18]

In spite of the title of his book, *Muslim Society*, Gellner actually does *not* invoke explicitly the Orientalist thesis that religion (Islam) determines (North African) social structure. Gellner focuses on the *nature* and *role* of the religion of Islam *in* a complex (pastoral-tribal, sedentary-urban North African) society. His main point is that Islam (in North Africa) embraces various types of social structure. To explain the two styles of religious life, he argues that they are embedded in two types of social organization: segmentary-tribal pastoral and urban mercantile in centralized but weak states. In the pre-modern period, however, "Islamic" (North African) society reiterates "a-rotation-within-an-immobile-structure": a pendular pattern rather than a linear type of social transformation. This, of course, changes in post-traditional Islam as a consequence of contact with the West, including the rise of strong central states.

When he attempts to explain contemporary ("post-traditional") forms in Islam, Gellner reverts more explicitly to another Orientalist theme by reasserting the thesis of the homogeneity of all Muslim societies: "For all the indisputable diversity, the remarkable thing is the extent to which Muslim societies resemble each other."[19] Gellner finds this homogeneity puzzling, especially in the absence of a central authority on faith (i.e., a church). He contends that the elements that constitute the "Islamic social syndrome fall into two main groups: the ecological/technological, and the ideological."[20] The ideological is illustrated by his analysis of the bases of "Islamic" legitimation. Gellner's analysis fails to take into consideration or explain the emergence of nonreligious-based legitimation in Arab and other nations in the modern Middle East[21] and the varying degrees of separation-linkage between religion and state in the various societies whose populations profess Islam: for example, Saudi Arabia as compared to Turkey.

Although Gellner does not elaborate on the role of Islam in the emergence of modern Arab society, he nevertheless poses the classic Weberian problematic of religion, rationality, and capitalism:

> By various obvious criteria—universalism, scripturalism, spiritual egalitarianism, the extension of full participation in the sacred community not to one, or some, but to *all*, and the rational systematization of social life—Islam is, of the three great Western monotheisms, the one closest to modernity.[22]

Contradicting Weber's conclusions, Gellner contends that the patterns of scripturalist puritanism and hierarchical ecstatic mediationism found in Islam may explain both why it was not the birthplace of industrial society and why in the end Islam may be the most suitable to industrialism.[23]

While Gellner only touches on the Weberian problematic, it is directly addressed by Maxime Rodinson in *Islam and Capitalism*.[24] This book was an early step toward the deconstruction of Orientalist myths concerning Islam's role in the formation of social and economic structures of Muslim society. *Islam and Capitalism* is commonly viewed as an attack on Weber's thesis on religion and capitalism, but that is only one aspect of its analysis. Rodinson reexamines Islamic history, socioeconomic formations, and the ideological currents of the Muslim world in a political economy framework.

Rodinson confronts directly the issue of whether Islam was an obstacle to capitalist development in the Muslim world. He presents the argument that Islam was not the determining factor in the Muslim world's failure to achieve capitalism by critically deconstructing the Orientalism of Weber's and Marx's conceptions of Muslim society. Historically, the Muslim world clearly had a strong capitalistic sector based on commerce and merchant capital. In fact, the density of commercial relations based on private capital gave the Muslim world the most highly developed capitalistic sector in history up to the sixteenth century. Since Marx argued strongly for the importance of commerce and merchant capital as a necessary precedent for capitalism, why did this sector not become predominant and lead to full capitalism as in Europe?

To form a conclusion to this question in terms of the nature of Islam is to base the argument on ideological rather than materialist factors. Rodinson shows that Islam is not monolithic and is perfectly capable of adapting to the changing economic needs of society—in Weberian terminology, of rationalizing itself. Rodinson's purpose is to refute the conception of ideology as a causal factor in economic development. Rather, he argues, religious ideology and practice are conditioned by social realities. For him the development of capitalism was due to "conjunctures of events and the more or less permanent factors. . . . If primitive accumulation of capital [in Muslim society] never attained the European level—all this was due to factors quite other than the Muslim religion."[25]

Rodinson's call for anchoring the analysis of religion in material social relations is not adopted by Clifford Geertz. In *Islam Observed*, Geertz defines the subject thus: "religion is a social institution, worship a social activity, and faith a social force."[26] His is a comparative study of social and religious transformation in the two geographical extremes of Islam: Morocco and Indonesia. He begins and concludes his book with an exposition of "the Moroccan man" as contrasted to "the Indonesian man," and Moroccan society ("strenuous, fluid, violent, visionary, devout, and unsentimental, but above all, self-assertive")[27] as opposed to Indonesian society ("the national archetype is the settled, industrious, rather inward plowman of twenty centuries, nursing his terrace, placating his neighbors and feeding his superiors").[28] In Indonesia the impact of Islam and Dutch colonialism had differential consequences on the various classes. The peasantry, for example, "folded back upon itself in a paroxysm of defensive solidarity"[29] causing a form of "cultural involution" and syncretic religious expression. In Morocco, Islamic orthodoxy became reaffirmed as a result of centuries of aggressive fundamentalism.

Like Gellner, Geertz gives much significance to the rise of the centralized activist nation-state and the parallel increase in influence of scriptural Islam. In both Indonesia and Morocco, religion took on an even more pivotal role as a result of colonialism: "Before, men had been Muslim as a matter of circumstance; now they were, increasingly, Muslims as a matter of policy. They were *oppositional* Muslims."[30]

But "in both Indonesia and Morocco, the prologue to nationalism coincides with the epilogue to scripturalism."[31] According to Geertz, the nation-state replaced religion as a means of identification and brought about the ideologization of religion. In short, although dealing with profoundly pivotal periods in the social history of the two societies, his focus, approach, and conclusions are conventional and reflect standard Western interpretation of the impact of the West on Islam.

An insightful analysis of Islam is provided by Michael Gilsenan in his book *Recognizing Islam: Religion and Society in the Modern Arab World.* The style and tone of this text offer a clear contrast to the patronizing approach of Geertz: *recognizing* Islam as opposed to Islam *observed.* Gilsenan forthrightly admits to a conscious attempt to *construct* the meanings of Islam in modern society. He introduces his subject as follows:

> I have come to write about . . . class opposition, groups and individuals using the same signs and codes but seeing events in quite different ways, concealed significances in social life, complex relations to wider historical changes in power relations and the economy. Finally, and not least, it draws attention to the danger of stereotypical images of another society and another religion.[32]

Gilsenan's text provides a vivid, detailed, and comparative analysis of the various aspects of the religious phenomenon placed squarely in the context of the broad political and economic processes which over the last century (at least) have integrated the societies that profess Islam into modern global history. He investigates the social meaning of the "hidden layers" and "concealed motions" of religion in relation to the socioeconomic and political transformations through the medium of new class formations. Accordingly, he identifies the social changes wrought within the varied societies he studied, especially the new classes, and assesses the meaning of Islam in these contexts. The portrait that emerges is complex, subtle, and contextual. As he notes in the conclusion: "Different and sometimes mutually exclusive apprehensions and practices of Islam are emerging that separate societies and classes as much as they unite them."[33]

Unlike Geertz with his broad sweep or Gellner with his model building, Gilsenan fleshes out some of Rodinson's theoretical questions and gives a more substantial appreciation of the role of Islam in modern Middle Eastern societies. All four authors differ substantially from Levy, with his classic Orientalism. The idealist underpinnings of Levy's approach have been progressively discarded: somewhat by Geertz, more by Gellner, and completely by Rodinson and Gilsenan. To use contemporary social science jargon, for Levy religion (Islam) is an independent variable determining all other social and political institutions, while for the latter four it is a phenomenon to be explained, a dependent variable. In this sense the progress of the discourse has been from Orientalism to sociology of religion.

In the decades prior to the 1980s, Islam as a political force attracted relatively little attention. Since the Islamic revolution in Iran, however, a new emphasis on the study of Islam by all types of Western social scientists has produced a vast literature. Much of this output is commissioned or inspired by government policy concerns and thus focuses on "radical Islam" in the narrow political sense. Ironically, prior to the Iranian revolution and its anti-Western rhetoric, political Islam and Islam as culture were seen by Western scholars and policymakers as a pro-Western countervailing force to radical (Arab) anti-imperialist secular nationalism. The conventional wisdom on Islam at that time emphasized its conservative religiosity and anticommunism.

The Iranian revolution and the rise of Arab, Turkish, and other Islamic political movements upset this simplistic political equation and undermined the received wisdom. Nevertheless, instead of being inspired to initiate a new and innovative discourse on Islam and the role of religion in modern Arab, Iranian, and other Muslim societies, many Western analysts merely revised standard Orientalist interpretations to accommodate these new realities. They maintain that the Islamic discourse and the Islamic political dilemmas are continuous, permanent, unchanging and insoluble now as they were upon Islam's genesis,[34] and that this permanent core explains the reemergence, structure, dynamics, and hostility to the West of contemporary political Islam. In a review of B. Etienne's *L'Islamisme radical*, Gilsenan notes: "Etienne, too, is in this sense a fundamentalist: he believes that the basic terms, the fundamentals of Islam set in the first years of the prophetic mission, motivate the tradition of the present day."[35]

R. H. Dekmejian's *Islam in Revolution: Fundamentalism in the Arab World*, a study commissioned by the U.S. government, presents the whole expanse of Islamic history as characterized by fundamentalist eruptions endlessly occurring and recurring in the context of societal crisis: ". . . the causal relationship between spiritual-social-political turmoil and fundamentalist ascendance has been a recurrent pattern in Islamic history . . ."[36] For Dekmejian, the Islamic fundamentalist is a fanatic (he uses the Arab term *mut'asib*) who exhibits a severely pathological psychological profile. Although he presents no evidence, Dekmejian constructs this pathological syndrome through mere assertions: infantile premature integrism, paranoia, alienation, and authoritarianism. In Dekmejian's text we see a transparent wedding of simplistic Orientalism with unsubstantiated assertions based on modern psychology, sociology, and political science. This fusion of Orientalism and modern social science is not limited to the analysis of Islam. It is the core framework of modernization theory, to which we now turn.

III.   Modernization Theory

The grand theory and abstracted empiricism that C. Wright Mills criticized in American sociology was produced in the United States in the post–World War II period. It reflected the self-congratulatory liberal ideology of the postwar economic boom. Talcott Parsons, the outstanding representative practitioner of grand theorizing, inspired a whole generation of sociologists and other social scientists. Parsons's functionalism aspired to explain the structure and functioning of society, and also to provide a model of social change for non-Western societies along the lines of Western capitalist development. Functionalist theory gave birth to modernization theory for the non-Western world, itself a grand conceptualization, a master theory claiming to capture the essence—the dilemma and the solution—of non-Western underdevelopment.

The underpinning of this theory is a social science paradigm incorporating a syncretic but unintegrated theoretical formulation: neoclassical economic theory, functionalist social theory, and pluralist political theory. This syncretic paradigm was coupled with a positivist methodology. Structural functionalism became so pervasive that research questions and data categories were all couched in terms of this formulation. Social scientists had either to employ this dominant paradigm as bases for their research or to suffer professional delegitimation and marginalization. This dominant social science theory conceived of sociopolitical conditions in America and the West as self-perpetuating and universalizable ones which, when applied in other areas, would bring similar economic growth and well-being.

The essential thesis of modernization theory is the existence of a global unilinear social history in which the West advances along a continuum and the non-West remains behind. Hence, the blueprint of change for the non-West is emulation of the West, as stated forthrightly by Daniel Lerner: "What the [West] is . . . the Middle East seeks to become."[37] Modernization theory as a grand theory of Third World dynamics was expressed in all the modern social-science disciplines.[38] In sociology it achieved a central and prominent position; witness the work of Marion J. Levy, S. N. Eisenstadt, N. Smelser, and others.[39] Modernization theory was operationalized in social-psychological terms (D. Lerner) and in sociologistical terms (Hoselitz and others).[40]

In Middle Eastern studies, modernization theory was informed by Orientalist categories in the context of the emergent area studies approach. The earliest attempts, highly Orientalized, are those of Carleton Coon and Raphael Patai.[41] In sociology, two principal efforts stand out: Morroe Berger's *The Arab World Today* and C. A. O. van Nieuwenhuijze's *Sociology of the Middle East: A Stocktaking and Interpretation.*[42] Both Coon and Patai conceptualize Islam as the determining power of Islamic culture. Berger, on the other hand, is more impressed by the forces of change—the operationalized categories of modernization theory: urbanization, industrialization, education, nationalism, etc. Although Berger notes the impact of these changes on the structure of social hierarchy, he dwells largely on the nature, size, and role of the "new middle class"—a favorite variable of modernization theorists.

In sociology, the Orientalist influence expressed itself especially through the "culture and personality" approach, elaborated by Patai, Hamady, Lerner, and others.[43] Patai's and Hamady's interpretations were crude and methodologically questionable, relying heavily on opinions of other Orientalist authorities (the citationary method), while Lerner's approach was much more sophisticated both theoretically and methodologically, reflecting the developments of postwar quantitative methods.

In his book, Berger attempts to integrate Orientalism with functionalist modernization theory. He raises some of the typical problematics and policy concerns of this paradigm that emerged in the 1950s: population growth, economic development, and political-ideological currents (nationalism). He also analyzes the modernizing role of the new middle class, especially the military elite, reflecting the then-common issue of stability and change in the non-Western world. The two parts of this text remain unintegrated, as if they are separate essays on two separate realities. This illustrates the limits of both approaches; Berger utilizes Orientalism to analyze and interpret the micro-sociological aspects of Islamic Middle Eastern society(ies), and employs modernization theory to describe macro-sociological trends. Interestingly, this reflects the flaws of postwar American sociology in general. Apart from the highly removed grand theory, American sociology underwent extensive development at the micro- and middle-range levels, especially in its empirical studies. These three levels remain basically separate and unintegrated, a situation exacerbated by the theoretically fragmented state of mainstream American sociology.

The theoretical and conceptual/methodological problems that plagued Berger's text are evident in van Nieuwenhuijze's *Sociology of the Middle East: Stocktaking and Interpretation,* a text of 819 pages, 21 tables and 11 maps. Van Nieuwenhuijze intends to present a comprehensive study of the Middle East. While Berger restricts his analysis principally to the core countries of the Arab East, van Nieuwenhuijze includes the whole area conventionally labeled the Middle East, including all the Arab countries from the Atlantic to the Gulf as well as Turkey and Iran. Van Nieuwenhuijze consciously begins by warning of the pitfalls of (Western) ethnocentricism and eschewing "aprioristic" Orientalism.[44] He thus wants to move farther away from Orientalism and utilize modern social science in the form of modernization theory. As noted in the foreword by Kemal Karpat:

> A new understanding of Middle Eastern society and its modernization could be achieved by analyzing in the greatest possible detail the internal structural transformation of this society, the emergence of various social groups, their interrelations, and their impact on culture and government. Thus, a factual, empirical approach to the study of the Middle East, free of value judgments or cultural assumptions, should yield satisfactory results. The approach, in addition to replacing the fallacious reliance on Islam as the only key to the understanding of the Middle East, may also define the true place, function and evolution of religion in the total transformation of Middle Eastern society.[45]

This quotation identifies van Nieuwenhuijze's theoretical orientation and defines the tasks he undertakes. After a general introduction in which he establishes the Middle East as a culture area (an anthropological concept), he spends half the book (nearly 400 pages) "in the greatest possible detail" factually and empirically describing "features of the Middle East as a region, and as a culture area." This includes not only geographical/ecological features, but also resources, communications, human densities, and cultural/linguistic diversities. It is an account of the history and macro-features of the region, including a comparative survey of the sub-areas. The second part—the interpretation—is in turn divided into two sections: dimensions of morphology and modalities of continuity. The morphological analysis closely follows Berger's "patterns of living," including family, tribe, village, city, and the community of Islam/nation-state. These are standard Orientalist/anthropological divisions of

Islamic Middle Eastern society as epitomized by the mosaic model, which also includes the "cultural minorities." Van Nieuwenhuijze's interpretation of Middle East society is unique, due not to his use of the mosaic model, nor to his treatment of women and youth ("categories aside" as he refers to them), but to his argument concerning Middle Eastern "social rating." The categories he introduces in this book are elaborated in a later, edited tome, *Commoners, Climbers and Notables.*[46] According to van Nieuwenhuijze, the articulation of Western society is manifested through stratification, the principal form of societal integration. However,

> the way in which Middle Eastern society achieves its own distinctive articulateness cannot be called social stratification. Nor could the aggregate self-identification of Middle Easterners, as members of ever so many distinct social units of many kinds—a self-identification that after all will determine the mode and degree of integration characteristic of the Middle Eastern societal patterns—be called by this name.[47]

Islamic Middle Eastern society is a "composite society," pluralistic and mosaic-like, integrated only "insofar as it converges upon a core," a core that is cultural (i.e., Islam).[48] "There is parallelism rather than integration." This principle is "unlikely to manifest itself as a stratification criterion".[49] Van Nieuwenhuijze does not deny that there are "ascendant categories," or "elites," and "intermediate categories." He merely argues that the principle of stratification as a mechanism of articulation is alien to Middle Eastern society. He thus takes issue not only with the use of the term "stratification," but also with the notion of "middle class" as conceptualized in the work of Berger and others. In short, he denies not only the conceptual relevance of such categories of analysis but also the existence of classes, strata, and a Middle Eastern stratification system qua system.

Curiously, despite his disclaimer against Orientalism, van Nieuwenhuijze reverts to the standard Orientalist societal morphology and differentiation ("diffraction," as he terms it) of the Islamic Middle East. He elevates the cultural (religious) element to a deterministic core factor, characterizes the social structure as a patchwork mosaic of social configurations, underplays or eliminates the economic-productive foundation and class differentiation, and ends up as Orientalist and idealist as Berger. Also like Berger's, his work fails to link the macro-sociological process with the institutional and micro-level patterns in any overarching theoretical formulation. His theoretical reconsideration of stratification theory is pedantic, oblivious of the fast-changing social realities of the Islamic Middle East.

Modernization theory's inability to apprehend the Middle East is perhaps nowhere more evident than in its application to one country—Lebanon—once celebrated by Western social scientists as the regional model of runaway capitalist development. The celebration of Lebanon's liberalism, entrepreneurship, democracy, and therefore "modernity" in *Politics in Lebanon,* edited by Leonard Binder, was surpassed only by Daniel Lerner's *Passing of Traditional Society* and by Elie Salem's *Modernization Without Revolution.*[50] Only Michael Hudson's insightful analysis rose above the ideological limitations of modernization theory and made the counterpoint regarding this small *Precarious Republic.* However, the precariousness that Hudson identified was limited to the political realm and did not extend to the contradictions inherent in modern Lebanese society.[51] Samir Khalaf, despite the collapse of Lebanon, is still interpreting *Lebanon's Predicament* in the idiom of modernization theory as "the dialectics of tradition and modernity."[52]

Nor is modernization theory capable of apprehending total Palestinian social reality. Joel S. Migdal's book, *Palestinian Society and Politics,*[53] is a case in point. Published in 1980, the book covers Palestinian society from the nineteenth century to the present. It is heavily Orientalist-modernizationist in conception, organization, and method, focusing on the classical analytical units of the village (peasants) and the city (elites), and their interaction. It contrasts sharply with Roger Owen's edited *Studies in the Economic and Social History of Palestine in the Nineteenth and Twentieth Centuries.*[54] Owen's book places Palestine in the political economy of European imperialism and the Zionist colonial project. Owen additionally raises the theoretical problems of conceptualizing Palestine in the nineteenth century and under colonial rule in the twentieth century. He presents three conceptualizations: Mandate Palestine as a typical European colony; Palestine as constituted by two separate, coexisting communities (Arab and Jewish), each with its own social, economic, and political arrangements; and Palestine as constituted by two sectors, one capitalist (principally Jewish) increasingly dominating the other, precapitalist (principally Arab).

Problematic as Mandatory Palestine is to study theoretically, the problem of conceptualizing Palestinian society after 1948 is even more challenging. For example, studies of Palestinians in Israel are often narrowly conceptualized or empirically erroneous. Khalil Nakhleh notes:

> . . . the questions most of these studies raised . . . often related to undefined sociological processes which Western social science has generated (e.g., modernization), rather than to the basic ideological underpinnings of the State of Israel which created the minority status of the Arab population in the first place . . . Such a persistent avoidance is

purposeful, and it can be understood mainly in terms of an *a priori* adherence on the part of these researchers to the major ideological construct of political Zionism.[55]

Nakhleh's critique raises two important issues: that the dynamics of the social structure of the "Arabs of Israel" are conceptualized in terms of the unchanged, stagnant nature of traditional Arab patterns (as if they were still living in Ottoman times); and that Israeli researchers employ a methodological dichotomy which masks contradictory ideologies and moral judgments regarding the status of the Palestinian community inside Israel.

Talal Asad presents a trenchant critique of this kind of scholarship. Asad's deconstruction of Abner Cohen's *Arab Border Villages in Israel* is masterly, not only demystifying the Orientalist foundation of Cohen's anthropology but also articulating a radical perspective of political economy for understanding the history, structure, and dynamics of Palestinian village society under Israeli rule.[56]

Elia Zureik, author of a good theoretical study on the Palestinian community inside Israel (*The Palestinians in Israel: A Study in Internal Colonialism*)[57] states that Israeli social scientists ignore the impact of Zionist practices in such processes as the proletarianization of Palestinian peasantry, as they generally do in interpreting the structure and change of Palestinian society altogether. While this work is theoretically and methodologically original, his schematic sketch of the stages of transformation of Palestinian societal structure lacks a theoretical formulation to explain the reasons/causes for these shifts and for the character of the sociohistorical stages. Missing is a contextual conceptualization of why the development of Palestinian social structure does *not* take place in isolation from the capitalist political economy of the region and the globe, but rather is an integral part of the dynamics of Euro-American imperialism.

Several sociological studies analyzing the post-1948 social reality of the Palestinians have gone beyond the confines of Orientalism-modernization. For example, Rosemary Sayigh, in *Palestinians: From Peasants to Revolutionaries*,[58] uses oral history methods to record and analyze the structure of pre-1948 Palestinian society, the process of its destruction (uprooting and dispersal), the structure of the new reality (as refugees in Lebanon), and its revolutionary revival. Sayigh lets the Palestinian people speak for themselves to explain their motivations and actions rather than theorizing about them. What emerges is a fascinating portrait. On the other hand, *The Sociology of the Palestinians*,[59] edited by K. Nakhleh and E. Zureik, is the first sociological work that simultaneously considers Palestinian communities inside Israel, under occupation, and in the Arab host countries. It utilizes various theoretical conceptualizations of contemporary social science. For example, the Palestinians are analyzed as special minorities in the political economy of Arab host countries and as a "dependent" community in the West Bank and Gaza. Further, *Occupation: Israel Over Palestine,*[60] edited by N. Aruri, analyzes comprehensively the process and consequences of Israel's colonization of the West Bank and Gaza. These are among a handful of innovative studies of the Palestinians that have overcome the polemical and adversarial accretions and constraints of Orientalism and modernization theory, which are particularly unsuited and irrelevant to the Palestinian experience.

There are few straightforwardly sociological studies of Middle Eastern social institutions. One such study on family structure by W. J. Goode examines the change from extended- to nuclear-family organization in Islamic Arab society. This work was criticized theoretically through a case study by S. K. Farsoun, who concluded that the demise of the "functionally extended family" is far from evident in societies where the public institutional order is undeveloped and where a modern "civil society" has not yet asserted itself.[61]

Anthropologists and sociologists during the post–World War II period conducted a number of ethnographic and other village, town, and urban studies. These are too numerous to cite and review here. One major example is John Gulick's descriptive ethnographic study of Tripoli. The most interesting efforts are probably Janet Abu-Lughod's studies of Cairo and Rabat.

Abu-Lughod's approach to dealing with Arab-Islamic cities has undergone significant transformation since her first major work on Cairo, published in 1971.[62] Her second book on the topic of urban society, *Rabat: Urban Apartheid,*[63] published in 1980, offers a brilliant treatment of social transformation as evidenced through urban development. The difference between the two works illustrates an evolution of her own perceptions of the sociology of the Middle East. In *Cairo,* she conceptualized the analysis in Orientalist terms and used the main Orientalists among her major sources (e.g., Gibb and Bowen, Brockelman, etc.), whereas in *Rabat* she draws more on a political economy framework and on neo-Marxist sources, notably Samir Amin and Kenneth Brown.

Abu-Lughod sets her argument concerning Rabat's transformation in the context of Morocco's integration into the sphere of European domination and the consequent transformation of Moroccan society. In terms of this process she lays the groundwork for her later rejection of the concept of the "traditional Islamic city." She also rejects the idea, which the French, among others, espoused, that precolonized Morocco was a stagnant, insulated entity.

Abu-Lughod provides an explicit explanation of her own epistemological transformation and a lucid critique of her earlier Orientalist approach to the "Islamic City":

> My own book on Cairo fell into the trap set by the Orientalists by accepting many of the earlier authorities about the nature of the Islamic city. The edifice they had built over the years seemed to me a strong and substantial one. Only gradually did it become clear how much a conspiracy of copying and glossing had yielded this optical illusion.[64]

Abu-Lughod rejects the notion that characteristics of cities in the Arab world, or other areas where Islam is the religion, are "Islamic" by nature. There is nothing Islamic about camels, arid climates, or small-scale market arrangements. She does, however, make the point that Islam was a crucial *contributing* factor in shaping cities within its realms.

> First, it made rough juridical distinctions among population classes on the basis of their relation to the Umma and thus the State. . . . Furthermore, the frequent inability of the state to transcend communal organizations and the laissez-faire attitude of the state toward civil society left important functions to other units of social organization which strengthened them. Since many of these functions were vicinal ones . . . and since many vicinal units were composed of socially related people, what we would call the neighborhood became a crucial building bloc of cities in the Arab world during the medieval and even later times. . . . Second, by encouraging gender segregation, Islam created a set of architectural and spatial imperatives that had only a limited range of solutions. . . . And finally, one returns to the system of property laws that governed rights and obligations vis-à-vis both other property owners and the state. Such customary laws and precedents set in motion a process whereby a pattern of space was continually reproduced.[65]

Abu-Lughod takes the issue of urban mosaic structure from its common application as a *cultural fact* to a debatable *problematic* which must be viewed in a more sociopolitical manner as the juridical and spatial distinction by neighborhoods. She concludes by saying that it is not by edict that Islamic cities have similar characteristics (in those cases where they do have), but rather by a set of conditions that set in motion processes that generate common solutions to common problems (i.e. gender segregation and property laws).

In this auto-critique, Abu-Lughod contributes to the decolonization of sociology of the Islamic Arab world and presents an example of theoretical innovation for apprehending modern Islamic Middle Eastern society(ies).

IV. Sociological Eclecticism

The post–World War II emergence of the Middle East as pivotal not only to American political institutions but also to superpower rivalry encouraged, and perhaps hurried, many scholars and journalists into writing about the Middle East. The need to understand current events and social, economic, and political details is, ironically, a strong factor behind the demise of traditional Orientalism, which is more concerned with the dead past than with the living, puzzling present. It is this urgency of the present that pushed the established Orientalists into "area studies" and to a large extent into modernization theory. This odd mixture was further diversified by the specialized interests of the different disciplines and by their particular methodologies. A great number of scholars with and without the knowledge of the languages and cultures of the area produced a dazzling array of works dealing with all aspects of society(ies) of the region. As American involvement in the Middle East increased, social-scientific, historical, and cultural investigations have increasingly appeared. This has been evidenced by the growing number of university centers and departments, the growing size of the various associations concerned with Middle Eastern studies, the number of presentations in their conferences, and the proliferation of journals, books, and anthologies.

These products are extremely diverse, not grounded in any unifying theoretical or methodological framework. It is in this sense that we describe them as eclectic, competing paradigms vying with one another and against the backdrop of politicized and ideologized Middle Eastern studies. The demand for general texts on the societies of the region led to the proliferation of anthologies. These anthologies, in turn, reflect the changing theoretical/ideological tenor of the times. Early ones, such as *Readings in Arab Middle Eastern Societies and Cultures* (1970), edited by Lutfiyya and Churchill,[66] were heavily Orientalist in terms of conception, subject matter, and authorities. Similarly Orientalist in conception and execution is M. Milson's *Society and Political Structure in the Arab World* (1973).[67] A more empathic collection is the 1970 two-volume anthology edited by Louise E. Sweet, *Peoples and Cultures in the Middle East: An Anthropological Reader.*[68] While its first volume covers the conventional anthropological concerns, the second volume introduces varied studies dealing with emergent theoretical and substantive trends. In 1977 Saad Eddin Ibrahim and Nicholas S. Hopkins edited and published *Arab Society in Transition: A Reader,*[69] which addressed the rapidly changing character of the Arab social order.

More recently, two anthologies have been published that reflect the newer theoretical and substantive interests: development and political sociology. The first is Talal Asad and Roger Owen's *Sociology of Developing Societies: The Middle East*[70] and the second is *Arab Society*,[71] edited by Samih K. Farsoun. Asad and Owen organize the varied readings on the Middle East into three sections: the international context, the state dimension, and the social structures and transforming processes. The book focuses on the parameters of "development" in the Middle Eastern political economy. Farsoun's book, on the other hand, presents comparative political sociological analyses of the regional oil economy, as well as theoretical chapters by Hisham Sharabi and Edward Said. These anthologies reflect the coming of age of Middle Eastern studies in which a haphazard eclectic approach is being challenged on its own ground by analyses with thematic and theoretical unity.

Two books falling into the eclectic category approach which have been widely accepted are *The Arab Predicament*, an interpretive essay by Fouad Ajami,[72] and *The New Arab Social Order: A Study of the Social Impact of Oil Wealth* by Saad Eddin Ibrahim.[73] Although Ajami's book is not a sociological study of Arab society, it nevertheless deals, in part, with Arab intellectuals' thought concerning Arab society, politics, and practice since 1967. The book was written for a Western audience and uses Arab intellectual critiques of their society(ies) and polities. The tone of the book is derogatory of Arab political culture. The book is divided into three distinct parts: how the Arab intellectuals depicted the Arab crisis after the 1967 defeat, the dilemma of Egypt as a mirror of the overall Arab dilemma, and the political problems in the post-1973 war period— especially fundamentalism. Ajami presents an unabashed, old-fashioned Orientalist and idealist interpretation, and makes no attempt to utilize the modern methods of political science. His explanatory concept is "political culture"—comprehensive, uniform, classless, and seemingly determinant of political dynamics. His interpretation is sweeping psycho-history not unlike that of the classical and certain modern Orientalists.

Ibrahim's more serious sociological study is attuned to the interplay of the relationship between data and generalizations, although ungrounded in an overarching theoretical formulation about the nature of society and change. He sees the impact of oil on the (*Mashriq*) Arab social order as equivalent to the fourth tidal wave that has overtaken the Arab homeland, after the colonial experience, modern science and technology, and the nationalist struggles for independence.

It is the multiple and complex facets of oil as "energy source, technology, money, geopolitics, and manpower" that, in interaction with extant social structures, have produced a host of social and cultural changes which, in the aggregate, constitute the new social order: the emergence of new classes, status groups, demographic allocations and dislocations, values, behaviors, and social cleavages.[74] Despite its comprehensive-sounding title and statement of purpose, the book is a study of the causes and consequences of inter-Arab labor migration, particularly between Egypt and Saudi Arabia. It is largely descriptive and derivative in its causative argument from a simple economic model of supply and demand (of labor). The sociological discussion, especially on values, consists more of empirical observation than theoretical analysis. Although the book is largely descriptive, it is an important contribution to our understanding of contemporary Arab society as it shatters many of the intellectually restraining myths of Islamic Middle East society as static, mosaic-like, fixed in its values and customs, and unchangeable in its religion.

Finally, we should conclude this section by referring to the fact that the varieties of disciplines, disciplinary concerns, grand theory, or low-level hypotheses of Western, particularly American, social science that produced the vast multidisciplinary literature on the Middle East also generated research inspired by specific methodologies. Survey research, the methodological tool of Western sociology, has been extensively applied to the Islamic Middle East. These studies are too numerous and varied in scope and focus to summarize and evaluate. The limitations of survey methods in Third World contexts are too evident and well known to articulate here. Suffice it to say that Monte Palmer and his colleagues have collected, organized, and synopsized most published surveys in one compendium, *Survey Research in the Arab World.*[75]

V. The Dependency School

In Latin American studies, traditional approaches and modernization theory have been confronted directly by dependency theory, a perspective through which indigenous Latin American intellectuals attempted to comprehend the social reality and dynamics of their own societies. This theoretical perspective could not be ignored by Western, especially American, Latin Americanists. Nor, because of its sheer critical mass, could it be undermined or twisted into a serviceable referent for establishment theory. Indigenous Latin American discourse, a product of the transformations and struggles of Latin American peoples, literally imposed itself on Western social science literature. The result was that the indigenously inspired Latin American discourse became the central perspective defining the issues and parameters of Latin American studies.

In contrast, Islamic Middle Eastern Studies have not been informed by some of the innovative and critical discourse of the region's indigenous intellectuals. The renunciation of traditional social theories on Latin America, Russia, and China has not extended to the Islamic Middle East. Western social science of the Middle East, despite its own internal contradictions, has been relatively successful in resisting critical or radical intellectual alternatives.

The environment of contemporary Middle East studies has encouraged the extension of positivist and uncritical norms among professional social scientists. This has reinforced a tacit and at times explicit consensus based on the static Orientalist interpretations that have produced a relatively closed circle of conventional ideas and authorities. However, challenging paradigms have made some inroads in their effort to dismantle the bulwark of Orientalized knowledge.

Dependency theory has emerged in Middle East studies as one of the principal alternative perspectives to modernization theory and Orientalism. Indeed, the dependency discourse in both the intellectual and the political domain has spread to all parts of the Third World, where it has become a common discourse of opposition. The theory is premised on the idea that dependency is a situation in which the economic and political structure of one society is conditioned by the development and expansion of another to which it is subject. The social, cultural, economic and political features of the subject (dependent) society are the products of unequal relations with the dominant society. More specifically, the Western industrial capitalist core states are self-sustaining and exploitative of the dependent peripheral or satellite countries of the Third World. Further, the development of the core is directly linked to and responsible for the underdevelopment of the periphery. This basic conception has generated a common discourse of intellectual and political opposition in much of the Third World, including Iran and the Arab world.

Consider, for example, the book edited by Baha Abu-Laban and Sharon Abu-Laban, *The Arab World: Dynamics of Development,* which attempts to interpret these dynamics in terms of a combination of class and dependency theory.[76] Specifically Abbas Alnasrawi, in the chapter on the dependency status and economic development of Arab states, traces the rise of Arab dependency historically, tracing its evolution and the role of oil in dependent growth. He notes income rising with dependency in seeming contradiction of a central perception of Third World dependency.[77] According to standard dependency theory, one of the most consistent features of dependent growth is the inability to generate surplus investment capital resulting in an accumulation of foreign debt. The Arab oil-producing states not only have, until recently, accumulated vast capital surpluses and achieved extensive infrastructural development, but also have become lender nations. And yet they remain dependent (i.e., subject to the constraints of the dominant industrial capitalist core) economically, politically, and militarily. Further, their social structure, political institutions, and policies are derivative from their dependent relation to the capitalist core.[78]

Jacqueline Ismail's *Kuwait: Social Change in Historical Perspective*[79] analyzes the transition of Kuwait from colonial status to post-colonial dependency as a result of the influx of British capital, technology, and know-
how for the development of oil production and marketing and the ideological and institutional stabilization of local elite rule. Upon attaining
political independence, Kuwait and the rest of the Gulf mini-states had
ruling elites whose self-interest was guaranteed by continued collabora-
tion with foreign (British and later American) economic interests. This
local-foreign alliance has shaped all aspects of the economy and polity of
oil-producing states of the Arabian peninsula and Gulf.

In Latin American and African dependency, indebtedness has been
the pivotal factor in the reproduction of dependence and socioeconomic
backwardness. That is not the case in the oil-rich Arab states. To be
comprehensive, dependency theory must be expanded to take into consideration the unique situation in that part of the Third World. Abdul-
Khaleq Abdulla, in a study entitled *Political Dependency: The Case of the
United Arab Emirates,* argues that dependency literature overemphasizes
the economic factor.[80] In the case of the UAE, and by implication the
rest of the oil-producing states, dependency is reproduced and conditioned by the "autonomous role of . . . political factors." In this and
similar studies, a theoretical qualification of classical dependency theory
is presented. Dependency as a construct, and its presumed responsibility
for underdevelopment or distorted development (including commensurate social processes of overurbanization, rural change, and institutional
paralysis), and the authoritarianism of the Arab states, are major focuses
of this new genre of analysis. It has been extended to the cultural domain
and has been utilized as a descriptive more than an explanatory model
by many others.

The best example of this latter approach is Halim Barakat's study of
Arab society, *Contemporary Arab Society.*[81] The problematic Barakat poses
concerning "Arab society" builds upon the issues that indigenous intellectuals and many of the political movements of the twentieth century have
confronted: the questions of Arab identity, Arab integration (unity), and
the existence of an Arab *society,* not merely an Arab world or "societies."
Barakat's book is in the nature of a social psychological interpretation
anchored in contemporary social structure. As such, it is short on analysis
of the economic structures and institutions that undergird the class divisions and political conflicts. Nevertheless, the effort is remarkable in its
breadth, sensitivity, and attention to social problems of contemporary
Arab society.

The most influential dependency theorist writing on the Arab world
is Samir Amin. In 1970 Amin published an essay under the name Ahmad
El Kodsy in the book *The Arab World and Israel.* His essay, "Nationalism

and Class Struggles in the Arab World," provided an outline of his theory of unequal development for the Middle East, which was later expanded and published under his own name in *The Arab Nation*.[82] He addresses the themes of a materialist history of the Arab world from the Islamic conquests to the advent of European imperialism in the region.

According to Amin, the early social formations of the Arab world, located at the crossroads of the major areas of civilization, were predominantly commercial in character. Surplus accumulation did not come from exploitation of the area's own rural inhabitants (as in feudal Europe), but rather from the profits of long-distance trade. In other words, "it was an income derived, in the last analysis, from the surplus extracted by the ruling classes of the other civilizations (the ones linked together by the Arab world) from their own peasantries."[83] Amin emphasizes the urban nature of Arab society, unlike those who characterize Arab societies as predominantly peasant based and rural. According to him, the pastoral subsistence economy contributed people and animals, but no surplus. Therefore, the rural areas remained marginalized, in contrast to the cities along the trade routes.

Amin bases his support for the concept of a historical Arab nation on such factors as geographical contiguity and common language, as well as the existence of "a social class which controls the central state apparatus and ensures economic unity in the life of the community."[84] In the Arab nation, this class was the merchant-warriors, and the social formations were commercial. Due to the dependence on trade, the fate of the dominant class was always tied to factors external to its own society.

As the Arab world became integrated into the world capitalist system, there was no indigenous class fully capable of establishing an independent hegemonic control over part or all of the region that had constituted a nation during the heyday of overland trade. The class that emerged, based on state capitalism, was incapable of assuming any real national hegemony. This class, representing only a minority of interests, remains dependent in the global system on those states constituting the core.

Amin addresses the issue of why capitalism first developed in Europe rather than in the Arab world or some other region of the world. He explains that pre-capitalist modes of production, all constituting some form of tributary mode, were at different stages of development. European feudalism was the most underdeveloped, whereas the Arab world, with its centralized state, was more advanced and thereby more stable. Due to its stable nature, the Arab world could "absorb developments in the means of production without bringing into question the relations of production."[85] Thus European feudal society was better suited to go beyond itself and develop new relations of production, leading to the advent of capitalist accumulation and development. By this same logic, now that areas of the Third World, or the dependent nations in the world system, are disadvantaged in terms of modes of production, it is easier and more imperative for them to transcend capitalist relations and develop into socialism. This is the theme of his latest book, *Beyond Capitalism.*[86]

The significance of this global historical materialist perspective explains the crisis Arab society faced when long-distance trade began to disappear. Amin's contribution to the understanding of social transformation in the Arab world is to undermine the doctrines of both Eurocentric Marxists and Orientalist historiographers. Arab history and society do not lend themselves to European specific conceptions. To say that the Arab world is underdeveloped in relation to the West and that the society is fractured and without clear direction at this stage is not to say that the reasons are cultural or religious, but rather that the global political economic order and the relations of production at this time force the Arab world into a situation of dependence.

Another critical influence, the historiography of Fernand Braudel, has had a special impact in the United States, producing a unique variant of the dependency school—the world system approach developed by Immanuel Wallerstein. A recent study in Arabic by Khaldoun Al-Naqeeb, *State and Society in the Gulf and the Arabian Peninsula,*[87] is distinctly Braudelian in style. It matches, for the region, the historical sweep of Amin's global work and Wallerstein's historical detail. Al-Naqeeb's purpose, however, is not the explanation of the development of dependent capitalism in the region. Rather, it is a political sociology of the states and societies from a macro-perspective. His purpose is to explain the contemporary character of the peninsular (oil-producing) state and the nature of the relationship between state and society.[88]

In the pre-capitalist period, the peninsula and the Gulf developed a "natural economy" in the context of a mercantile world economy. This was based in the Arabian Sea and the Indian Ocean and existed until the end of the seventeenth century. Given the absence of a central power in control of the region, Al-Naqeeb offers an explanation for the rise of this "natural economy" characterized by long-distance trade, the tribal connection on land, and a circulation of tribal elites in the greater peninsula region.

He traces the disintegration of the "natural economy" and the political structural consequences of European imperialism beginning in the eighteenth century. The "natural economy" and commensurate political system collapsed fully with the rise and consolidation of British hegemony in the whole region from India to Africa and the littoral of the Arabian peninsula. The British ruled the Indian Ocean and the Arabian and Red seas as well as the Gulf. By the second half of the nineteenth century the indigenous mercantile (long-distance trade) capitalists were turned into petty merchants and agents of monopolized European manufactured and strategic goods.

Al-Naqeeb details this transformation and the changes it wrought on the social and political structure of the region: collapse of artisan production, rise of specialized export production such as pearls, reproduction of socioeconomic patronage relations, and most significantly, the stabilization of tribal elites under British protection. This ended the long-established traditional and classical pattern of tribal elite circulation. It is the dynasties that were protected by and dependent on the British during this period that emerged as the rulers of the modern oil-producing states. In the context of the discovery of oil, these dynasties, still under British protection, established the "rentier state" of the post–World War II era and set the stage for the emergence of the contemporary "authoritarian state."

Al-Naqeeb analyzes the unique features of the oil-based rentier state. Outstanding is the expenditure or redistribution of oil revenue, as distinct from conventional states, which collect taxes and revenues from varied sectors of the economy and the population. The ruling dynasties behaved as if national oil revenues were their private income. This explains why they appeared to be political regimes that *owned* the state.

By monopolizing the sources of wealth and power under foreign protection, the ruling dynasties were able to create the contemporary "authoritarian states." The authoritarian state came into being by the penetration of civil society and the transformation of its institutions (educational, cultural, religious, etc.) into organs of control and mechanisms of mobilization for solidarity with the state (that is, the ruling dynasties). These institutions have become mere extensions of state apparatuses. A second feature of the authoritarian state is the overwhelming domination of the economy, leading to a structure best described, according to Al-Naqeeb, as state capitalism. Finally, the authoritarian state ensures its continued rule through the use of coercion and terror.

The authoritarian ruling dynasties monopolize power and wealth not only through the penetration of civil society and coercion, but also by preventing the emergence of autonomous sociopolitical groupings. Thus, the authoritarian state of the Peninsula and the Gulf prohibits the establishment of political parties, independent trade unions, etc. Instead, it allows the rise of informal and at times semiofficial corporatist pressure groups based on tribes, sects, religious functionaries, extended families of the new middle class (technocrats and bureaucrats), and house trade unions. Just as political independence led to institutionalization of the Balkanized mini-states, so has the corporatism of the authoritarian state led to modern-day institutionalization and politicization of tribalism and sectarianism. For Al-Naqeeb, the authoritarian state is not merely a system of rule but a political expression of a socioeconomic system, or better, a mode of production of dependent state capitalism. Farsoun earlier advocated a similar argument concerning the oil-poor Arab states of the Mashriq.[89]

The application of dependency theory to Middle East studies has shaken the sterile discourse of Orientalism-modernization. First, it has placed the Middle East societies in the global context historically and contemporaneously, thus contesting the conception of a closed cycle of social patterns advanced by the idealist mode of analysis. In the new perspective, Islam does not determine the structure and dynamics of society. Its role fades considerably and religion/sect is viewed as one among several relevant institutions and sources of ideology in this materialist social conception. Further, this notion of social change rejects the simplistic unilinear modernization model in favor of a more concrete account of the history of the region as it becomes differentially integrated into the global system.[90] It is through this framework that the issues of development and underdevelopment of the region are addressed.

Dependency theory has also allowed scholars to investigate the internal structures and processes of the various societies with a fresh and innovative perspective especially in relation to processes of polarization and hierarchization internal to single countries and among the states of the region. The international system that produces dominant/dependent relations reproduces the same relations nationally and regionally.

The application of dependency theory to the Middle East nevertheless suffers from the same deficiencies it generally suffers elsewhere. Despite all the significance of the concept, none of the studies systematically document in detail the actual patterns of economic, military, and other dependence of Middle Eastern peripheral societies on the Western industrial capitalist core. More difficult still is to analyze how these dependent relations shape indigenous social structure, government policy, ideology, and political culture. Al-Naqeeb confronts these issues, as do some others. But a great deal of work remains to be done. Perhaps this is because of the inherent conceptual indeterminacy of the dependency construct, including its concepts of development and underdevelopment, as Nadia Ramsis Farah argues.[91] Further, the strong emphasis on external linkage downplays internal factors which in any case are often considered mere reflections or extensions of those external linkages. The theoretical paradigm which allows a more comprehensive (internal, external) approach to comprehending the problems of social transf)rmation—structure, dynamics, and development—is the modes of production and social formation approach of the Marxist intellectual tradition. To this we shall next turn.

VI. Political Economy: Modes of Production and Social Formation

Before we assess the recent and concrete applications of the modes of production and social formation approach to Middle East studies, it is important to review its antecedents. We have noted the dependency theorists above. However, other materialist historians and social scientists have also made important strides in the development of a political economy of the Middle East. Consider, for example, the contributions of Roger Owen.

Owen offers a significant contribution to political economy in *The Middle East in the World Economy, 1800–1914*.[92] This economic history anchors the region in the global political economy of the times, permitting us to build an understanding of Middle East economics and social structure. He constructs a view of the patterns and dynamics of European penetration into the area and the manner, scope, and character of the articulation of European capital with the precapitalist Middle East. One shortcoming of Owen's text is its inability to give a detailed account of internal economic relations within the Middle East, due largely to the fact that applicable information was not recorded by the Ottoman authorities. (On the other hand, Yusif Sayigh, using a neoclassical model, provides a comprehensive account of Arab states' economies in the contemporary period.)[93]

Amin ignores the hegemonic perspectives of Orientalism and modernization theory, while Owen directly challenges some of its masters. Bryan Turner has frontally attacked Orientalism and staked out a discourse on the Middle East based on Marxist political economy. His seminal critique deconstructed not only Orientalism but also Marx's writing on the Orient and its ideological accretions. Turner's book *Marx and the End of Orientalism*, published in 1978, clarifies the debate and the various schools of thought on Marxist analysis for the Middle East.

Turner finds Marxism the natural alternative to the inadequate conventional sociology so prevalent in Middle Eastern studies, but he rejects "any teleological versions of Marxism which, for example, treat history as a series of necessary stages and thereby relegate the Middle East to a stage prior to 'real history.' "[94] He contends that an Althusserian approach is "adequate to the task of undermining Hegelian Marxist interpretations of the Middle East."[95]

Turner undertakes the deconstruction of Marx's Orientalism by providing an overview of his theory of the Asiatic mode of production (AMP hereafter), asserting that Marx's theories in this area, unlike his theories on the capitalist mode of production, were neither fully developed nor thoroughly consistent. Turner faults Marx's early writings on Asiatic

society and his proposition that colonialism could lead to social transformation.

Marx and Engels defined the AMP, with the internal structural flaws
of Asiatic society, as characterized by "self-sufficient village communities,
the dominance of the state as the real landlord, the absence of classes, the
ability of the social structure to absorb changes resulting from dynastic
conquest."[96] Marxist theory has been interpreted by some as a propaga-
tion of the idea that capitalist expansion creates the necessary conflict for
revolution and therefore that colonialism is a necessary stage in the
development of capitalism in noncapitalist, non-European areas.

Turner uses the writings of Shlomo Avineri, an Israeli social scientist,
to illustrate the argument of those Marxists who see colonialism and
Western penetration as a necessary stage in social development. Avineri
uses Israel as an example of the progressive entity in the otherwise
backwards region, thus justifying Israel's creation and expansion. Turner
quotes Avineri: ". . . 'the more direct the European control of any society
in Asia, the greater the chances for the overhauling of its structure and
its ultimate incorporation into bourgeois, and hence later into socialist
society' (Avineri, *Karl Marx on Colonialism and Modernization*, 1968,
p. 18)."[97] Turner criticizes Avineri's approach on the grounds that he
ignores some of Marx's commentaries that criticize colonialism, exagger-
ates Marx's dependence on Hegel, and misrepresents the effects of Israeli
modernization on the Palestinians. But the main difficulty Turner has
with Avineri and other Orientalist Marxists is their dependence on the
faulty AMP.

According to Turner, studies of the Middle East that displace this AMP
with the articulation of three modes of production (pastoral nomadism,
prebendalism, and feudalism) would present a viable framework for
analysis:

> Such an approach would in principle allow us to conceptualize intra-
> class conflicts within the dominant power bloc, crises within pre-capital-
> ist modes of production and transformations of modes. In short, this
> approach to the Middle East would avoid the ideological and theoretical
> difficulties of the conventional AMP which assumed no real history, no
> internal contradictions and no classes. An adequate characterization of
> modes of production would also counter the argument that Marx's
> analysis of social formations requires an oversimplified view of a two-
> class model of class structure. The mosaic model would consequently
> be replaced by a theory of class based on an analysis of modes of
> production.[98]

Although Turner ignores, for the most part, the writings of dependency theorists relating to the Middle East, he concludes his book by summarizing the applicability of Marxist analysis in a Third World context, drawing similar conclusions. According to Turner, this approach requires a certain amount of revision of Marxist theory:

> My counterargument is based on the argument that once the global centers of capitalism had been established, the conditions for development on the periphery were fundamentally changed. The internationalist theory of development fails to grasp the significance of this global relationship and consequently persists in posing futile questions about spontaneous capitalist development. The dominant character of development on the periphery is combined inequality and unevenness. Capitalism intensifies and conserves pre-capitalist modes of production so that there is no unilinear evolutionary path from 'traditional society' to 'modern society.'[99]

Turner's ultimate point is that every social formation has a mode or modes of production. The issue is to establish applicable means for analyzing the Middle East. Certainly bourgeois sociology has proven incapable of rising to the task, but Marxism also needs critical elaboration for an application to Asiatic societies, including those of the Middle East.

Mahmoud Abdel-Fadil's study, *Social Formations and Class Structures in the Arab Nation,* is an application of the articulation of modes of production approach attempting a comprehensive analysis of class structures in the Arab world in the period between 1945 and 1985.[100] Abdel-Fadil anchors his analysis of the classes and strata and their transformations in the varied and distinct social formations of the Arab world—formations that are products of the articulation of pre-capitalist modes of production with the capitalist mode, itself varied and multi-staged. To do this, Abdel-Fadil provides a critique of the classical Western mosaic model of Arab social organization and the Orientalist view, both of which he dismisses as bankrupt. Further, he rejects the contention that traditional Arab social structure is unstratified along socioeconomic lines. In refutation of this thesis, he cites numerous classical writings identifying social classes and stratified economic groupings.

Abdel-Fadil identifies several pre-capitalist modes of production and their respective strata: the Asiatic mode, especially in Egypt; the pastoral-tribal mode, especially in the Arabian peninsula and parts of the Sahara; and the tributary mode of production in much of the rest of the Arab world. These are abstract conceptual formulations of pre-capitalist systems of production, and any concrete analysis will have to address the role of long-distance trade in the region as well as the dynamics and mechanisms of change within precapitalist social formations. Specifically,

Abdel-Fadil stresses that analysis must be undertaken to determine how the Asiatic and tributory modes gave way to the emergence of an Eastern feudal mode of production with distinctive specificities as central (Ottoman) authorities weakened.

Given these varied and complex social formations, the class structures of the Arab regions are quite distinctive, as are their unique and specific routes of historical formation. Often the class structures exhibit patterns, elements, and mixtures of pre-capitalist orders, castes, and even occupational groupings with classes and strata derivative from the specificities of the patterns of capitalist penetration of the region. In analyzing these structures, he addresses directly the issues of the articulation of class and stratum with sect, caste, ethnicity, and tribe in the region—articulated structures that have a direct bearing on the relations of production, the distribution of income and power, and political dynamics. The specificities of the process of capitalist development(s) in the region have had a significant impact on Arab class formation and class structure: contractual bourgeoisie, bureaucratic bourgeoisie in state capitalism, and newly capitalized fractions even in labor-exporting Arab states. The oil economy has also had important consequences: increased social mobility and accumulation of capital.

Abdel-Fadil's broad effort to draw a picture of the class formation and class structure in the whole of the Arab world during the post-World War II period contrasts with the more detailed analysis of social-class organization in Iraq by Hanna Batatu. Batatu's purpose in *The Old Social Classes and the Revolutionary Movements of Iraq*[101] is not merely identification of the class structure and the relevant social classes, but rather an analysis of Iraqi society and politics utilizing a stratification framework. This pioneering effort successfully combines the dialectical use of Marx's conception of class and Max Weber's notion of status groups to comprehend and chart out the complex Iraqi social structure over the last century. Specifically, Batatu documents the transformation of the old status groups (i.e., the tribal *shaykhs*, religious *sayyids*, Sharifian officers, and Kurdish Aghas) into the new social classes (landed aristocrats and mercantile capitalists) based on the private ownership of the means of production.

Batatu does not enter into the issues of the articulation of the modes of production as Abdel-Fadil does, and his analysis is far less theoretical. Abdel-Fadil's effort sets forth the theoretical and methodological problematics of the articulationist school as applied to the Arab world: a new genre elaborated upon and debated by others.[102] The modes of production and social formation approach has been criticized as too structuralist and lacking in the integrated application of the role of social classes in apprehending social dynamics. Thus, Abdel-Fadil's unique contribution is his attempt to derive and characterize the Arab class structure in terms of the varied social formations that are based on several articulated modes of production.[103]

This new discourse promises a rewriting of the social history and political economy of the Arab world. Perhaps, finally, Middle East studies will have the opportunity to transcend the flawed establishment paradigms.

VII. Conclusion

By facing the shortcomings of sociology of the Middle East, we are confronted with the two elements that comprise any sociology—theory and method. The empirical categorizations that predominate in the study of the Middle East have been survivals of and defined by their Orientalist and modernizationist origins. For a long time, these areas of research guided certain considerations and interpretations while precluding others. However, critical theories have not only challenged categorizations and conceptions of Orientalized knowledge, but also introduced alternative ones in the emergent effort to construct a comprehensive knowledge of Middle Eastern societies. A decolonization of Middle East sociology would entail a simultaneous elaboration of theoretical frameworks and a reevaluation of empirical methods and concepts. One without the other would reproduce the current state of underdevelopment within Middle East sociology. Theory in isolation from empirical validation would produce flawed and acontextual theoreticism. Likewise, any development or modification of empirical categories devoid of theoretical guidance and structuring would produce sterile surveys with little relevance. Like that of Orientalist categories, the adaptation of materialist constructs is inappropriate if those constructs are merely borrowed from elsewhere. For the relationship between theory and method, every concept has meaning only within a whole problematic that founds it. It is a serious methodological problem to give new interpretations to concepts or paradigms created in an antithetical theoretical framework. What is needed is an approach in which theory and method are coordinated to devise an analytical framework and a discourse to fit the Islamic Middle East.

Decolonizing the social sciences' approach to the Middle East, therefore, entails not only the deconstruction of Orientalist conceptions and modernization theory, but also the construction of a theoretical framework that can apprehend empirical reality. There is no indigenous alternative that has been obscured or mystified, in part due to Western intellectual hegemony. Nor is there any completely viable radical alternative already in existence with a fully integrated theoretical and methodological approach. Granted, significant contributions have been made by studies that employ methods contrary to Orientalism in its various forms, and by studies that directly attack Orientalism and modernization theory and expose them as ideologically biased and therefore methodologically questionable. We contend, however, that there is a need for intensive and rigorous constructive theoretical formulations to guide future sociological studies of the Middle East.

The intellectual tools for such a decolonization process do exist. Critical theoretical formulations have generated innovative and creative analyses and interpretations of society and culture. Critical perspectives such as neo-Marxism, structuralism, post-structuralism, and feminist theory have served as epistemological challenges to existent dominant paradigms. These approaches remain, however, insufficiently applied to sociological studies of the Middle East and have not been fully fleshed out in their application to the Islamic world. Similarly, challenging Third World paradigms (dependency theory, pedagogy of the oppressed, liberation theology, etc.) emanating from Latin America offer theoretical models on which to build.

The most important issue for developing a sociology of the Middle East is the generation of an integrative approach that displaces Eurocentric analyses and methodologies. We stress "integrative" as a means for altering the existing state of the social sciences, which is rigidified disciplinary exclusionism. Thus, the focus must be on a macro-sociology that informs and is influenced by other fields of study. The critical approaches mentioned above are suitable for this type of macro-perspective.

Notes

1. Talal Asad, *The Idea of an Anthropology of Islam* (Washington: Georgetown University Center for Contemporary Arab Studies, 1986), p. 7.

2. Edward W. Said, *Orientalism* (New York: Pantheon Books, 1978), p. 3.

3. See Talal Asad, "Anthropological Texts and Ideological Problems: An Analysis of Cohen on Arab Villages in Israel," *Review of Middle East Studies*, no. 1 (1975): 1–40; Ralph Coury, "Why Can't They Be Like Us?" *ibid.*: 113–33.

4. Samih K. Farsoun, "Culture and Dependency: Cultural Invasion of the Arab World," in *Comprehensive Plan for Arab Culture* (Tunis: Arab League Economic, Cultural and Scientific Organization, 1986), pp. 1185–1206. In Arabic.

5. See Janet Abu-Lughod, "The State of the Art in Studies of Middle Eastern Urbanization," ms. 1986.

6. E. Terry Prothro, *Child-Rearing in the Lebanon* (Cambridge: Cambridge University Press, 1961). See also Daniel Lerner, *The Passing of Traditional Society* (Glencoe, IL: Free Press, 1958), pp. 169–213.

7. Ernest Gellner, *Muslim Society* (Cambridge: Cambridge University Press, 1981), p. 1.

8. Reuben Levy, *The Social Structure of Islam* (Cambridge: Cambridge University Press, 1965).

9. Arthur Jeffrey, "The Family in Islam," in Ruth N. Anshen, ed., *The Family* (New York: Harper, 1959).

10. Ralph Coury, *op. cit.*, p. 115.

11. *Ibid.*, pp. 122–127.

12. Pandelis Glavanis, "Historical Interpretation or Political Apologia? P. J. Vatikiotis and Modern Egypt," *Review of Middle East Studies*, no. 1 (1975): 70, 71.

13. *Ibid.*, p. 70.

14. Bryan Turner, *Marx and the End of Orientalism* (London: George Allen and Unwin, 1978), p. 39.

15. Janet Abu-Lughod, "The Islamic City—Historic Myth, Islamic Essence, and Contemporary Relevance," *International Journal of Middle East Studies*, May 1987.

16. H. A. R. Gibb and H. Bowen, *Islamic Society and the West*, Vols. I and II (Oxford: Oxford University Press, 1950, 1957).

17. Gabriel Baer, *Population and Society in the Arab East* (New York: Praeger, 1964).

18. Bryan Turner, *op. cit.*

19. Ernest Gellner, *op. cit.*, p. 99.

20. *Ibid.*

21. See Michael C. Hudson, *Arab Politics: The Search for Legitimacy* (New Haven: Yale University Press, 1977).

22. Ernest Gellner, *op. cit.*, p. 7.

23. *Ibid.*, p. 65.

24. Maxime Rodinson, *Islam and Capitalism* (New York: Pantheon, 1973).

25. *Ibid.*, p. 57.

26. Clifford Geertz, *Islam Observed* (Chicago: University of Chicago Press, 1968) p. 19.

27. *Ibid.*, p. 8.

28. *Ibid.*, p. 11.

29. *Ibid.*, p. 13.

30. *Ibid.*, p. 65.

31. *Ibid.*, p. 73.

32. Michael Gilsenan, *Recognizing Islam: Religion and Society in the Modern Arab World* (New York: Pantheon Books, 1982), p. 11.

33. *Ibid.*, p. 265.

34. Michael Gilsenan, "Apprehensions of Islam," *Middle East Report*, no. 153 (July–August 1988): p. 33.

35. *Ibid.*, p. 33.

36. R. Hrair Dekmejian, *Islam in Revolution: Fundamentalism in the Arab World* (Syracuse: Syracuse University Press, 1985), p. 11.

37. Daniel Lerner, *The Passing of Traditional Society*, p. 47.

38. W. W. Rostow, *The Process of Economic Growth* (New York: Norton, 1952); E. E. Hagen, *The Economics of Development* (Homewood, IL: R. D. Irwin, 1968); C. P. Issawi, *The Economic History of the Middle East, 1800–1914* (Chicago: University of Chicago Press, 1966); S. P. Huntington, *Political Order in Changing Societies* (New Haven: Yale Univer-

sity Press, 1968);D. E. Apter, *The Politics of Modernization* (Chicago: University of Chicago Press, 1965); L. W. Pye, *Aspects of Political Development* (Boston: Little, Brown and Co., 1966); R. Bendix, *Nation-Building and Citizenship* (New York: J. Wiley and Sons, 1964); M. Halpern, *The Politics of Social Change in the Middle East and North Africa* (Princeton: Princeton University Press, 1963); J. Bill and C. Leiden, *Politics in the Middle East* (Boston: Little, Brown, 1974); Raphael Patai, *Golden River to Golden Road: Society, Culture and Change in the Middle East* (Philadelphia: University of Pennsylvania Press, 1962); C. S. Coon, *Caravan: The Story of the Middle East* (New York: Holt, 1958); H. A. R. Gibb and H. Bowen, *Islamic Society and the West* (London: Oxford University Press, 1957); Bernard Lewis, *The Middle East and the West* (Bloomington, IN: Indiana University Press, 1964); M. Ma'oz, *Ottoman Reform in Syria and Palestine* (Oxford: Clarendon Press, 1968).

39. Marion J. Levy, *The Structure of Society* (Princeton: Princeton University Press, 1952); S. N. Eisenstadt, *Modernization: Protest and Change* (Englewood Cliffs, NJ: Prentice-Hall, 1966); N. Smelser, "Toward a Theory of Modernization," in A. Etzioni and E. Etzioni (eds.), *Social Change* (New York: Basic Books, 1964), pp. 258–74.

40. Daniel Lerner, *op. cit.*; Bert Hoselitz, *Sociological Aspects of Economic Growth* (Glencoe, IL: The Free Press, 1960).

41. Carlton S. Coon, *op. cit.*; Raphael Patai, *op. cit.*

42. Morroe Berger, *The Arab World Today* (Garden City, NY: Doubleday, 1962); C. A. O. van Nieuwenhuijze, *Sociology of the Middle East* (Leiden: E. J. Brill, 1971).

43. Raphael Patai, *op. cit.*; Sania Hamady, *Temperament and Character of the Arabs* (New York: Twayne Publishers, 1960); Daniel Lerner, *op. cit.*

44. C. A. O. van Nieuwenhuijze, *op. cit.*, p. 1.

45. Kemal Karpat, "The Land Regime, Social Structure, and Modernization in the Ottoman Empire," in W. R. Polk and R. L. Chambers, eds., *Beginnings of Modernization in the Middle East; The Nineteenth Century*, cited in van Nieuwenhuijze, *op. cit.*, p. xi.

46. C. A. O. van Nieuwenhuijze, *Social Stratification and the Middle East* (Leiden: E. J. Brill, 1965); van Nieuwenhuijze, ed., *Commoners, Climbers and Notables* (Leiden: E. J. Brill, 1977).

47. Van Nieuwenhuijze, *op. cit.*, 1977, p. 579; (See also van Nieuwenhuijze, *op. cit.*, 1965, pp. 7–9).

48. *Ibid.*, pp. 5790–80.

49. *Ibid.*, p. 580.

50. Leonard Binder, ed., *Politics in Lebanon* (New York: J. Wiley and Sons, 1966); Lerner, *op. cit.*; Elie Salem, *Modernization Without Revolution* (Bloomington, IN: Indiana University Press, 1973).

51. Michael C. Hudson, *The Precarious Republic: Modernization in Lebanon* (New York: Random House, 1968); see also, S. K. Farsoun, "Student Politics and the Coming Crisis in Lebanon," *MERIP Reports*, no. 19 (November 1973).

52. Samir Khalaf, *Lebanon's Predicament* (New York: Columbia University Press, 1987). See also his *Persistence and Change in 19th Century Lebanon: A Sociological Essay* (Beirut: American University of Beirut Press, 1979).

53. Joel S. Migdal, *Palestinian Society and Politics* (Princeton: University Press, 1980).

54. Roger Owen, *Studies in the Economic and Social History of Palestine in the Nineteenth and Twentieth Centuries* (Carbondale, IL: Southern Illinois University Press, 1982).

55. Khalil Nakhleh, "Anthropological and Sociological Studies on the Arabs in Israel: A Critique," *Journal of Palestine Studies* 6, no. 4 (Summer 1977): 61–62.

56. Talal Asad, 1975, *op. cit.*

57. Elia Zureik, *The Palestinians in Israel: A Study in Internal Colonialism* (London: Routledge and Kegan Paul, 1978). See also Ian Lustick, *The Arabs in the Jewish State* (Austin, TX: University of Texas Press, 1980).

58. Rosemary Sayigh, *Palestinians: From Peasants to Revolutionaries* (London: Croom Helm, 1980).

59. Khalil Nakhleh and Elia Zureik, eds., *The Sociology of the Palestinians* (London: Croom Helm, 1980).

60. Naseer Aruri, ed., *Occupation: Israel Over Palestine* (Belmont, MA: Association of Arab-American University Graduates Press, 1983). See also, Pamela Ann Smith, *Palestine and the Palestinians 1876–1983* (New York: St. Martin's Press, 1984).

61. William J. Goode, "The Islamic-Arab Family" in *World Revolution and Family Patterns* (New York: Free Press, 1963); Samih K. Farsoun, "Family Change in a Modernizing Society," in Louise E. Sweet, ed., *Peoples and Cultures of the Middle East: An Anthropological Reader* (New York: Natural History Press, 1970), pp. 257–307.

62. Janet Abu-Lughod, *Cairo: 1001 Years of the City Victorious* (Princeton: Princeton University Press, 1971).

63. Janet Abu-Lughod, *Rabat: Urban Apartheid* (Princeton: Princeton University Press, 1980).

64. Janet Abu-Lughod, *op. cit.*, 1987, p. 160.

65. *Ibid.*, p. 163.

66. Abdullah Lutfiyya and Charles Churchill, *Readings in Arab Middle Eastern Societies and Cultures* (The Hague: Mouton, 1970).

67. Menahem Milson, ed., *Society and Political Structure in the Arab World* (Atlantic Highlands, NJ: Humanities Press, 1973); Gabriel Baer, *Population and Society in the Arab East* (New York: Praeger, 1964).

68. Louise E. Sweet, *op. cit.*

69. Saad Eddin Ibrahim and N. S. Hopkins, eds., *Arab Society in Transition: A Reader* (Cairo: American University of Cairo Press, 1977).

70. Talal Asad and R. Owen, *Sociology of "Developing Societies" in the Middle East* (New York: Monthly Review Press, 1983).

71. Samih K. Farsoun, ed., *Arab Society* (London: Croom Helm, 1985).

72. Fouad Ajami, *The Arab Predicament* (Cambridge: Cambridge University Press, 1981).

73. Saad Eddin Ibrahim, *The New Arab Social Order* (Boulder, CO: Westview Press, 1982).

74. *Ibid.*, p. 2.

75. Monte Palmer, *et al.*, *Survey Research in the Arab World* (London: MENAS, 1982).

76. Baha Abu-Laban and Sharon M. Abu-Laban, eds., *The Arab World: Dynamics of Development* (Leiden: E. J. Brill, 1986).

77. Abbas Alnasrawi, "Dependency Status and Economic Development of Arab States," in Abu-Laban and Abu-Laban, *op. cit.*, pp. 17–31.

78. An example of the direct application of dependency theory is Samih K. Farsoun, "Changes in Labor Force Structure in Selected Arab Countries," in *Issues in Human*

Resources Development in the Arab Nation, introduced by A. Al-Adwani (Kuwait: National Council for Culture, Arts and Literature, 1978), pp. 103–18.

79. Jacquline Ismail, *Kuwait: Social Change in Historical Perspective* (Syracuse: Syracuse University Press, 1982).

80. Abdul Khaleq Abdulla, *Political Dependency: The Case of the United Arab Emirates,* unpublished Ph.D. dissertation, Department of Government, Georgetown University, 1985.

81. Halim Barakat, *Contemporary Arab Society* (Beirut: Center for Arab Unity Studies, 1984). In Arabic.

82. Ahmad El Kodsy and Eli Lobel, *The Arab World and Israel* (New York: Monthly Review Press, 1970); See also Samir Amin, *The Arab Nation* (London:Zed Press, 1978); Samir Amin, *Unequal Development: Accumulation on a World Scale* (New York: Monthly Review Press, 1976); Samir Amin, *The Maghreb in the Modern World* (Baltimore: Penguin Books, 1970); Bryan Turner, *Capitalism and Class in the Middle East* (Atlantic Highlands, NJ: Humanities Press, 1984); Roger Owen, "The Middle East in the 18th Century— An 'Islamic' Society in Decline: A Critique of Gibb and Bowen's Islamic Society and the West," *Review of Middle East Studies,* no. 1 (1975): 101–12; Roger Owen, *op. cit.,* 1982; Roger Owen, *The Middle East in the World Economy 1800–1914* (New York: Methuen, 1981).

83. Ahmad El Kodsy, *op. cit.,* p. 6.

84. Samir Amin, *op. cit.,* 1978, p. 81.

85. *Ibid.,* p. 89.

86. Samir Amin, *Beyond Capitalism* (Beirut: Center for Arab Unity Studies, 1988). In Arabic.

87. Khaldoun Al-Naqeeb, *State and Society in the Gulf and the Arabian Peninsula* (Beirut: Center for Arab Unity Studies, 1987). In Arabic.

88. See a more eclectic treatment in Hazem Beblawi and G. Luciani, eds., *The Rentier State* (London: Croom Helm, 1987).

89. Samih K. Farsoun, "State Capitalism and Counterrevolution in the Middle East," in Barbara H. Kaplan, ed., *Social Change in the Capitalist World Economy* (Beverly Hills: Sage, 1978).

90. See, Danny J. Reachard, *Social and Economic Integration Among Countries of the Arab East,* unpublished Ph.D. dissertation (Washington: Department of Sociology, The American University, 1987).

91. Nadia Ramsis Farah, "The Social Formations Approach and Arab Social Systems," *Arab Studies Quarterly* 10, no. 3 (Summer 1988).

92. Roger Owen, *op. cit.,* 1981. See also Roger Owen, *op. cit.,* 1975; S. Pamuk, *The Ottoman Empire and European Capitalism* (Cambridge: Cambridge University Press, 1987); and H. Islamoglu-Inan, ed., *The Ottoman Empire and the World Economy* (Cambridge: Cambridge University Press, 1987).

93. Yusif A. Sayigh, *The Arab Economy* (London: Oxford University Press, 1982).

94. Bryan Turner, *op. cit.,* 1978, p. 5.

95. *Ibid.,* p. 6.

96. *Ibid.,* pp. 14–15.

97. *Ibid.,* p. 27.

98. *Ibid.,* p. 52.

99. *Ibid.,* pp. 81–82.

100. Mahmoud Abdel-Fadil, *Social Formations and Class Structures in the Arab Nation* (Beirut: Center for Arab Unity Studies, 1988). Other studies utilizing the class structure

analytically include Mahmoud Hussein, *Class Conflict in Egypt: 1945–1971* (New York: Monthly Review Press, 1973); Claude Dubar and Salim Nasr, *Les Classes sociales au Liban* (Paris: Presses de la Fondation Nationale des Sciences Politiques, 1976); Bryan Turner, *Capitalism and Class in the Middle East* (Atlantic Highlands, NJ: Humanities Press, 1984).

101. Hanna Batatu, *The Old Social Classes and the Revolutionary Movements of Iraq* (Princeton: Princeton University Press, 1978).

102. Nadia Ramsis Farah, *op. cit.*

103. See also Samih K. Farsoun, "Oil, State and Social Structure in the Middle East," *Arab Studies Quarterly* 10, no. 2 (Spring 1988): 155–75, and Samih K. Farsoun, "Class Structure and Social Change in the Arab World," in Hisham Sharabi, ed., *The Next Arab Decade: Alternative Futures* (Boulder, CO: Westview Press, 1988).

6

Taming the West:
Trends in the Writing of
Modern Arab Social History in
Anglophone Academia

Judith E. Tucker

What is social history? What are the contours and parameters of a field that might, at its most ambitious, lay claim to be the historical study of *society* in all its senses? While social history has been variously defined as the history of social structure, the history of everyday life, the history of social solidarities and conflicts, the history of social classes, and the history of social relationships—in brief, an historicized amalgam of the social sciences—Charles Tilly has put these rather unrealistic claims to one side by suggesting that work in social history, at least European social history, has tended to revolve around a single core:

> European social history's central activity, as I see it, concerns reconstructing ordinary people's experience of large structural changes.
> The statement has a descriptive side and a normative side. As a matter of description, the search for links between small-scale experience and large-scale processes informs a large share of all the work European social historians actually do. As a matter of prescription, the linkage identifies the one enterprise to which all the others connect, the one enterprise through which social historians have the greatest opportunity to enrich our understanding of social life. Neither the effort to construct "social" explanations of major political events, the attempt to portray a full round of life, nor the search for past evidence bearing on present day social scientific theories—for all their obvious value—motivate the sustained, cumulative, and partly autonomous inquiry entailed by asking how people lived the big changes.[1]

"How people lived the big changes" and, I would add, how people made the big changes, strikes me as the stuff of social history across regions and cultures. Such an approach mounts an immediate challenge to the division of material into "macro" and "micro" categories that is treasured by most social science. The "big changes"—momentous economic transformations, shifts or breaks in political organization, and realignments in the contacts and power relations of different world regions—are clearly "macro" in the sense in which their effects are felt over a large territory and by significant numbers of people. Nevertheless they derive much of their import, if not, in some cases, their origins and shape, from the "micro" level. Indeed, I would argue that it is the way people lived these changes—the way they perceived, struggled against, accommodated, or actively encouraged them—that gives these changes their content as well as their historical meaning.

Such are the links we seek. We miss out on the ways in which people, in their daily lives and basic groupings, make history, when we curtain off certain "micro" spheres, or label studies of particular people (be they residents of a certain village or members of particular classes or genders) as interesting bits of a larger puzzle which, when assembled, will simply reflect the impact of the "macro" changes. In social history the "macro" and "micro" form a seamless whole: the major historical developments of the modern period are inextricably tied up with the multitude of ways in which people, as individuals, families, classes, and genders, made these developments possible.

Such a vision of history has informed the work of many social historians working on Europe and North America. In other world areas, however, the territory of social history is less well charted. In a recent book on the state of the art in social history, edited by Olivier Zunz, reviewers of Latin American, African, and Chinese social history can all agree that the field is new and relatively underdeveloped in their respective regions. While they set rather different agendas for future work, they do share a central concern that the models of Western history, and in particular the "big changes" of the West—the rise of capitalism, the emergence of the nation-state—can be very inappropriate and misleading points of departure in other world areas.[2]

To give these changes center stage is to assume, from the beginning, that the modern history of the entire world is ultimately derivative history, that it can and should be comprehended with Europe as the vantage point and referent. This is not to deny that the "big changes" in Europe did, in a very fundamental sense, transform the globe: the rise to global hegemony of the European powers in the nineteenth century reverberated across the continents as the "big changes" in Europe wreaked themselves upon the world. But to focus on this fact alone is to risk losing sight of the historical specificity of different regions, of the diversity of political arrangements, cultural expressions, and social relations that were, and still are, found in areas Europe entered. The subjugation of much of the "non-Western" world in the nineteenth and twentieth centuries did not spell the annihilation of all that existed before: even in

Latin America, where the exceptional might and brutality of the European invasion appeared to mow down everything in its path, the resilience
and long-term vitality of indigenous culture is now being recognized.[3]
The work of social historians, particularly in the non-Western world,
entails exploration of the richness of human experience that defies the
"Europe-take-all" view of modern history.

While I find these considerations directly relevant to our study of the
Middle East, Zunz's book does not help us further. The five major essays
in the book cover European, North American, Latin American, African,
and Chinese social history—the Middle East is completely missing. Surely
this lacuna reflects something more than an oversight on the part of the
editor: I suspect it reflects, unfortunately, the underdevelopment of the
field of social history of the Middle East even relative to Africa or China,
where practitioners are quick to stress what a fledgling their field is.
While, as we shall see, some very important work in social history has
been undertaken recently, we are still starting at a very basic point with
the social history of the Middle East in general, and the Arab world in
particular.

I focus in this paper on the writing of social history of the Arab world
and of the Ottoman Empire during the period in which it controlled
substantial amounts of Arab territory. The work under discussion was all
produced by scholars trained in North America or the United Kingdom.
Some Arab historians, based in the Arab world, have undertaken work
in social history, particularly in the areas of the history of the working
classes and the social bases of political movements. Their work, I believe,
has had a very different motivation, often different methodology, and a
different set of problems from those of their colleagues writing in English. It is, regrettably, beyond the scope of this paper.

Why has Arab social history been neglected in the United States? There
are, I believe, a number of reasons for the relatively slow start in our area.
First, there is the epistemological drag of Orientalism. The conception of
Middle East history as "Islamic" history—as the embodiment, however
partial or flawed, of Islamic values, ideas, and culture—almost completely
dominated historical writing up to a generation ago. While, as Albert
Hourani has pointed out,[4] the historical vision was transformed as the
ideas of Weber, Marx, and the Annales school seeped into the field in
the 1960s and 1970s, we cannot really speak of an epistemological break.
The effect of Orientalist distance from social history, foreign as it was to
both the approach and methods of Orientalist scholars, can still be felt.
The Orientalist approach, which emphasized the glories of early Islam,
the decline and decay of the period from the disintegration of the Arab
empires to the arrival of the West, and the partial recovery under the
impact of the West, necessarily neglected certain periods and topics.

The long twilight years, which included the seventeenth and eighteenth centuries, received little attention, while the focus on high culture and the political embodiment of the Islamic ideal at the state level precluded the study of life in its more popular guises. Today's historians, for the most part, are conscious of and vocal about the limitations of the Orientalist approach, but the weight of accumulated wisdom and training make for only gradual change.

There are, as well, more concrete barriers to the development of Arab social history in this country. As a field very dependent for its development in the United States on government and other monies that flowed toward research of interest to policymakers, Middle East studies (including the study of history) tended to deal with a set of "relevant" topics.[5] The inordinate attention paid to political history, and in particular to studies of foreign policy, can be partially understood in this light, as can the continued focus on the elite sectors of the population.

More mundane factors can also be at play. The difficulties of mastering Middle Eastern languages encourage work in European archives—which, in turn, skews research toward the diplomatic and political. Training in research techniques that is limited almost exclusively to reading the text— as opposed to the use of indigenous archival material, oral history, the artifacts of material culture, etc.—almost preordains the study of a literate elite.

I think many of these impediments to the study of social history are now being eroded, as funders grow more sophisticated and training in language and research techniques improves. Still, the major task looms. The enterprise of social history of the Arab world is still new and must stake out a terrain, and define that set of concerns and questions that will evoke the richest response. If, returning to Tilly, we want to ask "how people lived the big changes," in the modern Arab world, we first have to decide what these big changes were. What were the signal developments of the modern period, whether economic, political, or social, that framed human experience in the region? Most historians make implicit judgments, of course, in the way they plan their research and organize and interrogate their material. It seems to me that almost all recent historical writing in the modern Arab world circles around one of three poles of significant change: patterns in the growth of the state, the penetration of capitalism into the region, and the cultural impact of the West. While these three areas of change crop up as central explanatory features of the modern period for most historians, the understanding and evaluation of these changes varies widely: it is here, in the area of interpretation of change, that we need to set the field of social history on firmer ground.

The first task, then, is to sharpen our sense of what precisely the "big changes" were, taking care not to assume that the big changes of Europe—the rise of the nation-state, the development of capitalism—were automatically replicated in the Arab world. The added difficulty we confront lies in the historical fact of European ascendancy in the modern period. That Europe, as an economic system, a political power, and a cultural empire, played a profound role in the modern history of the Arab world is beyond dispute. But how do we weigh the role of Europe against the indigenous features of Arab society? How did the economic organization, political arrangements, and social and cultural life in the region interact with European pressures to produce the modern era? This question will be fully answered, I think, only as the field of social history matures and we come to understand better how the people of the Arab world experienced their history.

The Big Changes

Certain shared assumptions about the framework of this experience do seem to be present in the historical literature, taken as a whole. First, a striking feature of modern Arab history (and here I include the history of the Ottoman Empire, as inseparable as it is from Arab history from the sixteenth through the nineteenth centuries) is the focus on the state, and the recognition that the political institutions of the region were of weight and moment in the making of modern history. Such a focus has its own hallowed history: the Middle East of the nineteenth century posed itself as a problem, in the minds of Europeans, in the cloak of statehood—it was the Ottoman Empire, the once worthy adversary become the "Sick Man of Europe," that was the central focus of the region for nineteenth-century Europeans. In contrast to Latin America or Africa, where the indigenous states were, by and large, dismantled, the Middle East was equated with the history of a state, its rise, development, and decline. Nineteenth- and twentieth-century Orientalists, of course, viewed the Ottoman state in the modern period as a disparate set of institutions in full disintegration, kept afloat only by internal inertia and external restraint. The nineteenth-century state as a creaky anachronism from which the internal coherence and spirit had long fled lies at the heart of Gibb and Bowen's classic *Islamic Society and the West*, the capstone of Orientalist study of the empire.[6]

Scholarship of the last two decades or so has contested this view quite successfully. The importance of the state as such has remained a constant, but our understanding of the role of the indigenous state in the modern period has been transformed. Rather than a brake on the process of development in the nineteenth century, the Ottoman state is now viewed as a critical agent of change, a dynamic institution quite capable of instituting reform. Indeed, through a series of economic, political, and social measures taken in the *tanzimat* period (1839–1861), the state streamlined and rationalized its administration and prepared the ground, albeit unwittingly, for thorough European penetration.[7]

The picture that emerges is one of a state that, far from being incompetent and moribund, enjoys the services of a professional and experienced bureaucracy which, when brought to heel, can institute changes of great magnitude. As our knowledge of what the Ottoman state actually accomplished in the nineteenth century expands and the very real presence of the state in its own territory becomes clear, the emergence of the reformist state is coming to qualify as one of the "big changes."

Our picture of the state is complicated, however, by the relation between central authority and provincial power in the empire. The prevailing wisdom in the field has long held that the eighteenth and early nineteenth centuries were a period of unmitigated gloom: as the empire declined at the center and lost its hold on its territories, the provincial areas faced economic and political disintegration and sank into poverty and lawlessness.[8]

The problem here is one of perspective. From the vantage point of Istanbul, the pre-*tanzimat* era was indeed troublesome: the Empire's ability to control many of the provincial areas and collect revenues was impaired. The revolution in our understanding of the period, however, lies in the growing number of studies that question this conclusion from the vantage point of the provinces themselves. Crecelius has demonstrated how Istanbul's loss of control over Egypt, for example, allowed an eighteenth-century local ruler, 'Ali Bey al-Kabir, to consolidate his power, deal significant blows to a local elite which had siphoned off the country's revenues, and usher in a period of peace and stability, thereby promoting economic recovery.[9] In Palestine, Amnon Cohen sees the eighteenth century as a time of economic growth made possible by the strong, if somewhat brutal, local leadership of Shaykh Dahir al-'Umar and Ahmad Jazzar Pasha.[10]

Such studies reinforce the conclusions of local historians of the Arab provinces who, basing their work on local sources and popular lore, have tended to see the eighteenth century as one of significant achievement, at least among the ranks of the elite of urban and landed notables.[11] Such studies are still limited in number and tend to focus on the fortunes of a small official and economically privileged elite. Fortunately, however, the questions of power and prosperity in the eighteenth century are beginning to engage the attention of a new generation of social historians, and we can expect studies of this period to multiply.[12]

What are the implications for our understanding of the state in modern history? Were the establishment of foundations for an effective independent political power in the Arab provinces in the eighteenth century and the appearance of full-blown reformist states in the form of the Egypt of Muhammad 'Ali and the Ottoman Empire of the *tanzimat* the overriding political fact of life for the people of the region? How do we balance off the very real power and accomplishments of local rulers and bureaucratic states against our certain historical knowledge that their very existence as independent political powers was to prove ephemeral in the face of an expanding Europe? Robert Hunter has highlighted the increasing sophistication of bureaucratic structures in Egypt in the nineteenth century and the gradual incorporation of a significant middle class for which service to the state was an important source of livelihood and identity.[13] But what kind of impact did this state have on lower classes, whether urban or rural?

These questions, central to the construction of our frame for social history, remain to be answered. I can only attempt here to offer some initial reflections on the ways in which the particularities of the state in the region shaped modern history. Middle Eastern states did survive for most of the nineteenth century and, as a result, the people of the region were governed by an indigenous ruling group. Certain continuities ensued: some of the ruling families of the eighteenth century in Palestine, for example, were the officials of the nineteenth century and the bourgeoisie of the twentieth, while nineteenth-century Egyptian official *cum* landholding families still formed an important part of the political scene in the mid-twentieth century. While local rulers eventually were drafted, in almost all cases, into the service of European imperialism, the very fact that they existed, imbued with a firm sense of who they were and how deeply their roots reached into the past of their society, made them a repository of a distinctive cultural tradition. An enduring state, which sheltered the ruling group and provided them with employment, allowed them to survive the vicissitudes of contact with Europe. In this sense, I would suggest that the long, unbroken history of the state in the modern Arab world helped, in an immediate way, to preserve the language, arts, religion, and broad cultural identity of the region. Here instructive parallels can be drawn, I think, between the Arab world and China and Japan, where the continuity of the state institution and the ruling elite also preserved indigenous culture. Africa and Latin America, which witnessed far greater political disruption, sustained far greater cultural losses as well.

Herein lies a critical connection to social history: Until we acquire a far better idea of the relationship between state and civil society, we are at a loss as to how to account for the proven resiliency of state structures in the region. The old visions of the Ottoman Empire as alien Turkish oppressor, or the Egyptian state as instrument of the Turco-Circassian ruling caste, do not allow us to explore the intricacies of how people experienced state power and how they, in turn, buttressed or undermined that power in certain times and places. The extent to which the bulk of the population participated in the cultural world of the ruling elite and derived their identity from it constitutes a separate question of central importance to social history.

Historians have made a fairly strong case for the strength and continuity of the state in the modern Middle East, but precisely the opposite has been argued as well: for many, the striking feature of the state was a discontinuity bred by European penetration and colonial control. Not surprisingly, the case is argued most forcefully for areas where European penetration was particularly thoroughgoing: Abdallah Laroui's analysis of the colonial state in the Maghreb, for example, focuses on the break with indigenous tradition.[14] In the Arab East as well, the post–World War I dismantling of the Ottoman Empire and the carving up of its Arab territories among the European Powers ushered in a set of mini-states formally or informally dominated by their European sponsors. While the Powers generally aimed for continuity in government to minimize disruption, political aims introduced large elements of discontinuity as radically different approaches and personnel were required (in order to, for example, implement the British commitment to Zionism in Palestine).[15] Even in Egypt, where long state tradition and a consolidated territory worked to encourage continuity, the British insistence on fiscal solvency and tight control of the civil service introduced new policies and personnel.[16] The question is partly one of timing. The proponents of discontinuity focus almost exclusively on the disruptions of the late nineteenth and early twentieth centuries.

Certainly the European intrusion into the politics of the region closed off, to a certain extent, the history of the state in the twentieth century from its eighteenth- and nineteenth-century predecessors. Did this disruption constitute the signal difference between state formation in Europe and in the Middle East? Was this the break that fractured the relationship between state and civil society, that put the state on a path leading to ever-greater isolation from its population? Again, the historical literature does not address these questions in any systematic fashion. Our frame for social history needs a more coherent account of the impact of the colonial period on the state itself as well as popular perceptions of it.

Overall, the entire question of the state in the region calls for further historical investigation and a resort to social history: until we can better outline the changing characteristics of the state and its relationship to the population, the historical picture remains dim. Transformation of the state is undoubtedly one of the "big changes" of the modern period, but the precise nature of this transformation needs to be on the research agenda.

Capitalist development has proved another major and closely related pole of interest for historians of the region. Here we are on slightly firmer ground because, while still thin, research in this area seems more systematic and better focused. The neglect of economic history by Orientalist scholars may actually work in our favor here: with fewer dragons to slay, historians have been able to pose and pursue the central questions in a fairly straightforward fashion. There is general agreement, of course, that the development of capitalism in the Arab world, at least in its nineteenth-century form, derived directly from European penetration of the region. There is less agreement on the timing and characteristics of this development.

The pioneers in the field tended to sketch European economic penetration as a fairly rapid and totally transformative event. According to Issawi, Egypt, for example, moved in the nineteenth century from a subsistence to an export-oriented economy "accompanied by the breakdown of traditional feudal, communal, or tribal structures."[17] While Gabriel Baer, one of the first to devote himself full time to the social history of the region, raised questions as to how total the breakdown of social structures actually had been, he did write his history within the economic frame Issawi provided: the net transformation of the "subsistence economy" into an "export-oriented economy" aptly summarized, in Baer's view, the nineteenth-century experience.[18] This singular focus on the dramatic economic transformations of the nineteenth century, characterized by the demise of subsistence agriculture and local crafts in the face of the harnessing of the Arab economies to those of Europe, is now being modified in at least two significant ways. First, although there is no dispute about the significance of the nineteenth century and European penetration, certain important economic changes predated the nineteenth century. Second, in the nineteenth century itself, the process of transformation was uneven. In short, neither the "subsistence economy" nor the "export-oriented economy" was exactly that.

Much compelling new work is being done on the critical nature of pre-nineteenth-century economic change. The term "subsistence," for example, loses much of its meaning in the face of well-documented accounts of the active commercial life and long-distance marketing of agrarian communities. Surayah al-Faroqhi's study of sixteenth-century Anatolia, which illustrates the strong urban-rural ties and highly commercialized economy of the region, points to the kind of work that can and should be done in the economic history of Arab areas.[19] Peter Gran's study of the commercial revival in eighteenth-century Egypt, which spawned a cultural renaissance of sorts as well, sows real doubt about the standard view of a fragmented and inverted economy.[20]

Overall, we now know enough to be wary of positing the year 1800 as the ground zero from which economic development took off. The complexities of economic organization in the sixteenth century, and the absence of any solid evidence, as Roger Owen points out,[21] for economic decline in the seventeenth and eighteenth suggest that significant economic developments—including a rise in commercialization and even the growth of localized indigenous capitalism—occurred well before the nineteenth century.

If some of the economic changes of the nineteenth century were less novel than previously thought, recent work also shows that they transformed the region less thoroughly. Roger Owen's *The Middle East in the World Economy, 1800–1914* pursues as a major theme the unevenness of nineteenth-century economic change. Coastal regions most directly affected by European trade bore the brunt of transformation, along with the immediate hinterland, when it was suitable for commercialized agriculture. Elsewhere, however, in the long-established cities of the interior and in many parts of the countryside, the expansion of the European-based world economy did not annihilate the old: many indigenous crafts survived and flourished, and preexisting patterns of land tenure, technology, and capital accumulation and use persisted. While Owen's basic agreement with the Dependency perspective is reflected in the book's title, he is careful to eschew the extremism of early Dependency writers who held that European expansion wiped the slate clean. Much of his book is, in fact, concerned with the ways in which European commercial, financial, and political expansion intersected with the specificities of the region's economic arrangements.

But what were those specificities? The characterization of pre-nineteenth-century economic organization has sparked theoretical debates in Middle East history, a refreshing development in an otherwise rather untheoretical field not known for lively disagreement on issues other than that of the virtues of Orientalism.

The Marxist modes of production approach has, I think, generated some interesting and suggestive discussion. While I agree with Owen's remarks about the limitations, both theoretical and empirical, of the concept of precapitalist modes,[22] I do think the discussions about the characterization of the precapitalist mode in the Arab world have helped raise a number of critical questions. The "modes" approach can be the vehicle for a thoroughgoing interrogation of economic and political organization insofar as it demands knowledge of basic productive processes, the status of those who produce, and the role of the state and others in extracting the surplus. Before any systematic debate about precapitalist modes was joined, historians tended to employ the term "feudal" rather loosely to denote the devolution of economic power to local "notables" in the seventeenth and eighteenth centuries.[23] However, the very real and persistent role of the Ottoman state in the collection of surplus prompted attempts to rehabilitate the concept of the Asiatic mode of production. This had the advantage of underscoring the central role of state coercion in the extraction of wealth.[24] The classic version of the Asiatic mode, however, in which it appears as a static, nondeveloping social formation without significant levels of commercial activity, prompted Samir Amin to propose a new "tributary mode" which could accommodate the historical reality of the region—one of very active trade, large urban centers, and a powerful and coercive state.[25]

We cannot hope here to evaluate the various models, lacking as we do both space and basic information. I do think the debate has contributed, however, to our overall sense of the region before the nineteenth century—thanks to the emphasis on the interconnectedness of the economic and political and the need to study the nineteenth-century impact of Europe in the context of preexisting social formations.

The debate has also matured and deepened as historians have attempted to come to terms with the particularities of class structure bred by economic and political developments. Haim Gerber, in his book *The Social Origins of the Modern Middle East*, argues that the key to understanding modern sociopolitical events lies in the absence of a landed upper class in the region up to the nineteenth century, and the relative weakness of this aristocratic class when it finally did emerge.[26] It was, in effect, the preexisting agrarian system, in which the peasantry enjoyed control of the land, that was to condition the European economic impact into the twentieth century, impede the development of a strong, indigenous agrarian upper class, and, by extension, preclude class struggle. Gerber is critical of Dependency writers, whose theory, he feels, is not readily applicable to the region because it posits the strengthening of an indigenous landed upper class as the inevitable and key internal result of European encroachment, economic integration, and the peripheralization of the indigenous economy.

The historical absence of a landed aristocracy is not, however, incompatible with at least some Dependency approaches. Caglar Keydar, for example, in his *State and Class in Turkey: A Study in Capitalist Development*, describes an Ottoman agrarian regime very similar to that presented by Gerber but still argues for the peripheralization of the Ottoman economy in the course of the nineteenth century, a peripheralization accomplished through the good offices of a new indigenous merchant bourgeoisie, not a landed aristocracy.[27] Both writers agree that, compared with China or Russia, the Ottoman Empire did not allow a landed elite to oppress the peasantry, a difference that was to shape the political struggles of the nineteenth and twentieth centuries by effectively avoiding the great land-lord/peasant conflict that underlay much of the modern history of Russia and China. One of the difficulties in evaluating these promising discussions is the thinness of our historical knowledge of the rural environment, especially the peasantry, as we will see below.

What are the questions awaiting the social historian here? Clearly the economic transformation did not affect all areas and all people in the same way. The process was, and is, a complex one: European capitalism moved into the region at varying speeds and intersected with different forms of economic and social organization. The peasant in the highly commercialized Egyptian Delta, the artisan of Damascus, the Bedouin in the Syrian desert, and the merchant in Beirut saw different faces of this capitalism. What unified their experiences? The older version of total wrenching change in the nineteenth century has been modified, but does the new version have enough coherence to serve as the frame for social history? Again, the work needs to proceed on a number of fronts. Our understanding of modern economic history will continue to be circumscribed by the state of knowledge in social history. Signal economic developments, including the ways in which the growth of capitalism incubated new classes, can be described and understood only through close study of the lives of people who lived the period. Questions concerning the rate and extent of capitalist transformation will be answered, ultimately, by research into the ways people's productive activities and consumption patterns were changing.

The last, and most problematic, of the poles of significance for the historians of the modern period is the coming of the West as a culture. The Orientalist version of the East-West encounter revolved around a number of themes, all of which depicted, to varying degrees, the West as a vital, curious, and expansive culture which first sought knowledge of the East and then, by virtue of its innate superiority, transformed it as the East adopted Western culture, albeit in a fragmented and often superficial fashion. A key element in this analysis was, of course, the characterization of indigenous culture as "Islamic," in which values, world view, and modes of appropriation of knowledge derived directly from Islam. Bernard Lewis, for example, could write a book entitled *The Muslim Discovery of Europe* in which the innately incurious qualities of the "Muslim" world stand in stark contrast to the openness of the European world produced by the Reformation and Renaissance.[28]

Given such disparities, the outcome of the great encounter is foregone: the vastly more sophisticated, knowing, and self-conscious European culture forced the Muslim world to abandon the "old attitude of disdain and lack of interest. . . . At last Muslims were turning toward Europe, if not with admiration, then with respect, and perhaps fear, and paying it the supreme compliment of imitation."[29] The basic division of the field of Middle East history (which still predominates in most university courses and texts) into an "Islamic History" from the time of the rise of Islam to the late eighteenth century and a "Modern Middle East History" of the nineteenth and twentieth centuries subscribes to the view, perhaps unwittingly, that Islam defined the culture of the region until the modernizing impact of Europe.

A compelling and systematic critique of this version of history has, I think, been made by Edward Said, Bryan Turner, and the various contributors to the short-lived *Review of Middle East Studies* published in London in the 1970s.[30] I will not repeat their arguments here, except to say I feel relatively optimistic that their criticisms of the Orientalist version of the region—particularly of its essentialist and ahistorical aspects— have permeated the consciousness of an entire new generation of historians.

We have made far less progress, however, in the construction of an alternative. The culture of the Arab world did undergo significant change at deep-enough levels to qualify the cultural encounter with Europe as, indeed, one of the "big changes" of the modern period. We have yet, however, to outline the contours of this encounter, much less grasp its full nature. In distinction from the Orientalist tendency to divorce "culture" from its economic and political context, we need to situate the encounter squarely in the context of shifting power relations of West and East. The stark facts of imperialism and colonialism lie at the heart of the encounter, and as one looks at the Western imprint on intellectual life in the Arab world today, the full import of "cultural hegemony" becomes obvious.

Very few recent historical studies, however, venture into the cultural sphere. I suspect the very strong hold of Orientalism here, more than elsewhere, has discouraged historians from joining Talal Asad in the project of coming to terms with the Islamic discourse or any other significant feature of the region's culture.[31] The real possibilities of studying the cultural life of the region within a framework liberated from Orientalism have been suggested by Peter Gran in his *Islamic Roots of Capitalism.*[32] His study of cultural production in eighteenth-century Egypt seeks to demonstrate the vitality of cultural development as well as the ways in which a body of literature employing the language and symbols of the Islamic discourse might actually, following Gran's analysis, have been laying the intellectual foundations for the development of capitalism. Outside of Gran's work, however, I do not know of any historical study of modern culture that departs significantly from the Orientalist version of a stagnant indigenous culture revitalized by its response to, and appropriation of, the West. Nor does Gran himself deal with the nineteenth century, when, by all accounts, we do confront cultural disjuncture. Indeed, in the study of nineteenth- and twentieth-century intellectual history, the theme of Western-inspired renaissance, central to the work of Albert Hourani (*Arabic Thought in the Liberal Age*) and Hisham Sharabi (*Arab Intellectuals and the West: The Formative Years, 1875–1914*), was so entrenched until recently as to go virtually unexamined.[33]

In short, the East-West encounter, always taken as central to the modern history of the region, turns out to be one of the most impoverished research areas. We still lack a basic appreciation of the nature and depth of European cultural penetration: outside of a rather small group of Arab intellectuals, precisely what kind of impact did the West have on indigenous culture? Certain fields of knowledge—the Arab historiographic tradition comes to mind—were virtually annihilated by the embrace of Western epistemologies, but what, if anything, does this tell us about the persistence of cultural forms in other areas? How did the cultural production and identity of the vast majority of the population change? Did the enthusiasm for Western culture among the rising European-oriented middle classes disrupt their communication with other classes to the point where old social alliances came to be threatened? Many of the answers to these questions seem, in fact, to lie in the field of social history: only when we can trace the cultural encounter with the West as it was experienced by various social groups and classes can we hope to understand its full dimensions and import.

We have identified three "big changes" of the modern period recognized by the literature—a qualitative change in the power and reach of the state, the development of capitalism, and the impact of Western culture—which frame any study of social history. All these changes had something to do, of course, with Europe: the centrality of European expansion in the nineteenth century and the continued domination of the region by various Big Powers in the twentieth to what has transpired in the Arab world cannot be denied. While these changes are connected to the rise of the West, they are not, however, fully reducible to Western influence. Both the complexity of the political, economic, and cultural life of the region before the intrusion of Western power and the ways in which Western political needs, economic demands, and cultural missions intersected with indigenous society are key aspects of modern history.

We have not, as of yet, come to terms with this history, so that we still lack satisfactory answers to fairly basic questions, such as those of periodization (When does "modern" history truly begin?) and unit of analysis (Do we study the whole Arab world, the territories of the Ottoman Empire, or the Arab East in order best to capture the dynamic of development?). Social historians, insofar as they direct their attention to the human experience of the big political, economic, and cultural changes, and the human role in making these changes, will eventually provide, I think, many of the answers. By looking at a few of the studies in social history we now have, we can begin to see how the framework of the "big changes" is being employed, albeit implicitly, and consider how findings in the field of social history might, in turn, help refine that framework.

Examples of Social History

Most social historians have chosen to concentrate on one particular social group and on how one category of people—a class, a gender, a profession, etc.—experienced history. I confine my discussion here to how three such groups—peasants, merchants and artisans, and women—have been handled by social historians of the Arab world (and the wider Middle East when particularly relevant). The following is by no means a comprehensive survey of the literature (which remains, unfortunately, rather thin); I have tried, however, to select recent work representative of the different ways in which social historians and others have approached these groups in the Arab world.

Peasants

While trade and nomadic pastoralism have made important contributions to the economic life of the Arab world, the region has been overwhelmingly agrarian in terms of the pursuits of the vast majority of the population and sectoral shares in the economic base. The near dearth of historical writing of the peasantry thus comes as something of a surprise.

The neglect of the peasant arises, I think, out of the problem of sources common to peasant society everywhere and the particular bias toward the urban that developed within the Arab world itself. The paucity of sources derives from the simple fact that peasants, largely illiterate and lacking leisure, were unlikely to leave any written records of their activities and thoughts. Indeed, the few primary sources we have that purport to describe peasant conditions and customs in any detail prior to the twentieth century were written by city-dwellers whose attitude of unveiled animosity toward their subjects does not encourage confidence.[34] Peasants could not shake their bumpkin reputation, magnified in a society of long continuous urban traditions whose cultural life was inextricably intertwined (certainly in the mind of the city-dweller) with the past and present glories of Baghdad, Damascus, Cairo, and Istanbul. On the other hand, the basic material conditions of the peasantry might actually have been better documented in the Middle East region than in many other areas of the world because of the presence of the agrarian-based Ottoman state, which kept relatively good track of the rural sources of its wealth. Surayah Faroqhi's work on a group of late-sixteenth-century peasant villages near Konya in Anatolia, drawing on tax registers and Islamic court records that contained peasant inheritances, illustrates the ways in which state records can be used to reconstruct the material life of the peasantry.[35] Very few social historians have ventured, however, into the study of the Arab peasantry and the way they lived the "big changes."

The relationship between the peasant and the state does constitute a key theme of Gerber's *The Social Origins of the Modern Middle East*, discussed above. The Ottoman agrarian regime, as he describes it, was based on the security of small peasant holders who produced primarily for their own and local consumption. The state's desire to abort any embryonic competition for power, in the form of a landed upper class, predisposed the Ottoman bureaucracy and court system to enact and uphold a series of laws that protected peasant tenure. Certain practices, such as that of holding villages communally responsible for tax payments and intervening very little in internal governance, tended to build solidarity in the village community.

The sketch of a fairly egalitarian autonomous village in which small peasants controlled most land is drawn convincingly for villages in the vicinity of Bursa (Anatolia), the site of Gerber's own research. When he attempts to generalize these findings to other areas, especially the Arab East in the seventeenth, eighteenth, and nineteenth centuries, we feel on far shakier ground. The growing power in the eighteenth century of the landed "notables" in Palestine, some of them firmly based in the countryside, and the commercialization of agriculture in Egypt during the first half of the nineteenth century are only two examples of situations in which the autonomous village community surely must have been threatened. As Gerber himself acknowledges, we need far more research on peasant life even to begin to draw conclusions about the relationship of peasants to political power in the Arab provinces of the empire.

The Arab peasant's experience of the increasing power and demands of the state in the nineteenth and twentieth centuries has been studied, in part, in the context of peasant revolts of the period. Gabriel Baer argues that two factors—the increase in tax exactions occasioned by the state's growing ambitions and the imposition of a peasant draft—ushered in a series of peasant revolts in the first two-thirds of the nineteenth century in Egypt. Similarly, state centralization and the draft drove the peasants of the Arab East—especially in the mountainous terrain of Mt. Lebanon, the Palestinian highlands, and Jabal Druze—to rebel repeatedly against the Egyptian occupation forces and, later, the restored Ottoman government over the course of the nineteenth century.[36]

Baer stresses that peasant rebellions in the Arab world appear almost always to be directed against a state authority perceived as an oppressive outsider. This characteristic carries over into the Mandate period and the "peasant rebellions" against the French in Syria (1925) and the British in Egypt (1919) and Palestine (1936–38). If we search in the region for a rebellion that pits the peasantry against their logical class enemies, the landlords, the only salient example, according to Baer, is that of the Kisrawan peasant revolt in Lebanon (1858–61). The implication is clear: the agrarian-based state stood as landlord in relation to the peasantry and a major structural conflict, as a result, was that between the state bureaucracy and the peasantry, a conflict that grew more violent as the power and reach of the state expanded.

While I am not fully convinced that the nationalist movements in the twentieth century should be characterized as peasant revolts (we need much more evidence here), the other aspects of Baer's thesis are highly suggestive. We are dealing with an agrarian society that is not (with a few exceptions such as that of Kisrawan) feudal: the European model, as a result, is probably not very helpful. Indeed, the history of the peasantry in the modern period is tightly tied to the history of the growth of the state, certainly in the twentieth century, when, gradually, the private landlord came to play a more important role throughout the region. Keeping this central fact in mind, we have the beginnings of an approach to the study of how peasants experienced political change.

In the realm of the development of capitalism as well, there has been some pioneering work. Sarah Graham-Brown's study of the peasantry in Jabal Nablus in Mandate Palestine focuses on the kinds of change we expect to see when capitalism comes to dominate a rural sector.[37] She sketches a three-stage process of integration into the world market: first agricultural products become commodities; next, the means of production (land and tools) become commodities; and finally, labor power becomes a commodity. When she looks at the peasantry of Jabal Nablus, however, she notes that this process was, in fact, very uneven. Agricultural products were commoditized to a certain extent, but the arrangements governing control of land and tools changed quite slowly, with a general persistence of sharecropping. Labor power was transformed only partially with the maintenance of a large pool of rural labor.

Graham-Brown stresses the particularities of the Nablus district: its relative isolation in the hinterland and its share in the unevenness of economic and political development in Palestine as a result of British policies and the development of Jewish capital. I suspect, however, that the Nablus pattern was repeated, with variations, in much of the region. As imported capitalism entered only certain sectors, it transformed the economy piecemeal, allowing for the persistence of former economic arrangements as long as they served to provide markets, goods, and labor.

What did this mean for the peasant? Ylana Miller's study of rural

Palestine under the Mandate explicitly connects the economic disruptions bred by uneven development to the growth of the nationalist movement among the peasantry.[38] To what extent was the peasant unrest of the Mandate period and on into the 1950s in Syria and Iraq also the outgrowth of this uneven transformation, which commercialized agriculture but also, oddly enough, increased subjugation to the new landlord class? We need other studies to flesh out the impact on the peasantry.

In the third area of the impact of the West, we are even more at sea. To my knowledge, there is no historical study of peasant culture that deals with the ways in which the cultural developments of the nineteenth and twentieth centuries did or did not resonate with the peasantry. A major clue may lie in peasant participation in nationalist movements, critical in Palestine, Syria, Egypt, and Algeria. We await, however, closer studies of peasant participation in all these cases.[39] The work in this area has hardly begun.

Merchants and Artisans

A long history of major urban centers based on international and local trade as well as handicrafts made merchants and artisans highly visible social groups in the Arab world. The history of urban merchants and artisans in the modern period, while certainly far from complete, has received more attention than that of the peasantry. Sources are more abundant, because many merchants were members of a literate elite and because merchants and artisans alike played a role in urban politics that caught the eye of chroniclers, biographers, and officials.

The relationship of the merchant group to the state provides one major theme for historians of the modern period, although few go as far as Samir Amin in the identification of merchants with the ruling elite.[40] In his monumental study of the old social classes in Iraq, Hanna Batatu points out the extent to which Baghdad's merchants depended upon the state to secure and ensure a settled political situation. The all-important transit trade flowed through Baghdad only when law and order prevailed in the Iraqi valleys; in times of insecurity, other routes were chosen and the Baghdad-based merchants were left stranded.[41] The faltering of Mamluk rule in the nineteenth century and the reimposition by force of Ottoman control in 1831, strong enough to contain the Mamluks but not strong enough to secure peace and prosperity, disrupted trade routes and decimated local markets.

In Egypt, in contrast, early in the century, the merchants confronted a powerful state under Muhammad 'Ali. The big merchants of Cairo enjoyed a history of considerable political and economic power: as one of the key groups allied with the Mamluk ruling elite, they had managed, over the course of the eighteenth century, to grow richer and even to acquire land in the form of *iltizams*.[42] According to Afaf Lutfi al-Sayyid Marsot, Muhammad 'Ali initially also allied with the big merchants, an alliance based on their mutual interest in territorial expansion and mercantilist policies.[43] The fortunes of the merchant group soon fell victim, however, to Muhammad 'Ali's desire to exert state control over trade and his strategic dealings with European merchants at the expense of the indigenous group that had helped him consolidate power.

In short, the close relationship between the state and merchants proved both a boon and a bane to merchants in the region: they were protected but also vulnerable to changes in state policy. The perennial question why such an active and wealthy class did not sponsor a full-blown indigenous capitalism may find its answer, in part, in the comforts of this relationship. In addition, any mercantilist tendencies on the part of the state, as both Batatu and Marsot demonstrate, were nipped in the bud by growing European intervention in the form of trade treaties and the enforcement of Capitulations for European merchants.

The development of the state also influenced artisanal production, although in a less dramatic fashion. Artisans suffered in eighteenth-century Cairo and mid-nineteenth-century Baghdad when the state was too weak to secure their access to raw materials and markets. The rise of a more powerful state was not, however, without its own set of problems: the strangling regulation of crafts under Muhammad 'Ali is a case in point.

On the other hand, some of the new work on the organization of labor in the late nineteenth and early twentieth centuries suggests that the persistence of guild structures owes much to the relationship between the state and the guilds. Donald Quartaert, in his study of the late Ottoman Empire, views the modern state as heir to the close and mutually beneficial arrangements that bound the state and crafts producers in earlier Ottoman times. The guilds were the linchpin of the system, for the state could collect taxes through the good offices of the guilds and, in turn, owed guild members patronage and protection of their livelihoods. The porters' and boatmen's guilds of Istanbul, for example, enjoyed the patronage of the court in the Hamidian period, an association that may, in fact, have cost them power after the Young Turk Revolution.[44]

Overall, the old view of rapid marginalization of guild structures in the nineteenth century by the emergence of a modern bureaucratic state that reserved the regulation of urban occupations for itself must now be modified. Many aspects of "traditional" organization and identity lingered among both producers and service workers as a result, in part, of a specific history of political support for the guilds.

Historians have also been concerned with the growing marginality of merchants and artisans to the economic system in the nineteenth and twentieth centuries. On a political level, the significant increase in the power of the state enabled its official class to dispense with merchant allies. At the same time, on the economic level, the encroachments of European capitalism were weakening their economic base. That there was a powerful merchant class at all in the eighteenth and nineteenth centuries revises an old assumption in the field that the Muslim Arab trading elite had been put out of business during the sixteenth century by the discovery of the Cape route. Now the serious shift in the fortunes of the merchant class is situated squarely in the nineteenth century and attributed, by and large, to the growing competition they faced from their European counterparts or from fellow countrymen with European connections. Leila Fawaz has studied this process in Beirut, where the more lucrative long-distance trade of Europe rapidly came to be monopolized by Europeans themselves or by Christian Lebanese who were oriented toward Europe.[45]

Standard views of the impact of European penetration on artisans have also been revised. The notion that the importation of European goods virtually annihilated handicraft production in the region seems something of an exaggeration.

Certain crafts were, of course, hit very hard. Fred Lawson's article on the ways in which the extreme disruption of the textile industry in Upper Egypt generated artisans' rebellions (which most historians have erroneously identified as peasant rebellions) illustrates the severity of the European impact on the textile sector.[46] Elsewhere, however, as a number of studies have shown, a restructuring of the economy occurred, so that some crafts that found a ready local market or employed specialized skills, like carpet making, expanded significantly in the nineteenth century.[47] While we now have a sense of the aggregate figures involved, we know far less about the changes in the organization of craft production in most geographic areas.

The exception is Egypt. Important new work on the development of the working class in Egypt has enabled us to observe the mixed fate of the artisan more closely. Joel Beinin and Zachary Lockman, in their recent *Workers on the Nile: Nationalism, Communism, Islam, and the Egyptian Working Class, 1882–1954*, identify the Egyptian artisan, displaced by European economic encroachment in the later nineteenth century, as one component of the labor force in the large-scale industrial sector. Not all artisans, however, were displaced: many managed, after the demise of the guild system, to adjust to new methods and tastes and continue artisanal production. Indeed, up to the late 1930s, Beinin and Lockman say, the urban artisanal sector was both numerically and economically dominant.[48] It was this artisanal world that shaped the organization and outlook of labor well into the twentieth century. Ellis Goldberg, in another new study of workers in Egypt, has argued forcefully for the persistence of "guildlike associations," demonstrated by the incorporation of guild titles and forms of organization into the newly emerging trade unions of the 1930s.[49]

As certain forms of craft production became more oriented toward external markets and even relied on foreign capital, surely the life of the artisan was gradually transformed. We are beginning to understand, however, thanks to the interests of social history, the critical importance of artisanal production to the life of the region well after European encroachment presumably transformed the economy. While we now have a much better idea of the way development of the artisanate occurred in Egypt, the fate of modern artisans in other regions of the Arab world remains to be examined.

The last, and again the thorniest, question is that of cultural change. Peter Gran's book is unique insofar as it attempts to penetrate the cultural life of eighteenth-century merchants in Egypt.[50] The vitality and resources of the class enabled them to sponsor a cultural revival in which merchant *diwans* (salons) lent the forum for discussion and contact essential to the renewal of cultural production. This flurry of activity among the merchant class was to fall victim, however, to the state-building policies of Muhammad 'Ali, which deprived the merchants of their economic base and coopted the leading intellectuals of the day. Looking toward Europe as the rising challenge, the refurbished Egyptian state naturally tended to sponsor intellectual projects oriented toward the comprehension and appropriation of European knowledge. Here a number of questions central to the theme of cultural impact need to be pursued. To what extent did the priorities of the states in the region play a critical role in the undermining of indigenous culture? Did the loss of the relative autonomy of the merchant class seriously weaken a primary source of patronage for indigenous cultural expression? Did the specifically "Islamic" form of cultural production come to be associated with the culture of "losing" classes, leading to a loss of vitality and momentum of the discourse as a whole?

We have yet to see a parallel discussion of artisan culture. The interlocking of the artisanal guild structure with various Sufi orders in Egypt has been noted by André Raymond: the activities of the artisan class, from daily ritual to political rebellion, were colored by their Sufi connections.[51] The blows dealt to this cultural life by the state can be deduced from the ways in which establishment *'ulama*, with the state's backing, repeatedly attacked, in the course of the nineteenth century, the reputations and practices of the Sufi orders to which most artisans belonged.

The one systematic study of this process, by Frederic De Jong, does not, however, deal with the implications for the cultural world of the artisan.[52] Did the discrediting and marginalizing of the "lower class" Sufi orders spell cultural impoverishment for artisans? Did the discouragement of this form of indigenous culture, viewed as potentially insurrectionary by the state, leave the artisans without acceptable forms of cultural expression? The role of the state in the suppression of indigenous cultural life, and the way this process may have prepared the ground for the cultural imperialism of Europe, should be on the research agenda.

We have the beginnings of research into this question for twentieth-century Egypt. Beinin and Lockman's focus on the political role of urban workers allows for only passing references to the evolving culture of the artisan-*cum*-working class or, for that matter, the larger peasant-*cum*-working class. Goldberg, in *Tinker, Tailor and Textile Worker*, takes on the task of describing the cultural world of a working class that included urban artisans in Egypt of the 1930s and 1940s. The strong historical urban roots of this culture are apparent in, for example, the importance of the urban cafe as a locus of both cultural and political activities.[53] It lay beyond his scope, however, to analyze how this culture had evolved in the modern period or how an indigenous urban culture of the lower classes was or was not being transformed in the context of political and economic developments. We still await research on the cultural world of artisans and how, most importantly, that culture underpinned—or did not—that of the emerging working class.

Women

The history of women, or more broadly, the history of gender whether female or male, has received little attention from social historians of the Arab world, and this yawning gap in the historical literature has crippled our understanding of Arab history as a whole. Often excluded from overt participation in official politics, many economic activities, and the high culture of the society, women lived in a world defined by informal networks, "casual" economic activities, and popular culture. This was not, however, only the world of women: the majority of the precapitalist population, composed of the peasantry and urban lower classes inhabited this world as well. If we fail to comprehend women's activities, we fail to come to terms with the activities and institutions of most women and men alike.

The neglect of women's history stems in part, I believe, from the deeply ingrained view that, prior to the impact of Europe, Arab women were indeed a quintessentially oppressed group held in thrall to Arab men by

Islamic law, social custom, and sexual mores. Only as Western ideas about women penetrated the society was a debate about women's position joined which eventually brought change, however modest—in the form, for example, of the discarding of the veil and participation in nationalist movements.

This view does not encourage historical inquiry into the precapitalist period, for the truly and thoroughly oppressed have no history. It also reduces the history of women in the nineteenth and twentieth centuries to a history of Western ideas and the activities of a few elite women (whose important contributions should not be overlooked) in the area of formal politics.[54] This view neglects the very real role women played in indigenous society as well as the ways in which they experienced, and helped shape, the "big changes." Given the dearth of historical studies, we cannot do much more than suggest what might appear to be fruitful areas of research in light of our framework for social history, drawing, when available, on the few studies we do have.

Women probably experienced the growth of the state in a number of disparate ways. One of the most intriguing areas of research at present concerns the extent to which elite women wielded considerable political influence behind the scenes in the period preceding the rapid growth and rationalization of the state. While the formal politics of the Ottomans, for example, were indeed male defined and male run, the importance of the family to the political system, as a mechanism for political recruitment and alliance both in the Palace and out among the notable families of the provinces, provided an avenue for female participation. Study of the Ottoman royal *harim* by Fanny Davis reveals the ways in which the Sultan's concubines, sisters, daughters, and, above all, mother exercised considerable power. Using the good offices of the chief eunuch, they intervened in succession disputes, pushed for reform, and lent their considerable weight and money to social-welfare projects.[55]

Was this system of informal yet effective female influence eliminated by the political reforms of the nineteenth century? The exit of the chief eunuch from politics, for instance, does suggest that reforms in the bureaucracy and the institution of formal consultative councils narrowed the field for informal influence, and thereby for elite women's power. On the other hand, Margot Badran's studies of early Egyptian feminist movements illustrate the extent to which some upper-class women applied their experience of *harim* politics to the public-political sphere in both early feminist and nationalist movements.[56] This remains an area in which we need far more work.

On the other hand, the reformist state did pursue some programs that had a significant impact on women. The task of strengthening the country, for the Ottoman Empire and Egypt alike, called for state initiatives in the fields of health care and education that included the training of women as public health officials and licensed midwives and the establishment of a few state-run schools for girls.[57] The number of women trained and educated, as well as the number who benefited from their services, remained modest; this involvement of the state, however, did set a precedent for twentieth-century policies.

By the end of the nineteenth century, as most states in the region succumbed to European control of one kind or another, European views and colonial policies began to play a real part. Rosemary Sayigh has pointed out how a major justification of colonial rule, enunciated by British and French officials alike, was the degradation of women in "native" society, a condition to be ameliorated through the good offices of the European governors.[58] On the ground, however, the colonial state, as it functioned in Egypt, for example, did not actively pursue policies that promoted women's issues. Scant attention was paid to female education on the grounds of fiscal constraint, and, in general, the colonial rulers followed a hands-off policy on the woman issue, citing the perceived risks of alienating the "traditional" sectors from colonial rule. While I have examined colonial policies elsewhere,[59] basic studies of the chasm between official rhetoric and actual policy need to be done. The broader question—to what extent colonial rule actually retarded the development of indigenous positions on women's issues by claiming the territory as Western property but failing to implement any constructive policies— still needs to be addressed.

The notion that Arab women were closed off from the main economic activities of the society until the advent and development of capitalism brought them into the labor force in the twentieth century has been revised for several reasons. First, studies of *waqf* property and other urban real estate in the period preceding the arrival of European capitalism demonstrate the very active role women played in the urban economy as investors in, and managers of, property.[60] Second, the consistent contribution of the peasant woman to agricultural production has been noted.[61] Third, there is a real possibility that European capitalism, as it penetrated the region, may have actually narrowed women's economic opportunities. It did undermine certain crafts, such as textiles, in which women had been particularly active, and displace the indigenous Muslim merchant class to which some women belonged and in which women operated as important investors.[62]

We must be careful here, of course, not to lose sight of the real limitations placed upon women's economic participation by the practice among the upper classes of female seclusion and by the exclusion of women from most of the more skilled and better remunerated trade and artisanal sectors. Still, the sexual division of labor brought by capitalist encroachment did not necessarily work in women's favor.

The history of women's cultural life is, once more, rather poorly documented. The participation of women in elite culture, as patrons of architects and artists or as poets in their own right, has received some attention.[63] It suggests the extent to which the female poets, novelists, and artists of today are the heirs of an indigenous tradition that did, in fact, recognize the creative impulse in women.

At the level of popular culture, far less work has been done. The important connection of women to Sufi orders, for example, is often referred to in passing, but we lack any systematic study.[64] Most critical questions have yet to be tackled at all. Can we distinguish a specifically "women's culture"? If so, what did the development of cultural life along separate gender lines mean for the overall evolution of cultural expression in the society? To what extent were women disproportionately identified with the "heterodox" aspects of culture that came under attack from the state in the nineteenth century?

Moving to the issue of the prevailing views of women in the society, how did Western sponsorship of less gender segregation affect Arab women? Which groups in Arab society stood to profit from adopting Western views, and which perceived them as particularly threatening?[65] How does the history of the religious discourse on women in the modern period reflect a variety of social needs among different groups in society—their experience, in brief, of the "big changes"?

Clearly, in all aspects of the study of women and gender we have many more questions than answers. Work in Arab history has yet to make any significant contribution to our understanding of gender in general, despite the attempt by Mervat Hatem to argue the case for the particularities of its autonomous sex-gender system.[66] We just do not know enough about the history of gender in the Arab world to support the development of new theory in our area.

An overwhelming problem here lies in the ghettoization of women's history: the entire question of women and gender is relatively isolated from the field of history as a whole. It is very telling that all the social historians mentioned above who have written on peasants, merchants and artisans, or the working class mention women only in passing and offer no reflections on the issue of gender in the social group they are studying. Women's historians, in the field of Arab history and elsewhere, are trained as historians of the social history of their region and as a result enjoy a broad historical perspective. Their work, however, has yet to be recognized as central to the field. The implications of gender organization in the society for our overall understanding of economic development, the functioning and ideology of political institutions, or the cultural crisis are many. We need to move the study of gender, of the ways in which being a woman or being a man shaped human experience, to center stage.

Concluding Remarks

We still stand, in the field of Arab social history, on the threshold. The task of historians today is, I believe, twofold. We need to develop a broad understanding of the modern period, an understanding that can encompass the rhythms and features of the indigenous society as well as the patterns of European penetration. At the same time, we must continue to conduct the focused studies that can help us understand how people lived the period. The two tasks are reciprocal: while the broad understanding provides the framework within which we can orient our work and learn to ask the significant questions, the focused studies will help test and refine our broad understanding.

I have attempted here to argue that the work of the social historian is critical to this venture. Social historians are bridge builders. Through the investigation of the lives of ordinary people, they seek to span the big structural changes and the human realities. The field of Arab social history has been woefully underdeveloped as a result, I think, of the absence, until recently, of such bridge building. We have tried to comprehend the major political, economic, and social changes of the period without, in fact, knowing very much at all about the people who made and lived these changes. Lacking a firm sense of political culture, economic activities, or the social life of the Arabs of modern times, many historians have resorted to the view of modern Arab history as a reaction to the West tempered, in various ways, only by the traditional "Islamic" mindset.

Studies in social history are helping to revolutionize our approach to the modern history of the Arab world. Standard periodization in the field has come under sharp scrutiny: our sense of "modern" history as having everything to do with the coming of the West is being questioned as we pay more attention to the many continuities in forms of economic activity and political culture. From the little we now know of the experience of the peasantry, merchants and artisans, and women, we see that their history does not divide into a neat before and after, but rather reaches back into the Ottoman past and beyond.

That the nineteenth century brought disjuncture to the Arab world cannot be denied, but part of the task of social historians is to come to terms with the ways in which people used their past experiences, drawing on their accumulated knowledge of themselves to bridge the disjuncture and make their history a whole. Only then will we have foundations solid enough to sustain the refining of ideas concerning the "big changes" of the modern period.

Notes

1. Charles Tilly, "Retrieving European Lives," in Olivier Zunz, ed., *Reliving the Past, The Worlds of Social History* (Chapel Hill: University of North Carolina Press, 1985), p.15.

2. See Charles Tilly, *op. cit.*; Olivier Zunz, "The Synthesis of Social Change: Reflections on American Social History"; William B. Taylor, "Between Global Powers and Local Knowledge: An Inquiry into Early Latin American Social History, 1500–1900"; David William Cohen, "Doing Social History from Pim's Doorway"; and William T. Rowe, "Approaches to Modern Chinese Social History"; all in Zunz, ed., *op. cit.*

3. See William Taylor, *op. cit.*, pp.115–90.

4. Albert Hourani, "The Present State of Islamic and Middle Eastern Historiography," in Hourani, *Europe and the Middle East* (Berkeley: University of California Press, 1980), pp.161–96.

5. For elaboration of this point, see my "Middle East Studies in the United States: The Coming Decade," in Hisham Sharabi, ed., *The Next Arab Decade* (Boulder, CO: Westview Press, 1988).

6. H. A. R. Gibb and H. Bowen, *Islamic Society and the West* (2 vols.) (Oxford: Oxford University Press, 1950, 1957).

7. See, for example, Moshe Ma'oz, *Ottoman Reform in Syria and Palestine* (Oxford: Clarendon Press, 1964); and Haim Gerber, *Ottoman Rule in Jerusalem* (Berlin: Klaus Schwarz Verlag, 1985).

8. The view embodied in almost any standard text until recently. See, for example, Bernard Lewis, *The Emergence of Modern Turkey* (London, 1961); and P. M. Holt, *Egypt and the Fertile Crescent* (London, 1966).

9. Daniel Crecelius, *The Roots of Modern Egypt* (Minneapolis, MN: Bibliotheca Islamica, 1981).

10. Amnon Cohen, *Palestine in the Eighteenth Century: Patterns of Government and Administration* (Jerusalem, 1973).

11. See, for example, Ihsan al-Nimr's study of Jabal Nablus in which the eighteenth century shines as an era of glorious independence. Ihsan al-Nimr, *Tarikh Jabal Nablus wa al-Balqa'* (Nablus, 1975).

12. See Linda Schatkowski Schilcher, *Families in Politics. Damascene Factions and Estates of the Eighteenth and Nineteenth Centuries* (Stuttgart: Franz Steiner Verlag, 1985); and Abraham Marcus, *The Middle East on the Eve of Modernity: Aleppo in the Eighteenth Century* (New York: Columbia University Press, 1989). See also the recently completed Ph.D. thesis at Georgetown University by Dina Rizk Khoury, "Land, Power and Local Notables in the Ottoman Empire: The Province of Mosul, 1700–1850," which tackles the problem of the eighteenth century for the *vilayet* of Mosul in Iraq, and ongoing work by Ph.D. candidate Beshara Doumani at the same university focusing on the Nablus region in Palestine.

13. F. Robert Hunter, *Egypt under the Khedives, 1805–1979: From Household Government to Modern Bureaucracy* (Pittsburgh, PA: University of Pittsburgh Press, 1984).

14. Abdallah Laroui, *The History of the Maghreb* (Princeton, NJ: Princeton University Press, 1977), chapters 13 and 14.

15. Ylana Miller, *Government and Society in Rural Palestine, 1920–1948* (Austin: University of Texas Press, 1985).

16. R.L. Tignor, *Modernization and British Colonial Rule in Egypt, 1882–1914* (Princeton, NJ: Princeton University Press, 1966).

17. Charles Issawi, "Egypt since 1800: A Study in Lopsided Development," in Charles Issawi, ed., *The Economic History of the Middle East, 1800–1914* (Chicago, IL: University of Chicago Press, 1966), p. 361.

18. Gabriel Baer, *Studies in the Social History of Modern Egypt* (Chicago, IL: University of Chicago Press, 1969), p. 213.

19. Surayah Faroqhi, *Towns and Townsmen of Ottoman Anatolia: Trade, Crafts, and Food Production in an Urban Setting* (Cambridge: Cambridge University Press, 1984).

20. Peter Gran, *Islamic Roots of Capitalism: Egypt, 1760–1840* (Austin: University of Texas Press, 1979).

21. Roger Owen, *The Middle East in the World Economy* (New York: Methuen, 1981).

22. The complex nature of this process is well illustrated in Alexander Schölch, "European Penetration and the Economic Development of Palestine, 1856–82"; and in Roger Owen, ed., *Studies in the Social History of Palestine in the Nineteenth and Twentieth Centuries* (Carbondale: Southern Illinois University Press, 1982).

23. See, for example, Halil Inalcik, "L'Empire Ottoman," in Inalcik, *Studies in Ottoman Social and Economic History* (London: Variorum Reprints, 1985).

24. See Huri Islamoglu and Caglar Keydar, "Agenda for Ottoman History," *Review* 1, no.1 (1977).

25. See Samir Amin, *The Arab Nation* (London: Zed Press, 1978).

26. Haim Gerber, *The Social Origins of the Modern Middle East* (Boulder, CO: Lynne Reinner Publications, 1987).

27. Caglar Keydar, *State and Class in Turkey: A Study in Capitalist Development* (Verso, 1987).

28. See Bernard Lewis, *The Muslim Discovery of Europe* (New York: W. W. Norton, 1982), especially his conclusions, pp. 295–308.

29. *Ibid.*, p. 308.

30. Edward Said, *Orientalism* (New York: Pantheon, 1978); Bryan Turner, *Marx and the End of Orientalism* (London: Allen and Unwin, 1978); and extant issues of *The Review of Middle East Studies*.

31. Talal Asad, *The Idea of an Anthropology of Islam* (Washington, DC: Center for Contemporary Arab Studies, Georgetown University, 1986).

32. Peter Gran, *op. cit.*

33. Albert Hourani, *Arabic Thought in the Liberal Age, 1798–1939* (New York: Oxford University Press, 1962); Hisham Sharabi, *Arab Intellectuals and the West: The Formative Years, 1875–1914* (Baltimore, MD: Johns Hopkins University Press, 1970).

34. See the essay on Yusuf al-Shibini's treatise on peasants in seventeenth-century Egypt in Gabriel Baer, *Fellah and Townsman in the Middle East* (Frank Cass, 1982), part I, chapter 1, pp. 3–48.

35. Surayah Faroqhi, "The Peasants of Saideli in the Late Sixteenth Century," in Faroqhi, *Peasants, Dervishes and Traders in the Ottoman Empire* (London: Variorum Reprints, 1986).

36. See Baer, *op. cit.* pp. 253–323.

37. Sarah Graham-Brown, "The Political Economy of the Jabal Nablus, 1920–48," in Roger Owen, *Studies in the Economic and Social History of Palestine in the Nineteenth and Twentieth Centuries* (Carbondale: Southern Illinois University Press, 1982).

38. Ylana Miller, *op. cit.*

39. A signal new contribution here is the recently completed Ph.D. dissertation by Ted Swedenburg at the University of Texas (Austin) on the Palestine Revolt, "Memories of Revolt: The 1936–39 Rebellion and the Struggle for a Palestinian National Past" (1988). It relies heavily on oral histories and focuses on the consciousness of the narrative.

40. Samir Amin, *The Arab Nation.*

41. Hanna Batatu, *The Old Social Classes and the Revolutionary Movements of Iraq* (Princeton, NJ: Princeton University Press, 1978). See chapter 9, pp. 224–318.

42. See André Raymond, *Artisans et commerçants au Caire au XVIIIe siecle* (Damascus, 1973–74).

43. Afaf Lutfi al-Sayyid Marsot, *Egypt in the Reign of Muhammad Ali* (Cambridge: Cambridge University Press, 1984).

44. Donald Quartaert, *Social Disintegration and Popular Resistance in the Ottoman Empire, 1881–1908* (New York: New York University Press, 1983), p. 102.

45. Leila Fawaz, *Merchants and Migrants in Nineteenth Century Beirut* (Cambridge, MA: Harvard University Press, 1983).

46. Fred Lawson, "Rural Revolt and Provincial Society in Egypt, 1820–24," *International Journal of Middle East Studies*, 13 (1981): 131–53.

47. See Roger Owen, *The Middle East in the World Economy.*

48. Joel Beinin and Zachary Lockman, *Workers on the Nile: Nationalism, Communism, Islam, and the Egyptian Working Class, 1882–1954* (Princeton, NJ: Princeton University Press, 1987), p. 38.

49. Ellis Goldberg, *Tinker, Tailor, and Textile Worker: Class and Politics in Egypt, 1930–1952* (Berkeley: University of California Press, 1986).

50. Peter Gran, *op. cit.*

51. André Raymond, *op. cit.*

52. F. de Jong, *Turuq and Turuq-Linked Institutions in Nineteenth-Century Egypt* (Leiden, 1978).

53. Ellis Goldberg, *op. cit.* pp. 19–27.

54. For elaboration of these points, see the "Introduction" in my *Women in Nineteenth Century Egypt* (Cambridge: Cambridge University Press, 1985).

55. Fanny Davis, *The Ottoman Lady: A Social History from 1718 to 1918* (Westport, CT: Greenwood Press, 1986).

56. Margot Badran, "The Origins of Feminism in Egypt," in *Current Issues in Women's History*, eds., Jacqueline Zirkzee and Arina Angerman (London: Croom Helm, forthcoming).

57. See my *Women in Nineteenth Century Egypt*, chapter 3, pp. 102–31; and Fanny Davis, *op. cit.* chapters 2 and 3, pp. 33–60.

58. Rosemary Sayigh, "Roles and Functions of Arab Women," *Arab Studies Quarterly* 3, no.3 (1981).

59. See my *Women in Nineteenth Century Egypt*, chapter 3.

60. Abraham Marcus, "Men, Women and Property Dealers in Real Estate in Eighteenth Century Aleppo," *Journal of the Economic and Social History of the Orient* 26, no. 2 (1983), 137–63; Gabriel Baer, "Women and Waqf: An Analysis of the Istanbul Tahrir of 1546," *Asian and African Studies* 7, nos. 1–3: 9–28; Margaret Meriweather, "Women and Work in Nineteenth Century Syria: The Case of Aleppo," unpublished symposium paper (Washington: Georgetown University Center for Contemporary Arab Studies, April 1986).

61. Tucker, *op. cit.*, pp 16–63.

62. *Ibid.*, pp. 16–101.

63. See Fanny Davis, *op. cit.*, pp 217–44; also Caroline Williams, "Women and the Arts: An Historical Survey," unpublished paper (Washington, DC: Georgetown University Center for Contemporary Arab Studies, April 1986).

64. Julia Clancy-Smith is currently doing research on an important Algerian Sufi order of the nineteenth century headed by a woman *shaykhah*.

65. For a first and highly evocative article on this problem, see Juan Ricardo Cole, "Feminism, Class, and Islam in Turn-of-the-Century Egypt," *International Journal of Middle East Studies* 13 (1981): 384–407.

66. Mervat Hatem, "Sexuality and Gender in Segregated Patriarchal Systems: The Case of Eighteenth and Nineteenth Century Egypt," *Feminist Studies* 12, no. 2 (1986).

7

Studies of Anglo-American Political Economy: Democracy, Orientalism, and the Left

Peter Gran

However radical the potential of Marxist theory, most academic re-search on the Middle East by English and American writers employing the worldview of political economy or Marxism is not particularly radical. Often it does not differ appreciably from Orientalism, the dominant theoretical framework in scholarship on the Middle East in the United States and Britain. Most Marxist scholarship on workers, peasants, and other "radical" or progressive themes is hard to distinguish from the work of more conventional scholars. In fact, genuine intellectual controversy resulting from an open conflict between paradigms is rare in Middle East studies.[1]

This paper tries to explain the trajectory of this radical tradition by a political and cultural analysis of modern democracy. Middle East studies, it concludes, far from being a "failure," provide a key to explaining the enigma of the "failure of socialism" in the US and the UK The paper has three main sections: an analysis of structural features of democracy that have tended to retard the development of radicalism; an analysis of Orientalism, as a logical and natural aspect of the dominant culture of democracy and as a cultural tradition that serves to retard the develop-ment of a tradition of political economy in Middle East studies; and some concluding comments on feminist scholarship and on scholarship of the modern Islamic movements as potentially important for a radical tradition seeking to break away from its moorings in democracy.

I. Democracy—An Introduction

Since the 1960s, critical writers appear united in questioning the old political philosophy linking democracy to freedom and progress. Anar-chist writers in modern times emphasize the rise of bureaucracy, the factory, and other authoritarian structures as failures of democratic society. Marxist writers emphasize that bourgeois democracy is a phase that antedates socialism and is inferior to it. This paper adopts a position somewhere between these two worldviews. Following Antonio Gramsci's analysis of the "English Road," it argues that democracy is a structure of ruler and ruled, not simply a mode of production with autonomous economic behavior.

Gramsci's "English Road" is an analysis of bourgeois democracy as a structure in which the ruling class grants citizenship to the working class as a strategy to blunt radical culture and render it more dependent on the hegemonic culture than it is in political systems in which the peasantry is a major element. Peasants are far more distant from the dominant culture than are citizens. Democracies depend on racism to maintain the loyalty of the worker of the dominant race to the state; racism spawns guilt feelings and rationalizations of its persistence. One common rationalization is the "chosen people" ideology, which is central to Orientalism. A "chosen people" ideology separates the dominant race from the ordinary moral scrutiny of behavior imposed on the rest of humanity.

Because it has deep roots in Anglo-American democracy, Orientalism appears too much a part of common sense to be easily abandoned when ordinary academic criticism shows it to be unsound. Quite the contrary, Orientalism is still in place even after such criticism. Further, Orientalism has had much influence on the applications of political economy.

This is not to deny that Marxism potentially provides a critique of Orientalism, for it does. But, as Marxism developed in the democracies, it was supportive of Orientalism to a degree that cannot completely be explained by power imbalances characteristic of modern capitalism or colonialism.[2] Capitalism has contributed to all modern thought, but capitalism, as Gramsci showed in his study of Italian fascism, can coexist with a number of political and cultural structures, some of which are not Orientalist. It therefore seems that Orientalism in the United States and the United Kingdom is an element, and a very important one, of the hegemonic cultures rather than a product of capitalism as an economic system.

II. Orientalist Influence on Political Economy in Anglo-American Middle East Studies

Orientalism is the preeminent conventional discourse about the Middle East.[3] It is equally well known for its "romantic" interests—revelations, Golden Ages, and essences—as for its place in positivism, where it emphasizes data and "modernization." Modernization theory pictures the Middle East as undergoing a process of renouncing its old self and becoming more like the United States.

From both romanticism and positivism, Orientalism can reach Marxism. Evidence of this is that political-economist and Marxist approaches to the Middle East often do not even try to formulate an alternative radical position on many issues. This section offers some examples of political economy's borrowing from positivism and romanticism.

If one assumes, following romanticism, that the Self is the opposite of the Other, or, following positivism, that Self and Other are the same but at different stages, then other ways of viewing cultural difference are closed in advance. Orientalists try reforms, but they do not work. Take, for example, such ideas as the shared nature of the "People of the Book"; it is a recognizable strategy for overcoming "Otherness," but it has not worked either for liberals, such as Francis Peters, or for Marxists. Few liberals and even fewer Marxists find in the "one" book what they assume for the "Other." Thus while many Marxist studies rest on the assumed existence of a generic transhistorical consciousness of the revolutionary worker independent of the political system, this consciousness is seen as being imported to the Middle East, while in the West it has Jewish and Christian roots.[4]

Orientalists, with Marxists tagging along, commonly assume that an "Arab world" exists, based on the existence of a common language.[5] In other contexts, Marxists would be more than a little resistant to this romantic residue. They would hesitate to assume that a "world" exists of the English-, the French-, or the Spanish-speaking peoples. Yet here there is no quarrel. No Marxist sociolinguistics or class analysis of language exists in Middle East studies. Orientalists and Marxists alike seem to imagine that language facilitates not only communication but even social homogenization, and that miscommunication does not take place. Rather there is "correct Arabic" and colloquial. Further, no Marxist critiques exist of the study of Arabic grammar or of the existing linguistic categories such as the diglossia in deconstructionist critiques like the recent essay *Neo-Patriarchy* by Hisham Sharabi. Why do political economists who study the Middle East accept the concept of language as a central determinant of the political culture of the Middle East but not study it?

Political analysis, the study of the relationship of ruler and ruled, affords another area of positivist influence on Marxism. It is rare to find Marxists attacking the institution of area studies, although area studies are an obstacle for someone interested in political analysis. If, for example, one determines that Jordan is a "tribal state," would it not be more logical for a student of Jordan to compare Jordan to other tribal states, many of which are in Africa or Southeast Asia, than to follow the conventional political-economy methodology that plays a country like Jordan off against another Middle Eastern country, and often one such as Egypt, which has a different type of society altogether?[6]

In England and the United States, political economists have expressed very little opinion one way or another about the entire Orientalist formulation of the Islamic past; generally, political economists have tended to concentrate on recent times. They appear to accept the overview that a Golden Age of Islam existed, followed by a decline. In this formulation, a beginning and an end of science in the Middle East occurred shortly after "the translation movement."[7] This contrasts sharply with the scholarship produced by Marxists in the Middle East, who have wrestled not just with modern but with ancient and medieval history from within a materialist framework.

How seriously does political economy contend with that great pillar of positivist thought, "the coming of the West"? Not very seriously, I think. The concept plays an important ideological function for Anglo-American political economists. Political economists routinely invoke "the coming of the West" as a point of demarcation but then, like liberal positivists, add the qualification that significant change occurred only many years later. Political economists also accept that upon the coming of the West, whatever internal dynamic may have existed in the Middle East gave way to a dynamic of West and Third World. As we have little or no knowledge about the reproduction of life in the eighteenth- or early-nineteenth-century Middle East, when all this was changing, this assumption seems to be little more than an acceptance of modernization theory.

Orientalism surfaces as well in the economic analysis of the Middle East. Political economists commonly reproduce the assumptions of liberal trade theory. They argue that when British industrial goods reached the Middle East in the nineteenth century, people bought them because they were cheaper. But why should pricing, taste, and access to market have been such simple matters in the Middle East when studies of working-class culture elsewhere suggest how complicated such matters are?

Another example of this confluence of interpretation is the interpretation of the history of slavery. Slavery's importance to the economic history of the Middle East began in Biblical times; merchant capital in the Middle East and elsewhere has made use of slavery as a labor form until the present. This is the most rigorous view from a political-economy perspective; however, it is not commonly found in Western political-economy writings in general or on the Middle East. Rather, what is found is a more liberal view of slavery as part of pre-capitalism. Why do political economists of the Middle East not take up slavery? Its existence raises interesting questions about the nature of modern capitalism. The obvious conclusion is that it is distasteful. Thus the subject of slavery has been slighted by political economists and by liberals, and left to the most conservative Orientalists, who treat it as a racial question.[8]

Worse yet, for all their discussions of trade unions and strikes, political economists have written little showing that class conflict made any difference in the analysis of concrete historical episodes. In practice, a number of elite-mass type books on Egypt written by positivists differ very little from books by a political economist using the language of class.[9]

Both political economists and positivists are almost equally attached to Great Power analysis, oil politics, and studies of the PLO elite. Although political economists' sympathies may differ from those of positivists, this is not built into their methodology. A positivist can be as sympathetic to Arab causes as a Marxist. Indeed, American Marxists are often just as closed as any positivist to criticisms of Israel.

In sum, while it is conventional and usually correct to assume that political economy is quite different from positivism and more radical in its viewpoints in Islamic and Middle Eastern studies, this is not yet the case, at least not in the Anglo-Saxon world. The question why this is so is an important and apparently enduring one. A satisfactory answer requires at least two levels of discussion. The first level concerns the hold of the Middle East as a special place or "sacred geography" for all the ideologies produced within democratic cultures. The second is more general. It asks what type of political economy, the Middle East aside, is characteristic of democracy. In other words, it reverses a long-term trend of simply criticizing individual Americans and Englishmen who take up this field with a radical vision and have difficulties, and tries to explain their difficulties in structural terms.

III. The Middle East as Sacred Geography for the Democracies

Sacred geography is the link between the material structure of democracy and its cultural foundation that God in the Middle East told Christians and Jews that they were "chosen people." Democracies are political systems in which the working classes are in modern times given legal rights. Built into such a system is the problem of how to control the worker, how to prevent him from using those rights effectively. Ruling classes have worked out a solution based on racism. Racism is institutionalized; democracies all have a racial undercaste.

When racism is a fact of life, or "scientifically-based," citizens find themselves in an ethical dilemma. A characteristic solution is for dominant-race people in democracies to espouse officially a melting-pot ideology in which they do not really believe, while clinging more or less consciously to the old religions—repressing, in doing so, the obvious fact that blacks or Arabs are either as Christian as they, or, by extension, at least "People of the Book".

The "chosen people" ideology in the United States is old; it has a religious foundation in Puritanism. It lives on in contemporary secular manifestations such as the Peace Corps or World Bank, many of whose personnel believe, just as strongly as missionaries do, that they have a mission going beyond personal gain.[10]

The "chosen peoples" feel a special, pan-racialist affinity for one another. Among "chosen peoples," Orientalism is mass culture. Among the "chosen peoples" alliances exist to "keep the world safe for democracy." Israel, the only democracy in the Middle East, garners support out of the very social structure of other democracies and not simply government policies; this support overcomes (and perhaps coexists with) other indigenous ideologies—paradoxically including anti-Semitism. Support for South Africa is natural, too. Apartheid is a hated policy, but without question, support of whites for other whites is firm.[11]

However, democracies are psychologically vulnerable when confronted by an underclass who demand to be treated as humans, as the Palestinians do. If blacks demand civil rights too quickly, as Martin Luther King, Jr. did, or if Palestinians demand a state of their own, they trigger hysteria not only among the dominant race of the affected country, but also throughout the entire ensemble of democracies. Currently, Palestinians are seen as terrorists and creators of dissonance, not only by Israelis, but by Americans as well. Americans truly believe that Zion-forming or utopia-forming movements are the most idealistic of human endeavor.[12] But for democratic citizens who are Marxists, an undercaste such as the Palestinians can scarcely be studied correctly if their political liberation makes them an enemy of the democratic civilization, a civilization that political economy shares. A vulgar vanguardism appears; the life of an Israeli citizen becomes more precious or politically significant than the life of any member of an undercaste, e.g., a Palestinian peasant.

Political economists criticize Israel, but not its democratic system or its Orientalist worldview. Instead, the critics call for the destruction of the Jewish character of the state or endorse a Solomonesque bifurcation of Israel to make room for a Palestinian state. These positions are idealistic, remote from ordinary discussions of the transition from capitalism to socialism. In fact, they echo the critiques of Israel derived from positivism.[13]

Not only is modern Israel a democracy; it contains the sacral geography of all the other democracies. This point needs to be expanded to explain why Israel, of all the democracies, has been the subject of the least real analysis in political economy. Sacral geography contributes the stability missing in democracy. Life in a democracy offers unlimited personal freedom and change; it is thus by definition uprooted, or potentially so. In democracies, the study of history is alien to most of the citizenry; citizens of democracies rely heavily on the study of heritage, not history. To the Puritan mind, history implies tradition or resting on one's laurels. To rest on one's laurels is to be slothful. Puritanism encourages "heritage-ism" and presentism, because one's chosenness also emerges from one's present acts.

Thus, historical process, which is important to political economists, rather goes against the American grain. Students in this country must be *required* to take history.[14] Voluntarily, any history teacher will report, citizens send Israel, the symbol of both their heritage and of their identity, large sums of money. The United States and British governments have asserted that a special bond connects them to Israel. It follows that when a heritage approach replaces a historical approach, as is largely the case for the Middle East, one can predict that a very unsatisfactory under-standing of political economy will result. It is not surprising that the right wing in democracies actively promotes the study of heritage.[15]

A heritage approach to the Middle East not only undermines history as a study of social process; it alters the meaning of the key concepts of political economy, e.g., the concept of imperialism. Imperialism began in Marxist thought as a stage in the history of capitalism, a scientific concept describing both world and internal national developments. To-day, in standard political-economy studies of most regions, e.g., Latin America, the analysis of external influence must compete for space with the analysis of the internal social structure. By way of contrast, in the typical political-economy studies of the Middle East, the special link of the West not only precedes a study of the internal dynamic of the societies but replaces it. This is the case in a number of standard books on the role of the Shah in Iran, but also on the oil regimes in the Middle East. Israel, too, is often explained in terms of external factors—most often U.S. foreign aid. Studies are thus rare that analyze these countries in terms of an internal dynamic. Heritage or sacral geography appears to be the operative factor in the interpretation of the Middle East in Western political economy.[16] A focus on heritage frees one from the flux of history, but at a price: one's heritage, in contrast to one's history, is ultimately unexaminable. The rigid cultural consequences and downright errors that result affect the broad-gauge Marxist theoretical expositions as well as more limited monographs.

The special bonding of the West to the Holy Land affects not only the political-economy approach to the contemporary Middle East but the study of the era preceding the coming of the West as well. The Western Left usually portrays feudalism in the Arab world as a negative aspect of the Arab heritage. Marxists have therefore not looked to peasant struggles against feudalism to understand its breakdown. In general, they have emphasized "the coming of the West" as a necessary condition of the coming of capitalism or modern times. Clearly, this is also the Orientalist formulation. In contrast, studies of feudalism in the West focus increasingly on the role of the peasant in bringing on the crises of the feudal state.

As everything about the Holy Land is perceived as frozen, Islam, too, is taken as heritage in studies by modern historians. According to the dominant Durkheimian approach, Islam is a fixed orthodox creed; it has periods of reform, it responds to the West, but it never loses its unitary nature. It is not part of history as Western religions are. From all this, it becomes clear that sacral geography and Orientalism are logical components of democratic culture and that they influence the political ideologies formed in democracies, including Marxism and political economy.

IV. Characteristic Phases in the History of Democracy and Their Political-Economy Productions

Three different historical phases occurred in democracies during the past hundred years, each with its own cultural emphasis, including its political economy. One is the open-market liberalism of nineteenth-century England, which viewed the state as the Night Watchman. In England and America, this phase was eclipsed by another, a collectivist or welfare-state phase. In more recent times, Reagan and Thatcher have ushered in a partial return to the earlier liberal phase. A third possible phase arising in a crisis of the democratic state is Nazism. Each of these phases marks a different struggle for the Left, and a different variety of political-economy scholarship is produced in the process.

Let us now turn to the two main phases of recent Anglo-American democracy, collectivism and liberalism. By collectivism, we refer in the United States to the New Deal era and its aftermath, and in Britain to the somewhat wider experience correlated with the rise of the Labour Party. By liberalism, we refer to the phase associated in particular with the Reagan administration and the Thatcher government. We will emphasize the hegemonic manifestations of these phases in culture, saving the demonstration of their impact on the studies of political economy of the Middle East for the second half of the paper.

The dominant modality of the collectivist period was one that emphasized development through governmental initiative. Stalinism was the most available analogue within Western Marxism that seemed to fit the politics of public-sector democracy. Collectivist thought, including Stalinism, characterized American leftist culture from the New Deal to 1970, the date of the beginning of the contemporary era, the New International Economic Order.

In the collectivist era, the radical tradition of the US and the UK emphasized such themes as agricultural development and the abolition of malnutrition and poverty. Political economy helped to define these as problems of the Third World and to champion industrialization as a solution, so that development was seen as a precondition for social and political change. The British Labour Party developed a critique of colonialism, which it characterized as an obstacle to the development of the colonized nations.

In the United States during this period, the evolution of political economy was hampered both by the failure of the Left to control a major political party and by McCarthyism.[17] It was almost as though the U.S. government adopted state socialist practices in a spirit of preemption, and compensated for indulging in the moral decadence of welfare by extirpating the Satan within it, the American Left. In England, on the other hand, political economy seemed superficially to have a freer terrain because it developed as a part of the tradition that produced the Labour Party.

Close scrutiny blurs these differences. The autonomy of British working-class leftism was bought at a price: the acceptance of a genuine racial caste system in the universities and other intellectual centers, which left room for an establishment leftism, but of a very confined sort. In America, purges of the Left, e.g., the Palmer raids, and the hearings of the House Committee on Un-American Activities, and of course of Arabs and blacks, occurred because the caste system was not as dependable as in England.

Victims in democracies find the purges hard to resist or to stop. Springing from the ground of the righteous purification of the community of chosen people, purges often run their course with few counter-struggles. While this tradition of purges spanned both the liberal and the collectivist eras, it was in the latter that one found its greater impact.

In Middle East studies, purges went on longer than elsewhere. A discreet anti-Arabism has long functioned in the State Department and the Middle East centers and may have lasted well into the 1970s. In England, on the other hand, the more powerful racial caste system has all but marginalized even the most illustrious Afro-Asian scholars.

Looked at from the vantage point of our own era, it appears unfortunate that political economists of the collectivist period gave so much attention to American industry that they have devalued agriculture, and regarded productivity as synonymous with the health of our agrarian sector. American writers, caught up in the politics of collectivism, including many members of the radical tradition, seemingly ignore our own rural poverty, poor health, and malnutrition and emphasize the rural poverty of the Third World just as though they were Orientalists. Although poor health and poor nutrition have always been a feature of our society, it is the Orient that we picture as starving and filled with beggars, for "chosen people" are healthy, not starving or disfigured. In democracies, of course, disfigured people are very often put in institutions because it is considered inappropriate for the general populace to see them on the street, as we see them in Calcutta or Cairo.

The socialist tradition in democracies agrees; socialists also consider institutions the state's responsibility. It is perhaps only in the anarchist tradition that the political practices and ideologies prevalent in democracies are disputed and that social integration takes precedence over "normality" and "acceptability."[18]

In the liberal phase of democracy, dependency theory is the dominant form of political economist thought. Dependency theory emphasizes the competition between world trade patterns and world production patterns, whereas Stalinism subsumed trade under production. Dependency theory suggests that states are trapped in the world market and that they cannot develop apart from the world as a whole. Middle East studies were well placed for the liberal phase, for they had always emphasized the impact of the West and because the Stalinist epistemology had held little appeal. In fact, Middle East studies came of age in the United States and the United Kingdom in the 1970s, the heyday of dependency theory.

In political economist circles of the liberal age, Immanuel Wallerstein's world market variant of dependency theory began to influence the conceptualization of the breakdown of the Ottoman Empire and the peripheralization of modern Turkey. Samir Amin's slightly more optimistic concept of periphery capitalism also played a role in Arab studies.[19]

Most of the important commentators of the Left, e.g., Noam Chomsky, Edward Said, the *MERIP* group, and their British counterparts, published as independent journalists critical of the Establishment. During the collectivist period, leftist commentators were more likely to have a public-sector job and work for party papers. In effect, the kind of independent journalistic criticism developed by the nineteenth-century Liberal Age British critics of empire such as Karl Marx and Wilfrid Scawen Blunt was reborn in the 1970s. It survives and flourishes because the Left is essentially out of power in the liberal phases. The governments can rely on a slower delegitimization of leftist thought carried out by intellectuals with close ties to government. Both governments thus avoid direct confrontation with freedom of speech issues.[20]

Political economy always functions on the defensive. Usually its appearance reflects the battles it has been waging. In recent times, two kinds of intellectuals have utilized the literature of controversy to discredit political economy, and governments have patronized them heavily: the Neo-Durkheimians (of whom Clifford Geertz is an influential example) in the 1970s, and the Neo-Anarchists in the 1980s. As we have indicated, the political-economy tradition recognized these establishment assaults against it; yet, because it lacked power, it became a reluctant participant in the discourse.

Clifford Geertz became an establishment intellectual in the early 1970s, with the rise of symbolic anthropology. Symbolic anthropology has taken over the function of general theory from the Weberian developmental theory promoted by Anglo-American political scientists. In the process, the field of anthropology emerged from the narrow confines of kinship studies, a legacy of the colonial era, to an ever-widening horizon of theory formation. A Marxist anthropology emerged.

Geertz's theory fit the neo-liberal phase; his notion of domination was wider than the Weberian notion of central state institutions. Domination for Geertz included a control of culture shared both by the central state and by the rural elites, the groups that were fast becoming U.S. allies in this period. Geertz's theory is equally an attack on the Left. The symbolized world of elite communication so marginalizes the role of historical dynamics and so reduces history as a means of understanding culture that there is often no overlap.

What enabled Geertz and his English counterpart, the anthropologist Ernest Gellner, to survive the decade of the 1970s? For a time, their very subject matter protected them. In Morocco and Algeria, they had a strategic terrain. Very little radical critique existed, and the area-studies audience was too limited effectively to point out their technical flaws.[21] It was thus from this Orientalist terrain that a general ahistorical understanding of the world could be most effectively sustained in the 1970s.

By the late 1970s, Geertz's reputation began gradually to fall. By the early 1980s, the much more polished and more accurate work of an heir apparent, Michael Gilsenan, was already passé for readers requiring recognition of the complexity of social history when it was published. Throughout the 1970s, a Marxist approach to anthropology gradually gained ground and, though everywhere the underdog, it was notably stronger in American scholarship on Latin America or Africa than on the Middle East.[22]

In the last ten years, Neo-Anarchists have become the new cohort of intellectuals with ties to the Establishment. Neo-Anarchism has become the political expression of libertarianism. In it, the breakdown of community extends to the breakdown of the Self. Jacques Derrida and Paul De Man come to the US from the European right. Michel Foucault represents another strand of Neo-Anarchism struggled over by the Left and the Right, as, for example, in the dozen or more apparently well-funded journals on post-structuralism. In Neo-Anarchism, the Orient and specifically Morocco continues to be significant, as they were earlier for Geertz and Gellner, but at the expense of the region and of political economy. As we have already established, the study of these areas is among the weakest in political economy.

What is the intellectual project of the preponderant libertarian Neo-Anarchism? Apparently this tradition opposes both large-scale or "totalizing" social theory, e.g., political economy, and the more traditional positivist accumulation of knowledge. Like the Neo-Durkheimians, the Neo-Anarchists offer the ruling classes a cultural synthesis but one that has limitations. Neo-Anarchist writings evince a concern for the Fourth World, a concern for peoples endangered by states, and a desire for some new approach to the world independent of that of the old science or social science, held to be a form of imperialism. In Geertz's writings on Morocco, external reality existed; in Paul Rabinow's writings on Morocco, subjectivity or mind is the bedrock of reality.[23]

In effect, the weakness of political economy permits anthropologists and post-modernist literary critics to go to Morocco and produce hegemonic culture for the West. These scholars justify their eclectic and unrooted ethnographic approaches on the grounds that North African culture is not "scripturalist." If during the colonial period, French scholars never relied on Arabic sources, today this can be put to advantage by Americans.

This "specialness" of the Maghrib, the pretext for many of the new studies, is odd because specialists know it is unwarranted. The *'ulama* of the Maghrib have produced a vast body of Arabic language textual sources of the sort commonly relied on for scholarly work on other parts of the Arab world. It exists in the usual manuscript form in private libraries. The absence of political-economist studies making use of this material is a real lacuna.

V. The Radical Tradition in the United States and Great Britain

That Western leftists are all "citizens" and participants in the dominant culture was the argument of an earlier part of this paper. This can be demonstrated by direct references to the history of class struggle from the earliest years of American history until today. In the deliberations surrounding the drafting of the United States Constitution, it became clear that the founders of America were concerned with the dangers of factionalism. Factionalism could easily tear a democracy apart.

The subsequent history of the United States revealed continuing ruling-class attempts to protect the community and the freedom of civil society, and also to prevent popular community-based movements from bringing about change. Sometimes the ruling class sought to delegitimate third parties, sometimes merely to bring charismatic politicians into the two-party system. The most common solution in the case of the US has been to play off the East Coast against the core culture, and in the case of the UK, to play off the English against the Celtic fringe.

The academic study of the radical opposition in the United States and Britain has had problems with the interpretation of challenges to regimes. This, of course, bears on Middle East studies. In the past half century, scholars commonly have had a bias in favor of leadership and ideological coherence rather than movements of challenge, although the emergence of the former features have often presaged the late stages or the downfall of radical challenges. In the past ten years, a reaction to the older trends has appeared. A spate of studies of working-class culture has emerged that in many instances develops the detail to the point of losing the broader national political picture.

In the United States, the study of radicalism has been dominated by an East Coast school. This group emphasizes that radicalism was not indigenous to the new American culture, but was brought by immigrants in the late nineteenth and early twentieth centuries and encountered a great deal of opposition among Christian small-town Americans, who sided with the capitalists against it.[24] The East Coast school makes use of Lenin's theory of the American farmer as a safety valve. Lenin, like the East Coast Americans, maintained a "Puritan-like" theory of the uniqueness of America, the land where capitalism was achieved through consensus and without a revolutionary struggle.

There is a certain irony in all this. In the face of almost endless American popular self-assertion, the "correct" East Coast position continues to stress the absence of an indigenous revolutionary tradition. An alternative school, the American populist tradition, has been on the defensive in the past generation or two, although it has made a modest comeback with the shift of the industrial tradition to the South and the West. The position in East Coast thought is that the populist tradition ended in the late nineteenth or early twentieth century. This is now generally repudiated.

Most political economists in Middle East studies work within the East Coast radical tradition. This accounts for their East Coast loyalties in the ongoing conflict between the East Coast and the core culture, as well as for many of their typical concerns. First, the location on the East Coast explains political economy's thematic and theoretical attraction to modern-sector working classes and to working-class life, as for example in the writings of Herbert Guttman, rather than to work itself, or even the politics of work. In the political-economy tradition in Middle East studies, one thus finds more studies of the organized working class than of petty commodity production or of housework.[25] Sectionalism no doubt also reinforces the ideology of vanguardism.

On another level, sectional division also explains many failures of political economy to communicate as well as Orientalism does. Political economists can scarcely persuade Americans of Israeli imperialism if the core culture understands the Middle East as the Holy Land. The Holy Land serves as a warning to and a critique of the Godless East Coast.

Testimony to the continuing significance of the sectional conflict can in fact be found in a number of the more interesting debates in political economy. One example that is quite important for Middle Eastern studies is the debate over the relationship of merchant capitalism to modern capitalism. In this debate, the East Coast represents the line that separates totally industrial capital from merchant capital as in Marx's *Capital*. The interpretation is a natural one for any industrial region to espouse. *Capital* is a useful book for this polemic. *Capital* was a book of the English industrial world written against that older "nation of shopkeepers" that took trade to be capitalism. In it, Marx argued that the focus on exchange over production, like the focus on the commodity over its system of production, was an ideological device to mask the system of production and its prevailing division of labor. In *Capital*, Marx argued that the history of modern capitalism is a history of surplus generation through proletarianized labor, and that it first arose in Great Britain. An influential present-day exponent of this dominant position is Robert Brenner of UCLA.[26]

A core-culture or merchant-capital reading of Marx and even of *Capital* is, however, quite common. As the core culture has regained importance, its interpretation of Marx has begun to be recognized. Works like Maxime Rodinson's *Islam and Capitalism* are finding a wider audience among American and British radicals. As this occurs, the Althusserian *Reading Capital*, once popular in London and on the U.S. East Coast, has waned in importance. So has the Hegelian Marxist interpretation of Marx's *Capital*. These two traditional readings of *Capital* are challenged in the United States and the United Kingdom both by anarchism and by other recently discovered referential texts. Marx is no longer *Capital* plus a greater or lesser amount of the "Young Marx." In the 1970s, an English edition of *Grundrisse* appeared and undermined *Capital*'s clear distinctions between trade and production.[27] In the 1980s, Teodor Shanin, a sociologist from Manchester, published Marx's correspondence with various Russians. He characterized this collection as the work of a later Marx who saw the specialness of Russian history—a "Russian Road," in Gramsci's terminology.[28] As the title indicates, this work directly conflicts with the basic tenets in *Capital.* In *Capital,* Marx wrote of a general proletarianization as part of capitalism; in his correspondence, Marx acknowledges the role of Russian peasant production and trade.

In fact, the undoing of Manchester along with the Celtic fringe at the hands of postwar British governments is creating sectionalism. Thus it is an appropriate point of departure to analyze Marxist challenges to Marxist orthodoxy in England. Marxist orthodoxy—Communist or Trotskyist—with all its theoretical baggage is more at home in the dominant center, London, than elsewhere. Similarly, in the United States in the South and the West, the merchant is the capitalist; the Chamber of Commerce was and is his institution. Obviously, arguments about merchant capital as modern capital have an entirely different ring in Texas than in New York, the traditional American economic capital.

In *Islam and Capitalism,* a University of Texas Press paperback, Rodinson argued that certain themes in the Qu'ran and hadith are supportive of capitalist activity. He did not suggest thereby that religion causes trade nor that seventh-century Arabian history is interchangeable with modern capitalist history, but he analyzed their interrelation more as an overlap than as a sharp break. A continuous world market existed in the Islamic world. Merchants traded not just in luxury goods for the elite but in commodities of all types. Merchants were also involved in production.

Although Rodinson concedes to the dominant Western Marxism the distinction between capitalism as a sector and capitalism as a socioeconomic formation, his book was largely ignored by the American political-economy tradition in Middle East studies, just as this tradition ignored the writings of the better part of Middle Eastern Marxists whose writings occupy a similar terrain.

The most important writer to expound a "non-stageist" history of Mediterranean capitalism was the Italian Antonio Gramsci. Recently, Gramsci's writings have found a wide readership even on the East Coast and in London. His theory of the capitalist state and its role in politics overlaps with the concerns of contemporary political economists. Gramsci, however, also developed a theory of the history of capitalism in Italy, a history that might be termed heterodox. In his analysis of capitalism, Gramsci did not take the rise of the West or the Italian advanced region, the Piedmont, as a given. In fact, he postulated a deepening alliance of modern capitalism with feudalism in Italy as workers challenged the state. He did not predict that capitalism would collapse because of some built-in need to keep increasing the surplus. He found capitalists making concessions even to fascists simply to retain their control. Gramsci's theory, like Rodinson's, suggests that capitalism can function powerfully as one sector of a multi-sector economy, that capitalism is not necessarily less at home in peasant Italy or Egypt than it is in a democracy.[29]

Here the sectionalist conflict underlying the interpretation of *Capital* comes to a head. The more capitalism is defined in terms of politics and culture, following Gramsci or Rodinson, the further Marxist theory drifts from the standard East Coast reading of *Capital*. The more culture and politics emerge, the less central the modern East Coast experience is to the United States and the less justification there is for its hegemony over radical thought.

No one I have encountered in our field considers sectional influence an appropriate element of the analysis of scholarship in Middle East studies. The major analysis of the relationship between sectional issues and capitalism is found in writings on American history, e.g., Eugene Genovese's *The Janus Face of Merchant Capitalism*.[30] In our field, with the exception of some of Rodinson's work, the central focus both in the mainstream and on the Left is on the mutations we noted within the culture of the East Coast, e.g., the traditions of Weber, Durkheim, and Nietzsche.

In England, the conventional view among students of English history was that several factors had combined to minimize the interplay of sectionalism and the Puritan heritage. Today Puritan values that had been buried have reappeared and may even become the dominant trend in England. Since the 1960s, the British Left has advocated the rights of English workers, sometimes at the expense of the Commonwealth immigrants, and often at the expense of the Third World as a whole in matters of the runaway shop. Nonetheless, in a few years Great Britain underwent a major transformation and a commercial elite reasserted itself on top of a broken working class. In the process, the British Left split. The split seems to reflect the new British reality of economic sectionalism, which has replaced the older unity under the welfare state of the different peoples of the United Kingdom.

The segment of the Left concerned with the Middle East and other Third World regions, based in London or in the major universities, stayed Trotskyist. In these circles, Trotsky, the theorist of a combined and uneven development, became the theorist of the English working class as vanguard. Those Marxists who concerned themselves with the daily survival of the British people abandoned the high theory of the *New Left Review* from London for *History Workshop* from Ruskin College at Oxford, for the inspiration of the Open University at Milton Keynes, and for the publications of the Center for Contemporary Cultural Studies at Birmingham. This split gave each trend its special features: the effect on the reader from abroad of drowning in details of the ethnography of the lower classes when one reads Raphael Samuels; the feeling, when one reads an article in the ultra-internationalist *Economy and Society*, of being an outsider to some arcane scientific vocabulary.

British left-wing scholars of the Middle East in the last generation are deeply committed to critique. No doubt critique has been needed for a long time in Middle East studies, but why this exercise has been done at this time and within certain intellectual boundaries is a question worth investigating. I propose that it was made possible at this juncture by the two-fold situation of London radicals losing out on the domestic interpretation of England, inducing them to turn to the Continent and the Third World, and by the British Establishment acquiescing in the critique. This explains the contemporaneous publication by the Establishment of Marxist dictionaries, biographical dictionaries, and encyclopedias on the one hand, and journals like the *Review of Middle East Studies* and the *Gazelle Review* on the other. The critique project happened to begin as an international venture of American, British, and Middle Eastern scholars under British auspices. When the critique project went beyond what the British wanted, they toned it down. British scholars wanted an attack on Orientalism as idealism or vulgar materialism, not a critique of the Left, nor of democracy itself.

In the heyday of the critique project, Bryan Turner suggested in a well-known book that Marxism had driven Orientalism into eclipse, but this turned out not to be the case, even for Marxists. At approximately the same time, Perry Anderson, the editor of the *New Left Review*, the leading British journal of the Left, published his *Lineages of the Absolutist State*. In this work, Anderson compared the dynamics of several early-modern empires, following a Marxist approach. When he turned to the Ottomans, his sources and mode of presentation changed. He wrote as a traditional Orientalist, elitist and idealist; his analysis is static, not dynamic. A whole section of the book can be read either as an epistemological rupture or a political defense of the West and of the British state.

I read the best-known British book, Roger Owen's *The Middle East in the World Economy, 1800–1914* (1981), in the same way. It suggests uprootedness and isolation of a different order.[31] The "world" economy of Owen's title is actually the English Middle East trade. Non-English trade merits only occasional mention.

Clearly the British state is not just under attack for its policies to white people. The influence of Commonwealth ties and the militancy of the Commonwealth people in seeking "national" rights opened the way for radical journals such as *Race and Class* not found in the US A few books also have gained prominence in this atmosphere of cultural collision. Among them are works on the political economy of the Middle East, including Talal Asad's well-known *Anthropology and the Colonial Encounter* and Abd al-Latif al-Tibawi's critiques of British Orientalism. Their writing is forcing Islam and hence the Middle East to move from sacred geography to part of local British race relations. The corresponding works by Americans seeking a "national solution" would be works like Leroy Jones's plays. They are offset by the deeper trend in the US toward racial integration. Writers on Arab affairs such as Edward Said and Rifaat Abu al-Haj, reflect this.[32]

VI. Impact of Gender Issues and the Islamic Revival on Recent Political-Economy Writing

Since the early 1970s, the nationalist "core" culture in the United States and the United Kingdom has asserted itself over the internationalist one. The nationalist culture emphasizes respect for tradition and for religion. The tightening bonds of the communities of "chosen people" spell a setback for the more egalitarian civil rights tradition. It does permit status to those few women and blacks who qualify. Thus, one can have deepening poverty and greater success at the same historical moment. Not surprisingly, the mirror effect of Middle East studies to Western culture induces us to react at present to religious issues and women's issues.

A cursory glance at the progressive side of scholarship on race and gender reveals a surprising trend. A number of unfamiliar texts about Islam and women are appearing in translation alongside or even ahead of Western academic studies about their actions. This is not as common in other subspecialties, where scholars translate primary sources years after a field is organized—in other words, at a time when presumably a consumer market for certain foreign-language classics has been established. What can be deduced from this willingness in England and the US to consume unintegrated material is that it serves to validate Western culture. The "Islamic" treatment of women is reactionary. However, exposure to primary sources can lead to unpredictable results. Through these writings, some Western scholars have come to realize that Muslims and Middle Eastern women are not our opposites, nor are they the same as we, nor are they inferior. Given the felt need in the West for Orientalism—this despite the West's declining power in the Middle East—it remains to be seen how much cultural space these writings will be permitted either by governments or by mass opinions.

Let us briefly examine Western critical thought through its reactions to a well-known feminist writer whose first major book could be understood to validate our notion of the Orient as comprehensible or conventional but whose later works could not. The Egyptian novelist Nawal Sa'dawi became known in the West for her work *The Hidden Face of Eve*; among her later translated books is *Woman at Point Zero*. The first book is a quasi-bestseller in Western progressive circles concerned with the Middle East. It introduces the "forbidden" theme of female circumcision and other bad practices and calls for reform. The reason for the success of this book in reaching a Western audience is that it is easily subsumed into pre-existing categories of women in a democracy. A deconstructionist reading leads to the conclusion that Western women should be glad they are Western. The author complains of a practice which a different reading would lead us to conclude was fairly widespread in nineteenth-century America, but which was in the fullness of time and education overcome.[33] Naturally, most readers ignore what they want to ignore even in the text itself. Sa'dawi actually links her major themes to imperialism, which she holds partly responsible for the situation of women, and to Islam, which she criticizes but does not dismiss.

The second book, *Woman at Point Zero*, enters our circles more passively. It has been much less often reviewed; it points to experience that is uncommon or unlikely in a democracy. It is thus exotic and it is also threatening, or possibly transformative, as it suggests possibilities for women not commonly achieved in the West at a time when few in the West accept Egypt as a country to which we should compare ourselves.

In this second book, a middle-class female doctor of a woman's prison in Egypt records her meetings with a lower-class woman prisoner. This alone would make the story extremely avant garde. A "chosen-people" ideology makes the criminal or the prison a fairly taboo subject, so that unlike the Russian, our literature does not produce accounts of it. To begin with, the novel thus implies the question for a Western reader of why, if our democratic societies tend to have a very high per capita number of people in prison, our cultural relationship to them remains a remote one of stories of adventure or of escapes from prison.

The book is threatening because of two important features of the protagonist. First, the woman in prison is a peasant; yet, her life and experience are as vivid and as real as any we might find in our world of citizens. Second, she was abused as a child in her home; she fled and became a prostitute. Through bad luck, she wound up with a pimp, whom she killed, and then had the very bad luck to be arrested for his murder.

While progressives believe in the struggle of women for their freedom from man's domination, only certain forms of struggle meet their approval. Liberation is for the few at the top of society who have inherited money or earn it after an expensive education. Liberation from below can come only through socialism. Progressives tend to see prostitution as not natural but immoral, a practice that, if legitimated, could lead to the mass collapse of the family system. In a democracy, prostitution is sin.

But the attentive reader of Sa'dawi's book will note that the Egyptian context is different; the moral problem in Egypt is not prostitution but the role of the pimp. Thus the death of the pimp is a high point of Sa'dawi's story. In our democratic context, given prostitution, the presence of the pimp is taken for granted.[34] For American political economists, to read this book and try to interpret Egypt, as they did *The Hidden Face of Eve*, opens up the subject of the struggle of the whores for their rights, a struggle rooted in a profound and multi-faceted critique of conventional radicalism.

American and British feminist research have revealed that child abuse and spousal abuse are very common in democracies. But, our writers insist, these crimes are moments of abnormality that are not reinforced by the basic structures of our society and polity. I disagree. By dividing the world into public and private spheres, civil society in fact creates opportunities for this violence within the small, unequal world of the nuclear family. Perhaps it is to avoid confronting this distinguishing structural feature of democracy that it is made a subordinate one even by Western feminists, and even as a literary theme.

The power of women and the foibles of male institutions is the theme of a major Palestinian novel widely available but little discussed in the West, Sahar Khalifeh's *Wild Thorns*. In a manner reminiscent of American black writer Alice Walker, in *The Color Purple*, Khalifeh grounds her story in a material reality in which a racial undercaste has responsible local networks dominated by women, while the men can be irresponsible or worse. Both Khalifeh's and Walker's works are important political books because they cannot be easily rebutted either theoretically or in point of detail. In fact, they show how rigid as well as how underdeveloped political economy is in racial and gender issues. They also show that the analysis of lower-class women is not more difficult than other subjects for those who seek it. It does, however, require that political economists abandon their defense of Orientalism and bourgeois democracy. Feminists admire strong women and support the exposure of abuse by men. They have been the main Western audience for these works so far. The fundamental reliance of dominant feminism on democracy has, however, kept their numbers small. Alice Walker is an important "black" writer; Sahar Khalifeh is ethnography.

The involvement of Muslim movements in politics on a large scale and the claim of many Muslims that church and state are not separated in Islam challenge views long held by writers in the political-economy tradition. How does one proceed to the subject of Islam through the base and superstructure? As in the case of feminist struggle, it is too early to know if the challenge leads to change in the formulation of political-economy thought.

Certainly, the populist nature of Latin American liberation theology is

attractive to many liberal and radical scholars. Could this extend to
Islamic Marxism, e.g., to a writer such as Ayatollah Muhammad Baqir
al-Sadr,[35] thereby breaking some of the hold of Orientalist sentiment?

To conclude this study, I would like to speculate on the direction of
the radical trend in the United States and the United Kingdom in Middle
East studies. The Islamic Revolution in Iran has brought cultural concerns to the attention of political economy. This is no small achievement.
For example, Fred Halliday rewrote a part of his well-known book on
Iran to include a discussion of Shi'ism; however, it is still apparent that
the struggle of women in Iran can be twisted into a fantasy. The power-
lessness felt by Western women may inspire them to study the other as
revolutionary, essentially a continuation of Orientalism. One may thus
ask, will the dominant paradigms of modernization and political economy
eventually pigeonhole Muslim movements and Middle Eastern feminism
within their traditional emphases, or will our corner of the culture world
produce a deeper radicalism, one perhaps challenging the stock features
of contemporary "science"? Given the present configurations, a real possibility exists that Islamic Marxism or Middle Eastern feminism could make
Western political economy of the Middle East a new center of theory,
with a framework combining gender and race in a more global view of the
world than is available in Western radical thought currently—although as
the larger sense of this study makes clear, the propensity for "popular
Orientalism" is embedded structurally in our racial structure and our
family system, and will not be eroded without social change.

For the Left, there is no going back. Most are too aware how in the
case of Middle East studies, scholarly disdain for the people of the area,
bound up in the Orientalist problematic, can be exploited by the power
structure of a democracy. This exploitation has contributed to the legitimation of our foreign policy and wars and to the racism in our own
culture. In addition, Orientalism has caused hurt in the lives of many
individuals of Middle Eastern background who became citizens here only
to face discrimination. And much as the field is concerned with issues
such as the Palestine question, the Iranian revolution, and the crisis in
Lebanon, it is clear that, no matter what the outcomes will be, Orientalism
is likely to remain as a threat.

Notes

1. "Anglo-American Marxism" and the "Political Economy of the Middle East" are used
   as phrases of convenience. I try to comment on writers in French and Arabic when
   they appear in English translation and become part of the sociology of Anglo-American
   Marxism. Turkey and Iran are given less than proportional attention because I am less
   familiar with the politics of knowledge there.

   The position that Marxism and political economy are Orientalist is revisionary, as the standard view is that Marxism is a critique of Orientalism. Bryan Turner provides a clear statement of that view in his essay *Marx and the End of Orientalism* (London, 1978), referred to in the text.

While I am writing about culture and intellectuals, which is a central theme of Gramsci, my reading of Gramsci is "non-standard," in that I emphasize the affinity between Gramsci and Foucault in their theory of power. The anarchist element in Gramsci's analysis of power led him to view the organization of culture as an arrangement of building blocks or paradigms more than as a frozen synthesis.

Currently, the anarcho-syndicalist or Sardist side of Gramsci is less commonly discussed than the Hegelian, the Bolshevik, or the social-democratic side of his work. I found Leonardo Salamini's *The Sociology of Political Praxis: An Introduction to Gramsci's Theory* (London: Routledge, Kegan Paul, 1981) the most useful commentary. I would like to thank Talal Asad, Rifaat Abu al-Haj, Samih Farsoun, and Judith Gran for their comments on earlier drafts.

2. Edward Said in *Orientalism* (New York: Pantheon, 1978) was among the first radical writers to reflect on the Orientalist nature of classical Marxism. This has traditionally been a theme of religionists, e.g., Ali Shariati's *Marxism and Other Western Fallacies* (Berkeley: Mizan Press, 1980).

Because of Said's emphasis on the imbalance of power relations during the nineteenth-century colonial period, his analysis meshes with the dominant New Left political economy of the Middle East in the West and in the Middle East (referred to in note 1). This emphasis distances him, however, from the older European culture and economy, including its Orientalism.

3. For a summary, see my articles "Political Economy as a Paradigm for the Study of Islamic History," *International Journal of Middle East Studies* 11 (1980): 511–26; and "The Study of Medieval Islamic History, 1930's–1950's, in Three Well-Known Texts," *Review of Middle East Studies* 2 (1976): 47–56.

4. Examples of Islam as Self include Francis Peters, *Allah's Commonwealth: A History of Islam in the Near East, 600–1100 A.D.* (New York: Simon and Schuster, 1973); James L. Peacock, "Weberian, Southern Baptist and Indonesian Muslim Conceptions," in *Proceedings of the Southern Anthropological Society* (Athens: University of Georgia, 1975); and Peter Awn, *Satan's Tragedy and Redemption: Iblis in Sufi Psychology* (Leiden: Brill, 1987).

5. Samir Amin's *Arab Nation* (London: Zed, 1978) is an important if somewhat ignored essay that raises the question of how to understand the unity of the Arab world. Its conclusions conflict with the main trends of Western Marxism and area studies. Amin argues for the modernity of a capitalist-oriented medieval Arab world, which fell behind Europe less because of the Ottoman invasion than because of the defeat of the European peasantry, who were driven off the land and turned into cheap labor. Cheap labor proved to be a lasting advantage for the European capitalists. They used it to drive down production costs, and the resulting cheap goods led to European commercial advantages. Unequal trade led in time to political changes which divided the Arab world into a number of centers tied to European metropoles. Thus, for the present, the unity of the Arab world is submerged. With the era of decolonization and the New International Economic Order, the logic of Arab unity will reemerge on the surface again.

6. Abdallah Laroui's *Crisis of the Arab Intellectual: Traditionalism or Historicism* (Berkeley: University of California Press, 1976), is the work of a Moroccan writer reflecting on the difficulty of using the vocabulary of Marxism in the manner commonly found in the Arab East, and presumably in Egypt. Not much of modern Arab intellectual life has been of interest to Westerners, and until recently it has been the tribal-state

intellectuals who have had the hardest time being heard. With the recovery of an anarchist tradition in the West, several tribal-road writers have been "born." The Lebanese critic Adonis is an example, to judge from his much-heralded exposition of Arabic poetry as oral expression in *Introduction à la poetique arabe* (Paris: Sindbad, 1985).

The resurgence of Neo-Anarchism as a part of political economy or as a critique of political economy is treated below in several present-day political-economy contexts. The reader seriously interested in pursuing the theme in Islamic studies is advised to read Martin Bernal's *Black Athena: The Afro-Asiatic Roots of Classical Civilization* (New Brunswick: Rutgers University Press, 1987), a study of classical Greece which impinges in important ways on Islamic studies. Bernal challenges a distinction in Western thought that has been crucial for both Marxists and positivists. He argues that the European-ness of Greece was a scholarly construction of late-eighteenth-century classical studies, and that until that time scholars had followed the idea of Greece as Asia Minor.

Reinterpretation of the Hellenistic culture and commerce around its Afro-Asian component is an important part of Bernal's research. It suggests the need for a new kind of history of the rise of Islam written as an event comparable to the spread of Hellenism or the later English capitalism.

7. Contrast the odd reference to medieval issues in journals like the *Review of Middle East Studies* to the numerous systematic works appearing in Arabic, like the Lebanese Hussein Muruwwah's *Al-Naza'at al-Maddiyah fi al-Falsafah al-'Arabiyya al-Islamiyya* (Materialist Trends in Islamic Arab Philosophy), two volumes, published in Beirut in 1979. This book explicates not merely materialist trends in Islamic philosophy but the role of the critical intellectual in medieval Arab society as well. The work of the Syrian Tib Tizini deserves a full-length study. Among his books are *Mashru' Ru'yah Jadidah lil-Fikr al-'Arabi fi al-'Asr al-Wasit* (Project for a New Perspective on Arab Thought in the Middle Ages), published in Damascus in 1971; *Min al-Turath ila al-Thawrah* (From Heritage to Revolution) published in Damascus in 1979; *Al-Marksiyah wa al-Turath al-'Arabi al-Islami* (Marxism and the Arab Islamic Perspective), published in Beirut in 1980.

Hadi al-'Alawi combines Marxism with a study of the Islamic tradition as well in *Min Tarikh al-Tadhib fi al-Islam* (second edition, Beirut, 1987), which treats disputations on the use of torture in Islamic history, and is dedicated to the victims of torture in the contemporary reactionary and fascist Arab jails. Elements of a Tizini or a Hadi al-'Alawi will strike the Western reader as similar to the Christian Marxism of Mexican theologian José Porfirio Miranda. Arguably among the most serious thinkers in the Third World today, Tizini and al-'Alawi tend to be ignored in the West because they come from the Middle East. Had they come from Latin America, where Orientalism is not at work, they would be widely read.

8. A standard book of political-economy theory is by Elizabeth Fox-Genovese and Eugene D. Genovese, *Fruits of Merchant Capital: Slavery and Bourgeois Property in the Rise and Expansion of Capitalism* (Oxford: Oxford University Press, 1983). Mahmoud Ibrahim's revised UCLA dissertation, with the working title "On Capitalism and Early Islam," is a forthcoming publication of the University of Texas. Otherwise, I have found no well-known work explicating slavery and merchant capitalism focused on the Middle East.

9. See, for example, John Waterbury, *The Egypt of Nasser and Sadat: The Political Economy of Two Regimes* (Princeton: Princeton University Press, 1983).

10. The "chosen people" idea exists in a less pronounced form in Islam, *al-Sha'b al-mukhtar*. This idea contributes to the broader Mediterranean perspective about the early history of capitalism, democracy, and nation.

11. This is an alternative to various attempts at a unitary theory of Marxist concepts like imperialism. The interrelation among democracies is a discrete subject; it has a specificity quite distinct from other sorts of international relationships, e.g., United States relations with Mexico or China.

12. For an intellectual history of the word *Zionism*, see Regina Sharif, *Non-Jewish Zionism: Its Roots in Western History* (London: Zed, 1983).

13. Examples include a number of such highly insightful works as Nathan Weinstock's *Zionism: False Messiah* (London: Ink Links, 1979); Akiva Orr, *The Un-Jewish State: The Politics of Jewish Identity in Israel* (London: Ithaca Press, 1983); Uri Davis's *Israel: Utopia Incorporated* (London: Zed, 1977) and *Israel: An Apartheid State* (London: Zed, 1987); Fawzi el-Asmar, Uri Davis, and Naim Khader (eds.), *Towards a Socialist Republic of Palestine* (London: Ithaca Press, 1978) and in a sequel, *Debate on Palestine* (London: Ithaca Press, 1981).

14. Examples of a wider literature could include Jan C. Dawson, *The Unusable Past: America's Puritan Tradition, 1830 to 1930* (Chico: Scholar's Press, 1984); and Davis W. Noble, *The End of American History: Democracy, Capitalism, and the Metaphor of Two Worlds in Anglo-American Historical Writing, 1880–1980* (Minneapolis: University of Minnesota Press, 1985).

15. The first generation of critique of Orientalism promoted by area-studies specialists had to stress the common integration of the Middle East into the world economy, e.g., Joe Stork, *Middle East Oil and the Energy Crisis* (New York: Monthly Review, 1975); Helen Lackner, *A House Built on Sand: A Political Economy of Saudi Arabia* (London: Ithaca Press, 1978); and Ruth First, *Libya: An Elusive Revolution* (New York: Africana, 1975).

16. More recently, a return to an internalist approach, subsuming the political significance of oil revenue in Iraq to the wider social structure and to the development of Iraqi capitalism, is presented in the recently completed UCLA doctoral dissertation of Samira Haj, "Class Struggle and Political Revolution: The 1958 Iraqi National Revolution" (Los Angeles, Dept. of History, UCLA, 1987). A highly successful article possessing the same qualities is Alexander Scholch, "The 'Men on the Spot' and the English Occupation of Egypt in 1882," *History Journal* 29, no. 3 (1976).

17. A Stalinist work, V. Lutsky's *Modern History of the Arab Countries* (Moscow, 1969), was known but not often quoted. Radical books appeared in a *sub rosa* form like John Ruedy's *Land Policy in Colonial Algeria* (Berkeley: University of California Press, 1967); and *A Middle East Reader,* compiled by Irene Gendzier (New York: Pegasus, 1969). There appears to be no history of radical thought about the Middle East.

18. Anita Weiner, "Institutionalizing Institutionalization: The Historical Roots of Residential Care in Israel," in Zvi Eisikovits and Jerome Beker (eds.), *Residential Group Care in Community Context: Insights from the Israeli Experience* (New York: Haworth Press, 1986), pp. 3–20; and E. Shurka and V. Florian, "A Study of Israeli Jewish and Arab Parental Perceptions of their Disabled Children," *Journal of Comparative Family Studies,* 14 (1983), pp. 367–75. A more general statement based on the US is Wolf Wolfensberger, *The Origins and Nature of Our Institutional Model* (Syracuse: Human Policy Press, 1975).

19. Immanuel Wallerstein, *The Modern World System* (New York: Academic Press, 1974). In 1977, Wallerstein began the journal *Review,* which has encouraged writers on the Middle East with his perspective but also others. In its first issue, there appeared two influential articles for this field: Huri Islamoglu and Caglar Keydar, "Agenda for Ottoman History," pp. 31–57; and Anouar Abdel-Malek, "East Wind," pp. 57–67. Islamoglu has recently edited *The Ottoman Empire and the World Economy* (New York:

Cambridge University Press, 1987), which includes a study on the nature of the state, "Oriental Despotism in World-System Perspective," pp. 1–26, as well as "State and Peasants in the Ottoman Empire: A Study of Peasant Economy in North-Central Anatolia during the Sixteenth Century," pp. 101–59. For a quite different approach, emphasizing agency more than structure, see Anouar Abdel-Malek (ed.), *Contemporary Arab Political Thought* (London: Zed, 1983). Abdel-Malek has shown here and elsewhere the broadly populist nature of modern Arab and Third World thought.

20. Some disturbing examples of this are revealed in the violations of the freedom of the press in Thatcher's England and in the recent and fairly notorious attacks on David Abraham, a Princeton historian specializing in Nazi Germany. An example from the 1960s would be I. F. Stone's *Weekly*. Stone was the author of controversial but influential articles on the Arab-Israeli crisis in 1967.

21. Abdullah Hammoudi, "Segmentarity, Social Stratification, Political Power and Saint-hood: Reflections on the Theses of Gellner," *Economy and Society* 9, pt. 3 (1980), pp. 279–303, translated by Tanya Baker; on Geertz, the important review from a radical perspective was Talal Asad, "Anthropological Conceptions of Religion: Reflections on Geertz," *Man* 18 (1983): 237–59.

22. David Seddon, *Moroccan Peasants: A Century of Change in the Eastern Rif, 1870–1970* (Folkestone: Dawson, 1981).

23. Paul Rabinow, *Reflections on Fieldwork in Morocco* (Berkeley: University of California Press, 1977); Clifford Geertz, *Islam Observed: Religious Development in Morocco and Indonesia* (Chicago: University of Chicago Press, 1971).

24. For an East Coast view of American radical history, see Mike Davis, *Prisoners of the American Dream: Politics and Economy in the History of the U.S. Working Class* (London: Verso, 1986). The most famous modern radical book of the core culture is C. Wright Mills's *The Power Elite*. For the link between radicalism and Puritanism, see Michael Walzer, *The Revolution of the Saints: A Study in the Origins of Modern Radical Politics* (London: Weidenfeld and Nicolson, 1966).

25. The following could be used to illustrate some of the main controversies between Neo-Marxism and the left side of post-structuralism: Ellis Goldberg, *Tinker, Tailor and Textile Worker: Class and Politics in Egypt, 1930–1952* (Berkeley: University of California Press, 1986); Joel Beinin and Zachary Lockman, *Workers on the Nile: Nationalism, Communism, Islam and the Egyptian Working Class, 1882–1954* (Princeton: Princeton University Press, 1987); and on a broader level, Barbara Harlow, *Resistance Literature* (New York: Methuen, 1987) versus George Stauth and Sami Zubaida (eds.), *Mass Culture, Popular Culture and Social Life in the Middle East* (Boulder: Westview Press, 1987). Beinin, Lockman, and Goldberg create for the English-language reader a welcome alternative to a history of twentieth-century Egypt as a history of the Wafd Party elite. Building on trade union studies written by Egyptians in the 1960s, they add a Marxist vocabulary combining ideas of the colonial and post-colonial state with a notion of working-class culture. Staut, on the other hand, argues "that the Communication Revolution related to modern mass culture has led to the destruction of any 'meaningful' relationship between individuals and social institution." He aligns himself with the cultural pessimism of the Frankfurt School, as well as the idea of post-modernism (p. 65). Sami Zubaida in his essay on Khidr proposes this figure as an example of popular mythology which imposes itself on the narrative of modern times (*op. cit.*, p. 143).

   A writer who begins within the conventional Neo-Marxist framework, but who reflects on its limitations for the case of Iraq is Hanna Batatu, e.g., *The Old Social Classes and the Revolutionary Movements of Iraq* (Princeton: Princeton University Press, 1978).

26. T. H. Aston and C. H. E. Philpin (eds.), *The Brenner Debate: Agrarian Class Structure and Economic Development in Pre-Industrial Europe* (New York: Columbia University Press, 1985).

27. Maxime Rodinson, *Islam and Capitalism* (Austin: University of Texas Press, 1978); Karl Marx, *Grundrisse: Foundation of the Critique of Political Economy* (New York: Random House, 1973). For the reception of Althusser, see Ted Benton, *The Rise and Fall of Structural Marxism: Althusser and His Influence* (New York: St. Martin's Press, 1984).

28. Teodor Shanin, *Late Marx and the "Russian Road": Marx and the Peripheries of Capitalism* (New York: Monthly Review, 1983).

29. Antonio Gramsci, *Selections from the Prison Notebooks of Antonio Gramsci*, edited by Quintin Hoare and Geoffrey Nowell-Smith (London: Lawrence and Wishart, 1973), pt. 1, sec. 3, pp. 44–122.

30. "The Janus Face of Merchant Capital," in Genovese and Genovese, *op. cit.*, pp. 3–26.

31. Perry Anderson, *Lineages of the Absolutist State* (London: New Left Books, 1974); Roger Owen, *The Middle East in the World Economy, 1800–1914* (New York: Methuen, 1981).

32. Talal Asad, *Anthropology and the Colonial Encounter* (London: Ithaca, 1973); Rifaat Abu al-Haj, "The Social Uses of the Past: Recent Arab Historiography of Ottoman Rule," *International Journal of Middle East Studies* 14 (1982): 185–201.

33. Nawal Sa'dawi, *The Hidden Face of Eve* (London: Zed, 1980); *Woman at Point Zero* (London: Zed, 1983). The subject of female circumcision complained about in Egypt stands comparison to the same practice in the US, cf. Barbara Ehrenreich and Deirdre English, *For Her Own Good: 150 Years of Experts' Advice to Women* (Garden City: Anchor Books, 1979), p. 123. For anti-Orientalist writing on Middle Eastern women, see the discussion by Rima Hammami and Martina Reiker in the *New Left Review*, no.169 (May–June 1978). The Palestinian novel is Sahar Khalifeh's *Wild Thorns* (London: Al-Saqi Books, 1985). Among the critically minded researchers of today are Judith Tucker, Mervat Hatem, Leila Ahmed, and Soheir Morsey. Mervat Hatem's "The Politics of Sexuality and Gender in Segregated Patriarchal Systems: The Case of Eighteenth- and Nineteenth-Century Egypt," *Feminist Studies* 12, no. 2 (1986): 251–74, is a speculative and theoretical article that takes seriously the institutions of the Mamlukes and inquires about their sexuality and life-style. This article, like the Abu al-Haj piece cited above, shows us what has been lost by following the dominant nationalist approach to history and by dismissing the Ottoman past. An archival study is Judith Tucker, *Women in Nineteenth-Century Egypt* (New York: Cambridge University Press, 1985). Tucker relates women's history to monetarization of the economy, establishing a basis for the study of women independent of the state and Islam. A piece of radical feminist deconstruction is Soheir Morsy, "Zionist Ideology as Anthropology: An Analysis of Joseph Ginat's *Women in Muslim Rural Society*," *Arab Studies Quarterly* 5, (1983): 362–79. Leila Ahmed's "Women and the Advent of Islam," *Signs* 11 (1986): 665–91, an essay from her forthcoming book, offers a revisionist interpretation that fits with Mahmoud Ibrahim's dissertation on merchant capitalism (cited above).

34. A pioneer work on the struggle of prostitutes in a democracy is Judith Walkowitz's *Prostitution and Victorian Society: Women, Class and the State* (Cambridge: Cambridge University Press, 1980). Some recent evidence suggests that the prostitute may have gained more power vis-à-vis the pimp, cf. Barbara Heyl, *The Madam as Entrepreneur* (New Brunswick: Transaction Books, 1979), pp. 144–45. A very useful article, permitting comparison among the struggles of prostitutes in the different "historical roads" that comprise the Arab world is Evelyn Accad's "The Prostitute in Arab and North African Fiction," in Pierre L. Horn and Mary Beth Pringle (eds.), *The Image of the*

Prostitute in Modern Literature (New York: Frederick Ungar, 1984), pp. 63–76. The punitive attitude of Israeli society toward prostitution is more like that in the United States than like that in any other country in the Middle East, according to Ram Canaan, "Notes on Prostitution in Israel," *Sociological Inquiry* 32, no. 2 (1982), pp. 114–21.

On democratic structure and spousal abuse, see Elizabeth Pleck, *Domestic Tyranny: The Making of Social Policy Against Family Violence from Colonial Times to the Present* (New York: Oxford University Press, 1987); and Sheila Saunder's *A Study of Domestic Violence: Battered Women in Israel* (London: Anglo-Israel Association, 1982). The major study on abuse of Israeli women is in Hebrew, Barbara Sviriski's *Daughters of Eve, Daughters of Lilith* (Giv'atayim, 1984). A commentary on prison in the Arab world is Marilyn Booth's "Women's Prison Memoirs in Egypt and Elsewhere: Prison, Gender, Praxis," *Middle East Report* (November–December 1987), pp. 35–41.

35. Muhammad Baqir al-Sadr's *Falsafatuna* (Beirut, 1986) was translated in full by Professor Shams Inati (London: Muhammadi Trust, 1987). This provides a quasi-socialist view of Islam. If it were followed by Sadr's long critique of positivist logic and his parallel study of the problems of society and were linked to the career of Sadr's sister and put in the framework of their opposition to the Saddam Hussein regime in Iraq, Sadr would suddenly emerge as an understandable figure, a kind of organic intellectual of modern Iraq, to use Gramsci's phrase.

Index

Contributors

LILA ABU-LUGHOD, who is an anthropologist by training, is Assistant Professor of Religion at Princeton University.

LISA ANDERSON is Associate Professor in the Department of Political Science, Columbia University.

HALIM BARAKAT is Research Professor at the Center for Contemporary Arab Studies, Georgetown University.

SAMIH K. FARSOUN is Professor of Sociology at the American University, Washington, D.C.

PETER GRAN is Associate Professor of History at Temple University.

LISA HAJJAR is a Ph.D. candidate in Sociology at the American University.

HISHAM SHARABI is Professor of History and Omar al-Mukhtar Professor of Arab Culture at Georgetown University.

JUDITH E. TUCKER is Associate Professor of History at Georgetown University.